Greg Martin

Jonathan Mahler is a contributing writer for *The New York Times Magazine*. He lives in Brooklyn, New York, with his wife and son.

Praise for *The Bronx Is Burning*

"A wonderfully detailed, gritty story."

—*The Hartford Courant*

"[A] terrifically entertaining book."

—*New York Post*

"A rich canvas . . . an excellent new book . . . The result is a book that is roughly half-baseball and half-civic history, both elements treated with nuance and depth. . . . Mahler makes his two-pronged approach pay off, linking Koch, Jackson, Steinbrenner, and Murdoch together as the type of men who would lead New York to a new day."

—*Sports Illustrated*

"One of the pleasures of the book [is] to see such figures as they were becoming icons. But for Mahler, the real issue is what it all would mean. . . . A stirring portrait."

—*Newsday*

"Riveting."

—*Entertainment Weekly*

"Damon Runyon, where are you now? Mahler's rollicking evocation of New York in 1977—the year of Son of Sam, the year of the blackout, the year it refuses to Drop Dead, the year, dammit, the Yankees take the World Series—is full of Runyonesque characterizations, energy, and biting wit. . . . The bases are loaded and Mahler smokes it."

—Harold Evans, author of *The American Century*

"A love letter to a year . . . [Mahler] is at his best when he's unearthing the details that explain and complicate the era."

—*The New York Observer*

"Kaleidoscopic . . . a fast-moving, multilayered narrative that puts the city itself in the starring role. . . . In many ways, this book is a fascinating prelude to Tom Wolfe's novel *The Bonfire of the Vanities*."

—*Publishers Weekly* (starred review)

"Recounts the turbulent year in gripping, storylike detail."

—*Time Out New York*

"What a book! . . . A mesmerizing trip down into the dark recesses of racist politics and up into the bright lights of Yankee Stadium."

—Robert Sullivan, author of *Rats*

"Splendid . . . fresh and lively."

—*Daily News* (New York)

"Terrific . . . Mahler has done a wonderful job. . . . A compelling read . . . He shifts easily from baseball to history to political battles, never letting the narrative stall or drag."

—*Forward*

"You begin this book thinking, reasonably, that Bella Abzug, Billy Martin, Son of Sam, and Studio 54 can't possibly occupy the same narrative space, but as Jonathan Mahler's story of New York circa 1977 unfolds, the disparate, gritty elements start to resonate off one another. The result isn't harmony—the city has never known such a thing—but rather what a great book about New York should be: a story that's oversized, blaring, impossible, and true."

—Russell Shorto, author of *The Island at the Center of the World*

"A gold mine of great settings . . . delightful in its evident craft."

—*The Boston Globe*

"Mahler captures the zeitgeist with near perfection."

—*Library Journal*

"A terrifically entertaining, knowledgeable book about one of the most tumultuous years in the history of New York. . . . Read it and weep, read it and laugh."

—Kevin Baker, author of *Paradise Alley*

"Despite the odds against such a combination being successful, [Mahler] pulls off an expert historical double play by blending front-page political news and sports-page action. The result recalls the ambient atmosphere of the ethnic neighborhoods of Brooklyn and Queens, the natural argot of the precinct houses and of the locker rooms. . . . And it's all done with the knowing acumen and street smarts of an old-fashioned beat reporter."

—*Kirkus Reviews*

"An energetic synthesis of a year in the life of a great city in manic conflict with itself."

—Nicholas Dawidoff, author of *The Catcher Was a Spy*

"Jonathan Mahler takes us back to one tumultuous year in New York, and through masterful storytelling and rich portraits of the leading characters of the day reminds us that what defines and ultimately saves a city, in any era, are its outsized citizens. In Mahler's expert hands, they are flawed, fierce, brilliant, bickersome, and as indomitable as the metropolis itself."

—Michael Sokolove, author of *The Ticket Out*

"A fascinating city, a fascinating team, a fascinating time. This book took me back. Where were you in 1977?"

—Tim McCarver

THE BRONX IS BURNING

1977, BASEBALL, POLITICS, AND THE BATTLE FOR THE SOUL OF A CITY

JONATHAN MAHLER

PICADOR

FARRAR, STRAUS AND GIROUX
NEW YORK

 For information, address Picador, 175 Fifth Avenue, New York, N.Y. 10010.

www.picadorusa.com

Picador® is a U.S. registered trademark and is used by Farrar, Straus and Giroux under license from Pan Books Limited.

For information on Picador Reading Group Guides,
please contact Picador.
Phone: 646-307-5259
Fax: 212-253-9627
E-mail: readinggroupguides@picadorusa.com

The author would like to thank *The New York Times Magazine*,
which published a portion of this work in a slightly different form.

Designed by Gretchen Achilles

ISBN-13: 978-0-312-42702-3
ISBN-10: 0-312-42702-6

First published in the United States by Farrar, Straus and Giroux under the title
Ladies and Gentlemen, the Bronx Is Burning

First Picador Edition: April 2006
Second Picador Edition: July 2007

10 9 8 7 6 5 4 3 2 1

TO MY PARENTS

PROLOGUE

I grew up hearing stories about the New York of my father's childhood, the New York of the 1940s and 1950s. The working-class Jewish neighborhood in the Bronx that was thick with semidetached houses; the broom handles swiped from his mother's closet, the pink spaldeens sailing over manhole covers: That was my mythology.

The images were especially resonant because we lived so far away from this world, in Palm Springs, California, where the streets are named after Bob Hope and Frank Sinatra and the landscape alternates between spiky desert shrubs and golf courses. Those supernaturally green fairways, kept lush by constantly whirring sprinklers, were my reality; the bustling streets of New York were my dreamworld.

The California Angels played their spring training games in a small ballpark just a short bike ride from our house. We would get season tickets every March and dutifully cheer on the home team, which was owned by one of the community's many aging celebrities, Gene Autry. But I never cared much for the Angels. I knew that baseball loyalty was generational, not geographic. You don't choose your team; you inherit it. So I became a Yankees' fan from afar, methodically monitoring their daily performances through *The Sporting News*, *Sports Illustrated*, and our West Coast edition of *The New York Times*.

In the summer of 1977 we visited the city. I was only eight, but it didn't take long to figure out that this wasn't the place I had imagined. Whenever we climbed into a taxi, my parents promptly rolled up the windows and locked the doors. When I drifted toward a group of men dealing three-card monte, my mother quickly yanked me away.

The highlight of our stay was a Yankees' game. We took the

No. 4 train north from Eighty-sixth Street on a sticky July afternoon. My father, a starched white button-down shirt tucked stiffly into his high-waisted chinos, kept a firm grip on my arm as I tried to decipher the swirls of graffiti that covered our car. The train rumbled into one station after another. At each stop a dozen more people in Yankees caps and T-shirts pushed their way aboard. Finally, I saw the glimmer of natural light that meant we had crossed into the Bronx. The train climbed out of the tunnel, and there was Yankee Stadium. I recognized only one feature from the gauzy photographs in my Yankees books: the ring of white wooden trim running over the bleachers like a picket fence. It was the last vestige from the Yankee Stadium of old, an anachronistic detail on top of this concrete fortress. The ballpark was surrounded not by the cheerful brownstones and flower boxes that I had imagined but by grim tenements with screenless windows thrown wide open in the heavy summer air.

The team inside the ballpark also bore little resemblance to the neatly pressed, fair-haired Yankees of my father's generation–"heroes who summed up the ideals of manhood, courage and the excellence of an entire generation," as one of the bent-up paperbacks on my bookshelf described them. The Yankees of the fifties won with ease and grace. They scored eight runs in the first inning . . . and then slowly pulled away. The 1977 Yankees were racially and ethnically mixed. They were life-size, loutish. On the field they did everything the hard way, with the maximum of stress and strain on their fans. Off the field, they bickered, backstabbed, and demanded to be traded.

When I first embarked on this book four years ago, my intention was to write about the '77 Yankees against the backdrop of New York during this infamous era of urban blight. As the months passed, though, the city slowly advanced into the foreground, and the two stories became one.

I might have anticipated this. I moved to New York after graduating from college in 1990, and while it was obviously a much cleaner, safer city than it had been in the late seventies, I nevertheless felt nostalgic for the New York that I had caught only in fleeting childhood glimpses, a New York that still felt wild, unsettled. And so, as my research progressed, I sought out people who had once roamed this urban frontier: disco devotees who frequented underground dance clubs; cops who patrolled the streets during this period of soaring crime; firemen who fought the epidemic of arson that swept through the city's ghettos; gays who cruised the abandoned West Side piers; artists and musicians who homesteaded in cheap, dingy lofts in the postindustrial wasteland of SoHo.

On September 11, 2001, I happened to be researching the orgy of looting and arson that had accompanied the twenty-five-hour citywide power failure in July 1977. There are, of course, obvious differences between a localized blackout and a terrorist attack that killed thousands. Still, both were extraordinarily trying moments for the city, and I couldn't help pondering how different New York felt in their respective wakes. In the aftermath of 9/11, there was a sense that our tallest towers had been felled but that our foundation was more secure than ever. We were able to identify (if not locate) our enemy, and the rest of the country, not to mention most of the free world, was on our side. During the days and weeks that followed the blackout, New York had felt shaken to its core, and America had been anything but sympathetic.

At the same time, though, as it sank to a new low in the summer of 1977, the city was also revealing its endless capacity for regeneration. I gradually came to regard '77 as a transformative moment for the city, a time of decay but of rehabilitation as well. New York was straddling eras. You could see it everywhere: in the mayoral race, which featured a hotheaded radical (Bella Abzug), an aging creature of the city's smoke-filled political clubhouses (Abe Beame), and a pair of unknowns who went on to play starring roles in the modern history of New York (Ed Koch and Mario Cuomo). You could see it in Rupert Murdoch's reinvention of the *New York Post*, formerly a dutiful liberal daily, as a celebrity-obsessed, right-wing scandal sheet and in the battle to stop the spread of porn shops and prostitutes across midtown.

You could see it in the Yankees too. The team's two biggest personalities, Reggie Jackson and Billy Martin, were locked in a perpetual state of warfare, and it was hard not to see race, class, and the tug-of-war between past and future at the root of their dispute. Reggie Jackson was New York's first black superstar. He was also a perfect foil for the scrappy, forever embattled Martin, the hero of New York's fed-up working class and a powerful reminder of the team's–and the city's–less complicated past, the yellowing image of what New York had been and the still blurry image of what it was becoming.

This book is the story of that change.

PART ONE

1.

ON the evening of July 3, 1976, some fifty thousand New Yorkers sat on blankets in Central Park's Sheep Meadow eating picnic dinners, drinking wine, waving red, white, and blue sparklers, and listening to Leonard Bernstein conduct the New York Philharmonic in a surging birthday concert for the United States of America.

The next day, a Sunday, dawned bright and brisk. Millions of people set out early to secure spots along the waterfront, crowding onto the Belt Parkway in Brooklyn or staking out space on the West Side Highway, the pockmarked stretch of crumbling concrete and rusting steel that had been closed to traffic for two years now, ever since an elevated portion of the road had collapsed under the weight of a city dump truck loaded with asphalt. The water was scarcely less congested. Thousands of boats jockeyed for space in the New York Harbor, from yawls to sloops to runabouts. It was a forest of masts and sails, "an unbroken bridge of small craft that reached from the shores of Brooklyn to the coast of New Jersey," as the lead story in Monday's *New York Times* described it. Some boats dipped in and out of view in the chop; others circled idly, their sails bent against the breeze, waiting for the parade to begin.

It began promptly at 11 a.m., when the three-masted Coast Guard bark slipped under the Verrazano-Narrows Bridge. Fireboats sprayed plumes of red, white, and blue water. Cannons boomed. One by one, an armada of tall ships chugged north against the Hudson's current and a downstream wind: the *Danmark* (Denmark), the *Gorch Fock* (West Germany), the *Nippon Maru* (Japan), the *Dar Pomorza* (Poland), and on and on.

New York's five-foot two-inch Democratic mayor, Abraham Beame, watched the whole spectacle through his Coke-bottle-thick horn-rimmed glasses from the ninety-foot-high flight deck of the host ship, the gargantuan aircraft carrier USS *Forrestal*. By his side was none other than President Gerald Ford, who had only days earlier reversed his position and conceded to loan New York City five hundred million dollars—enough, for the moment anyway, to stave off bankruptcy. When the show was over, Beame, who was wearing a light blue seersucker suit and USS *Forrestal* cap, boarded a Circle Line craft that had been hired out to ferry dignitaries to the nearby shore. The boat strayed into the wrong channel and was seized by the Coast Guard. Beame laughed off his rotten luck, as did his wife, Mary. "If they put him in the brig," she joked, "it'll be the first vacation he's had since running for mayor!"

Darkness ushered in the biggest fireworks display in the city's history, thirty minutes of thudding guns and streaking rockets fired from Liberty Island, Ellis Island, Governors Island, and three separate barges. The splashes of color against the night sky were visible for fifteen miles around. Transistor radios were tuned to local stations, which played snippets of great American addresses, from Lincoln at Gettysburg to the Reverend Dr. Martin Luther King, Jr., on the steps of the Lincoln Memorial in Washington. After the last chrysanthemum exploded into thousands of beads of light, the crowd turned toward the Statue of Liberty and sang "The Star-Spangled Banner" as a helicopter towing a huge flag made up of thousands of red, white, and blue lightbulbs floated overhead.

Nobody wanted the party to end. Fortunately, there was another one just around the corner, the thirty-seventh Democratic National Convention. The last two—Chicago '68 and Miami '72—had been notoriously rancorous, but this one was guaranteed to be a love fest. The party's presidential candidate, the genteel Jimmy Carter, had already been anointed, and the city was primping for its close-up. Special repair crews were sent out to patch potholes in midtown, the Transit Authority changed its cleaning schedule to ensure that key stations would be freshly scrubbed for the delegates, and more than a thousand extra patrolmen and close to one hundred extra sanitation men were assigned to special convention duty. With the help of a hastily enacted antiloitering law, the police even managed to round up most of the prostitutes in the vicinity of Madison Square Garden. New York's holding cells were overflowing, but its streets were more or less hooker-free. A red, white, and blue crown glowed atop the Empire State Building.

Come opening night, July 12, the Garden was stuffed to capacity. Beame, who had been the first big-city mayor to throw his support behind the ex-governor of Georgia, welcomed the throngs to "Noo Yawk" in his Lower East Side monotone and then proceeded to hammer the administration of his erstwhile shipmate. "It has been Noo Yawk's misfortune, and the misfortune of this entire nation, that the very men who should have been healing and uniting this land have chosen instead to divide it!" the Mighty Mite thundered.

That night *Rolling Stone* magazine threw a big bash for Carter's campaign staff at Automation House on the Upper East Side. A month earlier the magazine had splashed Hunter S. Thompson's maniacal twenty-five-thousand-word profile of Carter—JIMMY CARTER AND THE GREAT LEAP OF FAITH—on its cover, thus sewing up the youth vote for the Democratic candidate. (Thompson insisted that the article wasn't an endorsement, but you would have to have been high to read it as anything less.) Pious Christian that he was, Carter may not have been rock 'n' roll ready—in a few years' time, a disillusioned Hunter would be comparing him to a high school civics teacher—but he'd do in a pinch. At least his campaign team, which included the likes of Jody Powell, Hamilton Jordan, and Pat Caddell, passed for young and hip, especially for a magazine that was aspiring to get out of head shops and onto newsstands.

The party was the hottest ticket in town, a strictly A-list affair—the drugs were to be contained to the bathrooms and closets—to which only an elite five hundred had been invited. Thousands more, including dozens of congressmen, turned up. The party started at 11 p.m. By midnight the doors had been barred, and taxis and limousines were still disgorging hundreds more. Lauren Bacall,

Senator Gary Hart, Jane Fonda, Tom Hayden, Warren Beatty, Carl Bernstein, Nora Ephron, Ben Bradlee, and Katharine Graham all were stuck outside, vainly brandishing their invitations. The scene inside was a little more subdued, as the Establishment (Walter Cronkite) mingled seamlessly with the anti-Establishment (John Belushi). At 3 a.m. the landlord of Automation House, the labor lawyer Ted Kheel, asked the magazine's thirty-one-year-old founding father, Jann Wenner, for a couple thousand dollars to keep the party going. Wenner shouted at Kheel for a few minutes before writing another check, and the booze continued to flow into Monday morning.

It was a bleary crew at the Garden that night, when the Democratic Party adopted a platform that promised, among other things, a "massive effort" to help New York. Twenty-four hours later Jimmy Carter was nominated. As the convention drew to a close, delegates, well-wishers, surely even some reporters sang along to "We Shall Overcome."

2.

ABE Beame might have been forgiven for imagining that those words were meant for him. The past few years had been abysmal, both for the city and, by extension, for its hapless mayor. The clinical term for it, *fiscal crisis*, didn't approach the raw reality. *Spiritual crisis* was more like it.

The worst part was that Beame had seen it coming. As the comptroller to his predecessor, John Lindsay—the equivalent of being lookout on the *Titanic*, as the columnist Jack Newfield once quipped—Beame knew just how precarious things were. On the damp, blustery day when he was sworn into office at the beginning of 1974, he'd grumbled about a newspaper editorial praising Lindsay for leaving the city in good fiscal health. "The man left us with a budget deficit of $1.5 billion," snorted Beame, slapping the paper with the back of his hand for effect as he foreshadowed his headache-filled future. In case he needed another reminder, President Nixon, who would soon know from greasy poles himself, summoned Beame to the Oval Office to tell him he was at the top of one. "And believe me," said an unsympathetic Nixon, "New York is a greasy pole."

Sure enough, New York's 104th mayor hadn't been in office one year when, in the fall of '74, he was forced to put a freeze on all municipal hiring. New York's lenders weren't satisfied. A few months later the mayor sacked New York City employees for the first time since the Great Depression. Now the municipal unions were steamed. Beame quickly caved and rehired some of the laid-off workers. By February '75, Beame was supposed to have gotten rid of twelve thousand of the city's three hundred thousand employees. A *New York Times* investigation revealed that only seventeen hundred were gone; the rest had merely been shifted to other budget lines. In April '75, Standard and Poors suspended its rating of the city's securities. New York was not considered a safe investment. The city was no longer able to sell bonds, its main source of capital. The iceberg had hit, and Gotham was taking on water.

Down in Washington, hat in hand, Beame received an unsolicited lecture from Treasury Secretary William Simon on the perils of New York's civic liberalism: the generous municipal salaries and pensions; the subsidized public transportation; the rent-controlled apartments; the free higher education. President Ford's equally unsympathetic response was summed up most memorably by the 144-point *Daily News* headline, FORD TO CITY: DROP DEAD. (Rejected drafts included FORD REFUSES AID TO CITY and FORD SAYS NO TO CITY AID.)

New York reacted to all this with predictable indignation, the rest of the country with just as predictable glee. The syndicated columnists Rowland Evans and Robert Novak understated the matter considerably when they wrote, "Americans do not much like, admire, respect, trust, or believe in New York." In political cartoons across the nation, New York became a sinking ship, a zoo where the apes were employed as zookeepers, a naughty puppy being swatted by a rolled-up newspaper, a stage littered with overturned props.

Reminders of the city's decline were already everywhere. In 1972 the *Tonight Show* had moved from midtown Manhattan to Burbank, California. To a generation that had grown up watching Jack Paar and Johnny Carson interview Broadway actors, cabaret singers, and jazz and rock stars—live from the show's studio at Rockefeller Center—this was the cultural equivalent of the Brooklyn Dodgers' moving to Los Angeles, the surest sign yet that America's cultural axis was tilting. Carson, who had engineered the move himself, never looked back. New York's travails soon became a running joke in his nightly monologues, which were now, in a symbolic triumph of Hollywood over Broadway, taped. Central Park was Johnny's favorite punch line ("Some Martians landed in Central Park today . . . and were mugged").

As for Beame, the time for tiptoeing was over. He gave thirty-eight thousand city workers, including librarians, garbage collectors, firemen, and cops, the ax. In anticipation of the layoffs, the police union had already distributed WELCOME TO FEAR CITY brochures at Kennedy Airport, Grand Central Station, and the Port Authority Bus Terminal, which came complete with a "survival guide" advising arriving tourists not to leave their hotels after dark or to ride the subways at any hour. On the July 1975 morning when five thousand cops were furloughed, hundreds of them amassed in front of City Hall, waving empty holsters and signs that read: BEAME IS A DESERTER. A RAT. HE LEFT THE CITY DEFENSELESS. From there they marched over to the Brooklyn Bridge, where they blocked rush-hour traffic with Police Department barricades. Once the flow of cars had been halted, they deflated tires and hurled obscenities and beer bottles at uniformed ex-colleagues who tried, unsuccessfully, to persuade them to clear the roadway.

Fear City also became Stink City when ten thousand sanitation workers walked off the job to protest the layoffs. The piles rose quickly, and ripe refuse was soon oozing from burst garbage bags and overstuffed trash cans, making it difficult for pedestrians to negotiate many of the city's sidewalks. Within a matter of days some fifty-eight thousand tons of uncollected garbage were roasting in New York's summer sun. Sanitation workers ensured that private collectors wouldn't be able to provide relief from the unremitting stench by sealing off the various dumps in the city's outlying areas.

Twenty-six of New York's 360 firehouses were shuttered, prompting waves of firemen to complain of minor injuries and request sick leave. Communities around the city staged angry protests. In Bushwick, Brooklyn, a poor neighborhood fighting a losing battle against arsonists, residents blockaded an engine company slated for closure and held hostage the fourteen firemen inside. An assistant Fire Department commissioner was dispatched to negotiate their release, and the residents took him hostage as well.

Library branches and public hospitals were closed and the subway fare jumped from thirty-five to fifty cents. More devastating still, at least symbolically, Mayor Beame ended 129 years of free tuition at New York's public colleges, including his alma mater, City College, the fabled gateway to middle-class life. That it was Abe Beame, and not his silver-spooned predecessor, John Lindsay, who presided over the dismantling of this great experiment in social democracy amounted to a bitter irony. He was, after all, one of its proudest products. Beame's parents had fled czarist oppression in Warsaw at the turn of the century for a cold-water flat on the densely populated Lower East Side. His father, a paper cutter and hot-blooded Socialist, toted his young son along to drink in the fevered calls for social justice in drafty high school auditoriums and dingy meeting rooms.

His father's ideological ardor never rubbed off on Beame, but his work ethic did. Beame's first job, in grade school, entailed walking through the tenements before dawn, knocking on doors to wake people who couldn't afford alarm clocks. When he was old enough, Beame joined his father at the stationery factory after school and on Saturdays. Free time was scarce, but on Sunday afternoons he occasionally splashed around the public swimming pool in the old Madison Square Garden on Twenty-third Street. His nickname was Spunky.

A degree in accounting from City College safely in hand, Beame got married, moved to Brooklyn, and started logging time at the local Democratic club in Crown Heights. What he lacked in personal magnetism, he more than made up for with tirelessness and fidelity to the Democratic Party. Beame was a veritable vote-gathering machine, the political equivalent of salesman of the month election in and election out. And so he gradually worked his way up, from doorbell ringer to club captain to party leader.

Beame's climb through the civil service ranks was equally slow and steady. In 1946 he was named assistant budget director of New York City. Six years later he was duly promoted to budget director. (His salary practically doubled—to $17,500.) He put in fifteen years of service in the budget office, accumulating a thousand days of unused vacation along the way. In 1961 Beame was elected comptroller. This appeared to be the end of his ascent. He was plenty smart, but he was no leader.

A failed campaign for the mayoralty in 1965 confirmed this impression. The Democratic candidate in an overwhelmingly Democratic city, Beame ought to have been the odds-on favorite. There were even some early attempts to turn his physical stature into an advantage by reminding New Yorkers that the city's greatest mayor ever, Fiorello La Guardia, was exactly the same height. La Guardia had been known as the Little Flower; several of Beame's allies started referring to him as the Little Giant. The nickname didn't stick. He was just Abe Beame the bookkeeper. His flat campaign speeches, often delivered from atop an attaché case so that he could see over the lectern, accelerated his undoing. His overbred opponents—the tall, blond, and eloquent Upper East Side Yalies John Lindsay and William F. Buckley, Jr.—did verbal pirouettes around the pride of City College's accounting department.

After being drubbed by Lindsay, Beame skulked out of politics. In a betrayal of his roots that would surely have broken his late father's heart, he became an investment banker. "I was probably earning twice as much money doing one-tenth the amount of work, and I had very nice, lavish offices and whatnot," he reflected later. But private sector life wasn't for him, so in 1969 Beame ran again for comptroller and won. Four years later, at the age of sixty-seven, he took another shot at the mayoralty.

Things were different now. He was the same Abe Beame; it was the city itself that had changed. New York was waking up from eight years of John Lindsay with a hangover. Like most benders, this one had started with unselfconscious giddiness and infinite expectations for the night ahead, and had ended with lipstick smudged, rouge faded, and a cold, hard look in the mirror.

In the beginning the question wasn't so much did Lindsay deserve to be mayor of New York as did New York deserve to have him. The hope was that he'd restore civility to New York on his way to the White House. The reality proved otherwise. His tenure started inauspiciously and got worse. Hours after Lindsay's inauguration the city's thirty-five thousand transit workers went out on strike and didn't return for twelve days. ("Mayor Lindsay eliminated subway crime on his first day in office," joked Sammy Davis, Jr.) Two years later Lindsay's experiment with community control in a predominantly black school district in East Brooklyn yielded an angry dispute between local parents and New York's predominantly Jewish teachers' union. A series of teachers' strikes followed, closing almost all the city's schools for the better part of two months. When the dust finally cleared, the historic alliance between the city's blacks and Jews had been shattered.

Yet for a while anyway, New York clung fast to the image of its strapping mayor, tie loosened, suit jacket slung casually over his shoulder. In this time of racial turmoil, Lindsay had kept his city riot-free, bravely taking to the streets of Harlem the night of Martin Luther King, Jr.'s murder to soothe an angry, distraught community. Campaigning for reelection in the summer of 1969, the unflappable Lindsay admitted that he'd made some mistakes, and like that year's Miracle Mets—who invited him into their champagne-soaked locker room parties—he marched on to improbable victory.

By the early 1970s, though, New York had a bellyful of disillusionment. Lindsay's attempts to reestablish confidence between the police and the people backfired when his idea for a civilian review board to consider police brutality claims was shouted down by the *Daily News* as "the property of . . . cop-haters." His antipoverty programs became bastions of corruption and created warring fiefdoms within the city's ghettos. And nothing divided New York as bitterly as Lindsay's grand plan to build several low-income housing towers in the middle-class neighborhood of Forest Hills, Queens.

Time and again, Lindsay's noble attempts to empower the underclass served only to alienate the working class. The city's population was diminishing; its welfare rolls were growing. Crime had risen faster in New York in the 1960s than in any decade since the thirties, and the growth had continued through the early seventies. Subway cars and stations were bruised with graffiti, a cry of anguish from the ghetto to some, a sign the city was spiraling out of control to others. A new consensus emerged: The mayor wasn't a man of the people after all. Clark Whelton, writing in *The Village Voice*, put it best: "John Lindsay is a creature of air . . . He could walk on air. The people he tried to lead couldn't." By the end of his second term Lindsay had become, in the words of one especially memorable magazine headline, AN EXILE IN HIS OWN CITY.

Thus did Beame's moment arrive. There was no seductive rhetoric, no risk of dashed expectations. He was New York's rebound lover. What's more, he was a bookkeeper, and New York's books were in desperate need of attention. Reluctant to cut services during this time of social upheaval, Mayor Lindsay had gotten into the habit of borrowing. "He knows the buck," Beame's campaign posters confidently, if blandly, asserted.

He had a funny way of showing it. Less than halfway through Beame's term, the city was careering toward bankruptcy. In the end it was Governor Hugh Carey and a coterie of financiers who managed to rescue New York. In the summer of '75, Carey created the Municipal Assistance Corporation (MAC) to oversee the city's finances and put Felix Rohatyn, the head of the investment firm Lazard Frères, in charge. Rohatyn rolled the city's debt into new bonds and with the help of the rest of MAC's principals—businessmen, brokers, and bankers all—brought them to market. It was, or so it seemed at the time, the final indignity for the municipal bookkeeper from the Lower East Side; benched, as a high-gloss team of Park Avenue suits bailed out the city to which he had humbly devoted his life.

3.

HOW far away those dark days seemed in July '76, as Beame sat in the Rainbow Room with a large party of Democratic well-wishers, the bright lights of the city shimmering in every window, a few hours after that final chorus of "We Shall Overcome." He couldn't help showing off the personal letter he'd received from Jimmy Carter, who promised the city complete support from the White House.

New York had been though hell, but in the summer of '76 there was reason for hope. It was a feeling more than anything, palpable, if not quantifiable, that the embattled city was on the edge of a new day. America's hostility toward New York had only reawakened the city's pride, and the bicentennial celebrations had confirmed its preeminence. Washington was the nation's capital, Philadelphia the birthplace of its independence, but when it came time to commemorate the country's 200th birthday, no one even gave it a second thought: New York would be the center of the action.

Los Angeles could have *The Tonight Show*; New York now had *Saturday Night*, a subversive ninety-minute sketch comedy show that had debuted less than a year before and was already capturing more than twenty-two million viewers a week. The counterculture was starting to migrate from San Francisco to New York, a trend evidenced by *Rolling Stone*'s plan to relocate from Haight-Ashbury to midtown Manhattan in the summer of '77. And just as America's bicentennial celebrations had awakened a nation's interest in its history, so one of the surprise best sellers of 1976, Irving Howe's *World of Our Fathers*, had rekindled nostalgia for a critical chapter of that narrative, the immigrant experience on New York's Lower East Side.

Bold new restaurants were opening, including the extravagantly refurbished Tavern on the Green. The food was forgettable—"Took home a doggie bag," wrote one critic. "The dog refused it."—but the vote of confidence in the future of Central Park wasn't. (*Take that, Johnny!*) The new Tavern was the brainchild of a man-child, the 264-pound Warner LeRoy, who had grown up in Hollywood on the back lots of Warner Brothers, which his maternal grandfather had founded. (One of LeRoy's earliest childhood memories was of skipping along the yellow brick road; after the filming had been completed, he got to keep Toto as a pet.) When the time came, though, LeRoy declined to take over the family business, and moved to New York instead. He had his own passion for entertaining and transporting that needed cultivating.

The downtown crowd had its place, One Fifth, so named for its Fifth Avenue address, a former NYU dormitory at the corner of Eighth Street. Its proprietor, George Schwartz, had opened the place in January '76, envisioning it as New York's La Coupole. In a sense, it was. "It started with fashion people and a woman named Larissa who made furs for rock stars," Schwartz recalls. "Suddenly all hell broke loose, and we were the 'in' place." Nineteen-seventies New York was not 1930s Paris, but the restaurant's decor—cruise ship art deco—provided a whimsical diversion from the dirty, deserted streets outside. Schwartz had picked up all the furnishings a few years earlier, when a 1930s Cunard liner washed up in the New York Harbor with a broken engine. Rather than foot the bill to have it repaired, the ship's owner auctioned off its contents. Schwartz bought the lights, chairs, port windows, and German brass sconces that had filled its first-class smoking room and reassembled them in his new restaurant. The wait staff was gay and gorgeous; the maître d' wore tails, a lorgnette, and heavily gooped slicked-back hair. The food was continental American. No one knew who the chef was; no one cared who the chef was.

Still farther downtown, on the 107th floor of the World Trade Center, the two inarticulate towers that had received such scathing notices two years earlier, was Windows on the World. *New York* magazine's food critic, Gael Greene, couldn't resist the symbolism when the restaurant opened for business in the spring of 1976. "Suddenly I knew, absolutely knew—New York would survive," she wrote. "If money and power and ego could create this extraordinary pleasure . . . this instant landmark . . . money and power and ego could rescue this city from the ashes."

The next president was going to help too. When Carter launched his general election campaign in September, the city's subway cars and buses were festooned with posters of his smiling Southern mug and his solemn vow, "I GUARANTEE THAT IF I GO TO THE WHITE HOUSE, I'LL NEVER TELL THE PEOPLE OF THE GREATEST

CITY ON EARTH TO DROP DEAD." On his final swing through the Northeast two months later, Carter showed up at a rally in the garment center with Beame by his side. Clasping the mayor's hand, Carter proclaimed, "Together, we can do anything." Two days before the election Beame summoned seventy New York City Democratic district leaders to Gracie Mansion and told them to make sure that everyone who was ambulatory got to the voting booths: New York could put its faith in J. C.

And so it did.

Without the impressive turnout in the city, Carter would not have won New York State, and without the state's forty-one electoral votes, Carter would not have won the election. The president-elect wasted no time inviting Governor Carey, Felix Rohatyn, and Mayor Beame to his plantation on a little island off the Georgia coast to express his gratitude.

As for Beame, the pained expression that he'd worn for the better part of the last two years was finally giving way to something approaching a smile. "I think we've turned the corner and seen the light at the end of tunnel," the Mighty Mite told reporters in the fall of 1976. By now the city had an election of its own approaching, the '77 mayoral election. Beame sent the word around City Hall that, expectations to the contrary, he'd be running again after all.

4.

THE Martin meltdown began with the usual epithet-laced rantings in the early innings of the fourth and final game of the 1976 World Series on October 21 and ended with a dramatic detonation in the top half of the ninth, when the Yankees' forty-eight-year-old manager picked up a foul ball and hurled it in the direction of home plate umpire Bill Deegan.

A predictable chain of events ensued. After being ejected from the game, which was virtually unheard of in the World Series, Billy Martin stormed out of the dugout and let loose a ferocious tantrum. Neck veins bulging, jaw clenched, he was eventually coaxed off the field. Passing back through the dugout before disappearing from public view, he delivered a swift kick to the bat rack. Martin's anger soon turned to shame—not at his behavior but at being swept by the Cincinnati Reds. He retreated into the trainer's room, which was off limits to the press corps, to sob inconsolably.

Over the course of the series he'd used every excuse, from the chilly temperatures of the night games (so scheduled to keep the TV advertisers happy) to the plastic grass of Cincinnati's Riverfront Stadium, an affront to his old-fashioned sensibilities. Now, curled up on the floor beneath the cold metal training tables, Martin was left alone with his crushing sense of disappointment—that is, until his boss, George Steinbrenner, barged in to berate Martin for embarrassing *him.*

Martin eventually emerged, bleary and broken, clutching a cup of scotch. A reporter asked, unnecessarily, if he'd been crying. "Yes. I'm not ashamed of it," Martin answered. "I'm an emotional guy . . . It hurts my pride, my ego, I guess, to lose like this." It hardly needed to be said. Alfred Manuel "Billy" Martin's desperate desire to win, to avoid losing, was already legendary.

It was, for the most part, the product of a lifetime of enduring slights, real and imagined. Even the moment in 1949 when he first became a New York Yankee, in retrospect one of the great moments of his career, was marred by what he took to be a sign of disrespect. He was, at the time, a bony young man with a big nose and jug ears, a second baseman for the Oakland Oaks. Upon hearing a roar from the crowd, he glanced upward and caught sight of a blimp overhead.

The news was wrapped around the electronic ticker: BILLY MARTIN SOLD TO YANKEES. "I was kind of mad when I found out the rest," Martin remarked later. "Oakland was paying me $9,000. When I went to the Yankees the next year they only gave me $6,000. But I knew I'd make it in New York."

Others weren't so sure. Martin was just a throw in on a larger deal for a highly touted outfielder named Jackie Jensen. The Yankees already had two second basemen, Jerry Coleman and Snuffy Stirnweiss. And what did they want with a runty banjo hitter like Martin, anyway? During Martin's first Yankees' camp in 1950, Casey Stengel hit him eighth in an exhibition game. "Next thing, you'll have me batting behind the batboy," Martin fumed. Opening day at Fenway Park the dead-end kid slapped a double in his first big-league at bat, then a bases-loaded single—in the same inning. ("Listen you," Martin told one reporter afterward, "the name's Billy, not Alfred, like you wrote it up. Don't forget it.")

Yet down to the minors he went. "I'll make you pay for abusing me like this!" a red-eyed Martin shrieked at the Yankees' general manager, George Weiss.

A month later Martin was back in New York, this time to stay. He bunked with a couple of other rookies at the Concourse Plaza Hotel, right around the corner from the stadium, so he could get to the ballpark early for extra batting practice. He peppered his coaches with questions and hollered like hell from the dugout. Before long, he'd scratched his way into the starting lineup. It helped that Martin had already endeared himself to Casey Stengel, who managed Martin—"that fresh kid who's always sassing everybody and getting away with it"—back in Oakland in '48. (During infield practice Stengel would cock his head and scorch a grounder at Martin. Martin would scoop the ball up, flash Stengel a limp wrist, and then throw it back to him.) In New York the writers had soon taken to calling Martin Casey's Boy. Martin, who had never known his father, called Stengel old man.

What Martin lacked in talent he made up for in grit. The same determination that had propelled this juvenile delinquent out of the sandlots of a dirt-poor, fatherless childhood near the docks of Berkeley—his grandmother had floated over from San Francisco with all her household possessions on a raft—drove him to overachieve as a big leaguer. After getting plugged in the face by a fastball near the end of his career in 1959, he started bailing out at the plate. Whenever he came up, he'd tell himself, loudly enough for the opposing team to hear: "Stay in, stay in, stay in." But Martin kept pulling out. So during batting practice he put on a wool warm-up jacket and instructed the pitcher to throw him a bag full of "bow ties," balls that were hard and inside. There he stood, his olive skin stretched tight across his face, his dark eyes narrowed in concentration, willing his uncooperative body into submission as one pitch after another buzzed beneath his chin.

In the field Martin never lost focus. During batting practice he would study the infield grass to see how aggressively he needed to charge slow rollers. Once the game was under way, he'd watch each batter's feet for a sense of which direction the ball was likely to go. He hated wearing sunglasses during games, so he trained himself to follow pop flies out of the corners of his eyes to reduce the risk of losing them in the sun.

Martin turned double plays as ferociously as anyone who had ever played the game, and his disproportionately long arms came in handy when he was pivoting on the bag and whipping the ball across to first. He tagged runners so they stayed tagged, and he wasn't above swiping his glove across their jaws if he felt they deserved it. Sitting next to Ty Cobb at a banquet in San Francisco, Martin told the dyspeptic old-timer that if he had played during his era, Cobb would have come sliding into second spikes high on him only once: "After that, you wouldn't have had any teeth."

He was just a .250 hitter—and 75 percent of his hits were singles—but Martin got his knocks when they mattered most. A 1956 profile in *Sports Illustrated* labeled him "The Damnedest Yankee of Them All." In his six full years with the team, 1951 to 1956, the Yankees won five pennants. Only once did they fail to make it to the World Series: 1954, the year that Martin did a brief tour in the army. His lifetime World Series batting average was a gaudy .333, but his most memorable series moment came on defense. With the bases loaded and two out in the seventh inning of the final game of the 1952 series against the Brooklyn Dodgers, Martin streaked toward home from the edge of the infield, his cap disappearing behind him as he charged, to spear a windblown pop fly at his shoe tops. Somehow, Martin had sensed that the Yankees' first baseman, for whom it should have been a routine play, had lost track of the ball.

Martin would have done anything to avoid losing, but winning came at its own cost. In short, his emotional makeup was not equal to the pressure, external or internal, of playing so far above his head.

When Martin first broke into professional baseball, his boyhood priest, Father Dennis Moore, who had supplied Martin's impoverished family with baskets of food, prayed that he'd get some wise counseling. "Life had made him most vulnerable," Moore once said. The priest's prayers went unanswered. Martin fought insomnia, hypertension, and what was then known as acute melancholia. His churning stomach kept him from eating for long stretches. What he did eat, he'd often puke back up. Martin tried to cope, popping sleeping pills and drinking bottomless glasses of scotch, but nothing could quite cure the distemper. "The guys who are happy playing ball are those who can adjust to the nuthouse they have to live in," Martin told Al Stump for a 1956 story in *The Saturday Evening Post*, a rare profile that got at the essential darkness beneath Martin's "peppery" exterior. "Some of us can. Some can't. I've never been able to get a good steady grip on myself in this racket."

Instability bred truculence. Martin's fists always seemed to be finding someone's face. "The Bible says you should turn the other cheek," Martin once said, "but God couldn't have known anything about baseball." Baseball brawls are famously harmless affairs marked more by frenzied flailing than real combat. Not when Martin was involved. Most notoriously, he pulverized a mentally ill Red Sox rookie, Jimmy Piersall, beneath the stands at Fenway. When Piersall was institutionalized for a nervous breakdown a month later, even Martin was embarrassed. His only defense, he remarked, was that he was just a step ahead of the men in the white coats himself.

Martin lived in constant fear of having everything taken away from him, and his paranoia wasn't entirely unjustified. He wasn't going to be able to fight off the younger, more talented players forever. What's more, it was no secret that Weiss, a wealthy German-American from Greenwich, Connecticut, figured the unstable, bellicose Martin for a bad influence on the team's biggest box-office draw, Mickey Mantle. (Martin was convinced that Weiss had hired detectives to trail him.)

Sure enough, at the beginning of the '57 season Martin lost his job to a twenty-one-year-old rookie, Bobby Richardson. Six weeks later, on May 15, he went out to celebrate his twenty-ninth birthday with a few teammates. After dinner at the chic steak house Danny's Hideaway and drinks at the Waldorf-Astoria, they made their way to the Copacabana to catch Sammy Davis, Jr.'s 2 a.m. show. The table of Yankees was soon exchanging heated words with a bowling team from the Bronx. In the tangle that ensued, a forty-year-old delicatessen owner was knocked out cold. YANKEES IN DRUNKEN NIGHTCLUB BRAWL, blared the next day's banner headline in the *New York Mirror*. Martin reportedly didn't throw the punch, but he wasn't going to rat out the Yankee who did. Weiss now had the excuse he needed.

There was a month to go before the trading deadline, and Martin twisted in the wind for its duration. On June 15, with the midnight deadline just a few hours away, the Yankees were in Kansas City playing the Athletics. Absent from the lineup, a fidgety Martin walked out to the bullpen to watch the game, hoping somehow that if Weiss couldn't find him, he couldn't trade him. The bullpen phone rang in the sixth inning, and Martin was summoned to the clubhouse. The Yankees' farm director, Lee MacPhail, delivered the news: The next day he should report to the other dressing room. He had been traded to lowly Kansas City.

Martin drank late into the night with Mickey Mantle and Whitey Ford, then returned to his hotel room and sobbed until sunrise. The following day he debuted at second base for the A's. In the eighth, Ford, on the mound for the Yankees, signaled to his old pal to expect a curve, then hung a slow, fat one over the middle of the plate. Martin sent it into the left field bleachers on a line. It was small consolation. "I was running around the bases and I wasn't even happy," Martin reflected later. For seven years he refused to speak to Casey Stengel, whom he blamed for failing to protect him from the Yankees' brass.

A few weeks later the A's were in the Bronx playing the Yankees. The archbishop of New York, Francis Cardinal Spellman, was at the game, and he called Martin over to speak with him during batting practice. Cardinal Spellman asked Martin how he liked Kansas City. "Oh, just fine, your eminence," he answered. A few minutes later Martin was back behind the batting cage, waiting for his turn. "How do I like it in Kansas City?" he muttered. "I wanted to ask him, 'How would *you* like it in Kansas City?' "

After an uninspired hitch with the Athletics, Martin knocked around the big leagues for several more years. As he bounced from one flagging franchise to the next, his arrival was almost always accompanied by the expectation that his famous intangibles—"pride, fortitude, and aggressiveness," as Dick Schaap described them in *Sport* magazine in 1959—would transform the club into a contender. They never did. Martin played hard, but his mediocre skills deteriorated rapidly, and he never really got over the trade. "I tried and I tried, but I couldn't get my heart into it," Martin later reflected. "From then on I was through. It was all downhill."

When the Minnesota Twins cut Martin in 1962, they offered to keep him on as a scout. Martin jumped at the chance. He was gradually promoted through the club's ranks and in the summer of '68 was named manager of its Triple A affiliate, the Denver Bears. The team was 8-22 when Martin took over and 65-50 when he left. His performance earned him a one-year contract for the '69 season with Minnesota's sleepy big-league club. "He will be either the greatest or the worst manager in the majors," the Twins' president, Calvin Griffith, said ominously as the season opened. For his part, Martin guaranteed the baseball fans of Minnesota the most exciting summer of their lives.

They got it. Martin managed the game just as he had played it: personally, emotionally, intensely. Before games he'd take infield among his men. During games he'd bound out onto the field almost every inning—his right hand jammed into his back pocket, just like his mentor, Casey Stengel—either to issue an instruction to a pitcher that could just as easily have been communicated from the bench or to argue a call, which he usually did with his jaw an inch away from the umpire's nose. More than once the scene ended with Martin getting the heave-ho and then kicking red clay all over the umpire's trousers. He was a micromanager who shifted fielders, called pitches, and forbade even his fastest men to run without his permission. Most managers enjoy engaging in postgame analysis, getting the chance to explain to the writers why they did this or that. Martin guarded his strategic decisions like state secrets: "What do you want? The whole country to read it, for chrissakes?" At night he'd routinely violate baseball's unwritten prohibition against bending elbows with the help. (No one knew this rule better than Martin. After all, he'd heard Casey Stengel repeat it at the start of every year: "One thing I want understood—I do my drinkin' at the hotel bar. Stay out of it.")

As a player Martin had checked the lineup every afternoon half expecting to find that he'd been left off it. As a manager he wanted his players to live with the same uncertainty. He was more than happy to platoon his biggest stars to help get the message across. If that star was also a pet of one of the know-nothing suits in the front office, so much the better.

Martin led the Twins to a division title, drew a record 1.3 million fans to Metropolitan Stadium, and forever endeared himself to the Twin Cities. He also blasted the front office—"the second-guessing sonsabitches"—for mishandling a promising minor leaguer, decked the team's traveling secretary in the lobby of a hotel in Washington, and ordered Vice President Hubert Humphrey to get his ass out of his dressing room.

But nothing quite compared with the scene that unfolded one night at the Lindell AC, a popular Detroit saloon where Martin and a number of Twins had gathered to drink on a road trip. One of Martin's pitchers, Dave Boswell, had refused to run laps after the game that afternoon, and the team's pitching coach, Art Fowler, sat down next to Martin and told him as much. Boswell came over after Fowler left and let Martin know he was going to kick Fowler's ass for snitching on him. From here the details grow sketchy, but the undisputed facts are these: Martin pummeled Boswell, who had a good three inches and twenty pounds on his manager, so severely that the doctor in the emergency room assumed that the pitcher had been attacked by someone wielding a pipe. (Boswell said later that he'd been pinned by a few of his teammates while Martin went to work on him.) To Martin, it was just part of the job. "I like to treat my players as men," he once remarked, "but sometimes they act like little boys and little boys have to be slapped down."

Griffith couldn't get rid of Martin quickly enough. "Prior to hiring him, realizing his explosive personality and his inexperience as a manager, I had numerous meetings with him to set policy and guidelines," he said. "I feel he has completely ignored our understandings."

Martin's firing drove the people of Minnesota into a foul fury.

Bumpers were plastered with "Boycott the Twins" stickers, and screeds poured into the *Minneapolis Star*, including one signed by 218 fans renouncing the team in protest. More than a few letters were addressed to Griffith himself. "In my judgment," wrote one outraged Twins' fan, "history will record your decision on Billy Martin along with decisions that were made by Henry Ford, Adolf Hitler, and Napoleon, when they took it upon themselves, in defense of their own egos, to determine what was good for all the people." A Teamsters' chapel, a natural constituency for Martin, threatened to cancel its season tickets. More surprisingly, though Martin had not a liberal bone in his body, his anti-Establishment, stick-it-to-the-man persona made him a cause célèbre among local campus radicals. At an anti–Vietnam War protest at the University of Minnesota, shaggy-haired demonstrators wore "Fuck Griffith" buttons and chanted, "Bring back Billy." "It's an out-and-out revolt by the Minnesota baseball fans," reported *The Sporting News*. "They feel they have been robbed of their loveable, scrappy, outspoken, toe-stomping Italian leader."

A year later Martin was back in baseball, this time as manager of the Tigers. Again, he improved the team's sagging fortunes dramatically, bringing home a divisional flag in his second season. Again, he inspired fierce loyalty among fans. Again, he quarreled with the front office and was ultimately fired. Martin managed baseball teams well, the joke went; he just wasn't very good at managing himself. The Orioles' Earl Weaver later put it in starker terms: "Billy understands baseball, he just doesn't understand life."

The Texas Rangers picked Martin up near the end of the '73 season. In the winter he pushed the club to sign Ferguson Jenkins, a tall right-hander who was coming off a dismal year with the Cubs. At the end of spring training Martin elevated an unknown twenty-four-year-old named Mike Hargrove from Class A ball. Jenkins won twenty-five games and was named Comeback Player of the Year; Hargrove hit .323 and was voted Rookie of the Year. Having transformed the team with the worst record in baseball into an 84-76 club, the first winning season in franchise history, Martin was voted Manager of the Year.

Martin pushed his men to play over their heads, much as he had. He expected a level of intensity that was difficult, if not impossible, to sustain over a 160-game season. He shortened the careers of numerous pitchers, giving them the ball on three days' rest and keeping them in games with their pitch counts soaring. Martin's management style didn't please everybody, nor was it intended to. "You hire twenty-five players. Fifteen of them are for you a thousand percent. Five are probably undecided and probably five don't like you," he said. "The secret is to keep that last five away from the undecided so you'll have twenty going for you instead of fifteen against ten."

Still, he was a brilliant tactical manager, a fact that even those who loathed him are apt to concede. "I didn't like the way he treated his players, myself included," says Ken Holtzman, who pitched for Martin in New York, "but as a field manager, in terms of the X's and O's, he was the best."

Martin, who had been known as Billy the Kid in his playing days, liked Texas. The gunslinging swagger suited him. He even started wearing lizard-skin cowboy boots and adopted a Southern drawl. The team's owner, Brad Corbett, set Martin up with a membership at a fancy golf club in Fort Worth. When he and his old pal Mickey Mantle nearly ran over Ben Hogan in a golf cart, Shady Oaks cut Martin loose. So did Corbett, in late July 1975. "He's the easiest guy in the world to work for . . . as long as you just do it his way," Corbett said. Martin of course took a different view. "I was the perfect guy to be crucified," he said, after smashing the five-hundred-dollar wristwatch that Corbett had given him for Christmas. In six years he had saved three teams and been fired three times.

Martin was licking his wounds when Bernie Tebbetts tracked him down fishing for trout in Colorado. Tebbetts worked for a man named Gabe Paul who worked for a man named George Steinbrenner.

At the time, the Yankees had not won a pennant since 1964, an eternity in Yankees years. A generation of New Yorkers was growing up thinking the Mets were the city's winning team. Such were the club's softening fortunes that when a Cleveland-based syndicate led by George Steinbrenner bought the Yankees from the Columbia Broadcasting System in early 1973, it actually paid a few million less for the franchise than CBS had nine years earlier. At the time of the purchase, Steinbrenner had made it clear he had no intention of involving himself in the day-to-day affairs of the ball club. "We plan absentee ownership as far as running the Yankees is concerned," he told *The New York Times*. "We're not going to pretend we're something we aren't. I'll stick to building ships."

A different reality soon emerged. Even after Steinbrenner was suspended from baseball in the fall of 1974 for making illegal contributions to Richard Nixon's '72 presidential campaign, no one doubted that he was behind the team's aggressive personnel moves. Most notably, in the run-up to the '75 season, the Yankees traded Bobby Murcer for the quick and powerful Bobby Bonds and signed Catfish Hunter, one of the best control pitchers in the game, to a five-year three-million-dollar contract. Hopes soared; hopes sagged. With two months left to play in the 1975 season, the Yankees were ten games behind the Boston Red Sox. Steinbrenner decided it was time to sacrifice his manager, Bill Virdon.

Tebbetts made Martin an offer that should have been easy to refuse: seventy-two thousand dollars a year, the same amount he had earned in Texas, plus a contract crammed full of onerous clauses. One prohibited him from criticizing the front office. Another stipulated that he could be fired, without pay, for failing to make himself available to management. He'd be on parole, and he hadn't even been arrested. Steinbrenner was familiar with Martin's gift for turning players and fans against a team's management, but he was sure he could break him. He started by calling Martin to tell him this was a one-time offer. If he wanted to manage the Yankees, now was his chance. Martin signed.

Steinbrenner quietly flew Martin and his wife, Gretchen, into New York and stashed them away in a midtown hotel under a fake name. For dramatic effect, he wanted the announcement made on Old Timers' Day, which was still a couple of days away.

On August 1, 1975, Bill Virdon managed his last game for the New York Yankees. The following day, a steamy one in New York, Billy Martin rode out to Shea Stadium, where the Yankees were subletting space while their own ballpark in the Bronx underwent extensive renovations. The faded pennants and championship flags of a bygone era had been dragged out of storage and draped over the outfield fences for the occasion.

Martin hid out in the clubhouse and waited nervously for his name to be called as the rest of the old-timers—Mantle, Ford, DiMaggio—ambled out of the dugout, doffed their wool caps, and lined up along the first base line. Much to Martin's chagrin, Steinbrenner had insisted that his new manager, a lifetime .250 hitter, be announced last, a position traditionally occupied by one of the true greats. Martin, by now dizzy with anticipation, finally trotted onto the field in his old uniform, No. 1. After eighteen years in the wilderness, Billy Martin was back in New York. He looked about the same at age forty-seven as he had in his twenties, only he was skinnier, a little more hunched, and he wore a mustache—"that mustache of recent vintage that gives him the look of a rather shopworn Mississippi riverboat gambler," as the *New York Post*'s Jerry Tallmer described it a few days later.

The crowd roared, but Martin was fixated on the smattering of boos; the quiet, steady man whom he was replacing was not unpopular. "They're booing right now," Martin said to himself, "but before I'm through everyone will be cheering."

Martin, who was neither quiet nor steady, decided to use the remainder of 1975 to take the measure of his men both on and off the field, to identify the crybabies and "alibi Ikes." But first he needed to make his expectations clear, and he did after his second day at the helm: "If you play for me, you play the game like you play life. You play it to be successful, you play it with dignity, you play it with pride, and you play it aggressively. Life is a very serious thing, and baseball has been my life. What else has my life been? That's why, when I lose a ball game, I can't eat. Sometimes I can hardly sleep. If you're in love with the game, you can't turn it on and off like a light. It's something that runs so deep it takes you over."

Over the following eight weeks Martin designated several players for trade, including Bonds, who'd spent the better part of the year fighting knee problems. A revered figure in San Francisco, Bonds had never felt at home in New York. With a few games to go, long after the Red Sox had clinched the pennant, he told Martin to scratch him from the lineup because his leg was bothering him. "No man's going to tell a manager whether he's going to play or not." Martin quietly fumed. Bonds's fate was sealed. At Martin's urging, he was soon placed on the trading block. "Just wait 'til I get them for a full year," Martin kept telling the team's director of publicity, Marty Appel, as the '75 season wound down.

In April 1976 the Yankees came home to the South Bronx. It was, more or less, the same place that the team had left two years earlier, but it bore no resemblance to the South Bronx in which Martin had played twenty-three years before that. Back then the neighborhood's main thoroughfare, the Grand Concourse, had been known as New York's Champs-Élysées (with Yankee Stadium as its Arc de Triomphe). Now metaphorists referenced Dresden, not Paris, when describing the area. The old Concourse Plaza Hotel, a stately building of red brick, had been shuttered after a brief and ignominious run as a welfare hotel. The South Bronx itself was losing ten square blocks, or five thousand housing units, a year to arson fires. Rows of private houses, apartment buildings, and small businesses had been gutted, leaving only blackened hulks in their wake. In the area surrounding the stadium, more than twelve hundred buildings had been abandoned. Empty lots were covered with shoulder-high weeds. Ten blocks from the ballpark, an unfinished five-million-dollar low-rise housing development, abandoned for lack of funds in 1972, was a thriving heroin den. When Charlayne Hunter-Gault, the first Harlem bureau chief of *The New York Times*, visited the Samuel Gompers Vocational-Technical High School in the South Bronx, she was confronted by charred classrooms and broken blackboards. Students passed around a bottle of wine during class. "It's very difficult to generate enthusiasm," one teacher told her, "when you feel everything is terminal."

Amid this wreckage was the newly renovated Yankee Stadium, not the blue and alabaster bauble of yore, but a concrete fortress, battleship gray, with an anachronistic ring of white wooden trim running across the top of its bleachers, a little touch of Norman Rockwell on this otherwise bleak canvas. Mayor Lindsay had sold the twenty-five-million-dollar renovation to taxpayers as "the centerpiece of another New York City neighborhood renaissance." Six years and a hundred million–plus dollars later, it was instead a powerful symbol of misplaced priorities, an outsize admission of urban failure. "It was Lindsay," explained one official in the comptroller's office. "First he got us pregnant, and then an abortion would have cost too much money." Mayor Beame, who had inherited the stadium fiasco from Lindsay, did what he could to distance himself from it; he was conspicuously absent from the grand reopening festivities. WAS THE STADIUM WORTH IT? *New York* magazine asked rhetorically in a photo essay on the debacle.

At least the Yankees were finally winning. As his team dominated its division, Martin's prediction came true: The fans *were* cheering him. During the golden fifties, the dynastic era in which Yankees didn't strain—didn't need to strain—a sweat-soaked Billy Martin had thrived despite his cockiness, scrappiness, and unseemly hunger to win. In the seventies, a very different time in the life of the ball club and its city, he flourished because of them. In September, Steinbrenner gave him a three-year contract extension. Beneath the surface, though, Martin's inner demons continued to torment him. As the wins piled up, the stakes mounted, and the prospect of losing became that much more sickening. Martin, who was always skinny, was now more gaunt than ever. Over the course of the '76 season, he shed 20 pounds from his six-foot frame, dropping to a mere 154. The crow's-feet around his eyes, which had first appeared during his playing days, deepened.

The 1976 American League play-offs, New York versus Kansas City, went the distance. The decisive game five was played on a chilly October night in the Bronx. The Royals jumped out to an early lead, but the Yankees came back and pulled ahead. Then, in the top half of the eighth, George Brett's three-run home run knotted the game at six, where it remained until the bottom of the ninth. The Yankees' first baseman, Chris Chambliss, was due to lead off the inning, the start of which was delayed for five minutes while the grounds crew cleared the field of the glass bottles that had been raining down from the stands for much of the game. Chambliss finally dug into the left-hand side of the batter's box and sent the first pitch he saw, a waist-high fastball, over the fence in right-center.

Now, bedlam. Before Chambliss arrived at first base, a torrent of fans had poured out onto the field. By the time he reached second, one had taken the bag out of the ground; Chambliss had to touch it with his hands. Weaving in and out of the growing crowd between second and third, he was knocked down repeatedly. One fan tried to take his helmet. Approaching third, Chambliss decided he'd had enough. He made a wide turn around the bag and headed for the dugout, which was already spilling over with fans, including Cary

Grant, whom Steinbrenner had brought down from his box for the postgame celebration. The Yankee players pushed through the crowds to find teammates to hug. For his part, Martin was busy recruiting a detail of cops to escort Chambliss back onto the field so he could touch home plate.

The brand-new ballpark was in tatters. Huge chunks of turf were uprooted, every base had been stolen, and the field was littered with garbage, from newspaper shreds to empty bottles of Hiram Walker brandy and Jack Daniel's. The Yankees had won their first pennant in twelve years.

The National League champions, the Cincinnati Reds, were favored to win the '76 World Series. Martin was, at least outwardly, unfazed: "I don't care what Pete the Greek says," Martin remarked, referring to the prominent oddsmaker Jimmy the Greek. "I never met a Greek who was a smart baseball player." But Martin's run was over. The Yankees dropped the first two games in Cincinnati. After losing game three in the Bronx, Martin threatened to give one wisecracking reporter "a good asskicking." He was coming unglued. By the time he exploded in the fourth and final game, few were surprised.

The grotesque tableau was imprinted on Martin's memory, and to make matters worse, he and his second wife, Gretchen, a former airline stewardess and the belle of her sorority at the University of Nebraska, split up shortly after the season ended. He spent the winter of '76–'77 alone in the Hasbrouck Heights Sheraton in New Jersey. Most afternoons found him listening to Jim Croce or sitting curled over a drink in a dimly lit watering hole, idly running his finger around the rim of a glass of scotch. When he wasn't replaying the World Series in his head or entertaining dark thoughts about what Steinbrenner was up to across the river, he was worrying about his teenage daughter from his first marriage, who'd been thrown in jail in Colombia after being accused of trying to smuggle cocaine out of the country in her panty hose. "I'd like to kill the sons of bitches who sent her down there," thought Martin.

5.

WHEN news of Rupert Murdoch's purchase of the *New York Post* first hit the *Daily News* and *The New York Times*—the sleepy *Post* had been scooped on its own sale—on November 20, 1976, the city's response was a collective "Rupert who?"

He'd materialized in New York overnight: a thick, sad-eyed, harried-looking fellow with an outsize head and furry eyebrows, more day laborer than press lord by the looks of him. The bottomless pockets said otherwise. So did a vast media empire, nearly two decades in the making, spanning both Australia and Britain.

Murdoch's father, Sir Keith, had been a legendary newspaperman himself, the proprietor of a chain of Down Under dailies that were meant to be his son Rupert's inheritance. Only by the time of his death Sir Keith had been forced to sell off everything but a controlling interest in one, the *Adelaide News.* So, called back from an apprenticeship at London's *Daily Express* at the tender age of twenty-two, young Rupert Murdoch set about reconstructing the empire that he had once been destined to inherit. Applying the lessons he'd learned on Fleet Street, he soon transformed a quiet, provincial afternoon paper into a thriving scandal sheet. A tabloid career was launched.

Murdoch built on his success in Adelaide over the course of the sixties. The Australian newspaper world was a vicious one, and Murdoch fought his way through one circulation war after another, routing numerous opponents who were much better armed. His burlesque formula—some sex, some crime, some news, and plenty of hysterical headlines—proved an invaluable weapon. Murdoch had an undeniable gift for the so-called screamer (SEX OUTRAGE IN SCHOOL LUNCHBREAK topped a *Sydney Daily Mirror* leader in which he reprinted confessional excerpts from the diary of a teenage girl).

Australia is a big country, but it didn't take Murdoch long to outgrow it. In 1968 he set his sights on London, where *The News of the World*, a rare holdover from the Victorian era, was on the block. Robert Maxwell, a British Member of Parliament, had fixed his eyes on the same prize, but he was no match for Murdoch, who loosed his accountants on Maxwell's books. Once *The News of the World* was his, Murdoch wasted no time smutting it up. He swallowed *The Sun* next, leading his first issue, in 1969, with a story about a trainer who drugged his horses (HORSE DOPE SENSATION). On page three was another sort of sensation, a photo of a topless sexpot. *Private Eye*, the British satire magazine, dubbed him "Rupert 'Thanks for the Mammaries' Murdoch." On Fleet Street he was known simply as the Aussie tit-and-bum king.

In 1973, Murdoch landed on American soil, snapping up a pair of broadsheets, the *San Antonio News* and its sister morning paper, the *Express*. Murdochization promptly ensued. KILLER BEES HEAD NORTH was the headline atop a story about a type of bee with a potentially fatal sting that had been spotted minding its own business somewhere in South America. "The visual clamor is so great that on some days less than twenty lines of body type—'news'—can be found above the page-one fold," wrote Griffin Smith, Jr., in a 1976 article in *Texas Monthly* magazine. "Serious world, national, state or even local stories are—well, they aren't." Circulation soared. Soon after, Murdoch launched an American supermarket tabloid, the *National Star*.

His next target was nothing less than the oldest continuously published daily newspaper in America, one of the last living links to the country's founding fathers, the *New York Post*. The Killer Bee really was heading north.

The *Post*'s own founding father, Alexander Hamilton, had himself never been one to underestimate the dark side of human nature, or what he preferred to call its "impulses of rage, resentment, jealousy, avarice and of other irregular and violent propensities." Hamilton met a tragic fate that would have made for great tabloid copy

(HAMMY SHOT, KILLED IN DUEL). The *Post*'s first editor, William Coleman, hadn't fared much better. He was bludgeoned to death from behind by a political opponent.

The *Post* overcame this inauspicious start and had a fine run through the middle of the 1800s under the editorship of William Cullen Bryant, who commissioned Civil War dispatches from fellow poet Walt Whitman. Things went downhill from there, though, and by 1935 the paper was running a distant third behind New York's other afternoon dailies, the *Journal-American* and the *World-Telegram.*

A gentleman named George Backer believed he had what it took to save the *Post.* Everything except for the money, that is. That was where his wife, Dorothy, came in. Dorothy Backer (née Schiff), a slender, elegant woman with sparkling blue eyes, long fingers, and an aquiline nose, was the granddaughter of Jacob Schiff, the most successful of the German Jewish bankers who'd made their fortunes in New York in the late 1800s.

Schiff reluctantly agreed to bankroll the *Post.* Backer, her second husband, called Dolly (as she was universally known) a "wonderful sport" for doing so. Schiff didn't intend to involve herself in the paper's affairs. She was, as she put it, "just a woman who had gotten sucked into another sort of monstrous country house." Backer assured her that the repairs wouldn't take more than a couple hundred thousand dollars. Soon he was hitting her up for another hundred thousand every month.

For a while Schiff was content to play the Upper East Side matron, limiting her role at the evening broadsheet to signing the checks as the paper limped along under her husband's uninspired hand. The late thirties were a great time for newspapering: There was a civil war in Spain, the rising specter of fascism in Europe, and the matter of Stalin's regime, which, depending on whom you believed, was ushering in either a new world order or another Dark Age. Across America, ideologies were crashing into one another like angry atoms. In New York the Little Flower, Mayor Fiorello La Guardia, was ardently pursuing his utopian vision for the city. Yet Backer's *Post* was bland, soporific, "a kind of gentleman's product," as one of his editors derisively put it.

Schiff grew tired of her husband and annoyed with his dilettantish approach to the paper. She wanted the *Post* to be less tweedy and even proposed moving to a tabloid format. Backer disagreed. "George resisted the idea of popularizing the paper, which he saw as vulgarization," wrote Jeffrey Potter in his 1976 biography of Schiff (a line worth remembering, foreshadowing as it did the debate over Murdoch's subsequent Murdochery). The paper's features editor, Ted Thackrey, agreed with Schiff and told her so. When Backer became sick with tuberculosis, his wife started spending more time at the paper with Thackrey, a dashing man brimming with ideas. When the Japanese bombed Pearl Harbor, he and Schiff worked side by side on the *Post*'s early edition. She was falling in love, with both Thackrey and the newspaper life.

Backer told his wife that he hadn't bargained for a career woman, and the two decided to divorce. That was just as well for Schiff, who was by now ready to move on to Thackrey. They were married in the office and after a one-night honeymoon moved into adjoining offices as coeditors and copublishers. Schiff traded in her dresses for slacks. They were more comfortable to work in, even if they hid what one of her numerous admirers had described as "the finest gams in New York."

During the forties the *Post*, now a tabloid, came into its own. Schiff and Thackrey called for bigger, snappier headlines and photos, more New York news, better columnists, flashier writing, a foreign bureau, and a Saturday magazine. "I'm fortunate in having average tastes—neither highbrow nor lowbrow—and although I'm interested in serious reading, I love gossip, scandal and human interest," Schiff told Potter.

The new *Post* was finally tilting toward its owner's interests. Politically it was staunchly liberal, a full-throated champion of FDR, who had, in fact, owned a piece of the paper while it hemorrhaged money in the twenties. (President Roosevelt was also very close to Schiff, who was a frequent guest at Hyde Park. There were even rumors that the two had been romantically linked.) But it was not liberal enough for Thackrey, who wanted to endorse Henry Wallace, a Stalin sympathizer, for president in 1948. Schiff would have none of it, and the copublishers wrote competing endorsements, he for Wallace, she for Thomas Dewey. By now they had diverged on more than just politics. The following year Thackrey quit the *Post* and the marriage.

His successor—at the paper anyway—was James Wechsler, the *Post*'s Washington bureau chief and one of the giants of twentieth-century American journalism. In his first edition as editor of the *Post*, Wechsler, a tiny pipe smoker who wore bow ties and suspenders, laid out his vision for the paper in an editorial headlined THE THINGS WE BELIEVE: "It has often seemed as if liberal journalism must be dull journalism on the theory that any interest in the variety of human experience is somewhat irreverent or irresponsible. We don't accept this grim view. A newspaper . . . is the record of how people lived, exulted and suffered in every phase of their existence. We know that all of you will not agree with us all of the time, but we vow that you will never be bored."

Wechsler kept his word. His specialty was crusade reporting, and no threat to democracy, no matter how well insulated, was safe. The paper took aim at the great Robert Moses, uncovering the human cost of his "slum clearance," and at J. Edgar Hoover, who subsequently ordered Wechsler's hotel room bugged and labeled him a "little rat." The *Post* published a twenty-four-part investigative series on syndicated columnist Walter Winchell, revealing his "frightening power to bully and browbeat" (Wechsler's words), and was predictably answered by bullying and browbeating. Winchell devoted countless column inches to demonizing Wechsler, at one point reporting that the editor and his wife had stayed home on their anniversary rather than brave the public shaming that would have greeted them at any New York City restaurant.

Most explosive of all was the *Post*'s seventeen-part exposé of the foremost demagogue of his day, Senator Joseph McCarthy. Headlined SMEAR, INC.: JOE MCCARTHY'S ONE-MAN MOB, it was the first in-depth look at "the hoax of the century," as the series described him. "America had known and survived other demagogues," Wechsler wrote in his 1953 memoir, *The Age of Suspicion.* "McCarthy's advantage was the peculiar depth and intensity of the crisis he was exploiting; the atomic bomb gave a new dimension to our fears."

The paper came under heavy fire in the wake of the series. Much of it was directed specifically at Wechsler, who had been a member of the Young Communist League at Columbia University in the thirties. Since leaving the party at age twenty-two, Wechsler had become one of America's most militant anti-Communists, but that was of little concern to McCarthy, who preferred to believe that one couldn't be both anti-Communist and anti-McCarthy. So the senator from Wisconsin hauled Wechsler before his tribunal, where he proceeded to rehearse the facts of the editor's brief Communist past and added to it all sorts of farfetched fictions, including the preposterous suggestion that Wechsler was still a closet Commie.

The competing papers lapped it up: POST EDITOR ADMITS HE WAS YOUNG RED; WECHSLER TIES BARED, blared a 1952 page one headline in the *Journal-American.* Unintimidated, Schiff stood by Wechsler, and her paper continued to gather steam.

By the middle of the 1950s the New York newspaper market was crowded, and the *Post* was by no means the city's biggest or its best, but it was profitable. It had carved out an intensely devoted constituency, in part because its sports section was the best in town. (Ernest Hemingway had the *Post* sent to him in Cuba so he wouldn't miss the offerings of its emotional star columnist, Jimmy Cannon.) In this arena anyway, the afternoon press time worked to the *Post*'s advantage. At the end of the workday, streams of men in fedoras would pick up a copy for a nickel en route to the subway to catch up on the afternoon baseball scores.

The *Post* shared the liberal politics of the *Times* and was every bit as literate, but it had a much streetier feel than the stodgy paper of record. "She [the *Post*] is the good indignant mama of New York City as *The New York Times* is its good gray papa," Jerry Tallmer wrote in a valentine to the *Post* in *Dissent* magazine in 1961. "Papa goes down to the firm and makes the money while mama keeps things hopping." A. J. Liebling opted for a different metaphor that same year, calling the *Post* "warm, shrewd, pretentious and insecure, like a first-generation Phi Beta Kappa student at Hunter College."

The *Daily News* catered to blue-collar Catholics, a traditionally conservative lot, while the prounion, pro–civil rights *Post* (not coincidentally, Cannon was Jackie Robinson's biggest booster) was the newspaper of New York's blue-collar Jews. It was also the paper of Murray Kempton, whose columns seemed to embody best the paper's ethos, its commitment to ennobling the struggles of the working class, while keeping a keen eye on the rich and powerful–comforting the afflicted and afflicting the comfortable, as the saw went. It was as well the paper of gentleman gossip columnist "Midnight" Earl Wilson–"nobody ever feared me," Wilson once boasted–who chronicled the city's nightlife six days a week in "It Happened Last Night."

Schiff decided to separate the *Post*'s editorial and news operations in 1962 and booted Wechsler upstairs to run the opinion pages. The paper's circulation was slipping, and people had been telling her that Wechsler's cause journalism was muscling out of the news hole too many sexy tabloid stories of crime and corruption.

The new editor was Paul Sann, a wiry, Runyonesque newspaperman who wore closely cropped hair and cowboy boots and was free of ideological encumbrances. Sann inherently understood something that Wechsler, in his crusader's zeal, had a tendency to forget: that the word *tabloid* didn't simply refer to the physical format of a newspaper; it spoke to a whole approach to fashioning a narrative. Tabloids were passionate, dramatic, melodramatic. Even when big issues were at stake, tab stories had to be driven, and unabashedly, by larger-than-life characters and defining details. With Sann making sure that the rapists and crumb-bums got the same play as the pols and the eggheads, the paper hit high stride. "Wechsler gave the paper its liberal political soul; but Sann made it a tough ballsy tabloid," wrote Pete Hamill, a Sann protégé, in his memoir *A Drinking Life*.

In December 1962 a citywide strike upended the New York newspaper world. Four major dailies died in its wake, and the *Post* would have keeled over too if Schiff hadn't broken ranks with her fellow publishers and negotiated her own settlement with the unions. (Murdoch pulled exactly the same stunt in the summer of '78.) In 1967, when the *Post*'s last afternoon competitor folded, the paper's circulation jumped from four to seven hundred thousand.

Yet even without competition, the *Post* was soon faltering as well. By the middle of the seventies the very notion of an afternoon newspaper seemed antiquated, particularly now that Vietnam and Watergate, which provided daytime copy that seemed too urgent to wait until the following morning to read, were passing into history. Between the two of them, the *Times* and the *News* had a lock on the city's advertising lineage. The *Post*'s brain trust, Wechsler and Sann, were aging; the paper's readers, New York's working-class liberals, were migrating to the suburbs in droves.

The *Post* grew dowdy in its dotage. Schiff's cheapness was partly to blame. Among her more memorable cost-cutting measures was the mandate that reporters obtain prior approval before placing overseas phone calls. The news hole, already shrinking as advertisements disappeared, was being overtaken by soft features and chalky profiles like "The Daily Close-Up." Investigative reporting was all but out: too expensive. The paper had thirty columnists, most of whom weren't exclusive to the *Post* and were instead bought on the cheap from a syndicate. Front-page news stories were picked up from the wires. One talented young writer after another left to seek his or her fortunes, or at least a living wage, elsewhere.

Earl Wilson was still dutifully filing "It Happened Last Night," but by the middle of the seventies the column had come to seem quaint, anachronistic. The rest of the media were busy discovering the new celebrity culture: Time Inc. launched *People*, Andy Warhol launched *Interview*, the *Daily News* hired people spotter Liz Smith. But the *Post* was still clinging to Midnight Earl and his jocular chitchat about the Great White Way.

Schiff remained a strong presence at the paper. (Her arrival at the *Post*'s offices was always preceded by her white-gloved chauffeur, Everett, carrying her loyal Yorkshire, Suzy Q.) She was still more than happy to impose her political will on her reporters and editors, demanding, for instance, a stem-to-stern rewrite of a profile of William F. Buckley, Jr., that she deemed too flattering. There was no doubt about it, however: The *Post* was adrift. "In the last days of Dolly the paper was really horrific," remembers longtime City Hall reporter George Artz. "When my stories on the Citizens Budget Committee became front-page news, I knew we were in trouble."

It's hard not to read something else into the paper's aimlessness. The trauma of the Lindsay years had eroded the populace's faith in New York's civic culture, which the *Post* had so assiduously nurtured with its expansive, old-fashioned liberalism. By the mid-seventies New York's predominantly liberal middle class was becoming an increasingly conservative lot. Somewhere along the way the *Post* had lost its raison d'être, and Rupert Murdoch, who like any self-respecting publishing tycoon yearned to sink roots in New York, had apparently found his.

Murdoch first met the *Post*'s silver-haired doyenne in the summer of 1974, at the East Hampton beach house of *New York* magazine's celebrated editor, Clay Felker. Murdoch could be charming. Even in her seventies, Schiff, who'd been married and divorced four times and still smoked Kools through a white cigarette holder, was not immune to charm, particularly when her seducer's sweet nothings included attacks on *The New York Times.*

Not long after, Murdoch asked Schiff if the *Post* was for sale. It wasn't the first time she'd been approached. Hearst and Newhouse, among numerous others, had made overtures in the past, though no one had offered to do much more than assume the paper's mounting debt. She hadn't been ready then, and she wasn't ready now, though she was closer than perhaps even she knew.

The *Post* logged a substantial loss in '75 and was en route to an even bigger deficit in '76. Schiff had no other businesses to help absorb the damage. An imminent change in the estate tax law was likely to make it prohibitively expensive for her to pass the paper along to her heirs. Yet another strike by the print unions was in the offing.

In the fall of '76 Schiff invited Murdoch to lunch in her office suite on the sixth floor of the *Post*'s shabby downtown digs. The two publishers sat at her luncheon table and ate roast beef sandwiches on rye bread–Schiff served corned beef to Jews, tuna to Catholics, and roast beef to Protestants–beneath a life-size papier-mâché statue of Alexander Hamilton. "I sensed that she was very tired," Murdoch later reflected. Secret negotiations began, and within three months they had settled on a thirty-one-million-dollar price tag.

Murdoch went off to a private dining room upstairs at "21" to celebrate with twenty of his most trusted colleagues. The corks were still popping come midnight. The group eventually stumbled downstairs and found Governor Carey and Tip O'Neill, then in his final weeks as Speaker of the House, at the bar. Murdoch and his crew joined them for a drink. James Brady, the editor of the *National Star*, suggested that they finish the night at Elaine's, where the media elite always finished its nights.

As was the custom, a few stretch limos were grazing in front of "21," hoping for some freelance fares. The *Star*'s ace reporter, Steve Dunleavy, suggested that they travel uptown in style. Murdoch shook his head; taxis would be cheaper.

"But, Boss," pleaded Dunleavy, "you just spent thirty million dollars on the *Post*. For once, let it be limos!" And it was.

The restaurant was closing, but its proprietor, Elaine Kaufman, was there to greet them. "You did it!" she screamed. "You fucking did it! You bought the *Post*!" The chef had already gone home, so Elaine made them breakfast herself. Brady remembers floating home sometime before dawn, his stomach full of scrambled eggs and bacon.

New York, a city of subway readers, gave Murdoch a warm welcome too. At a Christmas party Hamill, a true newspaper romantic who'd watched his beloved *Post* succumb to irrelevance in recent years, told Robert Lipsyte that he had high hopes. Hamill suggested that Lipsyte, a once and future *Times*man, do a city-side column for the *Post*.

"It could be great—me and Jimmy [Breslin] at the *News*, you and Murray [Murdoch had already rehired Kempton, also at Hamill's urging] at the *Post*," said Hamill. "We could really kick ass in this town." The *Post* had soon signed Lipsyte up.

"New York hasn't had a first-rate newspaper rivalry since the Great Strike of 1961," wrote Michael Kramer in *More*, a respected, if short-lived, journalism review. "And now, thanks to Australian newspaper magnate Rupert Murdoch, the good old days seem to be on their way back."

And what of Murdoch's briny recipe for success—the blood, the guts, the boobs? That would never play here, Kramer, *More*'s editor in chief, confidently said. "His mix for the Big Apple is going to be a good deal more sophisticated."

6.

The freer you make baseball in every respect, the better the game's going to be. We saw that with Jackie Robinson. Jackie liberated the game. He was free. Free to steal home. Free to turn a single into a double. Free to play the game with a sense of danger and urgency. That same sense of freedom should apply to free agency.

DICK ALLEN

SHORTLY before midnight on November 28, 1976, a camera crew from NBC-TV's *Grandstand* show assembled on the tarmac at John F. Kennedy International Airport and waited for the arrival of an American Airlines flight from Oakland. The papers were reporting that the Yankees were about to sign the cream of baseball's first crop of free agents, and NBC wanted to be there to record the athlete's reaction to his new home.

Figuring out what plane he'd be on had been easy enough. A staff member for the program called every airline that made the trip. "Hello. This is Mr. Reginald Jackson," he said, "I'd like to reconfirm my reservation on your flight to New York." After a few tries he reached an American Airlines representative who answered in the affirmative.

At a few minutes past midnight Reggie Jackson stepped off the plane and into the bracing East Coast air with a blonde on his arm. The cameras were now rolling. A *Grandstand* reporter approached his six-foot, 207-pound subject and poked a microphone in his bespectacled face: "Welcome to New York, Reggie!"

Jackson looked at the reporter, grinned, and asked, "What the fuck are you doing here?"

The thirty-year-old slugger who had outgrown the tag *superstar* long ago—*Sports Illustrated* preferred *superduperstar*—proceeded to baggage claim. He picked up his valise, slipped on the hooded otter jacket that he had paid thirty-five hundred dollars for a week earlier in a boutique on Madison Avenue, and climbed into the stretch limo that his new boss, George Steinbrenner, had sent to fetch him in the far reaches of Queens. It was black, with the Yankees' symbol on the passenger door and the understated yet unmistakable vanity plate, "NYY."

The team's director of public relations, Marty Appel, had arranged for a suite at the Americana Hotel in midtown. The concierge had assured Appel that Mr. Jackson was going to love it; Jimmy Carter and his wife had stayed there a few months earlier during the Democratic National Convention.

Mr. Jackson hated it: The room had twin beds. He called Steinbrenner and threatened to turn around and go back to California if the situation wasn't remedied immediately.

Steinbrenner woke Appel at his house in Tarrytown and threw a fit of his own. Appel worked the phones for a while and eventually managed to secure a suite at the Plaza. When he called the front desk at the Americana to deliver the good news, he learned that Jackson and his friend had already gone upstairs. The presidential suite would have to do. He had a big day ahead of him.

"I was always afraid of New York when I played there," Jackson says of his pre-Yankees days. "I wasn't really a city boy." He was a suburban boy, born in 1947—the year that Jackie Robinson made his debut with the Brooklyn Dodgers—and raised in a two-story house in Wyncote, Pennsylvania, a predominantly white middle-class town just north of Philadelphia.

Jackson's father, Martinez Jackson, had been a professional ballplayer too, only that was back in the 1930s, when the game was still segregated. He was a small but scrappy second baseman, just like his son's future nemesis, Billy Martin. Years later, long after he'd left baseball to go fight in World War II, Martinez filled his young son's ears with stories from his barnstorming days, tales of sleeping in flophouses, of creeping into Southern towns late at night so as not to draw the attention of the local rednecks, of facing such legends as Satchel Paige and Josh Gibson. The Newark Eagles had paid him seven dollars a game, plus a little extra pocket money for driving the team bus.

Reggie Jackson's friends called his father Skippy, short for Skipper, because he'd been a pilot in an all-black military unit. He was a proud man, a tailor and dry cleaner who quoted the Bible frequently and reprimanded his children for using sloppy diction. "His kids would be able to use the language and use it properly," as Jackson once put it. "He knew it would pay off eventually."

Martinez Jackson was by no means a role model. He was a born hustler, with a weakness for gambling and chasing women, whose wife left him when their youngest son, Reginald Martinez, was six. Martinez Jackson supplemented his income by bootlegging illegal corn liquor in their basement. Reggie's older brother Jim—Slugger, as he was known because of his tendency to get into fights—helped operate the still and always had a pocketful of large bills to show for it.

In other ways, though, it was a typical suburban American childhood, circa 1960. Jackson wore khaki pants or dungarees and plain white T-shirts underneath a Cheltenham High School letter jacket—blue and gold, with a big *C* embroidered on the back. He listened to WIBG, which played plenty of Elvis Presley and Buddy Holly. He tinkered with his cars, a maroon '55 Chevy 327 and a '49 Ford with a wheezy Olds engine. He hung out at the Jack Frost ice-cream stand with his best friend, George Beck, who was planning to go into the army after graduation. A couple of bars were usually willing to serve them beer, usually Ballantine's or Schmidt's; otherwise it was hamburgers at Kenyon's, the local diner. On a clear night, Jackson and Beck might scramble up the hill behind the church and talk about their futures while taking in the view. (Years later, when Reggie was a star with the Yankees and Beck was a truck driver, Reggie's aging father would call Beck and ask him to drive him to the ballpark to see his son play. "Beck?" he'd say. "It's Skippy. I need a wheelman.")

"I once had a long talk with Reggie about his childhood, and I asked him what he had gotten out of living in an upper-middle-class white neighborhood," recalls *Newsday*'s Steve Jacobson. "He fiddled around with the question for a while and came up with 'aspirations.' "

As a black kid in a mostly white neighborhood, Jackson had his run-ins with prejudice. On several occasions Beck, who is white, says Jackson deputized him to pick up and drop off his girlfriend so the girl's parents wouldn't know their daughter was dating a black boy. Still, Wyncote, with its burgeoning Jewish population, was a relatively progressive place. Jackson later called it "a neighborhood where race wasn't an issue." Moreover, this was a time of racial optimism; dreams of a marbled America swelled in the baritone of Martin Luther King, Jr. "The hoarded anger of generations, so long starved by despair, was now fed by hope," as historian Arthur Schlesinger, Jr., put it. Jackson's boyhood hero Willie Mays, who rose to national prominence from the slums of black-hating Birmingham, drove the point home.

Reggie Jackson graduated from Cheltenham High in 1964. It was an infamous year for nearby Philadelphia. Race riots engulfed the city, and a growing antiblack backlash found a convenient outlet in the Phillies' new third baseman, Richie ("Dick") Allen. An outspoken black militant with a giant Afro who drank beer before games and smoked in the dugout, Allen was pelted with bottles and batteries and ordered by jeering Philadelphia fans to go back to South Street with "the rest of the monkeys."

By then Jackson was en route to Tempe, Arizona. He had been marked for greatness from an early age, though his future was supposed to involve carrying balls rather than swatting them. Not that he hadn't been a hell of a baseball player in high school—pitching three no-hitters and batting .550 his senior year—it's just that the athletic scholarship specified football. Of course, as soon as Jackson's football coach at Arizona State University moved him from halfback to cornerback, a defensive position, his eyes started wandering toward the baseball diamond.

Rather than ask for a tryout, Jackson told a couple of his buddies on the baseball team how good he'd been in high school. Then he told them a few more times. Eventually they grew tired of hearing it and bet Jackson that he couldn't make the team. A few days later, after football practice, he jogged over to the Sun Devils' diamond. He took off his helmet and shoulder pads, grabbed a bat, and dug into the batter's box. He missed the first pitch by a yard. His small, mostly uninterested audience laughed. Then the fireworks began: a series of towering blasts over the fifty-foot palm trees beyond the fence in right field.

Jackson joined the freshman baseball team and struck out nearly every time up. His extraordinary athletic ability was never in doubt, though. All the student athletes at ASU had to take a developmental activities class, which involved a series of physical fitness tests—jumping, running, chin-ups, etc. Jackson finished first in his class; among his more impressive feats was throwing a basketball sixty yards. "That's when I realized that this guy was some kind of physical stud," says Jeff Pentland, who lived across the hall from Jackson in college and went on to become a major-league hitting coach.

During Jackson's sophomore year, his only season of varsity ball at ASU, he broke the school's single-season home run record with fifteen. It doesn't sound like much now, but at the time it was unheard of, largely because most colleges, including Arizona State, considered baseball a low priority and bought cheap, lightweight bats. He also became the first collegian to hit a ball out of Phoenix Municipal Stadium.

Jackson was still raw, unschooled, virtually unable to recognize an off-speed pitch; Gary Gentry, who went on to pitch for the New York Mets, remembered striking out a callow Reggie Jackson on three straight sliders. But even with the Wiffle bats that the athletic department provided, when Jackson redirected a fastball, it would sail across the Arizona blue sky as though he'd hit it off a tee. "Nobody that I ever coached hit the ball harder, including Sammy [Sosa], Barry [Bonds], and Gary [Sheffield]," says Pentland. "And that's giving those other guys as much respect as I can."

In the outfield, Jackson misjudged loads of fly balls, but he got great jumps and had a tremendously strong arm. When one of his teammates who was trying to make the transition from pitcher to outfielder complained about his throws sinking, Jackson told him to come to practice early the next day for some pointers. Jackson showed up late. He rode onto the field on his bicycle, wearing wing tips, khakis, and a madras shirt. He took one practice toss and then told his teammate to watch. Jackson proceeded to launch a ball from the fence in right field to home plate on a clothesline.

There would be time for fine-tuning later. Reggie Jackson was the second player chosen in the 1966 draft. He might well have gone first, his coach at ASU informed him, had the New York Mets not been put off by a line in his scouting report that said he had a white girlfriend. Instead, the Mets took a catcher named Steve Chilcott, who injured his shoulder and never made it off the farm, leaving Jackson to Charlie Finley, the owner of the Kansas City—soon to be Oakland—A's.

Jackson's tenure in the minor leagues was destined to be brief: a cup of coffee in Lewiston, Idaho, where he batted .300 and hit a memorable dinger that broke a window in the little house across the street from the ballpark, then on to Modesto, California, where he made his first fashion statement, Ban-Lon shirts and alpaca sweaters. Jackson's teammates in Modesto had heard all the hype about their new bonus baby, but they were nevertheless awed by his prodigious home runs and the thunderbolts he uncorked from the deep recesses of right field. Sure, he misplayed more than his share of balls and struck out way too much, but it was only a matter of time. "You knew that once he learned to discipline himself at the plate and became a better defensive player he was going to make it big," recalls Rollie Fingers, who came up through the minors with Jackson.

The following year, 1967, Jackson was bumped up to the A's AA franchise in Birmingham. It wasn't quite the same Birmingham that his boyhood hero Willie Mays had known, but it was close. There were no visible signs that the struggle for civil rights had started here, no memorials to the fight against segregation, no statues commemorating its heroes. The movement itself had long since moved on—"Bombingham" was considered a lost cause—and the city had settled back into its comfortable bigotry.

The bus arrived from spring training at Nineteenth Street North, the same Greyhound bus terminal where the Ku Klux Klan had assaulted the Freedom Riders as the local police looked on in May 1961. Reggie and two other black players were given cab fare and sent to the Gaston Motel, which had been bombed four years earlier in a failed attempt to kill the Reverend Dr. Martin Luther King, Jr.

Jackson spent a couple of weeks sleeping on the couch of the apartment of a couple of his white teammates, Joe Rudi and Dave Duncan. Rudi told Jackson that their landlord had threatened to evict them if "the colored" didn't leave. Rudi thought they all should move. Jackson said to stay put; he'd find his own place. That place was the Bankhead, a rare apartment/hotel that rented to blacks, with a rare coffee shop that served them. The other towns in the Southern League weren't much better. When the team bus stopped for lunch, Jackson's teammates frequently had to bring his food out to him. Fans hollered "nigger" and "black boy" at him from the stands.

Jackson withdrew. "Reggie pretty much kept to himself in Birmingham," recalls Fingers. "The only time we'd ever really see him was on road trips." Between the lines, however, the fledgling slugger blossomed. In 413 at bats with Birmingham, he hit .293, with seventeen home runs and seventeen stolen bases. One of those home runs was memorialized with an *X* painted more than halfway up the light tower in right field at old Rickwood Field. No one, not even Mays, who had played here for the Negro League's Black Barons, had ever hit one there before. With success came swagger. Jackson started cracking wise when he returned to the dugout after his at bats. He led the Birmingham A's to the Dixie World Series, was voted the Southern League Player of the Year, and was called up to the big leagues for the tail end of '67.

When the A's opened the following season, in a game that had been postponed for twenty-four hours because of the rioting in the wake of the assassination of Dr. King, Reggie Jackson was the starting right fielder. He went on to lead the American League in two categories that year: strikeouts (171) and errors (14). He also hit twenty-nine home runs, including one that he one-handed off the field foul pole in Oakland while his sprained right wrist was wrapped in a bandage. He worked every day with A's hitting coach Joe DiMaggio, who focused on getting Jackson to make better contact. He also convinced Reggie, who was still using those toothpicks he'd hit with at ASU, to move to a much heavier piece of wood. "Reggie is still green as grass," DiMaggio told one sportswriter. "We've just got to bring his talents to the surface. They're all there, no question."

Anyone who failed to take note of this twenty-two-year-old slugger in '68 could hardly miss him in '69, when he exploded like a pack of Roman candles, slamming thirty-seven home runs before the All-Star break. He landed his first fan club, Reggie's Regiment, and his first *Sports Illustrated* cover. Jackson cooled down considerably in the second half, once pitchers stopped throwing him fastballs and defenses started playing him three infielders on the right side, but he still finished his second full major-league season with forty-seven home runs.

Jackson's sophomore swoon arrived a year late. The trouble started with an off-season salary row with Finley. Jackson asked for sixty thousand dollars; Finley offered forty-five thousand. Ten days before the 1970 season started, they finally settled on forty-seven thousand—a thousand for each dinger—plus a four-hundred-dollar-a-month apartment in downtown Oakland.

Jackson struggled, and Finley ordered him moved down in the lineup. When that didn't help, Finley had him platooned and eventually benched. At one point he even threatened to send Jackson back down to the minors. When he did play, Jackson inevitably got frustrated and lost his temper, flinging his helmet, kicking the water cooler, emptying out the bat rack. After one strikeout he slammed his bat into the ground, snapping it in two.

It didn't help that he and his wife, his college sweetheart, had separated at the start of the season, after less than a year of marriage. When Jackson threatened one local newspaperman, a few of his teammates told the writer not to take it too seriously: "You know how fucked up he is this season." Fucked up enough to give his owner the finger when he crossed the plate after a grand slam, his first major-league grand slam, in September. Jackson ended the season at a dismal .237. The diminished number of at bats did not prevent him from leading the American League in strikeouts for the third straight year, with 135.

A pair of eyeglasses to correct his nearsightedness—whoever heard of a home run hitter wearing glasses?—and a season of winter ball in Puerto Rico made all the difference. At the center of an emerging A's dynasty, Jackson returned to form in '71, lifting his average to .277, with thirty-two home runs. But his most memorable drive of the year didn't count toward his season totals.

Measuring home runs is an inexact science; the flight of the ball is always interrupted before it can come to a natural stop. So six hundred feet is only the estimated length of the one Jackson hit in the '71 All-Star Game in Detroit. The ball would have sailed right out of the ballpark if it hadn't crashed into an electronic transformer on top of the roof in right-center, making the titanic blast only more dramatic; it looked as if sparks were actually going to fly. Even some of the old-time writers who had watched Babe Ruth couldn't remember seeing anything like it. Al Kaline, who had been with the Tigers for nineteen years, called it "the hardest hit ball I've ever seen in my life, here or anywhere else." Asked later where the ball, which bounced back onto the field, had landed, Jackson cracked, "Around first base."

The A's captured their division in 1971. In the off-season Reggie went into therapy. (This was the period, as Jackson later reflected, during which he came to realize that R-E-G-G-I-E did not spell J-E-S-U-S.) The following year—and in '72 and '73 as well—the A's won the World Series. Reggie Jackson became a superstar. His teammates called him Buck or Buck Tater—a modification of *long potato*, a Negro League term for a home run—or just plain Reggie.

Part of baseball's allure had always been the unintimidating appearance of its professional practitioners. "[T]he man in the stands could be forgiven if he felt that only the inexplicable accident of skill kept him from the field itself," Roger Angell wrote in the days before steroids and rigorous off-season weight lifting regimes. Reggie Jackson was the exception that proved the rule. He was a remarkable physical specimen at a shade north of six feet, 207 pounds. He had a blacksmith's biceps—seventeen inches around, the same size as Sonny Liston's. His comic book superhero's thighs (twenty-seven inches around), got him down the line in a hurry but were so overdeveloped that he was constantly pulling hamstrings.

Reggie loved the whole ritual of hitting. He'd mash his helmet over his Afro, adjust his glasses, and shift around his upper body to make sure that his shirt wasn't pulling too tight. He'd dig his feet into the dirt calmly but purposefully—first the back, then the front—making sure there were no stones beneath his spikes. Then he'd take a slow-motion practice swing, stretching his arms out as he eased the barrel through the strike zone, lingering for an extra second at the end, the tip of his bat pointing menacingly at the opposing pitcher. Most hitters free their mind of all distractions when they step up to the dish; Reggie became hypersensitized. He was acutely aware of the bias of the crowd, of the way his uniform clung to his body, of the feel of the lumber in his hands.

He was a guess hitter. Rather than zone—drawing an imaginary zone and hitting anything inside it—he would look for a particular kind of pitch (usually a fastball) and drop the head of the bat on the ball. When it was at the top of his shoes, he'd go down and lift it up. The ball appeared to be stuck to his bat for an instant, as though he were shoveling dirt. "I wasn't sure the first time I saw him," Ted Williams said in 1970. "The second time I was amazed. He is the most natural hitter I have ever seen." Most power hitters need to be taught to shorten their strokes in order to increase their bat speeds. Reggie had a long swing and remarkably quick hands. He was a natural at cat-and-mouse mind games too, intentionally flailing at a pitch early in a game to set himself up to see the same pitch again in the late innings, when more was at stake.

When you look at hundreds of images of Reggie at the plate, two start to recur. In one, the snapshot of the home run swing, his shirt is stretched tight across his chest, his bat is slung over his shoulder, and his chin is tilted up slightly to allow his eyes to follow the flight of the ball into the seats. In the other, the strikeout swing, Reggie is clutching his bat—"the dues collector," he called it—in front of his torso like a tent pole, his legs twisting around each other as if he were trying to screw himself into the ground.

"There's nothing I like better than hitting a ball hard—clean and hard," Reggie said in his early years. "The feel and sound of it . . . it's just beautiful." The only thing as satisfying as delivering a good line drive, he might have added, was delivering a good line. His father had warned him: Remember, you're colored. So too had Dick Allen, who gave the young slugger some hard-earned wisdom—to speak with his bat, not his mouth. But Reggie adhered to a different motto: If you don't blow your own horn, there won't be any music. "When you take over a pitch and line it somewhere, it's like you've thought of something and put it with beautiful clarity," Jackson told a writer for *Sports Illustrated*, finishing the riff with a line that couldn't have made *SI*'s headline writer's job any easier: "Everyone is helpless and in awe."

During batting practice, Reggie routinely flouted the rule prohibiting players from fraternizing with members of the opposing team. Rapping with the league's other home run hitters was worth the fifty-dollar fine. In his 1981 book *Mr. October*, Maury Allen recounts a typical exchange, this one between Reggie and the Red Sox's George Scott, who tied Reggie for the American League home run title in '75 with thirty-six:

> *"It was right in my kitchen," Scott would say.*
>
> *"Did you cook it?" Reggie would ask.*
>
> *"Smoked it . . . really smoked it."*
>
> *Jackson's face would break into a smile. He would soon be touching Scott's bat and rubbing the handle and inspecting the grains of finely crafted wood.*
>
> *"Me," he would say, "I gotta go hunt for them. No one throws Reggie one in his kitchen."*

One of Reggie's favorite rhetorical devices was the weather metaphor, with all its biblical overtones. "I am like a storm when I hit," he once told Herb Michelson, a writer for *The Sacramento Bee*. "First there's sleet. Slow, sharp sleet out of dark skies. Then comes a mass of clouds and a howling wind. And thunder. Very noisy, very frightening thunder. The wind now grows in intensity. Leaves are blowing everywhere off trees of every description. Limbs and boughs are snapping off and falling. There is a great noise. There is a heavy, heavy downpour all around." He was also like a storm when he missed. "Hurricanes ain't nothing but soft winds when Reggie starts missin' when he goes for the downs," he said.

Reporters began huddling around Reggie's corner locker as though it were a free buffet table. "In triumph or tragedy, there is something about the Athletics' Reggie Jackson that attracts attention," *The Sporting News* wrote in 1971. Reggie described what that something was in a Q & A with *Black Sports* magazine: "I want to be the dominating force. I want to control the situation. I want to control the ballpark. I've come out there to get everyone on my side, to draw the attention to me so I can beat you."

There was, naturally, plenty of envy in the A's clubhouse and no shortage of snickering behind Jackson's back. But for the most part, his teammates learned to take Reggie in stride. When he paraded around the locker room in a towel—a Baby Ruth in one hand, an Oh! Henry in the other—asking everyone what his candy would be called, he was greeted with helpful suggestions: "How about the Shit-head bar?"

Reggie's teammates knew that his personality took the heat off them, and they could see that he thrived on the melodrama. Sal Bando, the team captain and a schoolmate of Jackson's at Arizona State, remembers making an error that cost the A's a game in 1973. He left the clubhouse early and went to bed dreading the morning headlines. He knew too that he'd have plenty of time to stew over them; the team was flying off on a road trip the following day. "So I get up in the morning and pick up the paper, and the headline is REGGIE RIPS COACHES AND MANAGER," Bando laughs. "And at the very bottom of the article is 'Bando's error lets in winning run.' " On the plane that afternoon, A's manager Dick Williams stood up to say something to Jackson as he strode down the aisle. The slugger just brushed right by him. "The next thing you know," says Bando, "Reggie goes on a tear and carries the club for a week."

Reggie let his Afro grow; Black Was Beautiful, particularly in Oakland, the cradle of the Black Panthers. But it was more a fashion choice than a political one. In this era of rising black militancy, Reggie was fiercely color-blind. He started a real estate company with a friend from college—they called it United Development because Reggie was black and his partner was white—and on the road he roomed with Chuck Dobson, a white pitcher. "There are 200 million people in this country and 180 million of them are white," Reggie told a reporter for *Time* in '74. "It's only natural that most of my friends are white."

The women with whom he disported after his divorce in '73, a large group that included several of the A's hot pants–clad ball girls, were almost always white. (This preference became the subject of jokes among his teammates. He was once sitting with Yankees' third baseman Graig Nettles in a bar at O'Hare Airport when a good-looking, well-dressed black woman approached them. She told Reggie how much she admired him, gave him her business card, and invited him to call next time he was in Chicago. Cracked Nettles: "Do you have a blond wig?")

Out in Oakland, tensions occasionally arose between Jackson and his black teammates. Baseball had been integrated many years earlier, but social segregation was still the custom in most clubhouses. The A's Billy North, now a stockbroker in Seattle, once confronted Reggie, telling him that a number of the team's black ballplayers didn't feel they could count on him. A couple of months later the two men were swapping punches—with Reggie in the buff—on the locker room floor.

North and Jackson had a complicated relationship, one that North later described as love-hate. Jackson had taken the A's new center fielder under his wing when he first arrived in Oakland, but by the following summer they were barely speaking. This was Reggie's way. He could be compassionate and sympathetic in one instant and cold and vicious the next. "There was a schizo part of Reggie that he could control and a schizo part that he couldn't control," says Marty Noble, who got to know Reggie covering the Yankees for *Newsday* in the late seventies. "That made him like four different people."

Peter Gethers, the editor of Jackson's 1984 autobiography, got to see them all. He remembers working with Reggie one afternoon in his hotel suite in Arizona, where Jackson's last team, the California

Angels, trained. After weeks of frustration they had finally made some progress, and Reggie was buoyant. He told Gethers what a great job he was doing and invited him to meet him downstairs for dinner in a couple of hours, when he'd be finishing up an interview. Gethers went downstairs at the appointed time and found Reggie at a table with the reporter. "I start to sit down, and he looks at me as if he'd never seen me before," recalls Gethers. "He just glared at me and said, 'Can't you see I'm being interviewed?' " Gethers apologized and went off to McDonald's. "If I hadn't been such a young editor at the time, I would have told him to go fuck himself," Gethers says. "Plus he was Reggie. As mean and genuinely horrible as he was, he was such a star and could be so charming that you really wanted him to like you, which only made the self-loathing that much worse."

Reggie won the American League's Most Valuable Player award in 1973. The following June he landed on the cover of *Time* magazine. In July he received more All-Star votes than any player in the history of the game. A few months later Reggie was *Sport* magazine's cover boy, only with a twist: He was dressed as General Patton and interviewed by George C. Scott, who had played the title role in the 1971 film *Patton*. It was a clever pairing: Both Jackson and Patton were mercurial egocentrists consumed by an abiding sense of destiny. For the photo shoot, Jackson gamely donned the four-star helmet, the leather holster with matching revolvers, and the high-powered binoculars. But when the World War II jeep was rolled into the studio, he balked. "Hey, man," he said, "I don't want to be *that* far removed from my peers."

Of course he already was. Reggie was working on three books: an autobiography, an instructional guide to hitting, and a diary of the 1974 season that began, "My name is Reggie Jackson and I am the best in baseball." As his fame grew, says Bando, his A's teammates saw less and less of him.

In 1974 Reggie moved from a penthouse apartment in Oakland

to a $85,000 condo in the Berkeley hills complete with a view of the San Francisco Bay. By now he was making more money in endorsements and on land development deals than he was playing right field. He hired a brunette secretary to handle his bills and fan mail. He took out a $1.8 million insurance policy on his life. Like his dad, who always had a fleet of beat-up, nowhere-near-roadworthy Chevies out back, Reggie started collecting automobiles: hot rods, muscle cars, antiques, even a souped-up drag strip racer. His favorite, a Porsche, was adorned with tags that read "MVP 73." His '39 Chevy, with a new Cadillac engine, was even more conspicuous: "REG-9."

He even took up golf. When Vice President Ford heard this, he invited Reggie to join him for a round in Arizona. It was, Jackson joked, the first time he'd ever hung out with someone who was asked for more autographs than he was. Ford shot a 97, Reggie shot a 90, taking ten dollars off the future president.

He was part old-fashioned ballplayer—"an uninhibited colossus of a man," Harry Stein wrote in *Esquire*—and part newfangled black superstar in his designer jeans, snug-fitting turtlenecks, and Italian loafers, a male purse tucked under his bulging arm. Baseball is a game of nuances, of subtle rhythms, of almost invisible acts, but there was nothing nuanced, subtle, or invisible about the fast-talking, freewheeling Reggie Jackson and his thirty-five-inch, thirty-seven-ounce stick of fire-treated wood. He was the national pastime's first made-for-TV celebrity. But he still wasn't famous enough for his taste. After all, only one local paper had assigned a writer to cover the A's on the road. "I want to be nationally known," Reggie proclaimed after his team won its third straight World Series in 1974. "I'm not a household name yet."

Reggie hit .289 that year, with 29 home runs, 93 RBIs, and 25 stolen bases. It was an impressive season, and Finley rewarded him with a $5,000 raise, bringing his salary up to $140,000. In '75 Jackson hit a league-leading 36 home runs with 104 RBIs. When he and Finley were unable to agree on new terms for 1976, the A's owner unilaterally renewed his contract with the maximum allowable pay cut of 20 percent.

This was permissible under baseball's so-called reserve clause, a provision in the standard labor contract that yoked a player to his team for the duration of his career. The offending line, in paragraph 10-A, read: "[T]he Club shall have the right to renew this contract for the period of one year on the same terms . . ." Over the decades baseball owners had interpreted this to mean that each time the contract was renewed, the one-year option clause was renewed along with it. A player was, in other words, effectively "reserved" for life. The standard contract also gave the owner the right to reduce a player's salary by up to 20 percent, precisely what Finley did to Jackson in advance of the '76 season.

Today's salary excesses notwithstanding, it was an unjust system, one that promoted monopolies like Finley's and violated a player's basic right to seek the highest available price for his services. In 1976 it was finally struck down. Thenceforth players who had played out their contracts plus a single option year would have the right to test their value on the open market. Finley had no intention of paying Reggie Jackson, or anyone else for that matter, what would soon be the going rate for top-tier talent, so he decided to unload him instead. On April 2, 1976, the A's power-hitting right fielder was traded to Baltimore.

Reggie initially refused to go. Eventually he set a price for his services: $200,000. After weeks of haggling, Baltimore went as high as $190,000. Reggie conceded; he would play, but he wouldn't sign a new contract. He wanted to finish out the option year of his contract with the A's, so he would be a free agent at the end of the summer.

When Reggie showed up for a pregame press conference at the Baltimore clubhouse in pressed blue jeans and a black leather jacket on April 30, the 1976 season had already been under way for three weeks. His new teammates were seething. The Orioles had given up a fine hitter and a quality starting pitcher for Jackson. They didn't begrudge him the right to fight for more money. They just didn't see why he couldn't have done it after reporting for duty, like the rest of the nine unsigned Orioles.

The fans weren't much happier. When Reggie took batting practice after that night's game, some five hundred of them stuck around to boo him. It was a time-honored baseball tradition; even the beloved Joe DiMaggio had been barraged with hate mail from Yankees' fans when he held out for a raise at the start of the 1938 season. And Baltimore's new cleanup hitter wasn't just holding out; he was carpetbagging. He hadn't even rented an apartment in Baltimore, opting for a room at the Cross Keys Inn instead.

Reggie got off to a slow start. He'd been working out in the Arizona State gym, but he hadn't faced live pitching in months. He was pressing, overswinging, overstriding, hacking at bad pitches in an effort to cram four weeks of at bats into every trip to the plate. After such a high-profile holdout, the pressure to perform was intense. The value of his stock was plummeting by the day, and as it did, his decision not to sign a new multiyear contract with the Orioles was looking increasingly foolish. At the All-Star break Reggie was hitting an anemic .242.

Then, all of a sudden, he righted himself. Ballplayers tend to emerge from slumps gradually, with a well-placed ground ball, a handle hit, maybe a lucky flare. Not Reggie. "Something in him would get triggered, and he would literally burst," recalls Marty Noble. Between July 11 and July 23, Reggie collected eight home runs and nineteen RBIs. "By next month," Reggie told his manager, Earl Weaver, "I'm gonna take over this league."

Baltimore joined the pennant race, and Reggie was back to his old self. "Not enough papers here to carry my quotes," he gleefully told Cleveland's press corps on one road trip. His teammates were slowly warming to him. "You just have to understand that Reggie is Reggie," said Orioles' outfielder Paul Blair. "Once you understand what he is, it's easy to get along with him. He's just a different individual. He likes attention and he wants attention and that doesn't necessarily have to be a bad trait." Jackson homered in the first game of an August 14 twin bill with the White Sox, then followed it up with a grand slam in the nightcap. Next time up, Chicago's reliever, Clay Carroll, knocked him down with a chin-high fastball. Jackson threw his bat toward Carroll, and his Orioles teammates poured onto the field for a brawl.

Orioles' fans were less understanding, particularly as the season wound down and Jackson's departure became imminent. After going three for three against Angels' ace Frank Tanana, Reggie struck out in his fourth trip to the plate and was hissed. It was the same story when he homered in six consecutive games but failed to go long against Nolan Ryan in the seventh. Fans started flinging hot dogs at him from the upper deck. Not that their resentment kept them away from the ballpark; attendance was up a hundred thousand in 1976. (In Jackson-less Oakland, it was down three hundred thousand.) Did he have any words for soon-to-be-jilted Orioles' fans? "This is business," he said. "I can't worry about the fans."

On August 30 Jackson turned up on the cover of *Sports Illustrated*—his fifth but by no means last *SI* cover—with a big grin, the gold frames of his glasses glittering in the sunlight. HITTING A MILLION: NO. 1 FREE AGENT REGGIE JACKSON, read the cover line. "I just want to be free," Reggie told a reporter from *Black Sports*.

A few months later, on an unseasonably warm day in early November, Reggie Jackson flew into New York to have lunch at "21." His lunch date, George Steinbrenner, met him at the airport in a blue blazer and gray slacks. Steinbrenner's obedient salt-and-pepper hair was neatly combed. His smooth face smelled of expensive after-shave.

The Yankees had already signed one free agent, Cincinnati's Don Gullett, the stringy-haired Kentucky southpaw who had effortlessly shut them down in the first game of the 1976 World Series. Now they had their sights set on Jackson. Steinbrenner told his head of baseball operations, Gabe Paul, to take a vacation in Puerto Rico while he attended to the matter. By his own admission, Steinbrenner didn't know much about baseball, but he had a feeling for personalities. (The story goes that when he first bought the team and paid an on-site visit to the ballpark, he saw a player wearing his cap backward. "Get that man's name," he told one of his aides. The player was the team's catcher.)

Steinbrenner's shipping business had occasionally brought him to New York, but it didn't get him into "21." Now that he owned the Yankees he was a regular. In an earlier era, ballplayers who needed a break from Toots Shor's or the Stork had bellied up there, but these days it was the province of a more haute crowd—power mongers, plutocrats, movie stars, politicians, authors, agents. What better way to lure Reggie to New York?

Reggie wasn't impressed, at least not initially. Checkered tablecloths and cheap-looking furniture? Tin jets dangling from the ceiling? The place looked more like a saloon than a fancy restaurant. Shit, it wasn't even carpeted.

He and Steinbrenner were joined by a few of Steinbrenner's friends, including William Fugazy of Fugazy Taxi and Limousine, who introduced Reggie to some of the other swells. (Fugazy's days as a highflier were numbered: His company went bankrupt in 1997, and Fugazy himself pleaded guilty to shifting assets to avoid paying off creditors, whom he owed on the order of seventy-five million dollars. He was ultimately pardoned by President Clinton.)

Reggie had a steak. After lunch he and Steinbrenner took a walk. They started up Fifth Avenue, passed the hansom cabs in front of the Plaza, and strolled alongside Central Park for a few blocks before moving over to Madison. They walked into a boutique with fur pelts in the window. When they emerged fifteen minutes later, Reggie was carrying an otter jacket. (He soon added a fifteen-thousand-dollar full-length nutria coat to his wardrobe as well, a gift from Ben Kahn

Furs, prompting Reggie to joke that he was the first athlete to be endorsed by a furrier.)

Everywhere they went, people were calling out to Reggie. "I had been there before, but I really hadn't been there before. It was as if I had seen New York across some crowded room, caught her eye, but never got the chance to talk to her," Jackson remembered in his 1982 autobiography, co-authored by Mike Lupica. "Now I was talking to her, feeling her. Being seduced by her."

Steinbrenner helped Reggie conjure a vision of his life in Manhattan: an apartment in a tony Upper East Side building with a sweeping view of Central Park (an easy drive to the ballyard); fine restaurants; beautiful, sophisticated women. "The way you can talk," Steinbrenner added, "dealing with the media will be like eating ice cream."

The word was that Reggie was asking for $3 million for five years, an unprecedented sum that turned off more than a few owners. There was the additional concern that paying one player so much would foster ill will among the rest of the team. "I will not demoralize this club over Jackson," said M. Donald Grant, the chairman of the Mets. Steinbrenner's main competition in the Reggie Jackson sweepstakes was the burger baron Ray Kroc, owner of the San Diego Padres, and Seagram's heir Charles Bronfman, of the Montreal Expos. Kroc offered $3.4 million over five years; Bronfman said he was prepared to go all the way to $5 million.

Jackson decided to sign with the Yankees for a lot less. The *Daily News* explained it thus: "While George's competition was offering nothing more than filthy lucre, George offered filthy New York—beautiful, big, bustling, exciting, pressurized, hurrying, unfunctioning, sexy, cultured, glamorous, filthy New York."

Not that there wouldn't be filthy lucre: $2.9 million over five years, plus an additional $63,000 for a custom-made Rolls-Royce Corniche. It averaged out to $580,000 a year—less than O. J. Simpson, Jimmy Connors, and Julius Erving, but more than anyone else in baseball, or for that matter, the history of baseball.

"If this is Americana, we lost the Revolution," an architecture critic once observed of the European-themed banquet rooms of New York's Americana Hotel. It was in the gaudiest of the lot, the chandelier-encrusted Versailles Room, that the Yankees crowned their new king on November 29, 1976.

Reggie wore a brass-buttoned three-piece gray flannel suit designed by Geoffrey Beene (who was about to roll out a new line of Reggie Jackson menswear), a sky blue shirt, a wide, dark blue tie flecked with gold leaves, and black alligator shoes. A gold bracelet with R-E-G-G-I-E spelled out in diamonds sparkled on his right wrist, a few inches above one of his three Oakland A's World Series rings.

"Here is the replacement for Babe Ruth," the *World-Telegram*'s Dan Daniel, dean of the press box, had written when twenty-one-year-old Joe DiMaggio first appeared in New York forty years earlier. Now it was Reggie's turn. The two men couldn't have had less in common. DiMag was tall and slender, strong and silent—"slow to smile and reluctant to speak," as his biographer Richard Ben Cramer wrote. His face was blank, like an actor awaiting his lines.

Reggie had already written and memorized his. "I didn't come to New York to become a star," he told the crowd, "I brought my star with me." He seemed more like the replacement for a different Joe—Joe Namath, who was conveniently on his way to Los Angeles to finish out his career with the Rams. They both were miniskirt-chasing bachelors—Namath's penchant for black women matched Reggie's taste for blondes—with rocket launchers dangling from their sculpted shoulders and the cocksuredness to guarantee the city victory. "I'm going to be working the World Series, either for the Yankees or for

ABC," Reggie told the assembled masses, "and I don't think I'm going to be in the broadcasting booth."

Even the editorial page of *The New York Times* took note of his arrival. "Reggie Jackson is a flamboyant man whose self-confidence is matched only by his athletic ability," the paper editorialized on December 2, 1976. "By choosing New York, Jackson has become the Yankees' first black superstar, not to mention their first black millionaire."

Reggie Jackson's new manager, Billy Martin, followed the Steinbrenner-Jackson courtship in the papers with a growing sense of disgust. He'd had his eye on a different free agent outfielder, Joe Rudi, a soft-spoken right-handed hitter who fielded his position much better than Jackson. Of course, no one in the front office had asked him.

Reggie was the kind of player who liked to draw attention to himself, the kind of player that Martin tended not to like, and over the years he'd directed more than one of his pitchers to throw at Jackson. But what bothered the fatherless Martin most was all the attention that Steinbrenner had lavished on Jackson. "George was taking Reggie to the '21' Club for lunch all the time, and I was sitting in my hotel room the entire winter and George hadn't taken me out to lunch even once," Martin later complained in his autobiography.

If Martin was looking for a reason to mistrust the newest member of his team, he didn't need to look far. Never one to miss a slight, Martin noticed that Jackson had told one of the reporters that he was excited about coming to New York because he and "George" got along so well. "You're going to find out George isn't the manager," thought Martin.

7.

ON a cold, snowy night in the waning days of 1976, former New York congresswoman and noted liberal firebrand Bella Abzug summoned her closest confidants to her red-brick town house on Bank Street in Greenwich Village. After stomping the snow out of their boots and stripping off their overcoats, they filed into the parlor, which, with its worn velvet couches and peeling red paint, resembled nothing so much as a Venetian bordello. It was time to discuss Bella's future.

The question was whether she should run for mayor. Private balloting would have revealed a landslide against the notion. "Most of us were there to say that we were exhausted and that we hoped she wasn't going to do this," says Harold Holzer, who had been Congresswoman Abzug's press secretary.

Nearly everyone in the room was still recovering from Abzug's grueling 1976 Senate campaign. It had been a bad idea from the start. At the time Abzug was one of the most powerful members of Congress, which is to say that she'd come a long way since her arrival in Washington in 1970. She'd started her congressional tenure by offending the House doorkeeper—when he asked her to remove her ubiquitous hat before stepping onto the floor, she'd reportedly told him to go fuck himself—and then moved on to the president. Meeting Nixon for the first time at a black-tie dinner for freshman members of Congress at the White House, she told him her constituents were very unhappy that he hadn't withdrawn from Vietnam. "We're doing better than our predecessors," Nixon replied, pumping her hand and smiling. "Well, your predecessors didn't do very well, but you're doing worse and we have to withdraw immediately," said Abzug. Nixon quickly moved her on toward his wife, Pat. "Oh, I've been looking forward to meeting you," the first lady said. "I've read all about your cute little bonnet."

The House of Representatives—"a male, white, middle-aged, middle- and upper-class power elite that stand with their backs turned to the needs and demands of our people," as Abzug described it—was a far cry from the Upper West Side that had elected her. The joke around Congress went that asking Abzug to sponsor a piece of legislation was the best way to ensure its defeat. It wasn't exactly a joke: A researcher for Ralph Nader determined that her sponsorship was enough to cost a bill between twenty and thirty votes. Abzug's popularity with her colleagues sank to a new low in 1972, when her district was gerrymandered and she chose to run for reelection against William Fitts Ryan, a beloved elder stateman of New York's liberal reform movement who was battling throat cancer and could barely speak. Ryan won the race but lost the fight against cancer and died before he could be sworn in. In a special election to replace Ryan, Abzug beat his grieving widow.

Then the tides began to turn. As the seventies wore on, many of the causes that Abzug had been carrying on about—namely women's rights, gay rights, government secrecy, the war in Vietnam, and the nuclear arms race—no longer sounded so controversial. The erstwhile pariah became an emblem of the triumph of liberalism. "No one better than she reflects such success as the new politics has had," wrote the editors of *The New Republic*. "Gutsy and shrewd, she has earned the esteem and, in Congress, the cooperation of people who at first disdained her as a kook." Always a nervous eater, Abzug became larger-than-life as well as large. She cut a memorable figure playing in House volleyball games in her jodhpurs and white sailor's cap, which she'd had specially made by a clothing designer in Connecticut.

Abzug's place in Congress could not have been more secure. There was no good reason to give it up, especially to run for the Senate. Winning votes in the hostile hinterlands, where radical Jewish feminists were as alien as skyscrapers, would be next to impossible, which explains why Abzug and her staff spent 104 consecutive weekends crisscrossing the state, visiting each of its sixty-four counties. Arriving in one rural county in the northern reaches of New York, Abzug was informed that there had been a threat on her life. The following morning she ordered one of her aides to take the first sip of her orange juice.

With four other legitimate Democratic candidates in the primary, the competition for endorsements had been fierce. After much deliberation, the *Times*'s editorial page editor, John Oakes, settled on Abzug. The paper's publisher, Punch Sulzberger, wasn't happy with the choice. An aggressively assimilated descendant of German Jews, Sulzberger didn't like Abzug's loudmouthed, yenta style, the way she called people *bubelah* when she scolded them. He vetoed the Abzug endorsement and ordered up a new editorial in support of her principal opponent, Daniel Patrick Moynihan, who wound up edging her out by a mere 1 percent.

It was Ramsey Clark who played the spoiler. He was a long shot, but his left-wing credentials—as a lawyer he had defended the inmates at Attica and the students at Kent State—positioned him to snatch votes from Abzug. He also snatched a deep-pocketed celebrity supporter from her, Paul Newman. Not long after her defeat, Abzug was invited to cut the cake at the launch party for *US* magazine at Elaine's. She leaned over the cake, knife in hand, to discover the frosted face of Paul Newman, the cover boy for the magazine's inaugural issue, smiling up at her. "I'd like to circumsize him instead," she cracked, carving right in.

Conservatives rejoiced at Abzug's departure from Washington. "The spectacle of a Congress without her has plunged her supporters into a grief rivaling the Maoists'," cackled the editors of the *National Review*; "for at least two years, the Captor Nations will be short one representative in Congress."

By the end of '76 most of Abzug's former employees had moved on to saner places of employ. This was not saying much. The only oppressed minority that Abzug had no sympathy for was her staff. It wasn't just the twenty-hour days; it was the emotional torture in the form of expletive-streaked abuse. The expletives changed, but the message stayed the same: "How could you be so stupid?" The tirades were made the more unbearable by the fact that they all believed so deeply in her. They were, to a man or woman, committed liberals, peace activists and graduates of the women's movement. For all of the lash marks on their backs, they remained fanatically loyal to their boss. "To work for Bella, you had to either be a masochist or an ideologue," says Doug Ireland, whom Abzug referred to as a "fat cocksucker" whenever she was in a foul mood.

Now that everyone had settled comfortably into the living room of her brownstone, Abzug asked for candid responses: Could she be elected the next mayor of New York? Dora Friedman, Abzug's administrative assistant, spoke first, and she spoke in an us-against-them language Abzug understood. "I don't think you can do it, Bella," she said. "*They* would never let you win. *They* would find some way to turn the electorate against you." The rest of the group waited quietly for their chance to second Friedman's sentiments.

Abzug gritted her teeth and peered over her half-rimmed glasses. "Are you quite finished?" she asked.

"Yes," Friedman answered.

Abzug hoisted her roly-poly frame up out of her chair. "How dare you speak to me like that," she thundered in a voice that could, as Norman Mailer once put it, "boil the fat off a taxi driver's neck." She ranted and raved and huffed and puffed. She opened a closet door, then slammed it shut. She knocked over a few chairs as she stormed into the kitchen, then knocked over a few more as she stormed back into the living room with a can of Pepsi.

Finally, she sat back down, pulled the tab off her Pepsi, and asked if anyone else had anything to say. A cacophony of voices chimed in: "You should run, Bella . . . Yes, definitely run."

Her candidacy remained the worst-kept secret in New York for the better part of six months. As long as her announcement wasn't official, she wasn't subject to the equal-time law, meaning that she could chatter away on *The Merv Griffin Show* and the Sunday morning talk show circuit without having to share time with the rest of the candidates. There were also rumors that President Carter might have a job for her, possibly even chairwoman of the Federal Trade Commission, and she didn't want to queer that deal, however remote a possibility. (Mayor Beame, who was all too aware of Abzug's popularity in the city, called on President Carter to encourage him to find a place for her, but Carter had already been warned that she was difficult to work with.)

The groundswell of support was building, and Abzug helped it along with quotes like this: "Barbra [as in Streisand] is begging me to run." She even teased at her plans in a cameo on *Saturday Night* in an interview with Miss Emily Litella, the addled TV news editorialist played by Gilda Radner who confused Soviet Jewry with Soviet jewelry and busing children with busting them. "Nothing's wrong with New York that a change in leadership can't solve," said Abzug. "So Stella," Miss Emily replied, "does this mean that you're going to throw your cat in the ring? I hope not because I can't understand why politicians throw their cats in the ring. The poor cats can't even put on gloves. Why throw them in the ring?"

When she did finally enter the race at the beginning of June, Abzug did hurl her big black straw hat into the crowd gathered in front of her. "It just went straight down," remembers Holzer. "I thought to myself, 'This is a very bad omen.' "

8.

HAVING already gobbled up one New York journalistic institution, Rupert Murdoch was now hungry for another. His eyes alit on *New York* magazine.

New York had gestated as a newspaper insert inside the Sunday edition of the *Herald-Tribune* in the mid-1960s, was born as a standalone publication in the spring of '68, and came of age in the infamous era of white flight and urban blight. Not that you would have known that from reading the magazine. While the rest of the country wrote and rewrote the city's obituary, *New York* stuffed its issues with mash notes, stories that celebrated the city's outsize characters (from Roy Cohn to Frank Serpico) and embraced its consumer culture (from Gucci to Givenchy).

Its founder/editor was Clay Felker, a tall, good-looking man with tiny feet, who dated a slender redhead, the best-selling author Gail Sheehy, and rented a well-appointed Fifth Avenue duplex with a massive statue of George Washington on horseback in the living room. Felker's well-trained social compass—the product of his own small-town-boy aspirations to make it in Manhattan—tugged him inexorably toward the city's ever-shifting power center. Yet the midwesterner was a perpetual outsider in the Big City. The paradox served him as an editor beautifully: He was both sophisticated and wide-eyed.

New York magazine was an editorial triumph, one that spawned countless imitators in cities across America. As a business, though, it never quite found its footing. In the beginning, Felker had had no trouble wooing venture capitalists. None of them had any illusions about getting rich, but since most of them already were, that didn't much matter. The magazine offered great cocktail party cachet, and the charismatic Felker was irresistible. "Everybody wanted to know

Clay; everybody wanted Clay to like them," says Robert Towbin, one enthusiastic early investor.

New York's cash flow problems started early and never diminished. A year after the magazine's launch the company was already starved for money and offered its stock to the public at ten dollars a share. A ritual developed at the annual board meeting. The company's chairman, Alan Patricof, would review Felker's exorbitant expense account line by line, while he and Felker screamed at each other.

Felker was determined not to let money concerns interfere with his plans to build an empire. In 1974 he approached his board with a proposal to buy *The Village Voice*. The directors balked, so Felker arranged for a merger that diluted his stake in the new company to 10 percent and boosted that of the *Voice*'s principal stockholder, Carter Burden, to 24 percent. Not two years later Felker persuaded his board to bring out *New West*, a *New York* magazine for California. Circulation and advertising were soon outpacing expectations, but so were start-up costs. True to form, Felker was not exactly running a lean operation. Among other things, he leased a pair of Alfa-Romeos for two editors who had been flown in from New York to pitch in with the launch. He was also angling for a 25 percent raise to his $120,000 salary and some additional perks, including a house in the Hamptons.

By the fall of '76 the New York Magazine Company was hemorrhaging money. Relations between Felker and his board were strained. From the perspective of the directors, Felker's recalcitrance had become exhausting, and the cachet of being associated with the magazine had diminished as he had grown less and less willing to humor his investors.

For his part, Felker was increasingly convinced that the moneymen were conspiring against him. He wasn't entirely wrong. Patricof was certain that if spending continued at its current levels, the company would go broke the following year. He also knew that as long as Felker was in charge, they'd be lucky if spending remained at current levels. Patricof told Felker that something had to give. "Clay," he warned, "find your own solution to the problem. If you don't, we'll have no choice but to find one ourselves."

Enter Rupert Murdoch. Felker and Murdoch had been introduced by Katharine Graham, the publisher of *The Washington Post.* When Murdoch subsequently moved to New York, Graham asked Felker to show him around town. They became fast friends, lunching in midtown, lounging poolside on summer weekends in the Hamptons, and, on occasion, discussing possible joint ventures. The lowbrow Murdoch and urbane Felker were drawn to different sides of New York—Murdoch to its grime, Felker to its glamour—but both had been seduced by the City of Ambition.

In a cab after dinner in late November 1976, Felker confided in Murdoch that he was having trouble with his partners at *New York* and asked if Murdoch, a battle-scarred veteran of boardroom warfare, had any advice. "He [Felker] was not astute enough to recognize that what he was doing was like asking an alcoholic to sniff your drink," wrote Michael Leapman, one of Murdoch's British biographers. A few days later Felker filled in some of the details over lunch. Murdoch offered Felker a piece of unsolicited advice for future business dealings: Borrow whatever you need to own 51 percent of something. Scrimp and save and bust your hump, and buy the rest: "Then you don't have to take any crap from anybody."

Now Murdoch illustrated the point. Ten days later he called Felker. "I've been thinking about what we talked about," Murdoch said, "and I've got some ideas for you. Why don't you come by the office tomorrow?" When Felker arrived, eager to hear what his friend had in mind, Murdoch had another man with him. "This is Stan Shuman," Murdoch said, "my investment banker." Murdoch offered Felker five dollars a share for his stake in the company, twice the stock's current trading value, but half the price at which the company had gone public eight years earlier. Felker was, in his words, "dumbfounded." A couple of days later he called back to say no deal. Felker figured Murdoch would just drop it. Instead, he and Shuman drew up battle plans for a hostile takeover. They'd woo one big stockholder after another until they had commitments for 51 percent of the company.

The key figure was Carter Burden, an ambitious young man from an enormously wealthy Manhattan family, who disliked Felker. (The feeling was mutual.) In the waning days of 1976 Murdoch flew out to Burden's ski house in Sun Valley, Idaho, to present him with the offer; Burden was more than happy to accept. Felker tried to rustle up investors for a counteroffer and Katharine Graham was interested, but when their representative called Burden, they were told he was out on the slopes.

Murdoch had soon locked up all the necessary shares. Felker sued to prevent the transfer, but he had no case. What he did have was a fiercely loyal staff, which threatened to walk out en masse. One *New York* writer, Ken Auletta, made a private appeal to Murdoch's lawyer, Howard Squadron, who answered: "You are a very talented group and Mr. Murdoch would like you to stay. But if you do leave, he will get new furniture."

Months later Gail Sheehy, Felker's girlfriend, charged in a lengthy article in *Rolling Stone* that Murdoch had cynically cultivated Felker's friendship. A Murdoch biographer who knew the publisher socially, Thomas Kiernan, took a less conspiratorial view of the betrayal. He suggested that Murdoch had soured on Felker after watching him in action in the Hamptons and on the Upper East Side, that he had found Felker's "social pretensions irksome." Both explanations sound overdetermined. Murdoch, a chronic deal maker, had probably given very little thought to Felker at all.

As 1977 got under way, Rupert Murdoch took control of three major New York journalistic institutions, a feat that landed him on the cover of America's two largest newsweeklies. *Time* dropped his head on King Kong's body and pictured him lumbering across the Manhattan skyline: EXTRA!!! AUSSIE PRESS LORD TERRIFIES GOTHAM. "Not since Charles Foster Kane strode into the city room of the mythical New York *Inquirer*," *Newsweek*'s story began, "has anyone caused such an uproar in the tight little world of New York journalism."

Arriving at his office in early January, *New York*'s new editor, James Brady, discovered a line of people outside his door waiting to quit. (One young woman handed him a box with a note inside: "Fuck you, Brady.") But Brady had more pressing concerns. The only cover story in the bank was a hatchet job on Murdoch. Eventually things settled down, and the magazine continued to follow Felker's blueprint, though with a much lower-profile stable of writers.

Murdoch tried to replace the editor of the left-wing *Village Voice* but then changed his mind in the face of a staff revolt and subsequently left it more or less alone. The paper was already making a handsome profit, and anyway, he had big changes in mind for the *Post*.

9.

REGGIE Jackson passed through the doors of the dressing room of the Yankees' Fort Lauderdale spring training facility at a few minutes after 9:30 a.m. on March 1, 1977. The reporters were already waiting for him, their Bic Bananas poised.

Reggie's new uniform was also waiting for him. The only problem was that it didn't fit. "Say, uh, sir," he called over to the clubhouse manager, grasping unsuccessfully for his name, "my pants are too long."

Pete Sheehy, the veteran clubhouse manager who had given

Babe Ruth his first Yankee double knits and had chosen No. 5 for Joe DiMaggio, fetched an extra pair from Fred Stanley, the Yankees' shortstop, who was two inches shorter and forty pounds lighter than Reggie. "See," Reggie cracked, as he pulled the pants over his bulging thighs, "I'm already too big for my britches."

Reggie reported to camp a little bit overweight. He almost always kept himself in good shape in the off-season, lifting weights—no one grunted louder on the bench press—and running around Lake Merritt in Oakland, but this winter he'd been busier than usual. There were the free agency negotiations and his crowded schedule for ABC, which included postseason color commentary alongside Howard Cosell (who complained that Reggie was trying to steal his thunder), a "Sports Legends" TV piece on Joe Frazier in Philly, a "Superteams" competition in Hawaii, and a "Superstars" competition in godforsaken Rotonda, Florida. ("I gotta take a Rotonda," Reggie cracked, interrupting one interview there for a bathroom break.)

As he stood bare-chested in front of his locker that first day as a Yankee, three gold pendants dangled from his neck: the word *Inseparable*, a gift from an old girlfriend; a dogtag that read "Good Luck Is When Hard Work Meets Opportunity"; and an Italian horn that was supposed to ward off evil spirits. Reggie layered on several T-shirts and a nonporous plastic jacket to help him boil off those extra pounds. He fiddled with his wristbands and pounded his fist into his glove a few times, before setting it down. "No sense fooling with this," he said, "'cause they didn't sign me for this." In time Reggie laced up his spikes, clattered up the dugout steps, and joined the rest of the Yankees on the field.

A little later in the day he had his first exchange with his new captain, Thurman Munson. Lucky for both of them, none of the reporters wrote it up at the time.

"Hey, you have to run now," Munson told Reggie, as the slugger made his way toward the batting cage to take his licks. "The way we do it here, you run before you hit."

"Yeah," Reggie replied, "but if I run now, I'll be too tired to hit later."

"Yeah, but if you don't run now, it'll make a bad impression on the other players."

Reggie looked over at one of the Yankees' coaches, Dick Howser. "Should I run now or hit?"

"The hell with running," Howser answered. "Get in there and hit."

All winter the New York papers had been filled with speculation about how Reggie and Munson were going to get along. The forecast called for storms.

Munson's insecurities ran deep, but their source was easily located. His father, Darrell, had drilled hundreds of ground balls at young Thurman, refusing to stop even after a bad hop caught him on the mouth and blood was running down his chin. A truck driver, Darrell spent most of his time on the road. Once he surprised his son by showing up at a minor-league game. Munson went five for five with two home runs; his father told him he looked like shit behind the plate. When Munson made it to the big leagues, Darrell told reporters that he had gotten carried away with his self-importance.

The scars never disappeared, though Munson did what he could to erase his father from his life, past, present, and future. In his posthumously published autobiography, *Thurman Munson*, he devoted exactly two paragraphs to Darrell, and he would have left him out altogether if his wife hadn't intervened with the ghostwriter, Marty Appel. "When dad was around," Munson wrote, "everyone in the house, including mom, was intimidated."

For most of the seventies, Munson had another nemesis, the Red Sox's Carlton Fisk. The two men fought over the title of best catcher in the American League, and Munson was usually on the losing end, often despite the numbers. In '73, Munson hit .301 to Fisk's .246, yet Fisk was voted starting catcher for the All-Star Game. At one point during the following season Munson realized he was beating Fisk in every category except assists. He remedied the situation by dropping the third strike on seven straight strikeouts, each time picking up the ball and throwing out the runner at first, an assist in the scorebook.

Those who knew Munson described him as moody. His friend Sparky Lyle begged to differ. "When you're moody," Lyle joked, "you're nice sometimes." Not that Munson was the type to let anyone know how he was feeling. "He had this shell around him that was impenetrable," recalls Appel. "He could be going through incredible inner turmoil, and he'd be singing a commercial jingle from the radio." (One of his favorites was for Burger King: "America loves burgers, and we're America's Burger King.")

Munson was never able to relax around reporters. He hated the fact that every racial or genital crack he made in the clubhouse might turn up in the papers. "I don't understand the press," he once said, genuinely perplexed. "They write about what you say, not what you do." Often when newspapermen trolled the clubhouse for quotes, he would simply retreat into the training room. Even for a catcher Munson suffered from an unnaturally long list of ailments—leg spasms, pulverized knees, blurred vision, debilitating headaches—but when he stretched out on the trainer's table, what he was seeking most of all was refuge. If a reporter found the caustic catcher in front of his locker on a bad day, Munson might tell him to get out of his face. On a really bad day he might tell him to get the fuck out of his face. He was, in baseball clubhouse parlance, a red ass. "Munson was the classic chip-on-the-shoulder guy," says former *New York Post* Yankees' reporter Maury Allen, "only the chip was a safe."

Phil Pepe of the *Daily News* was a rare reporter who was close to Munson. One of the more senior of the Yankees' beat writers in 1977, Pepe had grown up in Brooklyn in the forties, fantasizing, like every other boy in the neighborhood, about playing for the Dodgers. In the fifth grade, Pepe, who was small and unathletic, glimpsed a more realistic future. He wrote a composition about Abe Lincoln that his teacher assumed was plagiarized until his mother came into the school to vouch for him. "Thurman had this gruff exterior, but he really was a pussycat," says Pepe.

But it was the gruff exterior that New York so adored: the squat body, the turbo-charged waddle, the dirty uniform, the droopy mustache, the jaw bulging conspicuously with chaw, the way he stood in the on-deck circle in his shin guards, idly swinging a doughnut-heavy bat, occasionally releasing a gob of blackened spit. That, and the fire that burned in his Ruthian belly. The fact is Munson couldn't be nasty enough. After making a costly error and then striking out in one game at the stadium, he was buried in boos. Walking back to the dugout, Munson lifted his right arm and gave the whole ballpark the finger. Next time up he was treated to a riotous, foot-stomping ovation.

In the spring of '77 Munson was coming off one of the best seasons—and worst off-seasons—of his career. The Yankees' new captain, the team's first since Lou Gehrig, had just hit .302 with 105 RBIs and caught an astonishing 155 games, a performance that earned him the American League's Most Valuable Player award. Munson kept it up in the postseason too, batting over .500 in the Yankees' losing effort against the Reds. Yet after going four for four in the fourth and final game of the World Series, Munson, his gray shirt darkened with sweat, walked into the interview room just in time to overhear Reds' manager Sparky Anderson belittle him to the press corps. A reporter had asked the champagne-soaked Anderson to compare Munson to Cincinnati's own backstop. "You don't ever compare anybody to Johnny Bench," Anderson matter-of-factly replied. "You don't want to embarrass anybody."

A few months later Reggie Jackson inked his five-year deal with the Yankees. The front office wanted Munson at the signing. The Yankee captain gamely donned a plaid sports coat and slapped his new teammate on the back, but he was put off by the spectacle. "Naturally, the press conference for Reggie was a mob scene, with him calling all the writers by their first names, and asking the names and affiliations of those he didn't know before responding," Munson later recalled.

Munson had another reason to be bitter. After news of the Reggie signing first broke, Munson reminded Steinbrenner that his contract stipulated he would always be the team's highest-paid everyday player. Steinbrenner, who liked Munson—even though it drove him crazy when the catcher came up to talk after batting practice and left clumps of red clay all over his office—bumped his salary accordingly from $165,000 to $200,000. The matter seemed settled. Before long, however, Munson had learned that Reggie's $200,000 didn't include deferred income ($132,000), a cash signing bonus ($400,000), an interest-free loan ($1 million), or the Rolls ($93,000). "My promise," Steinbrenner answered, "was that no Yankee regular would be paid more annually in his *weekly checks* than Thurman was."

The back-and-forth continued. The Yankee catcher threatened to try to buy out his contract; the Yankee owner skipped Munson's MVP banquet. They eventually came to an agreement that entailed a new contract and more money, but Munson was hardly thrilled. He knew he was still earning a lot less than Reggie.

10.

IN all of Billy Martin's years playing for Casey Stengel in the fifties, the Yankees had never put together a winning record in the Grapefruit League. Martin saw the logic inherent in this. The regular season was long enough. Taking exhibition games seriously wasn't just a waste of time, it was downright counterproductive.

March also represented Martin's best shot at reaching some semblance of an emotional equilibrium. The baseball life was the only life he knew. (To be fair, *Sports Illustrated*, in a 1956 profile, had proposed two other career options for him: "Billy would have been perfectly at home among the hot-blooded bravoes of Cellini's Italy, or among the unionists who organized Big Steel.") The baseball-less winter was torture, and the summer simply held too many opportunities for failure.

But for one fleeting month, March, Martin could spend his days stress-free on the ballfield and his nights stress-free at the bar. Better still, it was a Yankee tradition to invite the legends down to Fort Lauderdale to work with the younger players, meaning he could room with his old pal Mickey Mantle in a two-bedroom condo in Boca Raton. All Martin really wanted was to be left alone to lose in peace.

It wasn't to be. Not only did Steinbrenner expect his manager to win grapefruit games, but he didn't like his living so far from the ballpark, nor did he approve of his driving to games instead of taking the team bus. As the losses mounted—even the University of Florida had the Yankees on the ropes until a ninth-inning rally—so too did Steinbrenner's anger. "The man was driving me crazy," Martin wrote in his 1980 memoir, *Number One*.

In the late innings of a drubbing by the Mets—in a game televised back in New York no less—Steinbrenner ordered the team's traveling secretary to let himself into the manager's office and take away the keys to Martin's rental car so he'd have no choice but to ride the bus back to Fort Lauderdale from St. Petersburg. After the game, Steinbrenner stormed into the locker room and lit into his manager, demanding to know why he hadn't, as promised, played the starting team.

"I'm going to tell you something," Martin shouted back. "I'm the manager of this team, and don't you be coming into my clubhouse again for any reason."

"I ought to fire you right now," Steinbrenner answered.

"I don't give a shit if you do fire me, but you're not going to come in here and tell me what to do in front of my players."

The players quickly rallied to Martin's defense. "We don't need him [Steinbrenner] riding in here like the Lone Ranger," said pitcher Dock Ellis, who was also feeling underappreciated by the Yankees' owner. After a dismal '75 with the Pirates, Ellis had gone 17-8 in New York in 1976. In contrast with his rabble-rousing days in Pittsburgh, where, among other things, he'd worn curlers to the ballpark and pitched a no-hitter on LSD, Ellis had also been a model of good behavior. Now he wanted $500,000 for three years. The Boss was offering him $100,000 for one.

Steinbrenner took Martin out to breakfast the next morning, and the two negotiated a cease-fire. Steinbrenner apologized for berating Martin in front of the team; Martin agreed to take the bus.

One starter who was getting plenty of playing time was Reggie Jackson. The slugger's name kept showing up on the roster for road games, an obvious sign of disrespect for an established veteran. Reggie complained about it off the record to a few writers. When they followed up with Martin, the manager insisted that Reggie was asking to make all the trips.

"They were probably both half right," says Pepe. "I have a feeling that Reggie would say something like 'I'll go anywhere. I'm here to play,' and Billy was sticking it to him to rub it in, saying, 'I'm the boss; you go where I tell you.' " That went for the lineup too. Reggie, for whom hitting cleanup was a birthright, was batting everywhere from second to seventh, depending, as Martin put it, "on what I was trying to accomplish that day."

Reggie's new teammates weren't treating him any better. Most of them couldn't look at him without feeling that they were grossly underpaid. Unable to secure raises, seven returning Yankees remained unsigned for the better part of the spring. Like Munson, those who had signed felt even worse off. Graig Nettles, the Yankees' gold glove third baseman, had agreed to a $100,000, multiyear deal midway through the '76 season, before winning the American League home run crown. "When I signed my contract last year, I was one of the highest paid players on the club. Now I'm one of the lowest," he complained to a couple of reporters. "I guess I'm partly to blame because I just don't believe in blowing my own horn. It seems the guys who make money are the flamboyant, controversial guys. On this club at least."

Reggie had a simple response to this sort of talk: "Play out your option or shut the hell up." The way he saw it, he had taken a considerable risk by not signing a contract with Baltimore the year before. He could have gotten injured or simply folded under the pressure. Reggie had a point. Still, it's hard to imagine a situation that required more diplomacy, which did not come easily to him. Instead, Reggie talked incessantly about his various endorsement deals and made sure to rearrange his thick rolls of hundred-dollar bills in plain view of his teammates.

One afternoon Reggie asked a writer what his new teammates were saying about him. The writer told him that Sparky Lyle, the team's closer, had said it was nothing personal, but that the Yankees already had plenty of left-handed power. (They already had a pair of right fielders too: Lou Piniella and Oscar Gamble.) Lyle later acknowledged that it was something personal: "After George signed him [Reggie], when he told the papers, 'I didn't come to New York to be a star. I brought my star with me,' right then I knew. I said to myself, 'This guy is going to be trouble.' "

For Reggie, though, the biggest problem wasn't what the guys were saying; it was what they weren't saying. He felt excluded from nearly all the locker room needling, a rite of passage in the culture of the clubhouse. When he was razzed, it didn't feel good-natured. One afternoon in early March, Piniella asked him how he was doing.

"How you doin', Hoss?" Reggie answered.

"I'm not the horse, Reg," Piniella replied. "You're the horse. I'm just the cart."

With Munson, things were more complicated. The Yankee captain wanted badly to put the self-aggrandizing superstar in his place, but he also felt an obligation not to alienate him. So he veered between trying to establish a working relationship with Reggie and doing everything he could to maximize the newcomer's discomfort. Munson never gave the writers anything they could use—"What are you asking me for?" was his favorite response—but if you hung around the ballpark long enough, you were bound to overhear something revealing.

One afternoon Reggie was taking some extra batting practice. First baseman Chris Chambliss and Thurman Munson, the only guys left on the field save for a rookie pitcher, settled in behind the cage to watch. Reggie fouled off the first couple of pitches. Chambliss looked at Munson and cracked, "Show time!" Reggie took a few more cuts and finally connected, but the ball fell a few feet short of the fence. "Some show," scoffed Munson. "Real power!"

At least no one could question Reggie's work ethic. He got to the ballpark early and stayed late, running wind sprints across the outfield and pounding out sit-ups on the floor of the training room. At the end of the day he'd open the cuff of his jacket and let the river of sweat pour out. Then he'd peel off, and wring dry, each one of his T-shirts.

What they could question was whether he was worth all the fuss. "He's an average player, not even a real good player," said Jim Palmer, a former teammate with the Orioles. Bitter about his own contract woes, Palmer was being excessively ungenerous, but Reggie's credentials were hardly beyond reproach. He was bringing a lifetime batting average of .258 to New York and had never hit .300, not even in the minors. In five of his nine seasons in the big leagues, he had either tied or led the league in errors by an outfielder. The only record Reggie was on pace to break was the major-league strikeout record: His 1,237 put him well ahead of the reigning champ, Mickey Mantle, at the same point in his career. And the book on how to pitch to Reggie was as straightforward as they came: Stay up and in, so he can't unfold those powerful arms.

"I give Reggie Jackson all the credit in the world for one thing—he talked that man [George Steinbrenner] out of $3 million," Dock Ellis told a reporter for *Ebony*. "He's an average ballplayer who has a lot of power. But more than that, he's a helluva salesman and he sold himself. That's what you're supposed to do. Reggie conned 'em—it was one of the biggest cons in baseball—and I admire him for it."

Or was it Steinbrenner who had conned Reggie? The *Daily News*'s Dick Young speculated that the Yankees' owner had paid off kids and cabdrivers to yell out to Reggie when he first brought him to New York for lunch at '21.'

As the spring wore on, the pressure continued to bake the slugger's neck. It wasn't just Reggie, it was what he represented. This was the first year of free agency, the demon that owners and commissioners had been beating back since the creation of the game. Now that it was here, the alarm bells were clanging. Commissioner Bowie Kuhn was warning that free agency would drive some teams into bankruptcy and might even force the American League to fold. Baseball's nostalgists bemoaned the end of the hometown hero ("Who's on first? No, really, who's on first?"), fretted that the new salary scale would increase the distance between fans and players, and complained that free agency was turning athletes into entertainers. Baseball, a game of order, had been thrown into chaos. Even the seemingly timeless "Casey at the Bat" needed to be updated. In Russell Baker's retelling, Casey *deliberately* whiffs in order to avoid hitting the ball into the parking lot, where his Maserati is parked.

Doubts were working inside Reggie. Late in the spring he abandoned his plan to wear No. 42, Jackie Robinson's digits, opting for 44 instead. The expectations for the game's highest-paid, highest-profile free agent were high enough without inviting comparisons to a man who had hit over .300 while carrying his entire race on his shoulders. To add to the pressure, Reggie's agent, Matt Merola, who soon changed the last four digits of his phone number to 4444 in honor of his most lucrative client, was pitching candy companies on a Reggie Jackson candy bar.

By the end of spring Reggie didn't sound much like the man who had, only one month earlier, joked about being too big for his breeches. A new tone had crept into his interviews, not exactly humility, but a sense that no matter what he did it wouldn't be enough. "If I lead the league in homers and runs batted in and win the M.V.P. award and we win the World Series, they'll say, 'He should have done that. Look what they're paying him,' " Reggie told Murray Chass, the beat man for *The New York Times*. "If I don't do it, if I come short of it, if we don't win, it will be my fault. 'Steinbrenner fouled up, Jackson's no good, he hurt the club, he created dissension.' "

For the first time in his career Reggie was talking about the color of his skin. Asked one day about claiming his place in the storied tradition of the New York Yankees, Reggie pointed out that the old Bronx Bombers were all white and that their front office was racist and bigoted. "They didn't want no black superstars," Reggie snapped, deliberately letting his usually proper grammar lapse for effect. He was hedging his bets: If he didn't become a hero, at least he could be a martyr. "I don't know if I'm going to fit in here, man," he told *Newsday*'s Steve Jacobson out on a Fort Lauderdale fishing pier near the end of spring, indulging his taste for melodrama. "I'm a loner."

By the time the Yankees broke camp, Reggie was coming to resemble, or perhaps fashioning himself after, the solitary hero of his favorite book, *Jonathan Livingston Seagull*, the gull that yearned to soar like an eagle. (A dreamy poster for the book had hung over his bed in Oakland.) If Jonathan had managed to transcend his scornful flock, all those petty birds that felt threatened by his ambition, why couldn't he?

11.

AMBITION was about the only thing that Edward Irving Koch, the latest entrant into New York's 1977 mayoral race, had going for him.

Tall and exceptionally unathletic-looking with wide hips and narrow shoulders that looked even slimmer beneath the unflattering cut of his three-button Brooks Brothers suits, the fifty-three-year-old Ed Koch's wavy brown hair had been reduced long ago to a narrow band of graying fuzz that wrapped around the side of his head. His face was expressive, almost elfin, and he often wore the teasing look of an uncle who was about to pull a penny from behind your ear. The writer and critic Michael Harrington described it as the look of a "diffident, somewhat loveable *schlemiel*." Only 6 percent of the city had any idea who Ed Koch was.

The *Daily News* tucked the news of his mayoral candidacy into the end of a story on an unrelated subject. The *Times* deemed the March 4 announcement, in which Koch declared himself ready to captain the city "through its darkest hour," worthy of a separate article but noted in the second paragraph that his first challenge would be to "scotch skepticism over the seriousness of his candidacy." *The Village Voice* pegged him as "an early dropout," which would be right in line with his last effort, when he'd bailed out of the 1973 mayoral race after seven weeks. For the moment Koch's main competition was the incumbent, Abe Beame, and the borough president of Manhattan, Percy Sutton, but more candidates, including the well-known Bella Abzug, were expected to follow. His own campaign manager, David Garth, put his odds of winning at one in twenty.

The few New Yorkers who did know Ed Koch in the spring of 1977 thought of him as a lumpy liberal from Greenwich Village. A middle child, he'd been born in the Bronx, though his parents, Jewish immigrants from Poland, had started their New York journey in a scabby, peeling tenement on the crowded Lower East Side. Koch's mother, Joyce, worked in a garment factory and spent nearly all her paltry earnings on a tutor who taught her to read and write English. His father, Louis, signed on with a furrier and eventually became a partner in the business.

Safely on the road to middle-class, the Kochs abandoned the bustling ghetto for the relative tranquillity of a six-story apartment house on East 173rd Street in the Crotona Park section of the Bronx. A new elevated subway stop had just arrived in the neighborhood, and with it came thousands of immigrants, a modest new bourgeoisie in search of roomier apartments and a little open air.

When the Depression hit, most Crotona Park residents managed to stay put until the storm had passed. Louis was not so lucky. His fur business went bankrupt, and he was forced to move his wife and children back to a slum, this time in a dingy corner of Newark, New Jersey, where the Kochs shared a two-bedroom apartment with Louis's brother-in-law, his wife, and their two kids. Louis worked for tips at the hatcheck concession in a local dance and catering hall. (The hall's manager pocketed the twenty-five-cent fee per hat and coat.) At age twelve, Koch joined his father at the catering hall every evening at eight and often stayed until midnight. "Don't forget the hatcheck boys," they'd remind anyone who tried to escape without leaving behind a little loose change. Soon Koch was logging afternoons at the deli counter at a local supermarket as well.

Eventually the family socked away enough money to move into their own walk-up in Newark, and in 1941, the year Ed Koch graduated from high school, they relocated to a house on Brooklyn's Ocean Parkway, the wide, tree-lined boulevard that stretches from Prospect Park to the boardwalk of Coney Island. Koch had just finished his second year at City College when his draft notice arrived, and he was shipped off to Europe, where he became a specialist in denazification, the Allies' campaign to purge Western Europe of Nazis.

Sergeant Koch returned from the war in 1946, a heady time for middle-class New York. Mayor La Guardia's handiwork was everywhere: prepaid health insurance for all New York residents; twenty-two municipal hospitals; subsidized housing cooperatives; a five-cent subway ride that zigged and zagged across four boroughs. La Guardia spoke endlessly about beautifying New York, about finding new ways to lift the spirit of its citizens. His successor, William O'Dwyer, picked up right where La Guardia left off. On the heels of his election in 1945, O'Dwyer put Robert Moses in charge of a sweeping program of postwar public works construction. Moses went to work drawing up plans for a new East River waterfront that would stretch all the way from City Hall to midtown, a new Metropolitan Opera House, a new Carnegie Hall, a new Madison Square Garden, and towering new apartment buildings everywhere.

New York's neighborhoods were still largely divided along ethnic lines, but the rise of the working class—out of the 3.3 million people employed in New York City in 1946, upward of 2.6 million were blue-collar—had produced a sense of common struggle that often transcended these boundaries. Something else was happening too. A new generation was coming of age. It consisted of people like Koch, children of immigrants who had passed through Ellis Island earlier in the century. Their parents had clung fast to the comfortable shores of their ethnic ghettos. By contrast, Koch and his peers were eager to swim out into bigger waters. Yet at the same time, their humble beginnings fostered in them a passionate commitment to the underclass.

Like so many idealists of his generation, Ed Koch came under the spell of politics in 1952, when Adlai Stevenson made his first unsuccessful bid for the presidency. As a twenty-eight-year-old volunteer in the campaign, Koch armed himself with a small American flag and a soapbox and went from one Manhattan street corner to the next, railing against Dwight Eisenhower and his evil running mate, Richard Nixon.

Koch lived with his parents on Ocean Parkway while attending an accelerated program at New York University Law School, in the heart of Greenwich Village. He fell in love with the neighborhood: the brick town houses; the twisting tree-lined avenues; the cafés; the cheap Italian restaurants; the bustling street life; the small-town political ferment. Brooklyn was too provincial for a young man who'd been bitten by the political bug, and he was tired of his mother's nagging him to get married. Koch rented a small apartment on Bedford Street, which he shared with a roommate. Not long after, Koch found his way into the loft on Sheridan Square that served as the headquarters for the Village Independent Democrats. Formerly a support group for Adlai Stevenson, who'd run a second unsuccessful presidential campaign in '56, the VID had by now refashioned itself into a "reform club," an alternative to the machine-controlled organizations that had ruled Democratic politics in the city since the days of Tammany Hall. Koch was soon elected its president.

Greenwich Village in the late fifties was a neighborhood in transition. It was still predominantly Italian, but progressive young professionals were discovering its charms, as were beatniks. Few of these corduroyed bohemians lived in the Village—the nearby Lower East Side offered tenement apartments at lower rents—but they gathered there nonetheless, often at coffeehouses like the Figaro, named after the Italian barbershop whose former quarters it inhabited. Streams of people poured into the neighborhood each day, including more and more blacks (so-called A-trainers) from Harlem. They came to hear poetry, to listen to folk and jazz music, to browse the local bookstores, or simply to walk around and absorb the scene. Not since Edna St. Vincent Millay and the Roaring Twenties had the neighborhood's narrow streets swarmed like this. Much of the activity took place along MacDougal Street, which also happened to be studded with tenements densely populated with Italian-Americans, longtime Villagers who didn't like being kept up all night by the nonstop partying beneath their windows.

Tensions inevitably arose. Neighborhood thugs vandalized coffeehouses and extorted protection money from their owners, particularly those who catered to racially mixed crowds. Local cops shook down the same establishments for such minor infractions as not having enough soap in their bathrooms. When a legal loophole was discovered—most of these coffeehouses were offering entertainment without the requisite $150 cabaret license—the local Democratic boss moved to have them shut down. Washington Square Park too became embroiled in the battle over the character of the neighborhood. Older Villagers wanted it to remain a sanctuary; the new colonizers thought it should be a cultural center as well, with art shows, chamber music, folksingers, and guitarists.

In the "town-gown" struggle between the neighborhood's working-class Italian-Americans and its college-educated liberals, Koch naturally sided with the liberals. He formed the Right to Sing Committee to counter the campaign to eject the folksingers from Washington Square Park and drafted a change to the cabaret license law. When Koch ran in a local assembly race in 1962, he dubbed his platform "SAD" after its three linchpin issues: sodomy, abortion, and divorce. (He was for making gay sex and abortion legal and for rewriting the state law that considered adultery the only viable grounds for divorce.)

Despite an endorsement from Eleanor Roosevelt, Koch got his clock cleaned, but the following year he ran for district leader against the neighborhood's longtime Democratic power broker, the man known as the Bishop, Carmine De Sapio. A decade earlier it would have been the equivalent of taking on a Kennedy in Boston. By now, though, bossism was taking a beating in New York. The name De Sapio smacked of the smoke-filled rooms of Tammany, of the sometimes corrupt, always patronage-hungry old-time Democrats. Even De Sapio couldn't ignore the winds of political change: He traded in his trademark sinister dark sunglasses for a more subtly shaded pair, acknowledging that his old ones were "no asset for a political leader."

By now Koch had been hanging around the Village long enough to have some influential friends of his own, most notably Dan Wolf, part owner and editor in chief of *The Village Voice.* Wolf swung his feisty paper behind Koch, covering every twist and turn of his campaign, while missing no opportunity to attack De Sapio and his history of influence peddling. As the campaign wound down, it looked as if it could go either way. The night of the election reports swept into Koch's headquarters on West Fourth Street that turnout in the predominantly Italian South Village had been strong and that a good many voters had entered the polls chanting "five, seven, nine," the numbers of De Sapio and the slate of candidates from his club, Tamawa. Koch also knew that Labor Day had just passed, and some fifteen hundred VID members were not yet back from their summer homes in the Hamptons and on Fire Island. De Sapio had the lead with one district left to report, Stewart House, an apartment complex on East Tenth Street that was massive enough to constitute its own election district. Koch figured he was finished; one of De Sapio's running mates lived in the building. He was preparing to concede when the Stewart House returns were announced: Koch 165, De Sapio 77. Koch had won the election by 41 votes.

Mayhem ensued, and as buckets of rain fell outside, Koch clambered up onto the platform and cut through the racket. There was no time to celebrate. "This election can be stolen from us," Koch said. "Every captain must return to the polls right away with an able-bodied man. See that those machines are not tampered with." Dozens of campaign workers spent the night at their election posts, guarding the machines until they were picked up by Board of Election representatives the following morning.

Being known as the man who unhorsed De Sapio gave Koch mythic stature among the liberals of Greenwich Village, and Koch didn't disappoint. He came out early and loudly against Vietnam, championed busing white kids out of the neighborhood, fought to keep the black children in the care of a local shelter enrolled in a public school in the Village, and enlisted the NAACP to help him force the owner of a local Howard Johnson to integrate his waitstaff. He led a trainload of Villagers down to a civil rights march in Washington and spent his August 1964 vacation doing pro bono legal work for the ACLU in Mississippi.

Because he had such impeccable liberal credentials, few noticed that as the sixties wore on and the Village's once-quiet streets became more crowded, Koch began absorbing some of the conservative values of longtime locals. He was evolving in small but portentous ways, as he reconsidered his position on local hot-button issues like the concentration of gay prostitutes on Sixth Avenue and the endless proliferation of noisy coffeehouses.

In 1968, Koch ran for Mayor Lindsay's old congressional seat in Manhattan's so-called Silk Stocking district. It was a slot traditionally occupied by a wealthy, WASPy Republican, but liberalism was ascendant, and Koch was able to overcome his obvious handicaps. Once he was elected, his friends told him to hunker down and become a ten- or twelve-term member of Congress, to pick a committee, become its chairman, and help shape the legislative agenda of the nation. They were sure that he'd topped out.

Koch, like Beame and Abzug, aspired to more. He'd dreamed of becoming mayor for years—"I want to be like Fiorello La Guardia," he'd told more than one acquaintance—but now he was motivated by something else too: a desperate desire to come back to New York. Koch cut a lonely figure in Washington. At lunchtime on Capitol Hill, where he represented the interests of a district that encompassed the mostly poor Lower East Side, the middle-class communities of Turtle Bay and Stuyvesant Town, and the moneyed Upper East Side, he could usually be found eating by himself in the congressional cafeteria. He worked hard but was always impatient for Thursday night, when he'd hop on the Eastern shuttle—it took him exactly twelve minutes to get from the steps of the Capitol to National Airport—and return to his rent-controlled one-bedroom apartment near Washington Square Park.

Blissfully home in New York for the weekend, Koch, never much of a reader, would listen to Simon and Garfunkel or the sound track to *Man of La Mancha*, go to a movie and eat dinner, usually at one of the Village's countless Italian restaurants with red-checkered tablecloths and eponymous names—Emilio's, Monte's, etc. He might even host a small, informal dinner party, where he invariably served steak, wine (for which he refused to pay more than three dollars a bottle), cheese, a vegetable, and vanilla ice cream with chocolate chips on top. Come Monday morning, he'd wake up at five-forty, walk over to Washington Square Park to hail a cab, and catch the seven o'clock shuttle back to dreary D.C.

12.

YANKEES-hating, long dormant as the team's fortunes sagged, was finally returning to fashion on the eve of the 1977 season. In Cleveland, plans were already being hatched for a September "Yankee Hanky" day. Every fan would be given an "I hate the Yankees" handkerchief in which to blow his or her nose.

The Yankees were the only one of baseball's ten best teams that had gone shopping for free agents, and they had signed not one but two. A new Yankees' dynasty was in the offing, just like the one Martin himself had played for two decades earlier. Only the '77 team was going to start five blacks. Center field, where DiMaggio, Mantle, and Murcer had once roamed, was the province of a young man from the Miami ghetto, Mickey Rivers. Second base belonged to rookie Willie Randolph, who had grown up in the Samuel J. Tilden housing project in Brownsville, Brooklyn. And the new right fielder was of course Reggie Jackson.

During spring training, someone had asked Mickey Mantle if he had any advice for the team's newest slugger. Mantle suggested that he live outside the city, just as Mantle had done during his most productive years with the Yankees. Fewer distractions.

Reggie had other plans. One of Steinbrenner's real estate mogul friends set him up with a $1,466 corner apartment on the nineteenth floor at 985 Fifth Avenue, a white-brick building just down the block from the Metropolitan Museum of Art. It wasn't Reggie's first choice—the boards of several other Upper East Side co-ops had turned him away on the dubious grounds that they didn't rent to athletes—but it was magnificent all the same, a spacious two-bedroom with a twenty-four-hour doorman and a balcony overlooking Central Park. He was the only Yankee who lived in Manhattan, and his neighbors included the divorce lawyer Raul Felder; actress Cicely Tyson; writer/producer Mel Brooks and his wife, Anne Bancroft; and Mohan Murjani, owner of Gloria Vanderbilt jeans.

Reggie outfitted his place with crushed velvet sofas, Persian rugs, stainless steel bookcases, and lots of plants. (A more tasteful job than that of Namath, who had decorated his penthouse at First Avenue and Seventy-sixth Street with snow leopard throw pillows, a cheetah-skin bench, a black leather bar, and a wall-to-wall white llama rug.) He filled his refrigerator with Dr. Brown's cream soda, and hung two paintings in the living room, both Leroy Neimans, one a portrait of Reggie himself.

Reggie also rented two spaces at the garage around the corner, one for his burgundy Rolls—the silver and blue Corniche was still on order—and one for the blue Volkswagen Rabbit, a perk of spokesmanship. ("REGGIE JACKSON DRIVES A RABBIT??" the ad copy asked. "The only one I have to impress is me," Reggie answered.) No vanity plates; he was told they wouldn't last five minutes on the streets of New York. The rest of his fleet, including three more Rolls-Royces, which he called "a hedge against inflation," stayed behind in California.

The Yankees held their final preseason practice at the stadium in the hand-stinging cold on April 6. After a light workout, Martin kicked all the reporters and photographers out of the clubhouse and spoke to his men as they dressed. "All that crap in spring training is done. Now we are a team, helping each other, pulling for each other," he said. "Whatever happens in this clubhouse stays in this clubhouse. Don't hang your dirty laundry out in public. Hang it in my office, and we'll clean it up, just you and me."

The writers filed back in and had soon gathered around Reggie, who told them it was the best pregame pep talk he'd ever heard. "Billy was a different guy. He was all business, which was the opposite of spring training, when he let guys do their own thing," he said. "The way he put his foot down was good. He said, 'Damn it, c'mon, we're gonna be a unit.' " Reggie even put a positive spin on the disappointing news that he was going to be hitting fifth rather than cleanup. "It's the ideal RBI position," he told the writers.

The next morning, a clear and crisp one in the city, Reggie drove his burgundy Rolls up Madison Avenue to the ballpark. At Ninety-sixth Street, the town houses, white-gloved doormen, boutiques, and cafés of the Upper East Side gave way to the bodegas, squeegee men, hubcap hustlers, and cinder-block projects of East Harlem. Madison dead-ended at the Madison Avenue Bridge, which fed right into the South Bronx. He'd been assigned the second of five lockers immediately to the left of the clubhouse entrance—easy access for the writers ("Left face" would soon be the joke among the press corps) and plenty of elbow room for Reggie. The locker to his left was empty; the one on his right belonged to Ron Blomberg, a second-string first baseman who was out for at least a month with a knee injury. Next to Blomberg was Elrod Hendricks, a veteran bullpen catcher who'd be bound for the minors soon enough. Next to Hendricks was the quiet Willie Randolph. Munson was in the opposite corner of the room, adjacent to the trainer's room and near the rest of the clique of players who were especially close to Martin: Nettles, Piniella, and Catfish Hunter.

It was Reggie's first locker with a built-in mirror. As was his custom, he dressed slowly. "I have to put on my cosmetic touch," he liked to say. This time the pants fit perfectly, and his shirt was a size too small, just the way he liked it. He fastened the buttons, leaving the top one undone—a fashion statement, or, as *The Washington Post*'s Thomas Boswell once speculated, to give his considerable muscles room to breathe. "Reggie in pinstripes was dazzling," Roger Angell rhapsodized in *The New Yorker*. "The change of costume from his Baltimore colors and his old green-and-gold Oakland frontier getup reminded me of Clark Gable no longer in the Klondike or on the China seas but entering a drawing room in a dinner jacket." Ray Negron, a Yankees' clubhouse attendant at the time, puts it more succinctly: "That uniform fit him like a fucking Superman costume."

Interviewing Billy Martin before the game, Yankees' broadcaster Frank Messer approached the inevitable issue gingerly. "Billy, a word I don't like to hear, but it's been passed around so much—dissension. Do you feel that there will be any dissension on the ball club this year?"

"There's no dissension," Martin answered. "As far as this thing about who doesn't like who, that was something the newspapermen wrote about in the first couple days of spring training because they didn't have a game to talk about so right away they started looking for problems that aren't there."

"And there are no problems then as far as you're concerned?"

"None whatsoever."

Reggie's first at bat came with two on and two out in the bottom half of the first. Digging in, Reggie heard a roar in the upper deck. He stepped out of the box and looked up to see two men swapping punches. Reggie smiled, dug back in, fouled off a couple of pitches, and then hit a towering fly pulled down in the vastness of center field.

The show started in the fourth. Reggie hit a 3-2 pitch the opposite way for a single to open the inning, then raced around to third on a bloop from Nettles, bellyflopping headfirst into the bag for good measure. From there he scored on a suicide squeeze in a cloud of dust, narrowly eluding the mitt of the lunging catcher with a fadeaway hook slide. In the sixth, Reggie lashed another base hit, was nudged around to third, and then busted home on a wild pitch. As he approached the plate for the fourth and final time in the eighth inning, the Yankees now leading 3–0, the baying started in the seats behind third base: *Reg-gie . . . Reg-gie . . . Reg-gie.* Reggie inhaled the cheers, then sent the first pitch, a waist-high fastball, sailing toward the right field bleachers. The unkempt crowd of 43,785, drunk from beer and anticipation, stoned from first- and secondhand smoke, roared. The ball hooked foul. The chanting resumed. Reggie took a couple of balls, waved at a breaking ball, then grounded out to first.

"You hear that sound, *Reggie-Reggie-Reggie*, and it turns on your adrenaline," he told the mob of reporters surrounding his locker after the game. "It makes you feel liked. It makes you feel *loved.*"

It was a sound he didn't hear much over the course of the next month.

There were some isolated highlights. Take Reggie's first home run as a Yankee, which came during the season premiere of ABC's *Monday Night Baseball*, an eagerly anticipated event made all the more so by the Machiavellian machinations of Commissioner Bowie Kuhn, who was trying to persuade ABC's Roone Arledge to ban Howard Cosell from the broadcast booth. And the mammoth blast over the bunting on the upper deck of the newly opened Seattle Kingdome, the American League's first indoor ballbark.

Sweetest of all was Reggie's triumphant return to Baltimore on a misty night in late April. Orioles' fans welcomed Reggie back to

Memorial Stadium much as they had sent him off: with a barrage of frankfurters, lusty boos, and a banner that read REGGIE IS A BOZO. When he came to the plate in the top half of the first, Reggie kicked a few hot dog scraps out of the batter's box and spanked the first pitch he saw through the right side of the infield. The ball slowed to a crawl as it breached the soggy outfield, and Reggie got on his horse, stretching a routine single into a dramatic double, complete with a headfirst slide that sent his helmet skidding across the soggy infield. In the fifth, with a runner on first and the Yankees down 5–4, Reggie deposited a fastball into the Orioles' bullpen in right-center. Halfway between third and home, his familiar home run trot—head down, torso bent slightly forward—turned into a home run walk. When he finally arrived at the plate, he doffed his helmet to the hissing crowd. In the eighth Reggie doubled and scored again for good measure, giving the Yankees a 9–6 win.

For the most part, though, it was a shaky start for the best-paid man in baseball. As of mid-May, Reggie Jackson was hitting .250, with a mere five home runs. After dropping eight of their first ten, then winning fourteen of their next sixteen, the Yankees were hanging around first place, but their new superstar hadn't contributed much to the effort. And he was struggling mightily in the outfield. When Standard Brands announced its plans to unveil a new candy bar tentatively called Reggie, Reggie, Reggie at a press conference at "21" in early May, the joke went that Reggie already had a candy bar, Butterfingers.

Reggie was doing what he could to keep his perspective. After one Sunday morning clubhouse chapel service on the road, he stuck around for a private session with the minister. Emerging half an hour later, the red and gold Bible that he never traveled without tucked under his arm, Reggie told the writers that he felt much better: "I was reminded that when we lose and I strike out a billion people in China don't care."

But millions of New Yorkers did, and they were letting Reggie know it every time he waved at a bad pitch, grounded out, or bobbled a pop fly. Nor was he getting much in the way of support from his manager, who appeared to be gaslighting his right fielder. For Martin, when it came to Reggie no insult was too petty. As often as not, the slights didn't show up in the box scores. One night in Milwaukee, Reggie came to the plate in the top of the fifth of a tight game. With two outs and the speedy Mickey Rivers on second, it was a perfect opportunity for Reggie to drive in a run, which was, after all, what he did best. Instead, Martin had Rivers steal third, where he was cut down. Reggie returned to the dugout, glowering in disgust.

In the middle of May the Yankees flew to Oakland, Reggie's crucible, for a two-game set. The old A's dynasty had been all but dismantled by Finley's pre–free agency fire sale. Even in the best of times, attendance had been a problem at the Oakland Mausoleum; thus far this year the A's had been lucky to draw in the five digits. But on May 16, an unseasonably raw and windy night for Northern California, 32,409 fans came out to hector Reggie. They booed long and loud when his name was announced and longer and louder when he booted a ball in the bottom of the first. They booed just about every time he touched the ball and every time he didn't—in the event, a more common occurrence: Reggie whiffed three times, twice in a row against a pitcher who was making his major-league debut.

The following afternoon Reggie arranged to have a block of tickets set aside for some old friends. He was desperate to leave Oakland with some dignity. Vida Blue, the A's ace and the only member of the old Oakland team whose star could be found in the same galaxy as Reggie's, was slated to pitch against a virtually unknown twenty-seven-year-old rookie named Ron Guidry.

It was a doozy of a game, a 2–2 tie after nine. By the top of the tenth it was already the next day in New York, where Yankees' fans were watching the action on WPIX. For his part, Reggie was watching the action from the dugout. They played five more innings, it was still tied, and Jackson was still riding pine.

In the top of the fifteenth Martin needed a left-handed pinch hitter to face Oakland's right-handed reliever. Looking down the bench past Reggie, Martin's eyes lit on Dell Alston, who had never before been to bat in a big-league game. Alston doubled, igniting a game-winning rally.

"Yeah," Reggie told reporters in the locker room after the game. "I'm a mediocre ballplayer and I'm overpaid."

13.

IN the middle of May, New York's already crowded mayoral race absorbed one final candidate. The latest entrant had required a push. Governor Hugh Carey, who'd done the pushing, referred to him as "a brilliant sonofabitch." The less charitable knew him as "the Italian Hamlet" because of his penchant for equivocation. But where Mario Cuomo was concerned, most people who knew him were inclined to be charitable.

Carey had been after Cuomo, his secretary of state, to run for months. The results of a spring poll conducted by WMCA revealed why. The talk radio station asked the twenty-eight reporters who covered City Hall to predict who would win New York's September 8 Democratic primary, which, in this city of Democrats, was tantamount to winning the general election itself. Seventeen of the reporters put Abzug first; the remaining eleven went with Beame.

The governor couldn't stomach the prospect of either one. He blamed Beame for failing to apprise him of the depth of the city's financial problems, and he was convinced the left-wing Abzug would alienate the investment banks that were now so critical to New York's fiscal health. Moreover, having played such a central role in rescuing the city from the brink of bankruptcy in 1975, the governor figured he had earned the right to intervene in the city's political affairs.

Cuomo was still coming around when Carey summoned David Garth, Koch's campaign manager, to lunch at the Plaza. The governor had firsthand experience with Garth's genius. A few years earlier, when Carey was a fat, glib, graying Brooklyn pol with delusions of gubernatorial grandeur, Garth had overhauled his image and led him to an improbable victory over Howard Samuels, the well-connected head of New York's Off-Track Betting Corporation. Now Carey had a much easier job for Garth. "You've got to leave Ed," he told him. "I've talked Mario into running."

Garth was crushed—he'd tried to persuade Cuomo to enter the race himself before signing up with Koch—but he knew it wouldn't be right to switch horses now.

Not that Cuomo needed him. In 1977 New York, a city known for its electoral tribalism, had 1.2 million Jews, 1.5 million blacks, and 1.7 million Italians. And Cuomo had much more than a last name ending in a vowel to recommend him to voters.

The working-class *Daily News* had been the first to canonize Saint Mario, urging him to run a day after publishing a full-page editorial urging Beame not to. "[Cuomo has] high intelligence, a hard, realistic view of what needs to be done to save New York, a reputation for almost zealous candor, and a capacity to inspire," the *News* wrote in early April. *The Village Voice* followed ten days later with a profile titled "Cuomo Rising." It began: "Will New York's great smart hope run for mayor?" New York was experiencing a phenomenon that soon became familiar to all America: The longer Cuomo debated moving onto center stage, the larger his shadow loomed.

At the age of forty-four, Mario Cuomo embodied the contradictions that explain his diversity of support. He was a hard-knuckled ethnic tough who quoted Augustine and worked beneath a large portrait of Saint Thomas More. He was an outsider—he'd attended

St. John's University and, after being rejected by a dozen Manhattan law firms, had set up his law practice across the river on Court Street in Brooklyn—whose many friends on the inside included the editorial director of Random House, Jason Epstein. He was emotional and expressive, but introspective too, a practicing Catholic with a chronic existential twitch, a gifted athlete—before a career-ending injury, Cuomo had been a promising prospect in the Pittsburgh Pirates organization—who read voraciously and wrote daily in his diary. He was a committed liberal, but a realist too, a family man with five children and an intuitive grasp of the state of mind of New York's outer boroughs, the world from which he'd sprung.

Cuomo's father, Andrea, an Italian immigrant, started his life as an American digging ditches and cleaning sewers in New Jersey. When he'd saved up enough money, he opened a small grocery store in South Jamaica, Queens, and with the help of his two sons, he managed to keep it open twenty-four hours a day. Andrea led by example. His callused hands and undying devotion to his family, who lived above the store, spoke louder than any homespun homilies could. Theirs was a polyglot neighborhood dotted with first-generation immigrants. On the Cuomos' block alone, there were Italians, Irish, Czechs, Greeks, and Jews. An altar boy at his family's Catholic church and a *shabbos goy* at the synagogue around the corner, Cuomo was steeped in ethnic diversity from an early age.

The New Yorkers who knew Mario Cuomo—and in May 1977 it remained a relatively small group—knew him best from his involvement in the 1972 flap over a public housing project in Forest Hills. But before Forest Hills there was Corona, a community of Southern Italians tucked away in an untraveled corner of Queens, a quiet village of wood-frame and shingle houses whose residents toiled away at blue-collar jobs during the week and lounged around the neighborhood on weekends. This, at least, was the picture of tranquillity that prevailed until 1966, when word spread through the community that the high school going up in nearby Lefrak City was going to force the condemnation of sixty-nine houses in Corona. The residents hastily mobilized and hired a thirty-three-year-old lawyer, Mario Cuomo, to help them take on City Hall.

Four years and dozens of briefs later, the bulldozers were moving closer to Corona. Cuomo had exhausted his legal options with no visible progress. The whole business might have passed unnoticed into history—another community plowed under by City Hall, another idealistic young lawyer disillusioned along the way—had not a stocky, rumpled caricature of a newspaperman named Jimmy Breslin tumbled into the picture. One Sunday night in November 1970 a friend of Breslin's persuaded the writer to come along with him to a Corona homeowners' meeting at the headquarters of the local volunteer ambulance corps. The room was jammed; Breslin was impressed. He asked his friend whom they had representing them. "Just a little local lawyer," his friend answered.

As the friend continued talking, Breslin's attention drifted elsewhere, toward a tall, handsome man with dark hair and strong shoulders who had risen to address the group. He was holding the audience rapt as he eloquently reviewed the history of the conflict. After the meeting Breslin took this man, Mario Cuomo, out for a cup of coffee.

The Corona story was a natural for Breslin, who, as his editor Michael O'Neill once put it, believed that politicians needed to be beaten every morning in order to keep them attentive to the will of the people. Here was a working-class community—on Breslin's home turf of South Queens no less—getting bullied by some swinging elbows in starched shirts. It was a tragedy with a little flicker of hope that was almost extinguished, but only almost, which is just how Breslin liked his tragedies. Best of all, the Corona story had its own unlikely hero—"talent willing to be tortured," as Breslin wrote of Cuomo.

With Breslin's help, the so-called Corona Fighting 69 became a cause célèbre. Newspapers as far-flung as the *Los Angeles Times* editorialized in their defense. Thanks to a Breslin-brokered meeting at City Hall, Mayor Lindsay took note. Before long he had agreed to Cuomo's compromise solution. Lindsay liked what he saw in Cuomo, and a few years later he enlisted the young lawyer to help him put out the fire raging over the city's plan to build a low-income housing project in the middle-class neighborhood of Forest Hills, Queens.

The plan had grown out of a 1965 U.S. Department of Housing and Urban Development mandate requiring that cities use a large portion of their federal grants to build low-income housing in stable neighborhoods. At the time so-called scatter-site housing sounded like a fine idea to most white middle-class New Yorkers. They shared the dream of racial and economic integration, and they were ready, in principle anyway, to do their part to stop the spiral of poverty by opening their neighborhoods to poor families. Forest Hills, a community of predominantly liberal Jewish apartment dwellers, many of whom had firsthand experience with discrimination, seemed as good a place as any to give it a try.

But much had changed by the time Lindsay recruited Cuomo in 1972. For starters, the specifics of the plan had been unveiled. It called for the construction of three twenty-four-story towers, not exactly the modest, well-distributed buildings that the term *scatter-site* suggests. This wasn't breaking up the ghettos; it was consolidating and relocating them. What's more, as the bright idealism of the sixties gave way to the grim realism of the seventies, the concept of scatter-site housing had gone out of fashion, both in New York, where politicians were now touting "ghetto rehabilitation," and in Washington, where President Nixon was offering cash subsidies for the poor to pay for apartments wherever they could find them.

Having failed to consult with the people of Forest Hills before presenting the project as a fait accompli, Mayor Lindsay was taking most of the heat for it. Local protesters were picketing daily, waving placards that read: ADOLF LINDSAY—THE MIDDLE-CLASS WILL

BURY YOU; SAVE FOREST HILLS, SAVE MIDDLE-CLASS AMERICA; and LIBERALISM IS A GOOD IDEA UNTIL IT HITS YOU WHERE YOU LIVE. Led by the demagogic Jerry Birbach, the heavyset president of the Forest Hills Residents Association, demonstrators threw rocks and flaming torches through the windows of construction trailers. (Birbach threatened to lie down in front of the bulldozers if the project went ahead, an idea that his opponents quite liked.) Forest Hills was no longer about one project and one neighborhood. It was, in the words of journalist Walter Goodman, "a monument to many of our urban aches and pains . . . commemorating the ideals and the limitations of those who are trying to manage this poor city and the dangerously conflicting needs and emotions of those who are trying to live in it."

Cuomo spent several months at the center of the storm, often with his friend Breslin, a resident of Forest Hills, absorbing the arguments of both sides before presenting a compromise solution that called for the buildings to be halved to twelve stories. Birbach dubbed the new plan "totally unacceptable." His principal opponent, the Housing Authority's Simeon Golar, denounced it as "outrageous." Cuomo, it appeared, had done something right.

On October 26, 1972, the Cuomo plan went before New York City's Board of Estimate. A standing room-only crowd filled the board's white-walled chamber. On the right side of the center aisle were the Forest Hills residents and their supporters, easily identified by their "No Project—No Way!" pins and black armbands. On the other side were the mostly black defenders of the original project. The hearings opened with a moment of silence for Jackie Robinson, who had died of a heart attack two days earlier. The next twelve hours featured nothing approximating silence. The chaos inside was exacerbated by the chaos outside. Some three hundred tow truck operators, protesting the city's low towing fees, had ringed City Hall with their trucks, blocking traffic and leaning on their horns for the better part of three hours. Inside, a succession of speakers made their pleas to the board. Years of acrimony were compressed into one long, ugly day. "If you let these criminals into our fine middle-class community, our future blood is on your hands," warned one woman from Forest Hills. If the project isn't built in its original conception, answered a woman from the other side of the aisle, "you'll see blood in the streets. We'll all die together, and we'll take many of you with us." Mayor Lindsay was conspicuously absent, but his stand-in, the president of the City Council, called for extra policemen.

The sun set, and the raucous hearing finally drew to a close. The Board of Estimate overwhelmingly approved the compromise. Mario Cuomo had faced down some of the worst impulses of his city with humanism. He had recognized the misguided absolutism of the liberals who considered his compromise plan a betrayal, but he had never wavered in his commitment to the principle of integration obscured by their zealotry. At the same time, he'd refused to treat the Forest Hills homeowners like bigots, appealing to their sense of decency in his efforts to persuade them to change their attitude toward the project.

Eight years of the Manhattan-centric Lindsay had left the outer boroughs hungry for a candidate of their own, someone who understood life in the neighborhoods. In the wake of the Forest Hills compromise, Breslin and a few of Cuomo's other boosters urged him to run for mayor in 1973.

Cuomo agreed to test the waters with a series of breakfasts and speeches. By then he could see that New York's spiral of poverty was coarsening the spirit of his home borough, but he didn't intend to let that stand in the way of his liberal ideals. It would just require a little finesse. "You've got all these blacks and Puerto Ricans down in South Jamaica, where I was born and raised," Cuomo said in an address to a political club in Queens. "You think they're all bad because they're the ones coming up here, mugging and raping you and breaking into your houses. And you're saying, 'We don't want them in our neighborhoods. We don't want them anywhere near us.' . . . Well, the net result of that attitude is their poverty will get worse and they'll produce more muggers and rapists . . . The liberals come and tell you it's our moral obligation to help those people because we oppressed them—the blacks, anyway—for 400 years. That's what John Lindsay told you, right? However, here in Queens, how can I tell my father that? . . . He never punished a black, or hurt a black, or enslaved a black . . . Here's what you have to say to my father: Whether you love them or not, whether you have an obligation to them or not, is between you and God . . . But unless you do something about where they are now, how they live now, they will continue to come into your neighborhoods and mug and rape . . . You have to find ways to break up segregated neighborhoods. And most of all, you have to find ways to get them jobs. Real jobs."

In the end Cuomo decided not to run for mayor in '73. He made his first bid for elective office a year later, losing the Democratic nomination for the lowly job of lieutenant governor. It was a humiliating defeat for a man with so much political promise. Fortunately, the new governor, Hugh Carey, recognized that promise and asked Cuomo to be his secretary of state. Over the next few years, Cuomo mediated a rent strike at the huge Bronx housing cooperative known as Co-op City, investigated a scandal in state nursing homes, and played referee in a land dispute between New York State and the Mohawk Indians. In early 1977 Carey came to Cuomo with a new task: running for mayor. After a few months of hemming and hawing, Cuomo reluctantly agreed. "The governor had given me the opportunity to come into public service," he says. "I felt I owed him something."

Cuomo launched his mayoral drive on May 10 in his newly opened campaign headquarters in the working-class, immigrant-rich neighborhood of Rego Park, Queens. His wife, his children, his parents, his in-laws, and some twenty other relatives filled the rows of folding chairs to the left of the podium as he spoke: "The record of the administration is on the faces of all those among us who have lost their sense of hope—of every old woman who lives behind triple-locked doors, waiting for day to return, afraid to venture onto the night streets or once look up at the night sky."

In a poll of registered Democrats conducted a few days later, he was running a close third behind Beame and Abzug.

14.

IF *Sports Illustrated* was the *Time* magazine of the sports world, *Sport* was its *Esquire*, a slick monthly filled with well-marinated profiles and straight-to-the-wall photographs—dispatches from the American dreamland. When it first sprang to life in 1949, a smiling Joe DiMaggio and son Joe, Jr., on its cover, *Sport* was in the business of making heroes. By 1977 the magazine was more concerned with satisfying the public's increasing appetite for personality. That was why Dick Schaap, *Sport*'s editor in chief, had sent Robert Ward down to Florida in March to profile the newest member of the Yankees. It was a perfect match of author and subject. Ward was a surging, scenic writer who went on to make a small fortune writing for the television shows *Miami Vice* and *NYPD Blue*.

Reggie initially refused to cooperate with Ward, claiming he'd been burned by *Sport* before ("They wrote a piece that said I caused trouble on the team, that I have a huge ego"). Ward started on the piece anyway, hanging around the clubhouse, watching Reggie as he moved through camp, asking his various teammates to comment on their new right fielder. After a few days of this, Reggie agreed to a drink, as long as Ward agreed to tell him what the guys were saying about him.

They met at a bar called the Banana Boat. Reggie showed up in a windbreaker, which he promptly ditched, revealing a blue T-shirt on which the word SUPERSTAR! was spelled out in silver letters across the chest. It was from the TV show that he hosted, but the implication was clear.

Ward began by telling Reggie that some of his teammates had expressed reservations about him. "You see," Reggie said as they started in on their first round, "I've got problems the other guys don't have. I've got this big image that comes before me, and I've got to adjust to it . . . Also, I used to just be known as a black athlete; now I'm respected as a tremendous intellect."

They were just getting going when the old Yankees' Rat Pack—Mickey Mantle, Whitey Ford, and Billy Martin—settled down at a backgammon table at the other end of the bar. Reggie told the cocktail waitress, who was decked out in a green Tinker Bell costume, to send over some drinks on him. She returned with a message: "Whitey Ford appreciates your offer, but says he'd rather have your *Superstar* T-shirt." Ward glanced over and noticed Mantle and Martin cracking up; they had obviously put Ford up to this bit of hazing. Reggie stripped off his T-shirt and delivered it to Ford, who in exchange gave Jackson his sweater, a pink cashmere V-neck that must have been three sizes too small for the slugger's thick torso.

The encounter, coupled with Ward's report on Reggie's unpopularity among his new teammates, tripped something inside Reggie. In a sense, it was Martin who was the odd man out. Mantle and Ford were "living legends"; Reggie's legend was still in the making but well on its way. Of the four, only Martin would be condemned to a lifetime of faint praise adjectives like "scrappy," "feisty," and "hardworking." That was not how it felt to Reggie. He knew that he would never enjoy the kind of camaraderie with his teammates that Martin, Mantle, and Ford shared. Players were more transient in the nascent era of free agency, but more than that, Reggie was too self-centered to command much in the way of personal loyalty from anyone.

Back at the bar, Reggie stirred around the fruit in his piña colada and delivered himself of an unforgettable soliloquy. "You know, this team . . . it all flows from me," he told Ward. "I'm the straw that stirs the drink. It all comes back to me. Maybe I should say me and Munson . . . but really he doesn't enter into it . . . I've overheard him talking about me . . . I'll hear him telling some other writer that he wants it to be known that he's the captain of the team . . . And when anybody knocks me, he'll laugh real loud so I can hear it . . . I'm a leader, and I can't lie down . . . but 'leader' isn't the right word . . . it's a matter of PRESENCE . . . Let me put it this way: No team I am on will ever be humiliated the way the Yankees were by the Reds in the World Series! That's why Munson can't intimidate me. Nobody can . . . There is nobody who can put meat in the seats the way I can. That's just the way it is . . . Munson thinks he can be the straw that stirs the drink, but he can only stir it bad . . . Just wait until I get hot and hit a few out, and the reporters start coming around and I have New York eating out of the palm of my hand . . . he won't be able to stand it."

All the essential Reggie Jackson contradictions were here: the swaggering free spirit versus the self-conscious brooder; the supremely sure exterior versus the vulnerable interior; the desire to feel loved versus an unconscious need to feel alone, embattled, by way of motivating himself.

"Thank you, God," was all Ward could think as he scribbled furiously.

Jackson finally came up for air. "Are you sure you want all of this printed?" Ward asked.

"Yes," Reggie said, smacking his hand on the bar for emphasis. "I want to see that in print."

It was the sort of scene that magazine writers fantasize about, and because Ward didn't have to cover the ball club day in and day out, he didn't have to worry about alienating anyone. He flew back up to New York and emptied his notepad. He added some memorable flourishes of his own—"God, he looks like some big baseball Othello as he smiles at the gaggle of reporters who rush toward him, their microphones thrust out"—and filed the story to *Sport.* The whole office could hear his editor, Barry Stainback, howling as he made his first pass through Ward's copy. Stainback was soon walking up and down the halls, his face crinkled up into a big smile, as he read sections aloud to the staff.

Sport scheduled the story—REGGIE JACKSON IN NO-MAN'S LAND—for its June issue. Schaap messengered the galleys over to Sy Presten, an old-fashioned publicist who had been in the game long enough to have peppered the *Journal-American*'s gossip maven Dorothy Kilgallen with items about the Copa. The "straw that stirs the drink" quote was buried inside the piece. Presten broke it out in the headline of his press release, which he promptly sent to every sports desk in town. Within hours *Sport*'s phone lines were lighting up like a pinball machine.

Several years later, when Reggie published his autobiography—in vintage fashion, he dedicated the book to his biggest fan, God—he claimed that the whole conversation at the Banana Boat had been off the record, and that he had been misquoted to boot. Most sports heroes set out to "write" their life stories with mythmaking on their minds. The '77 Yankees were more concerned with settling scores, and no one had more scores to settle than Reggie. (He settled fewer than his publisher was expecting. The book, for which Reggie was paid a then-whopping three hundred thousand dollars, was a best seller but still fell far short of expectations.)

Reggie claimed that he had asked Ward if his story was going to be positive and that Ward had assured him that it was. "Bullshit," says Ward. "I told him that I was going to set the record straight. He interpreted that as yes because he's so egocentric."

"All in all," Reggie wrote, "it was the worst screwing I ever got from the press. And I've had a few in my day."

15.

THE first pitch was still hours away but the T-shirts were already on sale outside the stadium: "Boston Sux" and "Fisk Eats Rice," as in Jim Rice, the Red Sox outfielder.

Such was the state of the rivalry, reborn anew for every generation, between the Yanks and the Sox, on the afternoon of May 23, 1977. If a pair of outfielders, Ted Williams and Joe DiMaggio, had personified the battle in the 1940s and 1950s, the teams' warring catchers did that day: the tall, even-tempered, urbane Carlton Fisk and the stumpy, grumpy, caustic Thurman Munson. Boston versus New York in a nutshell.

Fisk, who'd grown up in small-town New England, couldn't stand playing in New York. "There are more people on that block than there are in Charlestown—and more rats and pollution on that block than in the whole state of New Hampshire," he told one of the Boston reporters as the Red Sox team bus rumbled through Harlem on the way to the Bronx. His hatred for New York was matched only by that of his battery mate, Bill Lee, who was slated to open the series. The prior season Lee had separated his shoulder in the bench-clearing melee that followed a collision at home plate. "George Steinbrenner's Nazis," as he called the Yankees, had caused him to miss almost all of '76, and he was just now starting to regain his arm strength.

Reggie, who was finally emerging from a one-for-twenty-six drought featuring ten strikeouts, had just started dressing when Munson padded by on his way to the trainer's table. There was a rolled-up copy of the new issue of *Sport* sticking out of the back pocket of his baseball pants. A few minutes later Munson sent the assistant trainer into the clubhouse to fetch Fran Healy, the Yankees' backup catcher and Reggie's only friend on the team.

At the age of thirty, Fran Healy was reaching the end of a brief and undistinguished career, a baseball lifetime spent warming pitchers and benches. In a year's time he'd be on the other side of the microphone, hustling down to the locker room after the game to interview his ex–Yankee teammates for WPIX.

The six-foot-six-inch Healy, who had a graduate degree in American studies, had taken an instant liking to Reggie during their first meeting a few years earlier. At the time Reggie was just barely holding off Healy's Kansas City teammate John Mayberry for the American League home run title. "I think he's gonna catch you," Healy told Reggie. "The only way he's gonna catch me is if he plays winter ball," Reggie replied.

In '77, Healy didn't bother renting a place in New York. If he didn't want to make the three-hour drive home to Massachusetts after a game, he spent the night at Reggie's. Now Healy walked into the training room to find Munson jabbing one of his bent-up fingers at the magazine.

"Have you read this?" Munson asked, incredulously.

"No," said Healy.

"He ripped me here, he ripped me there . . ." Munson read a few choice paragraphs out loud.

Healy listened quietly until Munson stopped.

"Gee, Thurm," Healy finally ventured, breaking the awkward silence, "maybe it was taken out of context."

"For four fucking pages?"

Batting practice followed an hour or so later. Reggie entered the cage last, shooing away a photographer as he did. Digging in, he noticed his teammates clearing out from behind the cage, leaving him to take his licks alone in the fading sunlight. It was a mild spring evening and a light breeze was blowing as Reggie silently drove one ball after another toward the right field bleachers.

Martin bumped Reggie down to sixth in the lineup that night. Reggie responded with a run-scoring line drive double on his first trip to the plate. Through six innings, it remained the only Yankee run.

Lee hadn't looked this sharp since separating his shoulder, and the Sox were clinging to a 2–1 lead when Reggie came up in the bottom half of the seventh. Lee left a sinker over the outer half of the plate, and Reggie flattened it, knotting the game at two.

Like a bouncer making sure that an ejected drunk had no designs on reentry, Reggie watched the ball complete its flight from the batter's box, then circled the bases briskly. By the time he reached home, he had worked up a head of self-righteous steam. Reggie stepped on the plate and headed straight for the water cooler on the first base side of the dugout, ignoring his teammates and manager, who had gathered at home plate for the requisite posthomer handshakes. "They didn't want me around? I was an outcast?" Reggie reflected later. "Fine, I at least wanted them all to know that I didn't have to have a picture drawn for me anymore."

If only he could have left it at that. In the top half of the next inning, Reggie overran a ball down the right field line, turning a single into a double. The run came around to score, and the Red Sox went on to win.

After the game Martin sat in an undershirt and pinstriped baseball pants fielding questions about the ten-week-old *Sport* interview. "Leadership is done by example, not by mouth," he told the pack of reporters assembled in his blue cinder-block-wall office. As for the snub, he suggested they speak to Jackson. Martin took a long pull on his Miller Lite before finishing the thought. "And while you're at it," he added, "ask him about the ball that got away from him in the right field corner to start the eighth. He probably forgets about those things."

The reporters found Reggie hunched silently over the sandwich table, picking at the potato salad. "Hey, Reg, why didn't you take the usual route back into the dugout, where your teammates were waiting to congratulate you?"

"I had a bad hand," Reggie said. That was about all he said, not counting the tongue flaying he gave Henry Hecht, whose paper, the *Post*, had just published Reggie's home address on Page Six.

The mob migrated instinctively to Munson's locker for a response. The Yankees' catcher initially refused to speak. Then the writers repeated Reggie's quote about his hand. "He said *that*?" Munson gasped. "Well, how about this for a quote: 'He's a fucking liar.' " And the article in *Sport*? "For a man to think Thurman Munson is jealous of anybody in this world he has to be ignorant or an imbecile. I'll kiss your butt if the New York fans think anybody likes to play baseball more than I do."

At the ballpark the following night, the city made its bias clear. The day's papers had been filled with stories about Reggie belittling and then snubbing the beloved Munson. Now, as Munson approached the batter's box working a big wad of chaw, the crowd roared. Reggie strode toward the plate a few minutes later and was jeered. Their respective performances conveniently conformed to the consensus in the seats. Reggie went hitless; Munson drove home the winning run in the seventh. "That's leadership," concluded Dave Anderson in the next day's *Times*.

Reggie continued playing the silent star after the game, wordlessly rubbing a few dollops of Musk lotion into his brown skin. He pretended not to have heard the first couple of questions thrown at him. Then he decided to answer a few in Spanish. ("I think he just told us that the pen of his aunt was on the table of his uncle," joked one reporter.)

Later Healy tried to make peace, remarking to Munson that Reggie's comments in *Sport* had been off the record. "So what?" Munson snarled. "He still said them, didn't he?"

The next time he crossed home plate, Munson ignored Reggie's outstretched hand in the on deck circle. Reggie tried to shrug the incident off—"I don't think he saw it," he ventured unconvincingly—but the rising sense of rage and humiliation was taking its toll. In the clubhouse his teammates *accidentally* kicked his equipment bag. Two Yankees asked to have their lockers moved farther away from his. One afternoon Reggie found a note reading "Suck My Ass" taped to the hanger that held his freshly pressed uniform. Even the soft-spoken Willie Randolph stared blankly into his locker when Reggie asked him several times what time they were supposed to report for batting practice.

Reggie asked Martin if he could call a team meeting to apologize. Martin refused, telling Reggie that if wanted to say he was sorry to his teammates, he should do so individually. Then Martin told the writers that Reggie had made the clubhouse rounds to ask forgiveness. To *Newsday*'s Steve Jacobson, it didn't sound like the kind of thing Reggie would do, so he asked around. Jacobson's hunch was correct: There had been no apologies.

Reggie's teammates continued to torment him. "Reggie fuckin' Manuel Jackson," Mickey Rivers said in early June, rising from his seat in the back of the team bus. "You got a white man's first name, a Spanish man's second name, and a black man's last name. No wonder you're all fucked up, man. You don't know what the fuck you are." For Reggie, the fact that Rivers had unintentionally mangled his middle name—confusing it with Billy Martin's—didn't lessen the sting any.

A few days later in Milwaukee, as the Yankees' bus made its way toward County Stadium, Reggie tried to even the score. "There goes Rivers in five years," he said, pointing out the window at the driver of a passing truck.

"Yeah," Rivers replied, "but at least I'll be happy driving a truck."

"Listen to me," scoffed Reggie. "Arguing with a guy who can't read and write."

"Better stop fuckin' readin' and writin' and start fuckin' hittin'," said Rivers.

Often Reggie found himself sitting next to the team's clubhouse attendant, a nineteen-year-old ex–juvenile delinquent named Ray Negron. Over the course of the season, Negron became Reggie's unofficial aide-de-camp, signing his name on baseballs, answering his fan mail, carting his gear to photo shoots.

Half Puerto Rican and half Cuban, Negron had come to the attention of George Steinbrenner four years earlier, when the Yankees' owner caught him and a few of his cousins spraying graffiti on the side of the stadium. The cousins got away, but Steinbrenner grabbed Negron by the collar and threatened to turn him over to the police. In tears, Negron had pleaded with Steinbrenner to let him go. Instead, the Yankees' owner put him to work as a batboy and general clubhouse grunt.

When he went to work for the Yankees in 1973, Negron was playing shortstop on his high school team and in a few city leagues. He had soft hands and a strong arm—not to mention the excellent tutoring that was a perk of his new job—and in 1975 the Pittsburgh Pirates signed him up, expecting big things. Negron reported to the Pirates' training camp in Bradenton, Florida, in the spring of 1976. He had no problem fielding his position, but he couldn't touch big-league pitching. He was released within a matter of weeks. He packed up and flew home to his mom's apartment in Queens, too humiliated to tell anyone he was back.

Word eventually got out, and Billy Martin called Negron to tell him to stop being such a crybaby and come out to the ballpark. Negron showed up, and Martin ordered him to pitch batting practice. Negron plunked the first batter he faced. When he nearly hit the second one, he got a bat thrown at him.

The next day Martin called Negron into his office. Negron was sure he was about to get fired. Martin pointed at some unopened cardboard boxes. "There's some video equipment in there, figure out how to use it," Martin told him. Negron couldn't hide his surprise. "I gotta think of something for you to do," Martin continued, "because you sure as fuck can't throw BP."

Negron had met Reggie once before he became a Yankee. Jackson was playing for Oakland at the time, and Negron went into the visitors' clubhouse to introduce himself. "Hi Reggie, I'm Ray Negron, the bat boy," Negron said. "Yeah, go get me some sanis, kid," Reggie replied.

Over the course of the '77 season, though, Reggie befriended Negron, and the two remained close for the duration of Jackson's tenure with the Yankees. Negron's favorite memories begin in 1978, after Reggie Jackson had won over New York. In Negron's recollection, being with Reggie then was like entering into a fairy tale. "Reggie was the king of the city, and I was the prince because I was his sidekick," he says. "Whenever we would walk out of his building, I could almost hear the whole fucking city saying, 'Reggie! Reggie! Reggie!' I would look at him sometimes, and I could almost think that he heard it too."

Reggie and Negron worked out at a gym near Reggie's apartment—"spot me, motherfucker," Reggie would command when he lowered himself onto the bench—and ran together in Central Park. Jogging one winter afternoon in the park, they came across a small school bus stuck in the snow. Reggie told all the kids to get off, then went around to the back and started pushing until the bus moved. "The kids are going crazy," Negron says, "and Reggie tips his hat to the bus driver and runs off."

16.

To the experts who study the psychology of sports in America, the Tom Seaver trade is much more than just a loss by the New York Mets. These sports psychologists view the trade as a serious loss to New York City . . .

EDWARD EDELSON, *DAILY NEWS*, JUNE 19, 1977

ON the morning of June 16, 1977, the city woke up to the news that the Mets had traded Tom Seaver to the Cincinnati Reds.

A wholesome, handsome, smooth-skinned former marine and current spokesman for Sears, Roebuck & Company, Tom Seaver had never enjoyed Reggie Jackson's national profile—clean-cut was a tough sell in the 1970s—but in New York anyway, he was a god. How could it be otherwise? After all, he had arrived in Queens in 1967 and in two years almost single-handedly transformed the hapless Mets from a comedy troupe into World Series champions.

Sputtering, mutinous fans promptly lit up the switchboard at Shea Stadium. "Mets fan reaction was so outraged," Paul Good wrote a few months later in *Sport* magazine, "that one might have imagined that Washington had traded Jimmy Carter for Idi Amin, even up." The Mets were playing at home that night, and security forces were beefed up for the game. Fans opted for an unofficial boycott instead; fewer than nine thousand turned out. Those who did show up came bearing Reds' banners, and SEAVER LIVES and WHERE IS TOM? signs. (The protests continued through the summer, and the Mets ended up drawing fewer fans than they had since leaving the old Polo Grounds in 1963.)

The loss of Seaver felt like the loss of hope, not for the Mets, who already were hopeless, but for the city itself. It was more than the man; it was the moment the man represented, that improbable pennant run during the glorious summer of 1969, when John Lindsay owned New York and the city still felt full of possibility. "For the years he [Seaver] worked among us, he was an ornament of New York," Pete Hamill wrote on June 17 in the *Daily News*. "He leaves behind a diminished city. This is not simply a sports story. It is a New York story . . . A city struggling for survival can't lose a single hero."

In a sense New York had lost two heroes, for there was a villain in the Tom Seaver story: the city's preeminent baseball writer, Dick Young. For more than three decades Young had been manning the press box for America's largest daily newspaper, the multimillion circulation *Daily News*. In the 1940s and 1950s, when Young covered the Dodgers, untold numbers of Brooklyn boys had teethed on his prose. He wrote audaciously, breezily, irreverently, and often badly, abusing puns, torturing metaphors, surrendering to hyperbole. But that hardly mattered. His copy had a street-wise, smart-ass New York feel to it. (Young on the Dodgers' departure from Brooklyn: "Preliminary diagnosis indicates that the cause of death was an acute case of greed, followed by severe political implications.") A few years after the Dodgers decamped, he moved over to the Mets' beat, hyping these lovable losers as New York's new people's team, delighting in their comic failures much as he had reveled in Brooklyn's tragic ones. Young was a social progressive too, one of the first men to knit the broader story of race into his sports coverage. In 1949, when Jackie Robinson won the Most Valuable Player award despite being unable to find lodging in numerous cities, Young wrote that he had "led the league in everything except hotel reservations."

In the sixties and early seventies, Young became the patron saint to a generation of whippersnappers, the so-called Chipmunks, a new breed of sportswriter who wrote with attitude and favored a look known as the Full Cleveland—mint green or baby blue polyester pants, a wide snow white belt, and flowered shirts with oversize collars that broke like tidal waves.

But as the seventies progressed, Young grew increasingly cynical. The proliferation of night games, of militant black athletes, of ballplayers who listened to loud music in the clubhouse, rankled him. His city was changing too. Young's New York was a place where men still wore suits and fedoras to ball games. He seemed to recoil from the modern spasms of the city. When the freshly renovated Yankee Stadium reopened for business in 1976, Young urged his Spanish-speaking readers to leave their cans of spray paint at home. He was the press box equivalent of a neoconservative. He still had his admirers—"Surrounded by left-leaning New York anti-establishment types, he has the courage to tell the truth," one of them wrote to the *Sporting News* in the summer of '77—yet Dick Young was no longer the voice of the New York sports fan but rather that of the city's blue-collar fury. The joke among his fellow newspapermen went that after reading Young's copy, you needed a handkerchief to wipe the spit off your face.

Young's problem with Tom Seaver—"Tom Terrific," or in Young's mock baby talk, "Tom Tewwific"—was that he had the gall to complain about his $225,000-a-year contract. And so the scribe hammered away at the ace. Seaver, Young wrote, was typical of the "selfish modern-day ballplayer"; he had "an extreme maturity deficiency"; he was "destructive to club morale," a "pouting, griping, clubhouse lawyer poisoning the team." Then came the knockout punch. On June 15, 1977, Young implied that Seaver's wife, Nancy, was jealous of Nolan Ryan's wife because Ryan was outearning Seaver. Moments after hearing the offending line from Young's column, Seaver demanded a trade. The following afternoon he was cleaning out his locker at Shea.

It was the *Post*'s Maury Allen who first reported on Young's role in the Seaver trade in a June 16 piece headlined DICK YOUNG DROVE SEAVER OUT OF TOWN. Allen was known for his ability to tap out a story in the time it took most of his colleagues to change their typewriter ribbons, but this had not been an easy one for him to write. Growing up in 1950s Brooklyn, Allen had idolized Young. In recent years, though, he'd watched his boyhood hero turn bitter, angry. "He expected things to be the way they were in the forties and fifties," Allen says. "But they weren't. The world was different."

17.

41st and 40th St. along 8th Avenue across from the Port of Authority is one of the wildest areas spread over from the Times Square district. Big stereo and material shops plus overnight fruit stands have sprung up years ago to remain part of the color among dusty grease smeared windows of shadowy lampless bars where all of the characters from out in the ocean strut in to mix with delivery boys and pimps, prostitutes and the rest and small con guys who lean against the neon fuzz of jukeboxes illuminated faces like 30's deco tobacco cards and weary workers who push hunks of stale roll thru greasy puddles of stew meat.

DAVID WOJNAROWICZ'S UNPUBLISHED JOURNALS, AUGUST 12, 1977

A 1977 New York City Planning Commission report counted no fewer than 245 pornographic institutions in the city. In 1965 there had been 9.

As early as 1975 Mayor Beame, who was old enough to remember when the marquees along West Forty-second Street billed George M. Cohan's latest musical rather than "live nude girls," had been vowing to "reverse the blight in this vital center of our city." But between the loopholes in city and state laws, the dwindling number of city policemen and prosecutors, and the need to avoid violating the civil liberties of his citizens, it had not been easy.

Ramping up to his reelection drive at the start of '77, Mayor Beame launched a fresh attack on smut peddlers, a citywide zoning plan that would ban "physical culture establishments" (bureaucratese for *massage parlors*, itself a euphemism for what were, in effect, brothels) and eliminate all other pornographic businesses in or near residential areas. But the proposal quickly became the victim of squabbling among the borough presidents, and by early spring it had been indefinitely shelved. Now the sex industry wasn't just thriving, it was spreading east to the area around Grand Central Station.

The city had lifted its licensing requirements for massage parlors in the late sixties, and they'd been proliferating ever since, often stepping in to fill the void left by midtown businesses that were either closing or leaving New York. By 1977 there were at least ninety-three of them in and around Times Square, Manhattan's biggest erogenous zone, a neighborhood studded with nude fortune-tellers, stores selling dirty books, twenty-five-cent peep shows, pornographic movie theaters, topless bars, topless-and-bottomless bars, and prostitutes (the antiloitering law that had been enacted for the Democratic Convention in '76 had long since been struck down).

In 1977, Times Square saw the opening of Show World, its biggest sex institution yet. Situated on the corner of Forty-second Street and Eighth Avenue, the heart of Times Square, Show World was a twenty-two-thousand-square-foot multistory sex arcade complete with video booths, live sex acts, and private rooms where naked women sat behind thin sheets of Plexiglas. Most sex emporiums were dark, mysterious. Show World, which announced its presence with a blinking neon sign, was bright, garish. Some four thousand people passed through its doors each day.

After his antipornography zoning plan had been tabled, Mayor Beame decided to try a more confrontational approach. During his antiracketeering crusade in 1934, Mayor La Guardia had taken to the streets to personally smash illegal slot machines. On an afternoon in late March, Mayor Beame led a pack of cops and newsmen on a series of pornography raids beginning with Jax 3-Ring Circus, a strip club on Fifty-third Street east of Lexington Avenue.

It did not go well. The modest mayor waited outside, while the policemen and reporters marched inside to find three nude women gyrating under spotlights. Moments later he stood blushing under the marquee amid the jostle of news photographers, half-clothed dancers, and fleeing patrons. Beame and one of his aides taped a "peremptory vacate order" sign on the club's window, and the thumping music and nude dancing promptly ceased. Within a few hours, however, a judge for the State Supreme Court ordered the Jax reopened.

And so New York's sex industry continued to boom. In the fall, a potbellied ex-McDonald's manager–cum–orgy entrepreneur named Larry Levenson opened Plato's Retreat in the basement of the old Ansonia Hotel on the Upper West Side. The Bronx-born Levenson, who was himself divorced, had been initiated into the world of swinging singles about a year earlier by a woman he'd picked up at a cocktail lounge in Sheepshead Bay, Brooklyn. From there it was a short trip to hosting private orgies; then, at the suggestion of a potential investor, a business opportunity in the form of New York's first nightclub with a mattress area.

For a place that celebrated sexual freedom, Plato's had a lot of rules. A man couldn't enter without a female date—the cover charge was twenty-five dollars per couple, plus an extra five dollars for a temporary membership—and a lifeguard supervised the orgies from a chair overlooking the mattress area. Drugs were not permitted, though Plato's gift shop sold small felt pouches that were suspiciously well suited for concealing Quaaludes. If you were wearing a towel around your waist, you were dressed modestly. Maximum occupancy was six hundred, and there was almost always a line of people waiting to get in. What was most remarkable about the crowd at Plato's was how unremarkable it was. "Those of us who used to take comfort in the belief that sexual excesses were historically the vices of the bored and jaded upper classes must now acknowledge that a sizeable portion of the middle classes are now indulging quite openly," wrote *The Washington Post*'s Judy Bachrach in an article about the club in early 1978.

In fact, New York's middle class was absorbing its appreciation for sexual excess not from Park Avenue but from the West Village. Sandwiched between the arrival of AIDS on New York's shores during the 1976 bicentennial celebrations and the first reported cases of the virus in 1978, 1977 was the last great year of unprotected, nonreproductive sex in the city.

By the summer of '77 the surge of political energy unleashed by the 1969 Stonewall riots had more or less run its course. For every gay New Yorker marching for equal rights, umpteen more were finding their way into gay bars, bathhouses, and discotheques, not to mention the city's most famous gay cruising zone, the abandoned West Side piers. The sixties were over. As Arthur Bell, New York's first openly gay columnist, put it in *The Village Voice* in early 1977,

"The movement made it possible to 'be gay,' " while the emerging gay sex scene "made it possible to be gay with impunity, to drop your inhibitions along with your pants."

This new defiance was reflected in gay fashion too. Femme chic had given way to macho chic. Platform shoes, tight-fitting Lurex, and European couture were out; bomber jackets, lumberjack shirts, and work boots were in. "It is getting exceedingly difficult to tell a homosexual from a longshoreman," reported *Christopher Street*, a short-lived gay literary magazine, in late 1976.

Clandestine gay bathhouses had been part of the city's shadow landscape for decades. (A 1933 tabloid reported on the phenomenon beneath a headline that blared, PASHY STEAM ROOMS PANDER TO PANSIES.) Police raids were common, particularly in the McCarthy-fueled late fifties and early sixties. But ever since Stonewall, New York's gay bathhouses had been coming out of their collective closet. The 1977 gay guides listed them all over the city: the Upper East Side, Harlem, Wall Street.

Gay bars were also multiplying; a growing number of them—the Anvil, the Mineshaft, the Stud, the Toilet—had dark rooms in the back for fornication. For several years, these so-called backrooms had been operating out of public view, but in early 1977 Arthur Bell introduced them to straight New York in a graphic dispatch from this seedy subterranean world, describing the "dimly lit or pitch-black chambers where whips crack and urine and Schlitz are often served in the same container . . . TV dinners for young men in a hurry."

Not everyone in the gay community approved, either of Bell's decision to go public with the backrooms or of the culture of the backrooms themselves. "Do you want to be forced back into the closet by a society which is growing sick of the revolting image of homosexuals which is being forced down its throats by those who are willing to sell us down the river in the media?" Michael Giammetta, publisher of *Michael's Thing*, a weekly magazine covering New York's gay culture and social scene, asked in late March. A few weeks later a sympathetic reader wrote in to the magazine to echo its concerns and bemoan the fact that the backrooms had eliminated all conversational foreplay: "the lack of verbal communication leaves one as lonely as before."

The new permissiveness of the post-Stonewall, pre-AIDS era produced a peculiar nostalgia for the more illicit sex of a disappearing era. When a new bathhouse called the Broadway Arms opened in the summer of 1977, it featured "the latest in backroom concepts," the IRTearoom. Modeled after the bathrooms on subway platforms, formerly favorite gay trysting spots, the IRTearoom boasted stalls lined with tiles coated with graffiti and urine stains. The screeching sound of subway cars was piped into the room to enhance verisimilitude. Another savvy bathhouse owner outfitted his establishment with an eighteen-wheeler to simulate the once-popular pastime of sneaking into the trucks parked in front of the meatpacking district's commercial warehouses for furtive late-night sex.

During the summer months much of the anonymous sexual activity in New York's gay community took place outside, and no place was more popular for al fresco sex than the Lower West Side's derelict, semienclosed piers. New York's gay waterfront had a long history, one dating back to at least the 1930s, when queer locals trolled for transient seamen in boardinghouses and saloons near the Hudson River. The city's shipping trade eventually dried up, but a gay subculture clung stubbornly to the piers.

By 1977 the stretch of piers from Christopher to Fourteenth Street—"the Casbah," as gay guidebooks had labeled them—thronged with gay life. They were a hot spot for nude sunbathers; a campground for a racially diverse group of gay teens who had either run away from home or been kicked out of the house; and, most famously, a bustling gay cruising spot. Many things contributed to the piers' erotic appeal: the slapping of the Hudson; the smell of commingling sweat and brine; the sense of discovery that accompanied exploring an abandoned site; the sense of danger that accompanied having sex on aging wood planks over a polluted river.

This "moist and rotting nighttown," in the evocative words of the *Voice*'s Richard Goldstein, was a proud product of municipal neglect. The insolvent city had written off its waterfront. Even in decay, New York continued to bloom, if in ways unforeseen.

18.

The thing I like best about Bella is that she puts on fresh makeup and tries to have her hair done before a demonstration.

A NEIGHBOR OF BELLA ABZUG'S, QUOTED BY *VOGUE* MAGAZINE

THE owner of the empty Buick showroom on Fifty-fifth Street and Broadway that served as the headquarters for the Abzug mayoral campaign didn't want his new tenant hanging posters in the windows, so her staff painted B-E-L-L-A in huge orange letters on the plate glass instead. Part of the showroom was given over to the Bella Boutique, where a big-breasted woman in a tight T-shirt and sailor's cap sold Bella knickknacks, including a button of Gracie Mansion with an outsize hat hanging off the side. There was a gay porn theater with a twenty-four-hour pickup scene across the street. Some mornings Jackie Mason, who lived in the neighborhood, would stop by and volunteer: "What can I do for Bella?"

Not that Bella herself was ever there. The only candidate without a day job, she was out crisscrossing the boroughs, a bullhorn affixed to her mouth, one of her big hats flapping on top of her head. Abzug's day started early, even if that meant powdering her nose in the back of her campaign car, a yellow Chevrolet Impala convertible.

She was a full-contact campaigner, a polka-dotted beach ball bouncing from one outstretched hand to the next. "How arya? I'm Bella Abzug. I think I'm gonna be your next mayor. So let's get to know each other," she'd say. "Give 'em hell, Bella," or, "You've got my vote," they'd say back. "Bella was always fabulous on the streets," recalls her press secretary, Harold Holzer, who had first met Abzug while covering her 1970 congressional race for a small Manhattan weekly.

Abzug even *looked* different when she was campaigning. Her scowl turned into a smile; her round face grew soft and pink. "Campaigning does the same thing for her that pregnancy does for some women," Jack Newfield once observed. When Abzug and her aides returned to their Fifty-fifth Street offices, usually after midnight, they'd head around the corner to the Stage Deli. The candidate would have the corned beef on rye, even though she was, notionally, on a strict sixteen-hundred-calorie-a-day diet designed personally by her friend Shirley MacLaine. (*US* magazine was already planning a feature on Abzug's weight loss regimen.) Back home after 1 a.m., she might call an old friend or two from the movement. When they complained about her waking up their kids, Abzug would assume an indignant tone: "What? Aren't you a liberated woman?"

Abzug's radical, protofeminist past was never far behind her. She was born Bella Savitzky in 1920, the year women got the vote, and grew up in a South Bronx railroad flat. She struck her first blow for feminism at age thirteen, when her father died and she flouted the rules of her family's Orthodox synagogue by reciting the Kaddish—the Jewish prayer of mourning reserved for sons, not daughters—before school every morning. She had learned to stump by weaving in and out of crowded subway cars as a teenager, raising money for the creation of a Jewish state. "I shook my can for the JNF [Jewish National Fund]," she would later say.

The Depression stirred left-wing passions in Abzug's South Bronx neighborhood, an enclave of first-generation immigrant idealists, many of whom had already lived through the depths of privation in the Jewish ghettos of Europe. By the time she was elected president of the student council at Hunter College in 1942, the *New York Post* was already referring to her as a "known campus pink." Before entering politics, she worked as an attorney, defending alleged Communists—McCarthy called her one of the most subversive lawyers in the country—and a thirty-six-year-old black man who had been convicted of raping a white woman in Laurel, Mississippi, on whose behalf Abzug appeared in court eight months pregnant.

Abzug became an early champion of gay rights during her 1970 congressional race, after her campaign manager, Doug Ireland, encouraged her to stump in the Continental Baths, the bathhouse/cabaret/disco in the basement of the old Ansonia Hotel. Abzug headed gamely up to the baths with no idea what she was in for and promptly called Ireland from a pay phone, screaming: "What the hell have you gotten me into? There are hundreds of guys up here wearing nothing but towels held together by Bella buttons!" Ireland talked her down, and Abzug addressed the half-naked crowd in a navy blue dress with white polka dots and a Calamity Jane hat. "I'm sorry that I'm not quite dressed for the occasion," she began. She was a huge hit.

In June 1977, after the citizens of Dade County, Florida, had voted overwhelmingly to repeal a local law banning discrimination based on sexual preference, New York's gay community sought solace from Abzug. The referendum was the work of Anita Bryant and her grassroots group Save Our Children. Campaigning on its behalf, the beauty pageant queen–cum–homophobic ideologue had worn her familiar winning smile, only now, instead of extolling the virtues of Florida orange juice, she inveighed against the "human garbage" who practiced "a lifestyle that is an abomination against the laws of God and man."

After learning that the referendum had passed by a two to one margin and that Bryant was spinning the victory as a mandate to take her campaign national, thousands of gay New Yorkers amassed in front of the old Stonewall Inn for an impromptu demonstration. A few hours later the crowd migrated to Abzug's West Village brownstone. It was now a few hours before dawn, and she was awakened by the rhythmic chanting: "Bel-LAH! Bel-LAH! Bel-LAH!" Her long-suffering husband, Martin, groggily told her she was hearing voices in her head. (No doubt, if Abzug *had* been hearing voices in her head, that's exactly what they would have been saying.) But Abzug was sure the voices were coming from outside. She rose out of bed, pulled on her bathrobe and slippers, and stepped out onto her stoop to find hundreds of gay men assembled in front of her Bank Street house. Abzug told them that the struggle for civil rights was a long one and reminded them to vote for her in September.

Abzug was New York's feminist earth mother. For the 1977 mayoral race, she decided to update her famous 1970 congressional campaign slogan, "*This* woman's place is in the House," with "Maybe it's time for me to return to the traditional role of women—and that is to clean up the mess they made!"

There were two ways to explain New York's ongoing fiscal crisis. According to one, the banks were the villains. Rather than stand by the city as it grappled with the loss of manufacturing jobs, they had panicked and abruptly dumped all their New York City bonds on an unsuspecting market. Under the other explanation, the labor unions were the bad guys. They had strong-armed City Hall into concession after concession until the public sector payroll was finally so bloated that it broke New York's financial back.

Most New Yorkers figured there was enough blame for both parties to share. Not Bella. "Everybody makes the unions the scapegoat, but it was the banks who accelerated the fiscal crisis!" she bellowed. Her first priority as mayor, Abzug vowed, would be to give all out-of-work civil servants their jobs back. At a small gathering in front of Engine Company 269, a red-brick firehouse in the heart of Park Slope, Brooklyn, that had been shuttered because of budget cuts, the candidate promised to reopen this and every other closed engine company in New York. "Right on, Bella!" one local shouted. "Right on, baby!" she yelled back.

No one did protests better than Bella. At a "Disarm" rally in the Columbia quad, she whipped the young crowd into a frenzy, blaming the violence plaguing New York's streets on America's militaristic culture: "A society that sanctioned the horrors of Vietnam, the unbridled growth of the Pentagon, and the CIA's involvement in the violent overthrow of the governments in Chile and Guatemala should not be surprised when so many Americans turn to individual violence and crime at home." At a red-lining protest in front of the Greater New York Savings Bank in South Brooklyn, she accused the banks of "destroying neighborhoods" by refusing mortgages to local homeowners and businesses. In the depths of Queens, she demanded that New York State revoke the licenses of real estate brokers who engaged in blockbusting, the use of racial scare tactics to provoke panic selling among white homeowners. In the executive dining room of CUNY's Graduate Center, she railed against the "traumatic contraction" of the hallowed institution, which had lost thirty-eight thousand students and a thousand faculty members over the past year, and cited the "moral imperative" to provide free higher education to the poor and disadvantaged.

Nothing got Abzug hotter than Westway, the city's plan to rebuild the West Side Highway south of Forty-second Street. The blueprints called for burying the highway in a concrete tube beneath the surface of the Hudson, then extending the deck above out into the river to make room for parks and office and apartment buildings. Westway won high marks from architecture critics like the *Times's* Ada Louise Huxtable, who described it as "a chance to reclaim the mutilated waterfront and West Side," and the business community was convinced Westway would promote development in a flagging lower Manhattan. Even setting such practical considerations aside, the symbolic implications were hard to ignore: To many New Yorkers, the very fact that the city was again daring to reach seemed worthy of celebration. Best of all, Westway would be free. The new road would be within the interstate highway system, meaning that the federal government would pick up 90 percent of the tab. The state would pay the rest.

But Westway also made a logical next front for the community warriors who'd spent the better part of the 1960s beating back large-scale development projects they feared would wreak havoc on the city's neighborhoods. To them, Westway flew directly in the face of New York's organically messy essence. It was a big patch that would never become part of the larger fabric of the city. Naysayers needed only point to *The Power Broker*, Robert Caro's magisterial 1974 biography of Robert Moses, to underscore just how destructive overzealous city planners could be.

The plan's critics had no trouble persuading Abzug to side with them. She sponsored a clever piece of legislation that would enable cities to swap federal funds earmarked for interstate highways for mass transit money. Instead of getting $1 billion from Washington to build an interstate highway, New York City could opt for $550 million to rehabilitate its subway system, a needy case if ever there were one. Framed as a choice between automobiles and subways, between lining the pockets of real estate developers and improving the lives of workaday New Yorkers, Westway became a perfect foil for Abzug, who saw her beloved city as an overgrown village, a place where the power belonged to the people, not to the men with green eyeshades and pocket protectors who had the nerve to talk about the "greater good."

Still, Westway lurched forward, winning the final go-ahead from Washington in early 1977. "Mayor Beame and the real estate speculators who support this project are willing to sacrifice the needs of 89% of New Yorkers who use mass transit to benefit the highway lobbyists," Abzug said one drizzly early summer night at the Church of St. Paul and St. Andrew on the mostly liberal Upper West Side. The crowd rose from its red-cushioned benches to applaud her, much as it had earlier in the evening, when she'd made her dramatic entrance, striding up the church's center aisle, arms pumping, hands thrust out in front of her body. "This is exactly the kind of planning for special interests which has brought our city so many times to the verge of bankruptcy!"

As much as they adored Abzug on the liberal Upper West Side, they loved her even more at Camp Tamiment, a pine-spiced summer resort some ninety miles southwest of the city in the Poconos. A group of trade unionists and socialists had planted stakes here in the 1920s, and it had quickly become a favorite summer retreat for New York's working class, who came in droves to sleep in rustic cabins, swim in a shimmering lake, and soak up lectures on totalitarianism. It was a requisite campaign stop for every New York City mayoral candidate.

In late June 1977 Abzug told the crowd at Tamiment that she knew exactly what had gone wrong in New York, this once-proud paradigm of New Deal plenty. It was a case of diminished expectations. "Almost every day we can read editorials in our leading newspapers telling us not to expect much from Washington and not to expect much from City Hall," she said, the beads of perspiration glistening on her red temples. "The people with this outlook say we will continue to lose jobs and population. They say let's encourage the poor to get out of town and let's tear down their neighborhoods. Let's continue to attack the unions because we have to drive down wages . . . They say let's get rid of free tuition and the municipal hospital system, shut down child care centers, senior centers, libraries and fire stations. They say let's fire teachers, guidance counselors and security guards, and let's get rid of rent control. Let's slash subway and bus service and crush more people into the trains, and maybe we'll even make them pay more for that memorable experience. That's not my vision and I know it's not yours. You have invested too much of yourselves, too much sweat, time and thought into our city to settle for a spiral of further cutbacks and reduced services that will only hasten the decline of New York."

Abzug, pure product of old New York that she was, clung stubbornly to her utopianism, convinced that if she shook her broken snow globe hard enough, she could make the flakes fall again.

19.

ON June 17, 1977, a warm, foggy Friday night at Fenway, Catfish Hunter had the worst outing of the worst season of his career.

Like Reggie Jackson, Hunter, the Yankees' brown-haired, blue-eyed, barrel-chested ace, had started on Charlie Finley's plantation. When Finley signed him in 1964, there wasn't a scout in the country who hadn't heard of this eighteen-year-old kid named Jimmy Hunter. They descended in droves on Hertford, North Carolina (population: twenty-two hundred), a little tobacco town on the banks of the Perquimans River, but Finley outdid them all, pulling up to the Hunter family farm in a long black limousine. Jimmy's sunbonnet-topped momma was hoeing weeds; her husband was rearranging the bacon in the smokehouse. Over a dinner of hog jowls and black-eyed peas, they talked business. Finley left a few hours later with a pair of smoked hams and a new right-hander.

All Jimmy Hunter needed was a nickname. Finley settled quickly on Catfish. He'd tell the press that Hunter had been missing one night and that his folks found him down by the stream with one catfish lying beside him and another on his pole. Hunter himself didn't see what was wrong with "Jim," but he wasn't going to argue with the guy who was about to write him a check for seventy-five thousand dollars. First things first: Finley wanted the buckshot—the result of a rabbit-hunting accident—removed from Hunter's right foot. He spent the '64 season on the disabled list and joined the A's partway through '65, having never pitched an inning in the minor leagues.

On a good day, Hunter's fastball topped out in the mid-eighties, and to the untrained eye his slider looked a lot like his curve, but a childhood spent throwing rocks, corncobs, and clods of dirt through a small hole in the family's barn door had served him well. He estimated that he could put the ball within three inches of his catcher's target 90 percent of the time; others figured his margin of error closer to one or two inches. The key to his control was his repetitive motion. "If you go out to the mound after he's pitched a game you'll see three marks: one where he stands when he's on the rubber, one where his left foot lands, one where his right foot lands," his former teammate Doc Medich told J. Anthony Lukas for a 1975 *New York Times Magazine* profile. "Most players leave the mound all scratched up like a plowed cornfield."

Hunter was arrogant on the mound and humble off it and didn't want the distinction blurred. (After pitching a perfect game for the A's in '68, he wouldn't allow his teammates to hoist him up on their shoulders.) He had the relaxed, almost sedated temperament of a Carolina farm boy and an easy, appetite-whetting delivery to match. In the wake of one particularly humiliating defeat at Hunter's hands, Milwaukee Brewers' manager Dave Bristol slammed shut the clubhouse door and lit into his team for the better part of an hour: "You guys call yourselves hitters? If you can't hit that puffball pitcher, you can't hit anybody!"

Hunter became available to the highest bidder in '75, after Finley had violated the terms of his best pitcher's contract by refusing to make certain agreed-upon deferred payments. The timing of the Great Catfish Auction, as the free marketeers on *The Wall Street Journal*'s editorial page approvingly tagged it, could not have been better. Hunter was fresh off a twenty-five-win season, the fourth year in a row in which he'd won at least twenty-one games. The Yankees promptly signed him to a five-year, $2.9 million deal. He was the highest-paid player in baseball, but the numbers are a bit deceptive. Deferred income and insurance payments accounted for $2 million of the total; $36,000 was specifically earmarked for scholarships for his children, $6,000 for a new Buick. The contract stipulated that Hunter pay for the license plates himself. Still, it was six times what he'd earned playing for Finley.

True to form, Hunter won twenty-three games for the Yankees in '75, but in '76 his right shoulder began bothering him. Martin added a fifth starter to give him an extra day of rest. Not one to miss a turn—he already felt guilty enough about getting paid so much to work forty days a year—Hunter pitched through the pain, soaking his right arm in a big tub of ice after each start. "If I can still throw where I want to and get hitters out, if it hurts and I can still do it, that's not pitching with pain," he told one reporter, "that's pleasure." He went 17-15 on the year and hoped that a quiet winter on the farm in Hertford would restore him to health.

It didn't. Hunter struggled in spring training in '77, his fastball hovering in the low seventies. A cortisone shot managed to right him in time for a strong opening day performance, but since then he'd been floundering. His aching body compelled unconscious adjustments to his near-perfect form. Martin's strict policy about discussing injuries with the press notwithstanding, the word was out that Catfish Hunter was not well. Concerned fans were even mailing him cures. One suggested that cranberry juice might help dissolve the calcium deposits in his arm. Hunter, who was missing as many starts as he was making, was desperate enough to start drinking a quart a day.

Hunter made his June 17 start at Fenway, but he didn't survive the first inning. The Red Sox binge began with a leadoff home run off the bat of Rick Burleson, an overachieving line drive that settled softly into the net atop the Green Monster. Hunter sucked some juice from his tobacco-packed cheek and went to 3-2 against Fred Lynn.

Lynn fouled Hunter's sixth pitch straight back. The seventh he deposited in the right field bullpen.

Hunter dug back into his hole at the right-hand corner of the rubber and retired the next two hitters. Then Carlton Fisk sent a fastball over the Monster and onto Lansdowne Street. Martin came out to the mound to make sure everything was okay. The Yankees' skipper had scarcely returned to the dugout when George Scott went deep, tying the major-league record for most home runs in an inning.

Four hits and four runs over two-thirds of an inning. Martin came back out to the mound and this time asked for the ball. Hunter walked off the field briskly, slung his warmup jacket over his shoulder, and clattered down the cement runway toward the locker room. He was finished, but for the Yankees the weekend had just begun.

20.

THE fog cleared overnight. Saturday was sunny, hot, and humid. By noon the narrow streets surrounding Boston's cozy ballyard were choked with people as the temperature climbed toward a hundred degrees. Along Yawkey Way a brass band played and sausages sizzled. Fenway drew its biggest crowd in more than twenty years, and twenty-five million more were tuned to watch the first-place Red Sox play the second-place Yankees on NBC's *Game of the Week.*

The Yankees scored two in the top half of the first. The Sox answered with Carl Yastrzemski's three-run blast into the center field seats, then piled on three more in the fourth. The Yankees scratched out another two runs, closing the gap to 7–4 before they took the field in the bottom half of the sixth, with starter Mike Torrez still on the mound.

Boston's Fred Lynn singled to open the inning, bringing Jim Rice to the plate. Torrez came up and in, and Rice, checking his swing, looped the pitch down the line into shallow right field. Rice slowed down as he rounded first. Reggie, who was playing the power hitter deep, moved in tentatively. Rice, seeing Reggie's hesitation, started for second. By the time Reggie's throw arrived at the bag, Rice had slid safely into second. Reggie put his hands on his hips in disgust. Martin ambled out to the mound to lift Torrez.

As reliever Sparky Lyle jogged in to spell Torrez, Yankee broadcaster Frank Messer filled the void with the usual patter: "The Boston Red Sox are leading 7–4, and Sparky Lyle will be coming in. Sparky is tied for the American League in saves with thirteen. Before the game, Billy was saying . . ."

"Uh-oh," interrupted Messer's longtime broadcast partner, Phil Rizzuto. "I'm sorry, Frank, but I think Billy's calling Paul Blair to replace Jackson, and Jackson doesn't know it yet. We're liable to see a little display of temper here . . . It's Reggie's own fault really. On that ball he did not hustle."

Rizzuto quickly searched his memory. In his long career in baseball, he could recall only one other occasion when a manager made a defensive substitution in the middle of an inning: Casey Stengel sending Cliff Mapes in for Joe DiMaggio. DiMag refused to leave the field.

"Oh, look at Billy!" Rizzuto intoned. "Is he hot!"

The Fenway crowd caught sight of Blair trotting across the field and let out a roar. Reggie, who was chatting with Fran Healy, his arms draped casually over the green fence of the bullpen, was practically the only guy in the ballpark with no idea what was going on. Healy told Reggie to turn around. Reggie glanced over his shoulder and saw Blair coming toward him. Reggie pointed at himself—*You mean me?*—in disbelief. Blair nodded.

"What the hell is going on?" Reggie asked.

Blair shrugged. "You've got to ask Billy that."

The NBC cameras followed Reggie off the field and into the dugout. Initially, he looked more puzzled than angry bounding down the dugout steps with his hands spread, palm side up, in an expression of utter confusion.

Martin was waiting for him, neck cords bulging, knees bent, arms dangling impatiently at his side. "What the fuck do you think you're doing out there?" he asked.

"What do you mean? What are you talking about?"

"You know what the fuck I'm talking about. You want to show me up by loafing on me. Fine. Then I'm going to show your ass up. Anyone who doesn't hustle doesn't play for me."

Now the fury was building inside Reggie too. He took off his glasses, set them down on top of his glove, and started moving toward Martin.

"They're gonna confront each other right there in the dugout!" *Game of the Week* broadcaster Joe Garagiola narrated as NBC's cameras zoomed in. They were close enough now for America to read Martin's lips: "I ought to kick your fucking ass."

"Who the fuck do you think you're talking to, old man," Reggie spit back. "Don't you ever dare show me up again, motherfucker."

Martin started after Reggie. "There they go!" said Garagiola. Ray Negron quickly threw a towel over the lens of the dugout camera, only it was the camera in center field that was recording all the action.

Yankee Coach Elston Howard grabbed Martin and pinned him against a pole. "Billy wants a little piece of Reggie Jackson, and he's being stopped by Elston Howard," narrated Garagiola. But Martin broke free. "There goes Billy—he is hot!" Now another Yankees' coach, Yogi Berra, grabbed him in a bear hug. ("I swear if Yogi hadn't stopped me I would have beaten the hell out of him," Martin said later. "Reggie's big, but I wasn't afraid of him.")

Mike Torrez told Reggie in Spanish to go into the clubhouse and cool off. Outfielder Jimmy Wynn wrapped his arms around him to make sure he did. "You don't like me—you've never liked me," Reggie yelled back at Martin as he made his way down the ramp.

"I was livid," Reggie recalled later, "but I wasn't going to fight him in the dugout."

He was going to fight him in the locker room. Reggie stripped down to his undershirt and uniform pants, leaving his spikes on so he wouldn't lose his footing on Fenway's clubhouse carpeting, and waited for the game to end.

Healy came running in from the bullpen to talk to Reggie a few minutes later. He wasn't worried about protecting Reggie from Martin—"I can assure you that Billy didn't want a piece of Reggie, not if nobody was around, anyway"—he was worried about protecting Reggie from himself. It took some convincing, but Healy eventually persuaded Reggie to shower and leave the ballpark before the game ended. Negron came down to the clubhouse to check on Reggie and to ask if he needed a cab back to the hotel. Reggie wanted to walk.

Red Sox vice president Gene Kirby escorted him out a side door, up a set of stairs through Gate E, and onto Lansdowne Street. Reggie slowly made his way back to the Sheraton in the steamy late-afternoon heat.

None of the Yankees were exactly surprised. "I knew it was just a matter of time before it happened," recalls Ken Holtzman, "but I figured it would be in the clubhouse, not on national TV."

In the locker room after the game, everyone refused to be quoted. Off the record, however, most of the players expressed sympathy for their manager.

The Sox went on to win 10–4. Martin fielded questions in Fenway's cramped visiting manager's office. "When a player shows up the team, I show up the player," he said.

"Did you think twice about pulling Reggie in such a close game?"

"We won last year without him, didn't we?"

"Did you consider a more conventional means of discipline?"

"How do you fine a superstar, take away his Rolls-Royce?"

"Do you think the incident was bad for baseball since the game was on national television?"

"I don't care if it went over the whole world."

Steinbrenner, who'd been watching the game on TV in Cleveland, wanted Martin to attend an emergency meeting with Reggie and the Yankees' head of baseball operations, Gabe Paul, at the hotel that night. Instead, Martin headed for Daisy Buchanan's, a bar on Newbury Street. Moss Klein, the Yankees' reporter for the *Newark Star-Ledger*, found him there chasing scotch with beer later that night. It took Klein a while to write his game story, which is to say that Martin was operating on a full tank. "When Billy was drunk, he would repeat things, and he'd adopt a Southern accent that got more and more pronounced the drunker he got," Klein recalls. "That night he kept saying, 'They're gonna say this was my fault. They're gonna say this was my fault.' "

Across town Reggie sat in his hotel room with a bottle of white wine. The phone rang. It was the Reverend Jesse Jackson. At the time the thirty-five-year-old reverend, looking for a new act to follow the civil rights protests of the sixties, was in the throes of an extended flirtation with the Republican Party. He and Reggie had spoken outside Comiskey Park earlier in the season. "He'd had a bad day at the plate, and I said, 'Reggie, the difference between popping the ball up and popping it out of the park is an eyelash of concentration,' " Jackson recalls. "You need to drop some of your distractions and focus on the ball." More than a few autograph seekers had confused the two men, whose similarities ran deeper than their imposing frames. If Reverend Jackson represented the modern-day civil rights leader, a man who used the media as his pulpit and lectured his advance men on the importance of "drama," Reggie was the modern-day baseball star. Everything about him, from his violent uppercut swing to his bristling, emotional aura to his colorful flights of rhetoric, was overstated.

Reverend Jackson was spending much of the summer of '77 away from his Chicago headquarters, touring the nation's inner city schools on a tough love crusade, urging young black students to start taking responsibility for their plight. It was not too different from the advice he gave Reggie when the slugger was thinking about quitting. Jackson told Reggie that this was the real world, that even if he was overwhelmed by New York's expectations, no one was going to feel sorry for him if he quit.

A little later, *Newsday*'s Steve Jacobson called from the lobby to ask if he could come up. His deadline was approaching, and he didn't want to file his copy without a quote from Reggie. Jacobson generously brought Phil Pepe of the *Daily News* and Paul Montgomery of the *Times* along with him. When they entered the room, Reggie was bare-chested, his gold chains dangling from his neck. Sitting open in his lap was his big red Bible. Mike Torrez, whom Reggie had recruited to act as chaperon—"cut me off if I get carried away"—was also on hand.

The reverend's words doubtless still fresh in his head, Reggie sounded uncharacteristically stoic. "I don't know anything about managing, but I'll take the heat for whatever the manager says," Reggie said, looking up from his Bible. "Thank God I'm a Christian. Christ got my mind right. I won't fight the man. I'll do whatever they tell me."

Before long, though, Reggie's emotions had taken over. "It makes me cry, the way they treat me on this team. I'm a good ballplayer and a good Christian and I've got an IQ of 160, but I'm a nigger and I won't be subservient. The Yankee pinstripes are Ruth and Gehrig and DiMaggio and Mantle. They've never had a nigger like me before." The exception was Steinbrenner: "I love that man. He treats me like somebody. The rest of them treat me like dirt." Reggie dropped down to his knees and began gesticulating wildly, the paranoid preacher who spied the devil's shadows all around him. "He was talking about how everybody wanted a piece of him and was coming after him and how nobody understood him," Pepe recalls.

On and on he went as Torrez sat silent and the writers scribbled madly. "I'm going to play the best that I can for the rest of the year, help this team win, then get my ass out of here."

21.

THE image that had been seared on the nation's consciousness, courtesy of NBC Sports, was now plastered on sports pages across the country: the brawny black slugger, his glasses removed and set aside, standing chest to chest with his scrawny white manager. Much of America grinned vindictively. *Los Angeles Times* columnist Melvin Durslag wrote that he expected no less. This was, after all, a team that played in the South Bronx, "one of the meanest places in America."

The New York beat writers steered clear of the race question. No one wanted to point an accusing finger at Martin, nor was anyone eager to contradict a black man's charge of racism. "Is Jackson persecuted or does he just feel like he is?" wrote Pepe. "It probably doesn't matter."

Yet the race issue was not so easy to set aside, especially considering that this wasn't Martin's first clash with an outspoken black player. When he arrived in Detroit in 1970, Martin had inherited the outfielder Elliott Maddox, a University of Michigan graduate and convert to Judaism whom Martin dumped as quickly as he could. After the trade Maddox heard from more than a few writers and ex-teammates that Martin's nickname for him was the Downtown Nigger. (*Newsday*'s Jacobson recalls hearing Martin use the n-word in reference to Reggie as well.) Three years later Martin and Maddox were reunited in Texas. Once again Martin encouraged a trade, this time to the Yankees. As soon as he arrived in New York, Martin drove Maddox out yet again. "I never liked his make-up, his laziness, his show-offishness," Martin told a *Sport* magazine reporter in 1975. "I think he wants to get hit so he can cry. What he needs is a good asskicking."

"Billy was a racist and an anti-Semite," Maddox says now. "He had a drinking problem, and he had psychological problems stemming from his childhood. Most people to this day will not come out and tell the truth about Billy, but I'm not gonna lie. The truth comes out about presidents after they die. Why shouldn't the truth come out about him?"

A few years after that fateful day at Fenway, Elston Howard, the first black Yankee, offered his take on Reggie and Billy's relationship to Maury Allen for his book *Mr. October*. "Billy was jealous of him, hated the attention Reggie got, couldn't control him," Howard told Allen. "The other part, the big part was that Reggie's black. Billy hated him for that. I believe Billy is prejudiced against blacks, Jews, American Indians, Spanish, anything if you don't bow to him. He can get along with blacks if they don't challenge him. But Reggie challenged him in every way. Billy was always hostile to him. Did everything to make him unhappy. Went out of his way to see him fail." (Howard had his own reasons to dislike Martin: In the spring of '77 he'd reported to Fort Lauderdale to discover that the Yankees' manager had given his job coaching first base, a position he'd held for nine years, to Bobby Cox.)

In the summer of '77, though, very few voices were heard in defense of Reggie. For the most part, New York was proud of Martin—their working-class hero, their link to a better era—for standing up to the arrogant, overpaid slugger. And the truth was, the narcissistic, chronically melodramatic Reggie didn't make for a very convincing victim. Most of Reggie's black teammates were unsympathetic to his cries of racism. Hearing Reggie complain in a hotel bar one night, an exasperated Chris Chambliss, the understated son of a navy chaplain, exploded. "Reggie, you know what you'd be if you were white? Just another damn white boy," he said. "Be glad you're black and getting all of the publicity you do, getting away with all of the shit you do."

Even the city's black newspaper, the *Amsterdam News*, sided with Martin. Early in the season Reggie had told a reporter for the weekly, America's largest black newspaper, that he was going to do everything he could to improve Harlem. In the wake of the Fenway series, the *Amsterdam News* decided it was time for a follow-up. "He says he wants to rebuild the rundown Harlem he's seen since he hit town at the start of the season in April," the paper reported on its front page. "But he's never taken the time to learn some of the problems of the community as he drives up Madison Ave. from his $1500 per month apartment at 80th Street and Fifth Ave. in his $27,500 foreign made car, across the 138th St. bridge and into Yankee Stadium where he earns $400,000 per year as a diamond super star." Unkinder still was this quote from a "well-known" psychiatrist: "He [Reggie] came into town thinking that his reputation was all he needed to upset it, but this is New York, New York where many come but few conquer." And then, for good measure: "He lacks the inner qualities and charisma of a Muhammad Ali, Joe Louis or Ray Robinson who were 'people's heroes.' "

Reggie should have been accustomed to this sort of treatment. Throughout his career it had often been other blacks, not whites, who'd made him aware of the color of his skin: teammates like Bill North in Oakland, old greats like Willie Mays, Billy Williams, and Ernie Banks, even his father, who'd never gotten a shot at the big leagues because of racism. "Remember you're still a colored boy," his old man would tell him when he complained about the way he was being treated. "Don't forget that. You have to act a certain way. You have to be a certain way." Reggie didn't blame his father for this, just as he didn't blame the elderly black woman who'd gotten angry at him one afternoon for cutting short an autograph-signing session. ("We helped make you. You owe black people something," she told him. "It's her generation," Reggie reflected afterward. "It's the only thing she knows.")

The dugout incident at Fenway proved to be something of a turning point for Reggie. Over the years he came to sound very different on the subject of race, speaking eloquently about how his own coming of age had traced the arc of the postwar emergence of his race: "I was colored until I was 14, a Negro until I was 21, and a black man ever since." He spoke out, forcefully and persuasively, against baseball's failure to integrate at the executive and managerial level. And in his inimitable way, Reggie embellished his story, writing in his autobiography and in a first-person article published by *Sports Illustrated* in 1987 that his Little League coach had benched him in a state tournament to avoid any racial trouble with his team's opponents from Florida and claiming that when he was injured playing minor-league ball, a hospital in Lewiston, Idaho, refused to admit him. (Score sheets from the state tournament indicate that Reggie did play; a subsequent Associated Press story revealed that Reggie had been admitted to St. Joseph's Hospital in Lewiston.)

22.

THE day after the dugout debacle, Billy Martin arrived at Fenway Park, his eyelids at half-mast, changed out of his wrinkled tan suit, and stalked silently into the outfield to shag flies during batting practice. It was the only way to avoid the nagging reporters and clear the thick fog inside his hungover head.

Even before he'd had to be restrained from attacking his right fielder on national television, Martin was having problems. His heavily favored team was struggling to stay in the pennant race. Nearly all his starting pitchers were getting lit up, and just about every southpaw in the league was shutting down his lefty-heavy lineup.

Since the start of the season Steinbrenner had been calling him on a nearly daily basis to share his unsolicited opinion that Reggie Jackson should be batting cleanup, which of course only strengthened Martin's resolve to hit him fifth or sixth. Alas, a manager can control his lineup, but not his roster. Steinbrenner went out and bought a new shortstop, Bucky Dent, despite Martin's devotion to his old one, Fred Stanley. He had also traded one of Martin's favorite pitchers, Dock Ellis, and refused to fill an open slot on the roster with Elrod Hendricks, the third-string catcher for whom Martin had been furiously lobbying. When Martin complained that not having Hendricks had cost the team a game—lousy pitching and execrable fielding were more likely culprits—Steinbrenner fined him twenty-five hundred dollars.

There was no reason to expect Martin was going to survive the Fenway crisis. He had met with Reggie and Gabe Paul, the unofficial liaison between Steinbrenner and Martin, first thing in the morning and it had not gone well. Martin's first mistake was referring to Reggie as "boy," which an even more sensitive than usual Reggie interpreted as a racial slur. Martin insisted that it was just an expression, but Reggie was not inclined to give him the benefit of the doubt. At the end of the meeting Jackson refused to shake his manager's hand.

Reached in Cleveland for comment on Saturday's events, Steinbrenner had sided with his high-paid slugger, telling a *Boston Globe* reporter that it didn't look to him as if Reggie had failed to hustle. What it did look like, he added pointedly, was that his ball club was "out of control."

The game got under way, and the Red Sox pounded the Yankees for the third straight day, sweeping the series and extending their lead over the American League's defending champions to two and a half games. Adding to the humiliation, the Sox closed their final frame of the weekend with three of the longest home runs in the history of their ballpark, including Jim Rice's five-hundred-foot bomb to dead center. Even little Denny Doyle, who hadn't homered since 1975, went deep.

Back in the lineup, Reggie stung a couple of line drives but went hitless on the day and looked wobblier than ever in Fenway's shadowy outfield. He was lucky to pick up only one error for overthrowing a cutoff man. Asked after the game if he thought all his troubles with Martin could blow over, he answered, "No way." On the plane to Detroit that night, he stewed in silence.

Early the next morning a newswire reported that Martin was going to be fired and replaced by one of his coaches, Yogi Berra. As word spread through New York, angry fans flooded the stadium and local radio and TV stations with calls. The phone in Martin's hotel room was vibrating nonstop with inquiries from reporters, but Martin was out. His old friend Phil Rizzuto had spirited him away for a round of golf. Rizzuto tried vainly to assure Martin that the story was wrong, that Steinbrenner was too smart a businessman to fire someone so popular with the fans.

Rizzuto was wrong. Steinbrenner landed in Detroit in the early afternoon with every intention of getting rid of his manager. Gabe Paul, Steinbrenner's long-suffering lieutenant, made the case for why this was the wrong way to go: Fire Martin, and it will look as if Reggie runs the team. The new manager will have lost all his authority before he even fills out his first lineup card.

For his part, Reggie was letting reporters know that he didn't want Martin to be fired either, at least not on his account. He figured that he had enough troubles without being blamed for costing the manager his job.

A few hours later Martin reported to the ballpark, changed into his road grays, and sat quietly on the bench during batting practice. The newsmen circled warily. Martin, still unsure of his fate, spoke softly and said little as Tiger Stadium, a tangle of girders scabrous with rust that had opened for business the same week the *Titanic* went under, slowly filled. Mark Fidrych, the Tigers' flamboyant ace, was slated to pitch. With the Yankees in town, all 47,855 seats had been sold. The rest of America would be watching too, via ABC's *Monday Night Baseball.*

Steinbrenner showed up in the clubhouse as batting practice was winding down and called the team together to tell them that he was giving Martin a reprieve, but that if they wanted to keep him, they had better get their acts together. And no more of this "race bullshit." Steinbrenner sent Gabe Paul up to the press box with the news. The elevator was out of order, and Paul, who'd collapsed after suffering a mild stroke back in the spring, was red-faced and short of breath when he arrived.

By now many of the writers were convinced there was something Freudian going on in the Reggie-Martin-Steinbrenner dynamic. Unable to win his boss's affection or respect, the fatherless Martin had been reduced to acting out, both against Steinbrenner and Steinbrenner's favorite son. "Martin was the emotional weakling of the trio," recalls the *Post*'s Henry Hecht. "Reggie could be a creature of his emotions, but Martin was a mess."

A few minutes before that evening's game in Detroit, Martin, who'd owned this gritty town when he'd managed here, ambled out to home plate for the lineup exchange. The Tigers' fans rose from their hard, narrow seats and welcomed him back with a thunderous standing ovation. "Wasn't that super?" Martin said, back in the dugout and beaming. Recalling that evening a couple of years later, he explained more fully the broad smile that had suddenly spread across his pinched face: "That must have really burned George's ass."

23.

IT wasn't all bad being Reggie Jackson in the summer of 1977; if nothing else, he'd made a new friend, Ralph Destino.

At the time Destino, the chairman of Cartier, was living in a swanky penthouse on Seventy-ninth and Park Avenue, just a couple of blocks away from Reggie. Between them, at Seventy-ninth and Madison, was a coffee shop with sticky banquettes and stainless steel tables called the Nectar where Reggie was taking his breakfast one morning when Destino's wife, a fetching Italian, strolled in. Reggie set about chatting her up. Naturally, he began by introducing himself.

Reggie Jackson? The name didn't ring a bell. Mrs. Destino figured he was just some guy coming on to her. When she got back home, she asked her husband if he'd ever heard of this Reggie Jackson. The following morning, Destino insisted that they stake out the Nectar. Sure enough, Reggie walked in, and they invited him to join them for breakfast.

Soon after, Destino and his wife separated. For the first time in many years he was a bachelor. The timing couldn't have been better; by now he and Reggie Jackson were buddies. "There was a mutuality of interest," Destino remembers. "He was being hammered by Billy Martin, and I was in a very distasteful divorce. He needed a pal, and I was available. There was nothing I could teach him about baseball, but I could show him New York—that I knew about."

And so Destino set his new friend up with his first model, a Bill Blass girl and the daughter of *Fantasy Island* star Ricardo Montalban. He also took Reggie to his first Broadway show, *They're Playing Our Song*. After the play they had a late dinner at Sardi's. From across the room Reggie spotted the actor Lee Marvin, who had just beaten back the first palimony suit ever attempted. Reggie raced across the room to introduce himself. "He told him how much he admired what he had just achieved," Destino recalls. "Lee Marvin said, 'I admire what you achieve too.' "

Under Destino's tutelage, Reggie became an expert on Cartier. He brought his dates to the company's flagship Fifth Avenue store and lectured them on the various watches. (One afternoon, while waiting for Destino, whose office was above the store, Reggie got behind the counter and pretended to be a salesman.) Cars, Reggie already knew, and he regularly ragged Destino about the Lincoln Town Car's Cartier edition, much as he teased Steinbrenner about driving domestic: "Lincolns are just Fords with big price tags."

Destino bathed in the reflected glory, as did his eleven-year-old son, who became a minicelebrity at his Upper East Side private school: He was the kid whose dad knew Reggie. "He'd come home and say my friend wants a Reggie Jackson autograph, can you get it for me?" remembers Destino. "So I would get a couple of them, but pretty soon ten kids wanted them, then fifteen. By that time Reggie's signature was very familiar to me, so my son would say I need fifteen Reggie Jacksons, and I'd say okay. And after he'd go to bed, I would write fifteen Reggie Jacksons."

When he didn't have a date with Steinbrenner at the Carlyle, Reggie continued to have breakfast with Destino at the Nectar. They'd hook up at night too. If Destino couldn't make it to the ballpark, they would meet an hour after the game at Jim McMullen's on Third Avenue between Seventy-sixth and Seventy-seventh Street.

McMullen's was by no means the hottest place in Manhattan. In fact, it wasn't even the hottest place on the Upper East Side, not with Maxwell's Plum still going strong over on Sixty-fourth and First Avenue. Warner LeRoy had opened Maxwell's in 1966, the year after the Stork Club closed, which in retrospect does not seem like an accident of history. If the Stork carried New York from the dark days of the Depression through its postwar optimism, Maxwell's, with its stained glass kaleidoscope ceiling, Tiffany lamps, and human buffet of bachelors and bachelorettes, arrived just in time to spirit the city through the swinging sixties and sordid seventies.

Reggie and Destino tried Maxwell's a couple of times, but once they had to wait for a table they vowed never to return. It was just as well. Maxwell's may have had swinging singles, but McMullen's had models. "At any given time," recalls proprietor Jim McMullen, "we'd have two, three, four tables of the most beautiful women you'd ever want to see." There was a simple reason for this: McMullen himself had modeled for Eileen Ford's agency, and the two were still very close. Ford lived right around the corner from the restaurant in a town house on Seventy-eighth Street and always had a handful of young models in from out of town staying with her. As a favor to Jim, she'd send them over to eat at his place.

The decor at McMullen's was understated—modern, with some art nouveau touches. The walls were natural brick, with a few carved wood panels and etched mirrors. The food was simple too, mostly grilled and broiled fish and meat and chicken pot pie, the specialty of the house. The priciest item on the menu, the shell steak, was $9.95. Broiled chicken with potato and a vegetable went for $6.75. The restaurant didn't take reservations, so the bar up front was always elbow to elbow, with jostling standbys four deep.

Reggie usually had the swordfish, occasionally a steak, with a glass of wine or two, or maybe a beer. He often wore Gloria Vanderbilt jeans, a Polo shirt and loafers, and he always sat at table no. 40, which was in a small alcove in the far right-hand corner of the dining room. There he was protected from the great unwashed, but he could keep an eye on the scene. "Reggie liked to be seen, noticed, and not bothered—unless you were young and pretty," says McMullen. (A few years later, when Reggie made a guest appearance on *The Love Boat*, the show's writers had some fun with this idea of the semireluctant celebrity. Reggie goes on the cruise incognito so he won't be pestered. Once he realizes that no one is recognizing him, however, he starts dropping subtle hints, then not so subtle hints. By the end of the cruise he's doing jumping jacks on the Lido deck in a Yankees' cap and sweats.)

Rudy Giuliani (then a young prosecutor), Donald Trump, and Cheryl Tiegs all were fixtures at McMullen's, as was Steinbrenner, but Reggie was the only ballplayer who ate there. "I used to get mostly professional tennis players—Rod Laver, Bjorn Borg, Chris Evert, John McEnroe, Vitas Gerulaitis," recalls McMullen. "It really was more of a hangout for tennis players. Baseball players tend not to be very sophisticated."

On any given night, you could set your watch by the evolution of the scene at McMullen's. At 6 p.m. the restaurant was filled to capacity with blue-haired, old-money Upper East Siders. With each successive seating, the crowd grew younger and more stylish. Out with navy blazers and dull penny loafers, in with backless dresses and eight-millimeter pearls. McMullen, suave and handsome with a thick mane of prematurely white hair, moved among each age-group flawlessly. By 1 a.m. twenty black limousines would be lined up out front on Third Avenue, waiting to transport revelers seamlessly to their next nocturnal playpen, Studio 54.

"We went to Studio 54 like it was part of the evening," says Destino. "It was so hot then that there would always be a throng on the sidewalk begging, trying to get in, doing anything that they possibly could. But Reggie would walk through that crowd like Moses through the river. The sea would part."

Reggie Jackson was living two different lives. Away from the ballpark, he was discovering New York, superstar-style, doing late-night laps around Central Park with a date, top down, Donna Summer or the O'Jays blasting.

At the same time, Reggie was starting to dread the game he loved. He was waking up in the middle of the night and wandering out to his balcony twenty stories above Fifth Avenue, where he'd stare out at the New York City skyline and wonder how he was going to make it through the summer. (At least this was the portrait he painted for a writer from *Esquire* a few months later.) "He was confused," Destino recalls. "He couldn't understand why his manager acted the way he did. He couldn't understand why the other players acted the way they did. What upset him was his failure to understand why. 'Why are they doing this to me?' "

24.

"NOW is the summer of our discotheques," wrote night-crawling journalist Anthony Haden-Guest in *New York* magazine in June 1977. "And every night is party night."

It would have been hard to argue with him. Studio 54, the discotheque that defined an entire era of nightlife, had opened two months earlier, and Paramount Pictures had just begun filming *Saturday Night Fever*. By the end of the summer disco would be America's second-largest-grossing entertainment business, behind only professional sports.

Disco even had its own top forty charts. In stark contrast with the protest music of the sixties, most disco songs were about dancing and disporting. This was no coincidence, nor was the timing of the explosion of New York's dance scene. "People have always lost themselves in dancing when the economy's been bad," Bob Casey, the president of the National Association of Discotheque Disk Jockeys, told a *Daily News* reporter in the summer of 1975, as the city was sliding toward bankruptcy. "The discos are now doing exactly the same thing that the big dance halls with the crystal chandeliers did during the Depression. Everyone's out to spend their unemployment check, their welfare: to lose themselves."

Like any fad that seems to erupt into the national consciousness, this one had been percolating below ground for years: in gay hot spots along the abandoned West Side waterfront, in the vacant sweatshops south of Houston Street, in the dingy recreation rooms of Bronx and Brooklyn housing projects, in the empty ballrooms of aging midtown hotels.

If New York's disco scene had a party zero, it was David Mancuso's Love Saves the Day bash on Valentine's Day 1970. Mancuso had been throwing informal dance parties in his $175-a-month downtown loft for years, but this time he sent out invitations and collected $2 at the door. The sound system, his stereo, already in place, Mancuso hung a bobbing mirrored ball from the seventeen-foot ceiling, inflated several hundred multicolored balloons, and lined the edges of the space with church pews so revelers would have a place to rest. The image on the invites—Salvador Dalí's melting clocks—was easily deciphered: Once you tumbled down the rabbit hole and into Mancuso's wonderland, all sense of time would be suspended. And it was. At daybreak a shirtless Mancuso was still spinning vinyl, and about a hundred people of varying ethnicities, sexual preferences, and classes were still clamoring for more. A weekly tradition was soon born.

The parties started at a little before midnight on Saturday and ran until six or seven Sunday morning. Mancuso handled the music himself, using two turntables to ease dancers from one song to the next, lifting them up, and gently coaxing them back down as he moved seamlessly between soul, rock, R & B, Motown, and Afro-Latino. Sometimes he turned off all the lights and just let the music play. When he did, the dancers invariably screamed. "Dancing at the Loft was like riding a wave of music, being carried along as one song after another built relentlessly to a brilliant crest and broke, bringing almost involuntary shouts of approval from the crowd then smoothed out, softened, and slowly began welling up to another peak," was how disco journalist Vince Aletti described the experience in *The Village Voice*.

Ignited by this small spark, an underground dance culture started to spread to other unmarked lofts and hotel ballrooms. "The whole scene was a response to the sixties," says Michael Gomes, an early disco devotee who moved to New York from Toronto in 1973. "Instead of changing the world, we wanted to create our own little world." In the mass of bodies, sexual boundaries became porous: "It wasn't gay or straight. It was just this blur where you were caught up in the music."

The ethos of this emerging subculture was continuous dancing. In its name, borders of neighborhood, class, and ethnicity were crossed. "From the Bronx, you could get on a train at certain parts of the night—two or three in the morning—and it was like rush hour," recalls Mark Riley, a Bronx resident and disco fanatic.

The Bronx's own fledgling dance culture, one that eventually blossomed into hip-hop, was simultaneously gestating. It was less formal than the new wave of discotheques; a DJ might set up his table in a playground, run extension cords into the nearest lamppost, and start playing. The Bronx DJs had their own style, pioneered by the Jamaican-born Kool Herc in the rec room of the housing project his family lived in, which featured quick, choppy cuts and talking over the music—future trademarks of rap that would not have gone over well in the Manhattan dance clubs. But there was stylistic overlap as well. "All of the DJs were blending songs together," says John Benitez, who started DJing at block parties and sweet sixteens in his South Bronx neighborhood in the early seventies before breaking into the Manhattan club scene.

As dance clubs multiplied, DJs turned into minor celebrities. They didn't just play music; they *made* music. Record companies soon discovered their ability to sell records as well. Not only were they deluging DJs with promotional singles and dispatching scouts to dance clubs, but they also began producing their own extended play disco mixes exclusively for the discotheques. None of the hard-core dance clubs sold alcohol, but there were always plenty of drugs, chiefly acid, amyl nitrate, pot, mescalin, coke, Quaaludes (also known as disco biscuits), and speed.

With their flashing lights and pansexual crowds, the new clubs were a far cry from the old dance halls where the first- and second-generation immigrant parents of outer borough teenagers and twenty-somethings had done the fox-trot, which caused some confusion. "What my old man doesn't understand is that you don't have to be a fag to be into this scene," Tony Pagano, a young man from Staten Island, told the writer Ed McCormack for the 1976 book *Dancing Madness.* Between the music's ecstatic peaks and the undulating tangle of bodies on the dance floor, it was impossible not to see a connection between sex and disco. (As *Esquire*'s Albert Goldman put it in 1978, "All disco is implicitly orgy.")

Manhattan socialites were dancing too. That was the crowd that most interested steak house impresario Steve Rubell—before getting into discos, he owned a chain of upscale Sizzlers called the Steak Loft—and his business partner, Ian Schrager. The question they faced in 1976 was how to get them to Douglaston, Queens, the site of their disco, the Enchanted Garden, a place where, on any given night, the seven blow dryers in the women's room outnumbered the VIPs on the dance floor. New York's disco diva Carmen d'Alessio provided the answer.

Since coming to New York in 1965, the Peruvian-born d'Alessio had worked as a translator for the United Nations and logged a stint in public relations for Yves Saint Laurent, but in more recent years she had discovered her true calling, party planning. When Rubell and Schrager first spotted her in the winter of '76, she was wearing a bikini and dancing on the shoulders of a tall black male model at a Brazilian Carnival theme party she'd organized. Rubell and Schrager persuaded d'Alessio to come work for them. For her first party at the Enchanted Garden, d'Alessio chose an Arabian Nights theme, complete with elephants, llamas, and camels.

In early '77, d'Alessio was asked to promote another disco. This one had not yet opened. It was to be housed in Ed Sullivan's old theater on Fifty-fourth Street and Eighth Avenue. Much of the funding was to come from art dealer Frank Lloyd—that is, until a court found Lloyd guilty of defrauding the estate of the late Mark Rothko. Lloyd absconded to the Bahamas, and d'Alessio turned to the owners of the Enchanted Garden for financing. Before long Rubell and Schrager had pushed out the putative front man and were planning an April 1977 debut for their new disco, Studio 54.

In addition to any celebrity whose address she could beg, borrow, or steal, d'Alessio sent invitations to everyone on the mailing list of the Ford Modeling Agency, Andy Warhol's Factory, and the Islanders, a group of several thousand gay men who summered on Fire Island. Come opening night, the place was mobbed. "My mother had to be carried in over the crowd," d'Alessio recalls.

Studio 54 took the escapist ethic of the disco scene to its absurd extreme. An outsize prop of the Man on the Moon shoveling a coke spoon under his nose, shirtless busboys in white satin gym shorts and sequined jockstraps, busty women hanging upside down from trapezes, a fifty-four-hundred-square-foot dance floor crowded with undulators, balconies crowded with fornicators—this wasn't about avoiding reality as much as it was about obliterating it. Yet at the same time, Studio's Rome-in-the-twilight-of-the-empire feel seemed very much in keeping with this moment in the life of New York. At a birthday party for Bianca Jagger not long after its debut, the rock star's wife was led around the dance floor on a white horse by a man and woman with circus costumes painted on their naked bodies, all to the strains of the Rolling Stones' "Sympathy for the Devil." If this wasn't a sign of the coming apocalypse, what was? "I don't know if I was in heaven or hell," Lillian Carter, mother of President Jimmy, reflected on her first visit there. "But it was wonderful."

The disco purists were not so sure, about either Studio 54 or the rest of the gaudy dance clubs that sprouted up around New York during the summer of New York's discotheques. With the rise of these new clubs, New York's disco DJs were playing to bigger crowds than ever before, yet paradoxically, their power was slipping. Radio stations were now catching on to disco, so the record companies no longer needed to cultivate club DJs. At the same time, the increased competition from radio disc jockeys made it harder for club DJs to "break" records, especially because many of the new discotheque owners expected their DJs to play songs that were already hits. And to play them repeatedly over the course of a single night.

There was also the matter of elitism. Gay blacks had been regulars on the private dance party circuit, but they were almost wholly excluded from Studio 54. Of course the door policy at Studio left almost everyone on the wrong side of the velvet cord. Not that being shut out wasn't worth something. "[T]he borough hopefuls knew that in all likelihood they wouldn't be admitted, but the experience still enabled them to enter into the celebrity script, albeit in a subjugated role," wrote Tim Lawrence in his definitive book about the 1970s New York dance culture, *Love Saves the Day*.

To hard-core dancers, the disco scene's evolution from sweat-soaked lofts to celebrity-studded spectacles—in retrospect, an irresistible metaphor for the city's own journey from the gritty seventies to the glossy eighties—was tantamount to its demise. Among other things, all the new clubs served booze, which made the dancing sloppy. Michael Gomes, who was now publishing a newsletter for DJs called *Mixmaster*, referred derisively to the drunk and stoned dancers at Studio 54 as "discodroids."

But disco's real enemy came not from within but from without. The official declaration of war can be found in the lead editorial in the premiere issue of *Punk* magazine in January 1976. Titled "Death to Discoshit!," it began: "Kill yourself. Jump off a fuckin' cliff. Drive nails into your head . . . OD . . . Anything. Just don't listen to discoshit."

If disco music was euphoric, hypnotic, punk rock was assaultive, relentless; if discos like Studio 54 provided an escape from the ugliness of New York, its punk analog, a urine-stained dive on the Bowery called CBGB, embraced and indulged it.

Punk was a New York creation, though in 1977 it was easily mistaken for an English one. Not only were the Sex Pistols in the process of overshadowing New York's punk bands, but in late May a new display appeared in the windows of Macy's at Herald Square. Scattered among a half dozen motorcycles were eight female mannequins in cutoff denim shorts, spiky hair, and sixteen-dollar T-shirts adorned with cigarette burn holes, safety pins, and such slogans as "Boredom," "Burnt," and "Punk Rock Lives." To help sell this new line of clothing was an accompanying ad blitz for the "fashion trend that's making heads turn on London streets." (For those who were looking for something a little more upscale, the British designer Zandra Rhodes's collection of ripped gowns was available, starting at a thousand dollars.) The *New York Rocker*, a fanzine that championed the city's emerging downtown rock scene, reacted with predictable outrage in its July–August 1977 issue, accusing the English punks of cashing in on "the fruits of New York's labor."

In 1977, rock writers were just getting around to tracing the lineage of New York's punk scene, which began, by common assent, in the late sixties with the Velvet Underground's operatic odes to the city's junkies and drag queens. A few years after the Velvet Underground came the New York Dolls, a band of outer-borough boys with a devoted following of arty bohemians and protopunks. This was the era of Andy Warhol–inspired glam rock, and with their platform heels, dark red lipstick, and satin hot pants, the Dolls looked normal enough, though there was something tartier, trashier about their aesthetic—gutter transvestite, as it was known. Onstage they strutted with a theatricality that matched their costumes; one *Village Voice* writer described their lead singer, Staten Island's David Johansen, as a cross between Mick Jagger and Marlene Dietrich. If you closed your eyes, though, you heard songs about quotidian New York life set to a straightforward garage band sound. The city had no rock 'n' roll clubs at the time—it had been years since New York had anything approaching a rock scene—so the Dolls were reduced to playing at the Mercer Arts Center, a group of performance spaces carved out of an old Greenwich Village hotel.

Attempts were made to take the Dolls national. They produced two unsuccessful records and even did some touring but broke up in 1974 in the middle of a two-week run in Florida, largely because their Queens-bred guitarist Johnny Thunders (né Genzale) needed an excuse to get back to his heroin connection in the city.

By then the hotel that housed the Mercer Arts Center had collapsed, and Television, a rock band fronted by two teenagers who'd run away to New York to become poets, had talked their way into a Lower East Side biker bar whose name, CBGB, stood for country, bluegrass, and blues. Other protopunk acts including Blondie, Patti Smith, and the Ramones, soon followed. At a time when rock 'n' roll connoted suburban stadiums, a rock scene was born on, of all places, the Bowery. "Broken youth stumbling into the home of broken age," wrote Frank Rose, noting the irony in *The Village Voice* in the summer of '76.

One by one, New York's new bands signed record contracts. The Ramones, of Forest Hills, Queens, released their first album in the spring of 1976. "Their music swept the Bowery," read the accompanying ads in music magazines. "Now it's gonna sweep the nation." It never quite did; the record peaked at 111 on the *Billboard* charts. The Talking Heads, another one of the most popular bands at CBGB, wasn't doing much better. Their 1977 album, *Talking Heads '77*, barely broke 100. Touring the country that summer in the wake of its release, the band found itself playing mostly at pizza parlors.

But even if these bands weren't catching on in the heartland, they were at least taking their rightful place on the sound track for 1970s New York, ensuring that punk rock would forever evoke the dirty downtown streets where it had been born.

25.

WITH Bella Abzug and Mario Cuomo now in the race, David Garth adjusted the odds for his candidate, Ed Koch, from twenty to one to forty to one.

As befits a master image shaper, Garth, a small man with a round face and stubby fingers that were, more often than not, pinching a slender brown cigar, had carefully honed his own as a brash, brilliant, tough-talking, grudge-harboring control freak. The son of committed Jewish Long Island liberals, Garth had been bedridden with a severe case of rheumatic fever for much of his childhood in the late 1930s. Too sick to read, he listened to the radio broadcasts of Edward R. Murrow and H. V. Kaltenborn in the run-up to the war, igniting a lifelong love affair with the theater of American politics. Garth was always more than happy to help reporters connect the dots back to his youth. As a political consultant he was driven by the same fierce determination that had enabled him to defy one doctor's prognosis that he wouldn't live to age fifteen. When reality interfered with mythology, as it did with the apocryphal story of Garth's catching a plane in the driving snow to Milwaukee to scream, "Fuck you," at a campaign aide who had pulled his ads off the air in a presidential primary race, Garth would say it wasn't true and then invite the reporter to use it anyway.

In the early 1960s, when political consultancy was still in its infancy, Garth discovered the dark art of television. From the start he was shrewd enough to see that selling a political candidate was not the same thing as selling deodorant, and so he eschewed slickness for vérité, swelling music for silence, paid actors for real New Yorkers. In '65, he led the handsome John Lindsay out of the studio and into the streets, where the TV crews filmed him walking among the people, shirt open, hair uncombed. Four years later, when much of New York couldn't wait to kick its dilettantish mayor back uptown, Garth dreamed up the so-called Lindsay-eats-shit spot, featuring the incumbent, still-dashing but just world-weary enough to suggest an accumulation of hard-earned wisdom, earnestly confessing his mayoral sins to the camera.

Lindsay was easy. Garth simply had to nudge his actor into the most flattering light. With Koch he would have to create the character from whole cloth. Reflecting on the '77 campaign years later, Garth opted for a different metaphor: "Koch . . . was never the flashy guy who went out for the long pass. He was the Bronko Nagurski of politics, three yards and a cloud of dust."

But even a three-yard gain was going to be difficult unless certain obstacles were removed. Not only was Koch funny-looking and not especially charming, but he lived in Greenwich Village, had no girlfriend, and had never been married. Aside from ordering him to drop twenty pounds and to trade in his three-button Brooks Brothers suits for more stylish two-button ones, Garth couldn't do much about Koch's appearance, but he could at least head off the inevitable rumors of homosexuality.

Enter Bess Myerson, a leggy brunette from the Shalom Aleichem Cooperative Houses in the Bronx, a former Miss America—the first Jewish Miss America—and chairman of the Koch campaign. Twice divorced and still gorgeous at fifty-three, Myerson cut a lovely figure alongside the dowdy candidate. In addition to making sure that Koch's record of support for gay rights wasn't mentioned in any campaign literature, Garth set about cultivating the impression that he and Myerson might be more than just colleagues. "All the mommas would say, 'You make such a nice couple,' " Garth recalls, "and Ed would look at the ground and paw it quietly."

Garth's plan was to keep the focus on the issues, to somehow make a virtue of his candidate's lack of charm. Koch was unknown, but at least he wasn't disliked. It was no secret that New York was on the ropes. For the purposes of political narrative anyway, it was easy to put the starry-eyed Lindsay and the special interest–beholden

Beame as the one-two punch that landed it there. The result was the made-for-TV tagline: "After eight years of charisma and four years of the clubhouse, why not try competence?"

"The city was shaken," says Garth. "You couldn't go back to the Lindsay days, and you didn't want to go back to the clubhouse. You had to take a new course."

26.

Manhattan Island, at its center, inspires utterly baseless optimism—even in me, even in drunks sleeping in doorways and in little old ladies whose houses are shopping bags.

KURT VONNEGUT, *HARPER'S MAGAZINE*, AUGUST 1975

IN the early summer of 1977, as the mayoral candidates started jockeying in earnest to present themselves as the answer to the city's problems, New Yorkers were already creatively exploiting the very neglect that the politicians were decrying. Just as the gay community had colonized the abandoned West Side piers and graffiti writers were transforming unguarded subway cars into art installations, painters, sculptors, and entrepreneurs were repurposing empty factories and sweatshops in the area below Houston Street.

Most of these buildings had gone up in the wake of the Civil War and once bustled with activity. Over the decades, though, as New York lost its claim to the manufacturing capital of America, their occupancy rate began to fall. The increasingly deserted neighborhood gradually took on a melancholy, boulevard of broken dreams feel. In the late fifties a city planning commission characterized the area as a commercial slum and concluded that it was destined to deteriorate further unless something drastic was done.

That's exactly what David Rockefeller proposed in the early sixties. Rockefeller, the head of the Downtown–Lower Manhattan Association, envisioned SoHo as a gateway to Wall Street, complete with office buildings, luxury apartment towers, even a sports stadium. The linchpin was an idea first mooted many years earlier, an expressway that would cut across the width of lower Manhattan, linking the Holland Tunnel with the Williamsburg and Manhattan bridges. This was a time when the phrase *urban renewal*, the popular euphemism for leveling old structures and starting anew, was on every city planner's lips, and landmark preservation remained the exclusive province of antiquarian societies. The expressway seemed destined to become a reality.

Opposition came from a smattering of artists who were living illegally in these commercial lofts, hanging blackout curtains on their windows to hide the signs of nonindustrial life inside. With the help of some strategic picketing at the opening of a Leonardo da Vinci show at the Metropolitan Museum of Art in 1963—MONA IS NOT THE ONLY ONE WHO NEEDS A LEASA, read one placard—the artists won the right to remain in their lofts temporarily, as the details of the new expressway were ironed out.

In the latter half of the sixties, more visual artists moved into SoHo. They included Chuck Close, who paid $150 a month for an unheated loft on Greene Street (the massive freight elevators enabled him to get his outsize canvases upstairs), and the minimalist Richard Serra, who used the scrap metal and fabric that littered the neighborhood's bleak streets in his sculptures.

The derelict lofts of SoHo were also becoming popular among avant-garde jazz musicians like alto saxophonist Ornette Coleman, a leading pioneer of so-called free jazz, a formless, often dissonant alternative to bebop and fusion—one critic compared the sound to that of "a barnyard riot"—that was just beginning to find a following in the late sixties. Coleman bought two floors of an abandoned industrial building on Prince Street. He moved in upstairs, filling the three-thousand-square-foot space with sheet music and saxophones, and turned the storefront below into an avant-garde performance space called Artists House. Others soon followed his lead, taking two floors in empty lofts, one for living and one for playing, and subsidizing the cost with free-jazz rent parties. "In the 60s," recalled Rashied Ali, a drummer who leased a place on Greene Street, "you could get a loft for nothing–just to watch the building for a cat who didn't want to brush the bums off his doorstep."

Meanwhile, a formidable antiexpressway lobby was materializing, led by author–cum–neighborhood superheroine Jane Jacobs and a loose-knit coalition of Greenwich Village activists that included an ambitious young politician named Ed Koch, all of whom considered the expressway a threat to an indigenous New York neighborhood. They had the backing of the *Times*'s powerful architecture critic, Ada Louise Huxtable, who called attention to the grandeur of SoHo's old cast-iron structures and urged city planners to expand their definition of historic buildings to include commercial structures. The growing cadre of grassroots preservationists found a sympathetic ear in Mayor Lindsay, and in 1969 the expressway plan was finally scotched.

By now galleries had started following artists into SoHo. The first was Paula Cooper, who in 1968 rented a ten-thousand-square-foot, three-hundred-dollar-a-month space on Prince Street, next door to the only bar in the neighborhood, Fanelli's, a smoke-soaked nineteenth-century saloon with etched glass doors and signed photographs of old boxers that catered to the last of the local day laborers. The next year Ivan Karp, who'd worked for Leo Castelli for more than a decade, left the diamond belt of Madison Avenue to open his own gallery on West Broadway in a space formerly occupied by a dollmaker. Soon after, Castelli himself opened a SoHo outpost in an old paper warehouse. When he first visited the building, Castelli was just looking for inexpensive storage space, but he soon realized that it could also be used as a showcase for edgier work, including film and performance art. What's more, the neighborhood's griminess gave it authenticity. Castelli, an Upper East Sider, didn't need to be told that rich collectors loved coming downtown to visit artists in their natural habitat.

With the threat of the expressway gone, the battle over the South Houston district turned to zoning. Artists wanted to be able to convert their lofts legally into residential apartments, and public opinion was now on their side. The willy-nilly destruction of New York's architectural gems over the course of the sixties had galvanized the preservationists, and the charmless brick towers that were now shooting up bore witness to the devastating effect of urban renewal on the cityscape. Urban planners had discovered a new phrase, *adaptive reuse.*

By the early seventies something else had changed too. A decade earlier, when artists first petitioned the city to allow them to remain in their lofts, they were an embattled group of brooding bohemians whose manic splatterings meant very little to anyone outside the cloistered art world. But pop art, with its upbeat and accessible imagery, had stoked the interest of a new generation of viewers. Art was now big, bold, American, and the expansive galleries of SoHo, in contrast with the boutiques of Madison Avenue with their miniature European paintings, felt as though they'd been built to accommodate it.

To a city already casting about for ways to shore up its eroding tax base, SoHo's artistic community was looking more and more like an economic boon. The artists slowly won over City Hall, businessmen, bankers, and New York's emerging power brokers, the real estate developers. In 1971 loft living was legalized for artists. Two years later the neighborhood was officially declared a landmark district, ensuring that it would forever remain out of harm's way.

During the middle to late seventies the trickle downtown became a steady stream. The residents of nearby Little Italy feared that wild artists would soon be running through the streets. The transition was in fact considerably more subtle. The smudged, weary-looking men in denim shirts propping up the old mahogany bar at Fanelli's were, increasingly, no longer day laborers but painters.

To neighborhood nostalgists, these were the glory days. In his book *SoHo: The Rise and Fall of an Artists' Colony*, Richard Kostelanetz compared the SoHo of the seventies with a sprawling college campus. To continue the metaphor, the student center was Food, a cooperative restaurant/performance space run by a handful of artists, including the sculptor Gordon Matta-Clark, who famously went on to saw a suburban New Jersey house in two. The college paper was the *SoHo Weekly News*, which launched in 1973. There were even fraternity pranks disguised as performance art; Kostelanetz remembers one artist commemorating May Day by painting the names of Lenin, Marx, and Trotsky over local street signs.

Not everyone was enamored with the new SoHo. Some thought its monolithic identity contradicted the melting pot ethos of the city. The sculptor Donald Judd, who had bought an entire cast-iron building on Spring Street for sixty-eight thousand dollars in 1968, hated being surrounded by so many artists. "I don't want to bump into everyone I know on the streets," he complained in 1974. "I want to live in the real world."

This quasi-socialist bohemia wasn't destined to last anyway. In 1974, *New York* magazine named SoHo "The Most Exciting Place to Live in the City." "[A]lthough the outsides may suggest that the insides look like Ratso Rizzo's place in *Midnight Cowboy*, don't be deceived by the externals," the magazine reported, "For behind SoHo's industrial detritus, behind its rusty fire escapes, behind the Mr.-Otis-regrets condition of its elevators, and at the top of its *Les Misérables* stairways hides a robust middle-class materialism."

By 1977 the law that stipulated that all loft dwellers be certified artists was being blatantly ignored. New Yorkers with no connection to the local artistic community save for a shared taste for arched windows, exposed brick, and lots of cheap square footage were moving to the neighborhood. At the same time, a number of SoHo's once-struggling artists were getting famous, and the dealers who bought and sold their work were getting rich. (Those who were getting neither rich nor famous grew bitter. One put epoxy in the keyholes of all the galleries. Another spray-painted "SoHo Sucks, Bring Back the Trucks" around the neighborhood.)

Avant-garde jazz—loft jazz, as it had become known—was also in full bloom now. The rent parties and stripped-down performance spaces of the early seventies had given way to clubs and concerts. The *SoHo Weekly News* had been covering the scene for years, but by the end of the summer even *Newsweek* had taken note: "One of the many places jazz has found a new home is a sleazy area in lower Manhattan, where the phenomenon called loft jazz flourishes."

In September 1977 a former New York City public school teacher named Giorgio DeLuca unveiled SoHo's first supermarket. (Andy Warhol was among those who signed the guest book on its opening day.) For years people had been calling SoHo the new Montparnasse. The twenty-six-hundred-square-foot Dean & DeLuca would be its *fromagerie*, *patisserie*, and *boulangerie* all rolled into one. In later years the proud pioneers who had settled—or resettled anyway—this urban frontier would point darkly to the day, identifying it as the tipping point, the moment when their beloved neighborhood made the irreversible transition from scruffy artists' colony to theme park for the taste-fetishizing upwardly mobile.

By 1977, there was plenty to complain about. The average rent for a residential loft was climbing fast. The metamorphosis of SoHo had no doubt hastened the departure of numerous blue-collar jobs, and it was certainly doing nothing for those most in need, the city's poor. Some critics were even starting to wonder if the neighborhood was good for art. Writing in 1978 in the now-defunct journal *New York Affairs*, Carter Ratcliff accused SoHo's opportunistic artists and trendy galleries, which by then numbered nearly one hundred, of trivializing the "modernist struggle."

Yet it was hard not to be encouraged by the revival of SoHo. It wasn't simply the creation of a new tax base, nor was it the reaffirmation of the value of New York's most precious resource, real estate. As they gradually filled with people swimming against the suburban tides, these buildings that had once stood as ghostly reminders of the disappearance of manufacturing from New York were now being transformed into monuments to the city's resilience, powerfully evoking the past even as they hinted at a postindustrial future.

PART TWO

27.

New York makes one think about the collapse of civilization, about Sodom and Gomorrah, the end of the world. The end wouldn't come as a surprise here. Many people already bank on it.

SAUL BELLOW, *MR. SAMMLER'S PLANET*

WILLIAM Jurith left for work in the early afternoon of Wednesday, July 13. He was supposed to have the day off, but when a colleague told him that he needed to take care of some personal business, Jurith, who was putting his son through law school, volunteered to pick up his colleague's four-to-midnight shift.

Jurith was a system operator for Consolidated Edison. He had no training as an engineer, though he had done a tour as a radar technician during World War II. After the war he settled in Brooklyn, married, and took an entry-level job at Con Ed. He and his wife raised their family in a green clapboard house on a tree-lined street in the working-class enclave of Cypress Hills, Brooklyn. Jurith had been with Con Ed for twenty-nine of his fifty-six years, climbing steadily through the ranks, from emergency foreman to district operator to power dispatcher. Two years earlier he got the big bump to system operator.

The system he presided over for eight hours a day, five days a week, was the most complicated one in the world. When the Edison Electric Illuminating Company opened for business in 1882, it had the capacity to generate enough power to light four hundred lamps within one square mile in lower Manhattan. Now the company served all five boroughs and most of Westchester County, a total of nine million people.

The city's stringent clean-air regulations made it prohibitively expensive to depend on local generators that were required to burn costly low-sulfur oil rather than cheaper alternatives like coal. So

Con Ed built plants outside the city and bought power from neighboring states rather than make it. Most of that power came from the north–from the New England utilities, from a variety of generators upstate, and from hydroelectric plants in Niagara Falls that produced power on the cheap via kinetic energy. To import this power into the city, Con Ed relied on an intricate network of highways, more than a hundred thousand miles of cable, enough to circle the globe four times.

The lines ran down through Westchester County in a densely packed, narrow corridor before diving underground and joining Con Ed's web of high-voltage underground arteries. The service wasn't always perfect. Power failures, or at least the fear of them, had been a rite of summer in New York since 1965. In the late sixties and early seventies, as Con Ed lost a number of transmission lines to age, localized brownouts were commonplace. In more recent years, however, the company had undertaken an ambitious cable replacement program. In 1975 the city was brownout-free for the first time since 1963. Nineteen-seventy-six made it two in a row.

The system's first major test of '77 was now on its way. A blanket of hot, muggy weather was descending on the city like a giant steam iron. The arrival of a heat wave imminent, Con Edison's chairman, Charles Luce, went on a Sunday morning talk show to discuss his company's preparedness. Luce, a tall, slender Wisconsin native who wore a built-up left shoe to compensate for a limp, guaranteed New York that there would be no outages.

Jurith was stationed in the control room of Con Edison's Energy Control Center, a bleak, windowless building at Sixty-fifth Street and West End Avenue. The control room, the nerve center of the company's sprawling power system, was on the top floor. The unofficial dress code was short-sleeve dress shirts and short, wide monochromatic ties. Many of the various operators, monitors, and power dispatchers wore their hair neatly parted on the side and guzzled coffee with nondairy creamer and sugar.

The system operator sat at the front of the room. His job was similar to that of an air traffic controller, only instead of conducting planes through an intricate grid of highways in the sky, he conducted electricity through an intricate grid of highways underground.

Covering the wall facing him was a huge mechanized map known as the mimic board. The entire Con Ed grid was represented here. Meters indicated how much energy each generator was producing and how much power was flowing through every feeder. If there was a disturbance somewhere along the system and a circuit breaker was tripped, the corresponding line on the mimic board flashed green, indicating the line was open and thus not conducting electricity. When the line reclosed and resumed conducting power—generally within seconds—the corresponding line on the mimic board returned to red. In other words, in the inverted language of electrical systems, green suggested trouble, while red meant everything was okay.

There was a color monitor and keyboard on the SO's desk that provided him with more detailed information, including schematic diagrams for each generator, transmission line, and substation. To the left of that was his voltage reduction panel, a series of dials that allowed him to lower the voltage emanating from any given power station by 3, 5, or 8 percent. He used this panel rarely. Even when he did, voltage reductions nearly always went undetected by Con Ed customers.

Finally, to the right of the monitor was another panel, one that system operators prayed they'd never have to use. (Just the thought of it caused the sweat stains under the armpits of their shirts to grow.) This was the manual load-shedding equipment, thirty-nine buttons protected by plastic caps, one for each zone in the Con Ed grid. When the SO activated this panel—and not one ever had—it would mean only one thing: Some customers were about to lose power.

Energy consumption traditionally spiked during the dog days of summer. Demand peaked in the middle of the afternoon, when air conditioners were rumbling all over the city. On a hot summer day New York might burn through four times as much power as it would on an average spring afternoon.

Unlike gas, electricity can't be stored; it has to be used as it is generated. So as a day got hotter, the system operator had to anticipate the growing demand for power and find the most efficient ways to meet it. That meant bringing up generation with the help of gas turbines and special reserve generators known as peaking units, as well as contracting to buy additional power on the spot market.

On July 13 demand peaked at 7,264 megawatts at 4 p.m., just as Jurith was settling into his chair for the night ahead. The city's power needs would lessen from here. He'd spend most of his shift studying his monitor and easing off and shutting down generators, keeping pace with the demand curve as it slid south. The forecast for the evening was for continued heat and humidity, but no thunderstorms. Jurith figured he was home free.

By 7 p.m. all his supervisors, including the chief system operator, had called it a day. An hour later Jurith sent home most of the so-called turbine boys who manned Con Ed's four gas-powered turbine sites in the city. These turbines were primarily for peak-hour usage; they were expensive to operate and produced a relatively small amount of power.

At 8:37 p.m., Jurith looked up at the mimic board and saw green. Two circuit breakers had tripped in Westchester County, and a pair of high-voltage transmission lines had opened. There must have been a disturbance somewhere. Jurith stared at the board for a second or two, waiting for the lines to return to red, the sign that the short had passed and the cables had reclosed. They were still green. He blinked. A third indicator lamp in the same region had joined them.

The open lines led in and out of Buchanan South, a substation in a small town on the Hudson. Substations housed massive transformers that were required to convert the high-voltage electricity produced by generators into the low-voltage electricity used in offices and homes. In Buchanan South's case, that generator was Indian Point 3, Con Ed's behemoth nuclear reactor thirty-five miles north of midtown Manhattan. Built in the early sixties on the site of a former amusement park, Indian Point had been one of the world's first commercial nuclear reactors.

A horn blared. Jurith glanced at the mimic board. A needle was falling like the pressure gauge on a deflating tire—nine hundred megawatts, eight hundred megawatts, seven hundred megawatts—all the way to zero. It was Indian Point, his "nukie."

Either the mimic board was malfunctioning, or something was very, very wrong. Jurith punched a button on his communication console and was patched right through to Westchester's district operator. "Yeah, Bill," Westchester confirmed, "it looks like we lost the entire south bus [Buchanan], including Unit 3 [Indian Point] . . . The station operator tells me he saw lightning."

Behind Jurith, a teleprinter was spitting out a status report: W97 OOS. W98 OOS. Y88 OOS. INDIAN POINT 3 OOS. Three high-voltage transmission lines and Con Ed's most heavily loaded generator were all OOS—out of service.

It later emerged that the culprit was in fact a bolt of lightning at Buchanan South. Substations were designed to ground lightning strokes, but this one had slipped through. A short occurred, triggering the first two sets of circuit breakers.

The breakers were supposed to open the affected lines and isolate the problem until the fault dissipated. The fault did dissipate in less than a second, but the circuit breakers never reclosed to allow the flow of power to resume. In one case the problem was a loose locking nut; in the other, a critical circuit that had been removed for an upgrade had not yet been replaced. The third line tripped out when a protective timing device misread the disturbance, failing to recognize that the first two lines had already isolated the flash of lightning. Without an outlet for its power, Indian Point 3 had automatically gone into shutdown.

Electrical systems are designed so that if one generator goes down, another will pick up the slack. Sure enough, emergency power promptly started coursing down from New England. The trouble was, with three transmission lines out of service, the remaining lines were going to be shouldering a much bigger energy burden than they were built to handle.

At 8:40 p.m. a high-pitched alarm sounded on Jurith's desktop monitor. A key feeder connecting the Con Ed system to New England was exceeding its limit by a hundred megawatts. If the line wasn't deloaded right away, it was going to fry.

28.

ONE hundred and sixty miles north, in Guilderland, New York, home of the New York Power Pool, William Kennedy, a burly Irishman, was watching the scene unfold on his own mimic board, a twenty-foot-high, eighty-foot-wide map of New York State's entire power grid. Kennedy was the senior dispatcher for the power pool, the state's energy clearinghouse, an oversight body created for exactly such moments.

Kennedy called the Con Ed control room to make sure that they were "getting their dogs moving," revving up all its reserve generators. Every day Con Ed was required to report its emergency generating capacity to the power pool, so Kennedy knew exactly how

LEFT Laid-off cops protest at a demonstration on the Brooklyn Bridge in July 1975.

(NEAL BOENZI/THE NEW YORK TIMES)

RIGHT Mayor Beame uses a visual aid as he explains the state of the city's finances in early 1977.

(NEAL BOENZI/THE NEW YORK TIMES)

BELOW Boats crowd into the New York Harbor for the tall ships parade on July 4, 1976.

(NEAL BOENZI/THE NEW YORK TIMES)

ABOVE LEFT Casey Stengel gives Billy Martin a big hug in September 1952 after Martin's RBI-single in the 11th inning helped clinch the pennant for the Yankees. (BETTMANN/CORBIS)

ABOVE RIGHT Reggie Jackson after being selected second in the 1966 amateur draft. The young Reggie wouldn't say how much he expected to sign for, though he did say, "It's way up there." (ASSOCIATED PRESS)

RIGHT Reggie modeling his custom-made $7,000 fur coat the day after signing with the Yankees in December 1976. (ASSOCIATED PRESS)

LEFT Clay Felker (right) and Rupert Murdoch together in the Hamptons before their relationship soured. (JANIE EISENBERG)

ABOVE **Reggie takes a big cut on opening day in April 1977.** (ROBERT WALKER/THE NEW YORK TIMES)

LEFT **New York sided with Thurman Munson after Reggie criticized his leadership in an article in *Sport* magazine.** (JAMES HAMILTON)

BELOW **During the summer of 1977, Jimmy Breslin became New York's most famous newspaper columnist since Walter Winchell.** (JANIE EISENBERG)

ABOVE Bella Abzug peering over her half-rimmed glasses during the summer of 1977. (NEAL BOENZI/THE NEW YORK TIMES)

RIGHT Bella from behind. (JANIE EISENBERG)

RIGHT The crumbling Pier 52 was a popular spot for gay sunbathers during the summer of 1977. (LEONARD FINK, COURTESY OF THE LESBIAN, GAY, BI & TRANSGENDER COMMUNITY CENTER NATIONAL HISTORY ARCHIVE)

BELOW Bess Myerson chatting with Ed Koch in 1975. Two years later, the former Miss America would become a key figure in the congressman's mayoral campaign. (JACK MANNING/THE NEW YORK TIMES)

A glimpse inside a New York City subway car, circa 1977. (JAMES HAMILTON)

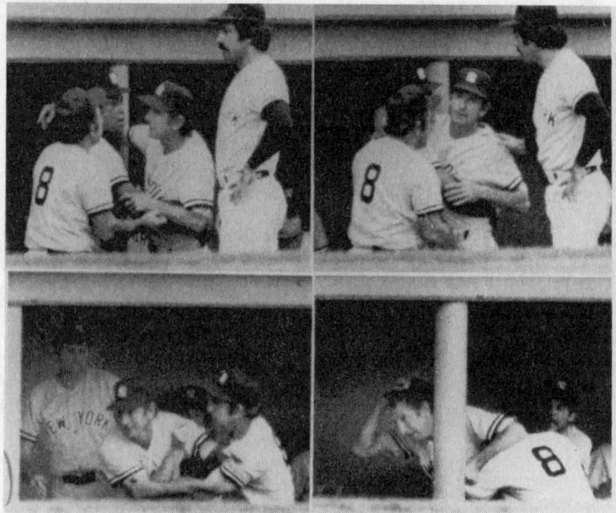

ABOVE Billy Martin being restrained from Reggie Jackson in the dugout at Fenway Park. (ASSOCIATED PRESS)

RIGHT Martin and Reggie walking into Tiger Stadium two days after their near-brawl at Fenway, as rumors swirl that the Yankees' manager will be fired. (THE DETROIT NEWS)

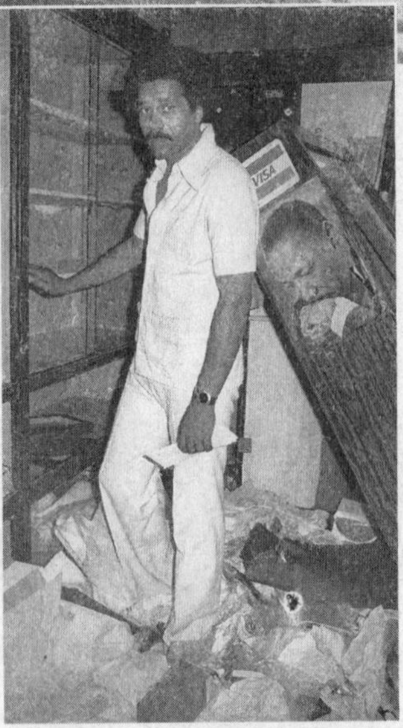

TOP **Looting on Broadway in Bushwick during the 1977 blackout.** (TYRONE DUKES/THE NEW YORK TIMES)

ABOVE LEFT **A cop swats a looter in Bushwick.** (BETTMANN/CORBIS)

ABOVE RIGHT **A Bushwick storeowner returns to his shop to find that everything has been taken.** (JAMES HAMILTON)

RIGHT **Two boys inside a cleaned-out store in Bushwick.** (JAMES HAMILTON)

RIGHT A house burns in Bushwick during the summer of 1977. (STEVEN SCHER)

BELOW David Berkowitz being led into a police precinct for booking. (FRED CONRAD/THE NEW YORK TIMES)

ABOVE LEFT Mayor Beame being kissed by his wife, Mary, as he concedes the 1977 Democratic primary. (JAMES HAMILTON)

ABOVE RIGHT Mario Cuomo campaigning at a beach club in Brooklyn during the summer of 1977. (JANIE EISENBERG)

LEFT The two run-off candidates at a debate during the 1977 mayoral campaign. (JANIE EISENBERG)

RIGHT Reggie turns and tips his hat to the crowd after his second home run in game six of the 1977 World Series. (LARRY MORRIS/THE NEW YORK TIMES)

BELOW Reggie trying to get off the field and into the dugout after the last out of game six. (LARRY MORRIS/THE NEW YORK TIMES)

much the utility had or at least how much it claimed to have. There was plenty of megawattage to offset the loss of Indian Point 3. It just might take a little while to get the backup generators up and running.

In the interim, Kennedy figured he'd help Jurith get his overtaxed lines deloaded. He told New England's power coordinator what was happening and instructed him to ease off a little. Then he asked Long Island's system operator if he could increase generation to pick up some of the slack. Long Island's capacity was limited, but the system operator offered to do what he could. "You guys in trouble, or what?" he asked.

"Yeah," Kennedy answered. "It's Indian Point 3."

At 8:45 p.m. Kennedy called the Con Ed control room again to confirm that the reserve generators were being fired up. He was told that they were.

Con Ed had two main sources of backup power in the city, steam units and gas turbines. The steam units worked like giant boilers. A furnace burned oil, which heated water in a boiler to produce steam. The steam pushed against blades to drive a generator.

The gas turbines (GTs) were faster and more efficient. Con Ed had brought them online over the course of the past decade, in response to criticism after the 1965 power failure that it didn't have enough electricity available within the confines of the city itself. GTs operate much like jet engines: They combine compressed air with fuel and then ignite the mixture of the two. The resulting gases push against the turbine blades to produce energy. Unlike steam units, the GTs, which were stationed in four sites around the city, could be operated by remote control.

At 8:55, Con Ed was still generating just 30 percent of the electricity that it had assured the power pool it could produce. The load on the line to New England was coming down, but not quickly enough. Kennedy couldn't figure out what was taking so long.

Jurith had a pretty good idea. Several of Con Ed's steam units were either down for repairs or operating at less than full strength. But the real problem was the gas turbines. The remote controls were out of service, so the turbines had to be manually jump-started by the turbine boys, most of whom he'd already dismissed for the night. Jurith tried to call his boss, Con Ed's chief system operator, Charles Durkin, at home in Westchester County, but couldn't get through. He instructed his deputy to keep trying.

Two minutes later, at 8:56, two more lines on the mimic board flashed green. Both were connected to a different tower along the same northern corridor. Lightning had struck again. This time one line grounded the electrical charge and reclosed without incident. The other didn't.

The line to New England picked up the additional load, and within a half second it had burned out. Con Ed was now left with a single feeder from the north, and it was way above its recommended load. The heat from the electrical currents was causing the line to expand and sag. If it dipped much lower, the cable would scrape the underbrush below. The contact would trip the circuit breakers, the circuit breakers would open the line, and the line would be rendered useless.

Con Ed had only three lines into the city, and it wasn't generating enough in-city power to meet demand. It couldn't get enough power from Long Island to make much of a difference, and the tie line connecting it to New Jersey was already so overloaded that the utility was threatening to open the line to protect its system. There was plenty of power available to the north—Ontario had three hundred megawatts ready to fly—but only one line to import it in on, Feeder 80.

Studying the big board, Kennedy could see no alternative. Con Ed was going to have to unplug some customers. He called Jurith.

"Bill, you better shed some load until you get down below this thing because I can't pick up anything except from the north, see?" It was a command that Kennedy had never issued. In seven-plus years in the power pool control room, he'd heard it only once before, back in '70 or '71.

"I'm trying, I'm trying," Jurith answered.

"Okay, fine," said Kennedy.

Kennedy bought Jurith a little more time with New Jersey by calling the dispatcher there and telling him that Con Ed was facing a "major emergency."

A few minutes later Con Ed's in-city generators still weren't producing enough power, the sole tie to the north was carrying an even bigger load, and Jurith still hadn't unplugged anybody.

At 8:59 Kennedy called him again. This time he was a little more insistent: "Bill, I hate to bother you, but you better shed about 400 megawatts of load or you're going to lose everything down there."

"I'm trying to," Jurith answered.

"You're trying to?" Kennedy asked incredulously. "All you have to do is hit the button to shed it and then we'll worry about it afterwards—but you got to do something . . ."

"Yeah, right," Jurith answered. "Yeah, fine."

Jurith still refused to activate the load-shedding panel. He may have resented the fact that Kennedy, who wasn't really his boss, was telling him what to do. He may have been clinging desperately to the hope that those three last feeders could support the system long enough for another solution to emerge. Probably he just couldn't bring himself to pull the trigger. Jurith's job was to keep people's lights on, not to shut them off. "We got the impression that he was disintegrating," recalls Carolyn Brancato, who directed the city's investigation into the events of that night. "He was in breakdown mode."

A couple of minutes later Jurith called Kennedy. He could see for himself, but he asked anyway: "Look any better?"

"No," Kennedy answered.

The high-pitched alarm on Jurith's desktop monitor had been whining for half an hour now. All three remaining feeders were exceeding their limits. The northern line, Feeder 80, was the most overtaxed. It was carrying fifteen hundred megawatts, 50 percent more than its short-term rating for extreme emergencies. Jurith knew he needed immediate relief. Never mind that losing Feeder 80 would send him right down the pipe—that those last two feeders would surely burn up from the additional load—he was going to open the line.

Jurith called the Westchester emergency supervisor. "I can't hold it," he said. "You're gonna have to cut out 80 for me."

"Feeder 80?" the Westchester supervisor asked in disbelief. "You want that cut?"

Kennedy intervened just in time. "If you cut feeder 80 then you're really going to be in trouble," he told Jurith. Once again he urged Con Ed's SO to shed load.

At 9:08, Jurith's boss, Charles Durkin, called in. The power at his house in Yorktown Heights had already been knocked out, but he was studying a map of the Con Ed power grid, which he kept with him at all times, by kerosene lamp. "You got some problems, huh?" Durkin asked. It was a gross understatement.

Jurith didn't notify Durkin that the power pool had been urging him to shed load for more than ten minutes. Instead, he told Durkin about his plans for Feeder 80. "Where's the power going to go if you cut it out?" Durkin replied. "You can't cut it out."

While Jurith was on the phone with Durkin, Kennedy called again on the green phone, a special dedicated hotline for emergency use only. Jurith's deputy, John Cockerham, answered.

"Tell Bill to go into voltage reduction immediately down there," Kennedy said. Jurith wasn't willing to shed load, so Kennedy hoped he might be less spooked by the idea of a voltage reduction. (Kennedy later testified that he was "getting desperate.")

At 9:13, Jurith finally moved his voltage reduction dials to 5 percent. The system load dipped by scarcely more than a hundred megawatts. Five minutes later he upgraded to an 8 percent reduction in voltage.

At 9:19, Feeder 80 drooped into a tree. Circuit breakers were tripped, and the line opened. Con Ed had lost its only connection to the north. The entire Westchester corridor was gone.

The two remaining lines—one to New Jersey, the other to Long Island—were hanging on somehow, but they couldn't last much longer. Jurith was still on the phone with Durkin, so Kennedy spoke to Jurith's deputy: "You got to shed load immediately or you're going to go right down the pipe!"

"All right, pal," Cockerham answered.

Durkin, who was without the benefit of a monitor, a mimic board, or overhead lights for that matter, was slowly coming around to the same conclusion. At 9:23 he told Jurith to do what Kennedy had been telling him for close to thirty minutes now: Start dropping load.

Con Ed's tie to Long Island, a feeder between Queens and Nassau County, was overtaxed and about to burn out. Kennedy told the Long Island Lighting Company's system operator to cut loose: "Go ahead, open it up, save your own system." Con Ed was now down to one feeder, a transmission line from Staten Island to Linden, New Jersey.

Kennedy made his final call to the Con Ed control room at 9:27. Cockerham picked up. "I'm going to tell you one more time . . ." Kennedy began.

By now, Jurith had finally activated the load-shedding panel. Cockerham could see him standing over it turning dials and pressing buttons. "He's doing it as fast as he can, pal," Cockerham answered.

Kennedy checked the load on the Linden tie, Con Ed's last lifeline to the outside world. It was still spiking. "All you got to do is punch a button to get rid of it," he pleaded.

"That's what he is doing right now," said Cockerham.

No more than thirty megawatts were shed. Something had obviously gone wrong. In all likelihood, Jurith failed to operate the load-dumping equipment properly. One investigation found that he turned a master switch the wrong way. Another suggested that he didn't lift the protective cover from the console before trying to depress the buttons.

At 9:27 the Linden tie opened. A few minutes later Long Island's system operator asked Kennedy for an update on Con Ed. "It looks like he is all by himself right now," Kennedy replied.

The Con Ed system was now officially islanded, cut off from all external power sources. It shifted much of its load to its biggest in-city generator, Big Allis, a thousand-megawatt steam unit in Queens. Like a circular saw fighting a losing battle with an oversize piece of wood, Big Allis's turbines ground to a halt. Seconds later the generator automatically shut itself down. The city's nine remaining generators buckled instantaneously under the increased load.

High in the sky over Queens, a cargo pilot watched the runaway vanish beneath him. He radioed the control tower: "Where's Kennedy Airport?" He was instructed to head for Philadelphia.

Ten thousand traffic lights blinked off. Subway trains froze between stations. Elevators, water pumps, air conditioners—everything sputtered to a halt. All five boroughs and most of Westchester County were suddenly without power. Save for the flashing red aircraft beacons atop the Citibank building and the World Trade Center and the flame in the torch of the Statue of Liberty, it was a total urban eclipse.

29.

New York City is simply too big. I have lived in it for too long to hate it, but I know it too well to love it. I am still a part of it, yet I feel removed, like a broken jockey who grooms horses. I earn my living caring for it, but I feel helpless because I know that I can't train it, or ride it, or make it win.

DENNIS SMITH, ***REPORT FROM ENGINE CO. 82*** (1972)

OFFICER Wilton Sekzer, a broad, mustachioed man, about five feet ten, with jowly cheeks and rheumy hazel eyes, was in the living room of his apartment in Sunnyside, Queens, when the lights went out. On the way into the kitchen to check his fuse box, he peeked out the window. The whole block was dark. Sekzer ran up three flights and swung open the metal door to his roof. The whole neighborhood was dark. He looked to the west, across the East River, to Manhattan. The familiar shapes of the world's most famous skyline all were blotted out by darkness. "Holy shit," Sekzer muttered to himself. "There's no lights on *anywhere*." Minutes later he was in his car and heading for work.

Sekzer's command, the Eighty-third Precinct in the bowels of Bushwick, Brooklyn, was exactly 5.3 miles away from the quiet, cheerful streets of Sunnyside. Driving through the blackness, the heavy air pushing through the open windows of his gold Chrysler Cordova, he remembered where he had been twelve years earlier, the last time New York was blacked out: the Mekong Delta, as a twenty-one-year-old helicopter door gunner. Now he was well into his thirties and married, with a boy of seven.

The Victorian-era station house of the Eighty-third Precinct was surrounded by buckling tenements and bodegas, its red- and yellow-brick façade buried beneath layers of grime. It was a beautiful building, though, one that recalled a distant era when constables patrolled New York's neighborhoods on horseback. The station house even bore its original City of Brooklyn seal. Turreted, with a corner tower and crenellated parapets, it looked almost like a medieval castle in miniature. Adjacent to it was a smaller building with big, rickety barn doors and a hayloft, the stable that once housed the police horses and now housed the commanding officer's car. A few doors down, on the corner, was the B&G, a seedy bar where the cops of the Eight-Three would get drunk and swap stories.

Sekzer had been sent to the Eighty-third Precinct from Emergency Services in the summer of '75, when the city's fiscal crisis forced the Police Department to lay off five thousand officers. Sekzer had only narrowly escaped himself. The list of "indefinitely furloughed" officers had clanked over the teletype machine, after a cacophony of bells indicating that an urgent message from the commissioner was forthcoming. Sekzer's captain proceeded to read all five thousand names in alphabetical order. The layoffs were based strictly on seniority. Most of Sekzer's classmates from the academy were sacked, but he was saved by his eighteen months of military service, which were considered time on the job. He was reassigned, though, as were most cops working in specialty crime divisions like Emergency Services. Down five thousand men at a time of soaring crime, the city's depleted precincts were going to need all the beat cops the department could muster.

Sekzer walked up the slate steps of the Eighty-third Precinct and checked in with the desk officer, who was still waiting for a call back from police headquarters about whether off-duty cops were going to be activated. Sekzer went down to the basement to the "lounge," a couple of ratty sofas and a silent black-and-white TV set, to kill time. When he came back upstairs a few minutes later, the word had come down: All active officers were to report for duty. Sekzer was officially on the clock. The desk officer told him to stay loose; he might be going over to Manhattan to "protect the big money."

A few minutes later the owner of a big furniture store in Bushwick burst through the station house doors in a rage. "What the fuck is going on? They're looting my business on Broadway, and you motherfuckers are standing here?"

"The duty captain walks up right behind him," Sekzer says. "This guy is screaming and screaming, and I don't blame him. And the captain says, 'All right, everybody in four-man cars. Go forth and do good.' "

The Eighty-third Precinct was not exactly a desirable assignment in 1977. The prior year it had confronted more criminal activity than any other precinct in central Brooklyn. Many truck drivers insisted on police escorts when making deliveries in the neighborhood. Some store owners had taken to wearing firearms on their hips. One block, Gates between Broadway and Bushwick, was so bad that two radio cars were required to respond to any call there. Three cops would enter the building in question while the remaining officer would stay behind to protect the squad cars.

One cop remembers being transferred from the Eight-Three into Manhattan in the 1980s. His new partner told him he had unholstered his gun six times in ten years. "Six times?" he replied, incredulous. "That was a good hour in Bushwick."

In 1977 the Eight-Three was predominantly white. The neighborhood it policed was overwhelmingly black and Hispanic, with a narrow strip of Italians along its western edge. "Our job was about arresting minorities," says one veteran of the Eight-Three. "That's what it was about."

About 130 officers called the Eighty-third Precinct home, meaning that at any given moment there were maybe 34 on duty, not nearly enough to police this crime-infested area of roughly 100,000 people. Working regular eight-hour shifts for five-day stretches was unheard of. There were simply too many people to arrest. "If you weren't doing at least a hundred twenty-five hours of overtime a month, don't you dare call yourself a collar man," says Sekzer. "You are not a collar man."

It didn't help that the fiscal crisis had virtually eliminated Police

Department support staff. It took anywhere from ten to fourteen hours for a cop to process a single perp. An officer first had to take his prisoner back to the precinct for fingerprinting, which had to be done by a detective. After filling out the arrest paperwork, he'd wait for a paddy wagon to take him and his prisoner to Brooklyn headquarters, where he'd give the fingerprints—and a buck for "expeditious service"—to another detective, who would hand them off to a clerk for processing. Mug shots were taken. Now it was off to the courthouse in downtown Brooklyn. While the prisoner was locked up downstairs, the arresting officer was up on the second floor at a bank of manual typewriters, most of which were broken or missing keys. He'd type out the official complaint with the help of the New York State Penal Code booklet attached to the typewriter. Finally, he took his paperwork down to the lounge and waited for the arraignment.

The Eight-Three's reputation was well established within the department. When the precinct's commanding officer first addressed his men a couple of years earlier, he had told them that his superiors described the precinct as a cross between a foreign legion outpost and a leper colony.

Rookies were taught a few important lessons when they reported for duty at the Eight-Three. Don't walk too close to the buildings (someone might drop a brick on you). Don't let neighborhood kids wear your hat (lice). Always check the earpiece on call boxes before using it (dog shit).

30.

UNLIKE Sekzer, Officer Robert Locklear was already on duty when the lights went out. He remembers people hanging out on Broadway, Bushwick's main strip, playing cards, drinking beer, trying vainly to catch a flutter of breeze. Now and then a train would rumble across the elevated tracks overhead, momentarily drowning out the sounds of salsa and disco emanating from the boom boxes below. Locklear, one of a small group of minority cops in the Eight-Three, and his partner had collared a murder suspect earlier in the evening—they found the guy frying chicken with his door open at the top of a tenement stairwell, in plain view of the dead body at the foot of the stairs—and were hoping the rest of the shift would be relatively quiet.

Locklear can't remember what he heard first, the sound of shattering glass or the store alarms. But he'll never forget what he saw when he looked down the block moments later: mobs of people materializing in the darkness. A local woman called the Police Department in a panic: "They're coming across Broadway like a herd of buffalo."

Cops gathering at the Eight-Three station house found it dark; the batteries were missing from the emergency floodlights that were supposed to kick in the moment power went out. "Hats, bats, and jeans"—riot helmets, billy clubs, and dungarees—were the norm. Officers were assigned to "combat cars" of four men, using every marked and unmarked vehicle at the precinct's disposal. They were ghetto cops. No one had to tell them to expect the worst. "This wasn't Park Avenue," Sekzer says. "This was the jungle. You could bet your ass there was going to be gunfire tonight."

Still, nothing could have prepared them for what greeted them on Broadway. Thousands of people were already out on the street; thousands more were pouring in from every direction. "If they had turned on the lights," one cop remembers, "it would have looked like the Macy's Thanksgiving Day Parade."

According to one police report, the looting had started at 9:40 p.m., only minutes after the onset of darkness. Marauding bands were sawing open padlocks. They were taking crowbars to steel shutters, prying them open like tennis-ball-can tops or simply jimmying them up with hydraulic jacks and then wedging garbage cans underneath to keep them open. They were pulling up onto sidewalks in tow trucks, slipping the big iron hooks under storefront gates, and ripping them clean off. They were punching through plate glass windows to grab the clothed mannequins inside, first with bare hands, later with towels wrapped around their fists. Four men wrenched a parking meter out of the ground and used it to batter open the door of a jewelry store. They filled cars, vans, trucks, and U-Hauls or simply carried their loot, be it sofas, television sets, or refrigerators, on their backs or in their arms. In the darkness, it was especially hard to miss the white washing machines bumping along Broadway, propelled by pairs of legs poking out underneath.

The most expensive shops were hit first: jewelry, electronics, and furniture stores. A teenager attached a chain to the bumper of a stolen truck and tore off the gates of a luxury item shop called Time Credit. He pitched a garbage pail through the window and filled the truck with TVs, air conditioners, and a rack of watches. After helping a fellow looter load a couch onto the roof of his station wagon, the teenager sped off. "At the onset of the blackout, the widely dispersed activities of those involved in criminality made it virtually impossible to prevent individual acts of vandalism and looting," William Bracey, the commanding officer for North Brooklyn, later reported.

The elevated tracks that ran above Broadway obscured the light of the slivered moon. In the darkness the cops started wading into the thick knots of people and making arrests. "You just grabbed 'em," says Locklear, who was patrolling the neighborhood in a battered gypsy cab. "There were plenty of them to grab on to."

Often the looter would drop the merchandise and run the moment he saw a cop approaching. The cop would give chase. If he managed to catch up with the looter, he'd tackle him, handcuff him, and go back to pick up the evidence, provided it was still there. Now he had to get his prisoner and the stolen property back to the station house. Short on cars and long on perps, he found it necessary to improvise. "I saw cars pull up at the station house," remembers one Bushwick cop on duty that night. "They'd pull four prisoners out of the back, open up the trunk, and pull two or three more out of there."

Robert Curvin and Bruce Porter, coauthors of *Blackout Looting!*, a study sponsored by the Ford Foundation in the wake of the blackout, divided the looters into three categories: the professional criminals, who were the first to start pillaging; the "alienated adolescents" who soon joined in; and the poor and not so poor, who either got caught up in the excitement or were motivated by "abject greed." Curvin and Porter interviewed one looter, a twenty-one-year-old man who lived with his mother and siblings in Brooklyn, who described the blackout as a gift from above. "It was like the man upstairs said I'm gonna put out the lights for twenty-four hours and you all go off, you know, and get everything you can . . . I was out there 'cause I'm a poor person and, like, you know, lock a hungry dog up with some food, you know he gonna eat it."

For the cops, there was no time for paperwork. All the stolen merchandise was piled up in the property room in the back of the station house. Polaroids were snapped of the cop with his perp. Time and place of arrest were scribbled on the backs. The prisoner was stuffed into a holding cell, and the arresting officer headed back out into the mayhem. Ordinarily prisoners were taken to downtown Brooklyn for processing, but the message had come down that all suspects were to be detained in the precincts in which they were arrested in order to conserve manpower on the streets and relieve pressure at central booking.

As the night wore on, some merchants started turning up to protect their property, but because most of them didn't live in the neighborhood any longer, everything was already gone by the time they got to their stores. Raphael Aboud, the owner of a shoe store on Broadway, arrived at his shop while it was being looted and was attacked. He ran to a nearby subway station, where he hid in the bathroom. Three cops eventually found him there and brought him back to the station.

At one point Sekzer and his partners followed a group of looters into a furniture store. It was pitch-black inside. The cops walked through with their flashlights but saw no one. There was a staircase in the back. Walking down into the basement, Sekzer heard voices. A lot of voices. There were at least thirty people down there. "We're all thinking the same thing," Sekzer recalls. "I'm not shooting anybody over this. If they come running at us to try and get out, then take care, send me a postcard."

The officers told the offending mob they were under arrest. Now the question was how to get them back to the station house. Sekzer and another cop went upstairs to commandeer a city bus. They managed to flag one down. The bus stopped, the door opened, and a police captain leaned out. "What the fuck is your problem?" he asked. The bus was filled with a detail of cops on their way to Brooklyn's central command for reassignment for the night. Unable to find a vehicle large enough to transport the mob of looters, Sekzer went back to the furniture store to confer with his partners. They decided to let the women and children go and call for squad cars to come pick up the men.

Bullets, as well as bricks and bottles, were raining down from rooftops. Meanwhile, WINS was reporting that there was "a party atmosphere" in New York. "These must be happy bullets," Kevin Cox, another cop in the Eight-Three, cracked to his partners. Many officers were using their guns repeatedly, usually with the intention of clearing hostile crowds and scaring off snipers. Some cops recall Emergency Services vans combing the streets, tossing out extra boxes of ammunition to officers in need. One cop says he and his partner shot on the order of 130 rounds. Another remembers talking to a shaken transit cop who had defended a token booth at an elevated subway stop by running back and forth between the two entrances, firing his pistol to keep the looters at bay.

At a little after midnight word spread that John and Al's, a sporting goods store on Broadway that sold firearms, was under siege. Just about every officer in Bushwick headed straight for it. They showed up in time to arrest seventeen looters, but dozens of guns and thousands of rounds of ammunition were already gone. At least some of the baseball bats had been left behind. One cop grabbed a Louisville Slugger to replace his nightstick, which he had already broken on a looter. The cops secured the location and turned it over to one of the store's owners, who stood guard the rest of the night with a high-caliber rifle.

Off-duty cops were slowly rolling in. Some, like Sekzer, just assumed they'd be needed. Others were responding to Police Commissioner Michael Codd's call-up order on the radio. Those without riot helmets were given air-raid helmets, teamed up, and sent out in the streets. The Eighty-first Precinct, which was just over on the other side of Broadway in Bedford-Stuyvesant and shared a radio frequency with the Eight-Three, had most of its men out on Broadway as well. For some reason, though, the Eight-Three received no backup from any of the city's quieter precincts.

31.

MAYOR Beame had just started in on a campaign reelection speech to a standing room only crowd of five hundred at the Traditional Synagogue in Co-op City when the lights went out. After he continued on in the darkness for a couple of minutes, promising to do something about the putrid smell wafting over from the

Pelham Bay landfill and to close all the porn shops in the area, his aides ushered him out.

The mayor climbed into his Chrysler and was spirited down to Gracie Mansion, where a candlelight strategy session was already in progress. After taking an aide's advice to lose the tie and roll up his sleeves—"it makes you look like a tireless worker"—Beame proceeded to a darkened City Hall. He invited a handful of newspapermen to lean over his shoulder and listen in as he grilled Con Ed's chairman, Charles Luce, who assured him that the city's power would be back soon.

Several hours later a bleary-eyed Beame officially declared war on the utility. Standing on a table outside the police commissioner's office, where he and his staff had relocated to take advantage of the emergency generators, he accused Con Ed of "gross negligence—*at the very least.*" (Luce knew a scapegoat when he saw one, quipping, "If we didn't have a Con Ed, we'd have to invent one.")

Beame did not follow his predecessor Mayor Lindsay's lead and take to the riot-torn streets himself. Such a tour, he explained to reporters, might just be a "stimulant" to more violence. Instead, he and his entourage visited the Upper East Side, where they stopped in on an empty fire station. Everyone was up in Harlem fighting the arson fires that had begun erupting shortly after the looting began. When he returned to police headquarters at a little after 5 a.m., Beame held another press conference in which he called on religious leaders to get into patrol cars and calm their communities. One of those who did, a priest in the Bronx, had his altar stolen while he was gone.

Some twenty-five hundred cops had been on the beat when darkness fell. Within minutes Police Commissioner Codd had ordered all officers to report for duty immediately, only instead of insisting that everyone try to find a way to get to his command, Codd told them to report to the nearest precincts.

This proved to be an enormous mistake. Ever since the 1962 repeal of the Lyons Law, which had required all cops to live in the city, police officers had been moving to the suburbs in droves. Most of those who continued to reside in the city lived in Queens or on Staten Island, so in the early hours of the blackout, there were hundreds, maybe thousands, of idle cops hanging around quiet precincts. Many were eventually reassigned to neighborhoods in need, but when they arrived in civilian clothes, without flashlights, helmets, or nightsticks, they were as good as useless. One South Brooklyn commander was thrilled to see a load of Staten Island cops pull up at his station house and disappointed when they stepped off the bus looking like what he described as "a tennis team."

Some cops simply ignored, or rather pretended not to have heard, Codd's call-up order. Morale in the department had been on the skids ever since the '75 layoffs. Mayor Beame's recent threats to put one cop in each patrol car in half the city's precincts as a further cost-cutting measure hadn't helped matters any. It perhaps explains why, as the looting peaked between midnight and 4 a.m., some ten thousand cops, 40 percent of the force who were neither on vacation nor on sick leave, had yet to check in.

32.

THE looting was by no means citywide. In some of the tonier areas of Manhattan, restaurants moved tables outside to escape the heat. Several stretches of First Avenue on the Upper East Side might have been mistaken for streets in Paris, were it not for the angled cars, headlights on, that made it possible for diners to identify what they were eating. At the Winter Garden Theater on Broadway, the cast of *Beatlemania* picked up their acoustic instruments and led the audience in a sing-along of Beatles' tunes. At the Metropolitan Opera, where the Canadian Ballet was performing, the orchestra's harpist did an impromptu solo of "Dancing in the Dark." Eight cast members of the nude revue *Oh! Calcutta!* were caught in the altogether. Unable to find their way backstage in the dark, they borrowed shirts and jackets from the audience. On Weehawken Street in the West Village, a gay orgy broke out. ("The small one block was a beehive of mad insane activity," one participant recalled in the magazine *Michael's Thing* a few weeks later. "Nudity was the rule; many guys were pushed against cars and performed upon with the full consent of everyone there.")

But not a single poor neighborhood escaped damage. In most cases the destruction outlasted the darkness, continuing well into the following afternoon. To this day the blackout looting of 1977 remains the only civil disturbance in the history of New York City to encompass all five boroughs simultaneously.

The authors of *Blackout Looting!*, the Ford Foundation study, counted no fewer than thirty-one neighborhoods that suffered considerable damage or theft. In white, working-class Queens and Staten Island, the damage was far less severe—mostly broken windows and missing display cases—but by no means insignificant.

In Manhattan's Alphabet City, residents started congregating almost immediately after the lights went out. "Subsequently," wrote the commanding officer for the local precinct, "these groups became unruly and began to smash and destroy windows and interiors of various commercial premises; looting of these premises began to occur." Patrolling officers were forced to evacuate the streets temporarily when looters started hurling objects at them from tenement rooftops. The looting continued along Avenues A, B, and C, from Houston up to Tenth Street, until ten the following morning.

More than a hundred blocks uptown, in East Harlem, outnumbered police initially tried to chase looters off and secure stores along Third Avenue. They soon realized that the looters were simply retreating to side streets and lying in wait until the officers were drawn to other locations. With the help of a busload of fifty-five cops who arrived from Queens at around 3:30 a.m., local officers began mobile sweeps, trapping looters by entering both sides of streets at once.

Over in West Harlem, Joyaria Ortega, a jewelry store on 144th Street, was one of dozens of shops cleaned out along Broadway. The owner's brother had arrived with his shotgun as soon as he could, but it was already too late. People were now picking through the heaps of glass shards, hoping something had been left behind. One cop, John Ryan, remembers finding a couple of the store's safes smashed open and emptied of their contents. Ryan made fifteen arrests that night, packing every one of his collars into the same ten by thirteen cell in the Thirtieth Precinct.

The pillaging reached all the way down into the Upper West Side. Between 96th and 110th streets along Broadway, store after store was damaged. Capri, a furniture store at 92nd and Amsterdam, lost everything, forty thousand dollars' worth of dressers, bedroom sets, mirrors, and sofas. "The size of the store didn't matter; who owned it didn't matter," the *Westsider* newspaper reported. "All that mattered was that they were there." Even the Twentieth Precinct, which ran from 59th to 86th Street, reported looting at thirteen stores and vandalism at several more. Between 63rd and 110th streets on the Upper West Side, sixty-one stores were hit. The emergency room at St. Luke's Hospital, adjacent to Columbia University, treated eighty people between midnight and 8 a.m., more than four times the usual number. Nearly all of them had suffered lacerations during looting or had been injured fighting with fellow looters over the spoils.

The Bronx was hit even harder than Manhattan. By 11 p.m., the showroom windows of a Pontiac dealership on Jerome Avenue had been smashed, and fifty of the fifty-five new cars parked inside driven off into the black night. Fifty-eight stores were looted along one stretch of East Tremont Avenue. "At the time of the blackout there were 38 officers on patrol," wrote the commanding officer of one Bronx precinct in his report to the NYPD. "Ten times that number would have been necessary to cope with the spontaneous incidents of looting, fires and attacks on police officers." The officers who were trying to cope with the bedlam were instructed to avoid using their sirens and turret lights, "so that a 'carnival' atmosphere is not spread."

A total of 473 stores in the Bronx were damaged; 961 looters were arrested. Virtually every Bronx precinct was forced to house prisoners in clerical offices and sitting rooms. Some dumped their excess at Rikers Island until it too was overcrowded. And still the looting continued.

It was worse yet in Brooklyn. On a five-block stretch of Crown Heights, seventy-five stores, including twenty shops owned by local Caribbean craftsmen, were hit. Sunset Park, Williamsburg, Brownsville, Flatbush Avenue—the list of ransacked areas goes on. More than seven hundred Brooklyn stores were plundered; 1,088 people were arrested.

Still, the character of the chaos in Bushwick was unique. "The crowds on Broadway in Bushwick seemed to possess a special kind of hysteria as the evening wore on," concluded Curvin and Porter. "This spirit appeared to lead them as much toward destruction and burning as toward looting."

It was a spirit born of the poverty and desperation of ghetto life. Yet what was so remarkable about Bushwick was that it had been a sturdy middle-class enclave just a decade earlier. The speed of its decline was dizzying. In ten years' time, a community whose roots in New York went back three hundred years had been virtually destroyed by greed, indifference, and good intentions. Worst of all, perhaps, few had even noticed. The South Bronx, Harlem, Brownsville—these were New York's ghettos, the symbols of a city in distress.

"Bushwick?" asked a puzzled reporter for New York's twenty-four-hour news station, WINS, when a local fireman called in during the blackout to fill the station in on what was happening there. "Where's that?"

33.

IN Bushwick the arrests peaked at about 1:30 a.m. By then there were two shifts' worth of cops—4 p.m. to midnight and midnight to 8 a.m.—out on the streets. The Eight-Three's holding cells, which were designed to accommodate one prisoner, had upwards of ten in each. When they couldn't squeeze in another body, cops handcuffed prisoners to radiators, to benches, to tables, to one another. (One popular method entailed cuffing five of them in a line, then cuffing the last guy to the first guy's ankles.) The rest were stuffed into a small courtyard behind the station house.

The property room was overflowing with merchandise. "P. C. Richard's was empty compared to that room," remembers one officer. "Sears, Roebuck? Forget about it." When the room was full, goods were redirected to a designated area outside the station where an officer stood guard.

By 2 a.m. the dispatcher was reporting only 10-30s and 10-13s—robberies in progress and officers needing assistance. Several cops remember being instructed to stop arresting looters. Even though they weren't hanging around to process their collars, the arrests were taking them off the streets for too long. Besides, the station house was running out of room for prisoners.

Instead, cops cracked their shins or gave them "turbans," copspeak for a bloody head wrapped in a towel or bandage. "You just wanted to stop the riot, so you beat up the looters with ax handles and nightsticks," recalls Robert Knightly, a bearded, mild-mannered veteran of the Eight-Three who is now a defense attorney for Legal Aid. "You beat 'em up and left them in the street. You catch them looting, you just smacked them down and left them."

Knightly chased one looter who was carrying a love seat. He caught up to the perp and knocked him down. The looter popped right up, as if attached to a spring. "I'm not like these people. I've got a job," he barked. "Oh, yeah?" Knightly answered. "Is today your day off?"

The station house was in chaos. When cops needed a breather, they'd drive a few blocks toward the Queens border, which was eerily quiet.

Several officers recollect being told to remove their shields and nameplates. The shields gave the looters a target to shoot at in the darkness. As for the nameplates, "They wanted this thing over as quickly as possible, and they didn't want anyone worrying about being identified," says one cop. The officer who had taken the Louisville Slugger broke it on a looter and yanked a metal riser out of the stairwell of an abandoned building to use as his new nightstick. It got him through the remainder of the night.

One cop remembers a looter running around beneath a building like an outfielder trying to get under a fly ball. "We were saying 'No, no way he's going to do this.' " He did. A love seat came crashing down on top of him from a couple of floors up. The looters were attacking one another too. According to one police report, a man was loading a van with stolen merchandise at Gates and Broadway. He offered an onlooker a hundred dollars to help. The onlooker declined. But as soon as the van was full, the onlooker stabbed the driver, took the keys to the van, and drove off.

Officer Frank Cammarata remembers chasing a looter up to the roof of a six-story furniture store with a few other officers. One thing led to another, and the looter went over the edge. A tree broke his fall. He looked up from the pavement, gave the officers the finger, and hobbled away.

By 3 a.m. the only hospital in the neighborhood, Wyckoff Heights, was a madhouse. A police administrator was stationed at the registrar's desk, filling out police reports while the registrar did intakes. So many people had cut themselves on broken glass that the hospital was running out of suture material. When officers came by to drop off the injured or simply to wash up and rest for a few minutes, nurses gave them packets of suture threads to keep in their pockets in case they needed them later.

Carl St. Martin, a medical student who lived on Bushwick's Greene Avenue, was helping stitch people up. A trim but muscular young man who wore a pooka shell necklace, a thin beard, and a full but tame Afro, St. Martin was home studying for his medical boards when the lights went out. Like Sekzer, he thought it was a fuse. "Then I heard noises in the street, people yelling. Within a matter of minutes people were going up to Bushwick Avenue to get stuff," he says. "The next thing I knew people were walking down my block with TVs on their backs. I remember one man carrying a sofa all by himself."

He also noticed that a lot of people were cut up from the glass. So he decided to walk up to Wyckoff Heights, where the overwhelmed emergency room was happy to put him to work. He sewed people up until close to dawn.

34.

WHEN the pricier shops and shoe stores had been cleaned out, the looters moved on to the supermarkets and bodegas. Even a taxidermy store on Broadway was hit, leaving a trail of eyeballs in the street.

After five hours there was little left to steal, but the worst was not over. Orange flames pierced the darkness; Bushwick was burning. Some of the looters, caught up in the insanity of the night, driven by the desire to destroy their neighborhood, or maybe just bored, were torching stores.

At one point two solid blocks of Broadway were ablaze. As fire trucks sped along the avenue, looters pelted them from the el tracks with rocks, bottles, bags of Goya beans. Cops tried to disperse the crowds at the various fire sites and protect the firemen so they could do their job. After the firemen abandoned one truck to seek cover from the objects raining down on them, a few cops climbed aboard and turned the water cannon on the crowd. The force of the stream sent looters skipping as far as half a block. Later the cops tried clearing the street by fastening a metal chain between two patrol cars and driving down either side of Broadway.

As dawn approached, exhaustion, as well as a growing sense of futility, had set in. A group of cops looked on as all the vehicles in a used-car lot were torched. The ad hoc bazaars had already begun: A $500 color TV set was going for $135, Pro-Keds basketball shoes for $5 a pair, a $200 Peugeot ten-speed for $40.

The sun finally rose, revealing endless piles of broken glass. Disembodied mannequin parts littered the streets like battlefield debris. Locklear sat on a curb in a daze, as streams of blackened water pooled up in front of him and a police helicopter buzzed overhead. Not only had the crowds on Broadway not diminished, they were larger than ever. "Ain't you guys have wives or girlfriends at home?" he asked a group of men busy picking through the litter. "Ain't you tired of being out here?"

With virtually no stores left to loot, the Eighty-first Precinct redirected all its men to the fire scenes to prevent people from harassing the firemen. "This tactic was successful," the commanding officer of the precinct reported, "but it was costly in that it tied up manpower and resulted in numerous injuries to police officers which were caused by thrown missiles."

In all, more than thirty blocks of Broadway, a distance of a mile and a half, were devastated overnight. One hundred and thirty-four stores were cleaned out; forty-five of them had been burned as well. "I remember a merchant on Broadway whose place was looted all to shit," says the Eight-Three's Knightly. "He was standing there, wondering why the police didn't stop them. I didn't have an answer. I guess because there weren't enough of us to go around."

Being black-owned offered stores no protection. One black proprietor, a pharmacist on Broadway, had managed to fend off looters without the help of the police. After staying all night with a loaded gun, he finally left his drugstore the next day to go get something to eat. When he returned a half hour later nearly everything was gone. Only after he squeezed off a couple of warning shots did the looters disperse. J. Walters, a local barber, had just rented out space for a new supermarket on Broadway. "I was almost ready to open," he says. Overnight he lost forty thousand dollars' worth of uninsured meat-slicing equipment. The supermarket never opened.

More than twenty fires were still burning along Broadway come Thursday morning, ten hours after the blackout had begun. The stifling heat was made more oppressive by the blanket of black smoke that hung heavy over the neighborhood.

After catching a ride home from the hospital, St. Martin went out to pick up his shirts at the dry cleaner. The store had been burned to the ground.

"Seeing the destruction," says Thomas Creegan, a redheaded veteran of the Eight-Three, "what was most upsetting was that you worked in this precinct. You worked with these people, you had taken care of them, and yet here they were, burning their own stores down. Where are you going to go come Friday? Where's that nice old lady in the tenement going to get her food?"

35.

In some ways, New York affects me like Venice. It's in danger of dying, so there's something tender about it. **PAUL MAZURSKY, FILM DIRECTOR**

BROADWAY separates Bushwick from Bedford-Stuyvesant, which was once a middle-class enclave too, a neighborhood of stickball, brownstones, and postwar optimism. As the fifties wore on, though, more and more of Bed-Stuy's working-class white families migrated to the suburbs. Lured by the promise of jobs at the Brooklyn Navy Yard, black families moved in to fill the void.

The jobs soon disappeared, and the steady white migration became a mass exodus. Still more poor black families, Harlem residents displaced by ambitious but ill-fated urban renewal projects, moved in. Still more white families moved out, often at the prodding of real estate agents who warned them to sell now because the neighborhood was turning.

Their prophecy became self-fulfilling: In 1965 the Department of Housing and Urban Development called Bed-Stuy "the heart of the largest ghetto in America." Federal antipoverty programs lined the pockets of local power brokers charged with administering them, rather than provide desperately needed first aid to a wounded neighborhood.

It was a familiar fate for much of Brooklyn in the late 1950s and early 1960s, yet it was a fate that Bushwick managed to postpone. Most of the neighborhood's housing stock, yellow-brick or three-story wood-frame row houses, was solid, if not fancy, and between its eleven breweries—longtime locals remember the pervasive aroma of yeast and hops—its knitting mills, and various other light manufacturing plants, Bushwick was less dependent on the dying navy yard for jobs than much of the borough. The beer barons who once lived in the mansions set back from the elms along Bushwick Avenue were long gone, but they had been replaced by doctors and lawyers.

The Italians were Bushwick's primary ethnic group, but there was still a smattering of Germans, as well as small pockets of blacks and Puerto Ricans. As an ethnic group, Italians tend to stick around neighborhoods longer than others, and Bushwick's six Catholic churches, and the culture that flourished around them well into the sixties, helped deepen their roots. The neighborhood featured an endless string of feasts for patron saints, complete with oompah bands and barefooted old women fighting through the crowds to pin a dollar bill to the statue of the Virgin Mary being paraded through the noisy streets.

Bushwick's best-known church was St. Barbara's, where Christmas Eve masses were so jammed you couldn't enter without a ticket. Modeled after St. Peter's Basilica, albeit with some Gothic touches, this hulking church cut an imposing figure among the neighborhood's modest row houses; its architects had wanted nothing to detract from its grandeur. Ornate moldings adorned the cream-colored façade. Inside, pastel murals covered arched ceilings beneath a two-tiered dome. On Sunday mornings the owner of the funeral parlor across the street left his doors unlocked to provide an extra bathroom for the fifteen hundred churchgoers. After mass, the crowd migrated to LaRosa's Bakery for hot bread. The congregation was overwhelmingly white, but not entirely so. St. Martin had been an altar boy at the church and a student at St. Barbara's parochial school. The school charged families tuition only for the first child, giving Catholic parents one fewer disincentive to reproduce and one more reason to stay put in Bushwick.

But change was coming to Bushwick too. Father Peter Mahoney, the monsignor at one of the neighborhood's Catholic churches, recalls returning from a three-month leave in the early sixties to discover that a hundred families had left his parish. Nearly all of them lived on the same block.

In 1965, Bushwick was denied Model City status. Unlike the slums on its southern and western borders, it was judged too white and too well off to qualify for federal antipoverty funds. The trouble was that the government had relied on six-year-old census figures. New immigrants, mostly Puerto Ricans, were already changing the ethnic and financial makeup of the neighborhood.

Bushwick soon received its first wave of welfare recipients, courtesy of East New York and Brownsville, where several twenty-block tracts were cleared for low-income housing projects. The displaced people were to be temporarily relocated to Bushwick. The new housing was never built.

The bulldozers rolled into Bushwick next. The city was going to replace the two-family houses and small businesses on two square blocks across the way from St. Barbara's with four fourteen-story housing projects, an elementary school, a community center, and a park. Neighborhood activists tried to fight the plan—"It wasn't urban renewal; it was urban removal," recalls Father James Kelly, one of those activists—but they were no match for the zealous idealists who dominated urban planning in the sixties. Many of the new occupants would be poor blacks and Hispanics. Local real estate operators pounced, calling homeowners to stoke their racial fears and stuffing their mailboxes with flyers warning them to sell before it was too late. Many were gone before the wrecking balls were set in motion.

The buildings were demolished, but weeds were soon growing in the rubble-strewn lot. Stray dogs, junkies, and winos moved in beneath a sign that read, URBAN RENEWAL ZONE. The twenty-three-million-dollar plan had been shelved, leaving a yawning hole in the heart of Bushwick.

Some of Bushwick's working class pulled up stakes, in most cases pushing east into Long Island. Others dug in their heels. On the night of Martin Luther King, Jr.'s assassination in April 1968, St. Martin's father and many of his family's neighbors—black and white alike—took to their rooftops with shotguns, ready to shoot any rioters who came near their homes. Several tense weeks followed. A number of Italian-owned neighborhood stores were vandalized, and Father Kelly spent hours in the Italian social clubs along Knickerbocker Avenue, trying to dissuade their members from retaliating. Gates started appearing on the windows of the stores on Broadway.

More simmering racial tensions bubbled over when local Puerto Ricans who had once steered clear of Bushwick's Italian enclave began frequenting a park where elderly Italian men gathered to play bocce. Fights became commonplace. One Italian man was stabbed in the heart with a switchblade and died.

Bushwick was bleeding. The Catholic Church undertook a study of its operations there to determine how to deal with the sudden and dramatic changes to the neighborhood. Buried in Mayor Lindsay's 1969 master plan for the city was this bracing *cri*: "Bushwick urgently needs almost every type of community facility and service—vest-pocket housing, schools, health services, parks, supervised recreation activities, language classes, low-interest loans to encourage improvement of private property, social services for every age group, cultural activities, libraries, more job opportunities, and training programs and improved sanitation and police protection . . . Bushwick's decline began almost overnight. And relatively little has been done because its problems were overshadowed by the enormous problems of neighboring slums."

Even those all too aware of Bushwick's woes couldn't have predicted what was coming next. When a house near St. Martin's burned down in 1969, neighbors expressed their condolences to the owner. Nobody thought arson. "We felt sorry for him," says St. Martin. "Insurance or no insurance, you didn't burn your own house down and put other people at risk. It was unthinkable. It just didn't happen."

It did, and it would, again and again. In 1972, Bushwick's two ladder companies, 124 and 112, went on more then six thousand runs, the unofficial benchmark of a severe social crisis. One block of

Greene Avenue, a short walk from St. Martin's, lost one house in '73, thirteen in '74, nine in '75, and forty-one in '76. Eventually the entire block was burned down.

By then St. Martin's mother, Irma, had packed up his seven siblings and moved out to Long Island. Carl wanted to stay behind in Bushwick. The family's three-story frame house on Greene Avenue would have fetched next to nothing if they'd tried to sell it, so he broke it up into rental apartments, keeping one on the third floor for himself. Eventually he learned to stop looking up from his medical school textbooks when he heard the scream of a fire engine.

Local firemen spray-painted signs on abandoned buildings. A single diagonal line meant that a building was structurally unsound, that firemen should enter only if absolutely necessary. Two intersecting diagonal lines, an *X*, meant a building wasn't safe: Do not enter, period. They were like tombstones for the doomed residents of a town confronting a deadly epidemic.

The fires were set by landlords who were tired of trying to evict delinquent tenants. They were set by vandals who intended to return for the plumbing systems, which were easier to extract and sell once the firemen had knocked down the walls. They were set by idle kids who wandered the streets aimlessly after school.

Sometimes ignition was preceded by the ritual removal of property, meaning that the fire had been started by a family that knew that Social Services was obligated to provide new housing and moving expenses to victims of disastrous combustion. Only a gasoline-soaked mattress would be left inside. "We'd go to a fire and the furniture would be out on the street and the building would be burning," recalls Santo Puglisi, a driver for Bushwick's Engine Company 271. (One Bushwick family was eventually accused of setting thirteen fires over the course of eight years, and bilking the city of more than forty thousand dollars in the process.)

When Puglisi first came to Bushwick in 1967, it was considered a soft assignment. His company's meals, eaten up on the third floor, were only rarely interrupted. When his company did respond to an alarm, they left the firehouse doors open. In 1976, Ladder 124, the "truckies" with whom Puglisi worked most closely, finished first out of 136 on the city's chart of most runs. Ladder 112, Bushwick's other ladder company, was second. Between 1975 and September 1977, there were four thousand fires in Bushwick. Tired of sliding down three flights' worth of fire pole mid-meal, Engine Company 271's firemen ponied up the cash to relocate the kitchen to the first floor. They also always locked the doors to the station house on their way out.

Local firemen tried to keep a sense of humor, jokingly referring to gasoline cans as Bushwick overnight bags. But mostly they found their work relentlessly depressing. Endangering their lives to save the neighborhood's aging housing stock came to seem like an increasingly senseless calculus; Bushwick was beyond redemption. They treated most blazes like garbage fires, the goal being containment.

It was a goal that was nearly impossible to achieve. Most of Bushwick's buildings had been built for German immigrants before 1910. More than half of them were made of wood and designed with air shafts over their stairwells. They burned like furnaces. Because they were usually connected via common cocklofts, the attic space between the roof and the ceiling, fires virtually leaped from house to house. The only way to stop one from advancing next door was to poke holes in the ceiling and try to draw the flames upward. There were two methods of accomplishing this, and both were perilous. Firemen could climb up the stairs through the smoke and heat and poke the holes from the inside or hover precariously on a ladder outside—right in the line of fire the instant the flames started licking toward the sky.

The dying neighborhood had a haunting beauty. "You'd be out fighting a fire until dawn," Puglisi recalls, "and riding back to the firehouse, you'd notice that there were fewer and fewer buildings. Then you'd start noticing the churches. Bushwick had a lot of churches. And the houses weren't blocking the view anymore."

Lisa Casuso, the fourth generation of Casusos in Bushwick, remembers sitting on the stoop of her family's house on Harman Street in the early seventies. With each passing year, the sound of the fire engines grew louder, the smell of smoke more pungent. The fires were getting closer. Once the engines came within a block or so of the Casusos' home, her parents started hosing down their small backyard to fend off the encroaching flames. Before long the fires hit Harman Street. By then most of the three-story frame houses had been abandoned. Unable to sell, their owners had simply packed up and left. When the Casusos' next-door neighbors did just that, her father took to the porch of the unoccupied house every evening to ward off potential arsonists. He sat in a folding beach chair, a shotgun in his lap.

More plans to replenish Bushwick's dwindling housing stock were hatched and aborted. A scandal in the city's Municipal Loan Program derailed a scheme to rehabilitate and fireproof close to one hundred deteriorating dwellings. Real estate agents called the remaining white homeowners to induce further panic selling. Speculators snapped up the houses on the cheap and stuffed them full of families on public assistance, exploiting their welfare subsidies to drive up rents for working people. Local banks stopped granting mortgages and home improvement loans in the area, calling it "too susceptible to heavy damage due to vandalism" and thus too risky for "prudent lending."

The Federal Housing Administration stepped in to help; the government would guarantee the loans. But what should have been a boon turned into a boondoggle when corrupt FHA credit inspectors conspired with sleazy real estate operators. The scam worked like this: Speculator buys a house for a pittance, then triples, even quadruples the price. Speculator pays off FHA credit inspector to approve a naïve prospective buyer. Buyer becomes owner. Buyer defaults on his loan. The FHA pays off the balance of the mortgage and then boards up the property. Speculator and FHA credit inspector move on to the next property.

As houses fell, crime rose. Both the numbers of robberies and the incidents of grand larceny doubled in the early seventies. In such an environment, any buffer from the violence was welcome. St. Martin's block was protected somewhat by the Spanish church on the corner. The drug dealers who hung out in front of the church didn't want any other criminals drawing attention to their activities.

A deacon was mugged at knifepoint in front of St. Barbara's. Attendance at Sunday mass dropped by more than half. Human excrement was found in a confessional. Wrought iron gates went up around the church, symbolically sealing it off from the community that it had once nurtured. The growing sense of spiritual desolation was mirrored by a physical one: The big beautiful church squatted among streets leveled by wrecking balls and arson. Now truly nothing was detracting from St. Barbara's grandeur. The effect was hardly elevating.

The church closed its parochial school in 1972. Between '73 and '77, the neighborhood's welfare population rose by more than eighteen thousand. By '77 some 40 percent of its residents were on public assistance; 80 percent were unemployed. Half of Bushwick's families were living on less than four thousand dollars a year. Bushwick High School, which had been designed for two thousand students, was supporting three thousand, roughly four hundred of whom dropped out every year. The neighborhood's infant mortality rate was the highest in New York City.

As Jim Sleeper wrote in *The Closest of Strangers*, his trenchant 1990 book about liberalism and race in New York, "By the mid-1970s, Bushwick was . . . a prison of traumatized welfare recipients reeling in rage and despair." In the darkness of July 13, 1977, that rage and despair found an outlet.

36.

IN the days after the blackout a damp, acrid smell permeated Bushwick. Fire-damaged buildings sloughed off large chunks of debris. Broken pipes burped brown water onto sidewalks. In the litter-strewn streets, people filled shopping carts with abandoned packages of meat.

Like the rest of the station houses in Brooklyn, the Eight-Three was told to hang on to its 133 accused looters for a couple of days, until central booking was ready for them. For Sekzer it was just as well. It was going to take him days to complete the paperwork for the 32 men he'd collared. Most of the precinct's prisoners had been wedged into an open courtyard between the cells and the property room. Several cops threw McDonald's hamburgers down to them from the detective squad on the second floor. At least one officer urinated on them.

During a few successive roll calls, sergeants asked if anyone had used his gun that night. No one wanted to deal with the paperwork that accompanied every shot fired, not to mention the elaborate examinations and reenactments mandated by the Weapons Discharge Review Board. (The department's policy on firing weapons into the air was nearly as strict as that on firing at someone.) In his report to the NYPD's chief of operations, the captain of the Eight-Three, John Menken, stated: "The Officers were subjected to provocations of bottle and other missile throwing, and the stress of attempting to contain the unrestrained lawlessness; however, no firearms were discharged."

William Bracey, the commanding officer for North Brooklyn, came through the Eight-Three to offer his commendation for a job well done, and without firing a single shot. "Where the fuck were you, Hawaii?" Sekzer chuckled to himself. In his own "unusual occurrence" report to the department, Bracey wrote: "[P]olice personnel performed in a most exemplary fashion and there were no instances when firearms were utilized."

On Saturday, July 16, Bushwick's Signorelli family hosted a big barbecue to use up all the meat that had defrosted when the power was out. Like the Casusos, Charlie and Vickie Signorelli had refused to leave the neighborhood, where they had met and fallen in love after World War II. At the barbecue, one family member started talking about how "the animals" had destroyed Bushwick. The Signorellis' son Gasper, a senior at City College at the time, shouted him down. "I defended the looters in my liberal reflexive way," he says, "but part of me was angry because I knew he was right. You couldn't defend stealing sneakers just because you can."

On Sunday, July 17, four days after the looting had started, two teenagers and a twelve-year-old set fire to an abandoned knitting factory. A few years earlier the Fire Department had urged the city to demolish the five-story building, which had already been the site of two three-alarm fires. Instead, it was slated to be converted into a low-income apartment complex. The fiscal crisis arrived before renovation could begin, and the building was now a popular hangout for local junkies.

The fire started at 1:40 p.m. in the basement, as temperatures outside climbed toward a hundred degrees, and spread with startling speed. Before long it had progressed from a three-alarm fire to a full-borough alarm fire, the equivalent of ten alarms. Flames were jumping across the street. A fire truck's windshield melted. Brick façades tumbled, and wooden houses collapsed, burying cars underneath them. More than fifty-five fire companies, including thirteen from Manhattan, were summoned to help, as were the cops on duty at the Eight-Three. All of the neighborhood's fire hydrants had already been opened by neighborhood kids looking for some relief from the unrelenting heat, drastically reducing the water pressure for the firemen.

Officer Cox of the Eight-Three and his partner were among the cops told to drive down the center of the street looking for survivors. Through their windshield, they could see the flames above their heads. When they emerged, having found no one, the paint on their car had blistered.

Firemen managed to get the blaze under control in about three hours, but by then it had destroyed twenty-four buildings in a four-block area, including a Methodist church. It was the city's biggest fire since 1963—"another sad day for Brooklyn," according to Borough President Howard Golden. As night fell, the Salvation Army was serving coffee to cops, the Red Cross was trying to find temporary housing for the two hundred newly homeless, and scavengers were picking through the rubble left behind.

It was an ignominious introduction, but New York had finally met Bushwick. In the weeks after the blackout a parade of columnists paid their respects to the battered neighborhood. "It is here, in the dirt and the smells and the heat," wrote Jimmy Breslin, "that New York must struggle to keep a crucial part of its city from falling apart." Martin Gottlieb and a team of *Daily News* reporters produced a heart-wrenching series on Bushwick's ills. In one of the articles, St. Martin told Gottlieb that he planned to stay put there and even open a medical clinic "to serve the people who now struggle to survive in the shell of a neighborhood." (St. Martin soon moved out, hours after being attacked by one of his tenants. When he returned to pick up his mail a month later, all the aluminum siding had been ripped off the house and his neighbors had run extension cords into his basement to use his power.)

For the Eight-Three, the bad summer got worse. In late August one of precinct's most beloved cops, a black officer named Joseph Taylor, Jr., the father of a three-year-old daughter, was killed in the line of duty. Taylor, who was thirty-four, and his partner, a laid-off cop who'd just been rehired, had been instructed to respond to an anonymous 911 call. Several men who'd just robbed a local McDonald's were on the third floor of a house on Linden Street, a relatively safe block. The officers checked upstairs and found no one there, so they descended to the first floor, to the apartment at the end of the narrow hallway. The officers knocked. They could hear people inside, but no one answered. They knocked again. Eventually someone inside cracked open the door, peeked out, and then quickly slammed it shut. Taylor's partner started trying to kick the door in. Taylor realized that if the people inside were armed, his partner would be leaving himself wide open and quickly pushed him away. As he was doing so, one of the people inside threw the door open, stuck the barrel of a sawed-off shotgun against Taylor's chest, and fired.

Sekzer, one of Taylor's best friends, took his body to the morgue and asked to be left alone. He lifted up the sheet to say goodbye to his colleague. "I could have put my fist through the hole in his chest," he says. "I remember thinking, 'At least he went quickly.' "

37.

NEW York's long night of looting was followed by another hot day, with temperatures climbing into the high nineties. The power still wasn't back. The streets were littered with debris, the skyscrapers empty, the subways hushed. Here and there a building burned for no apparent reason.

Con Ed needed to disconnect the entire system so that all its component parts could be inspected for damage. Then, once everything was reconnected, the juice had to be restored slowly to avoid any surges that might cause another failure. High-density areas were the first priority, creating a perverse situation: The depleted slums were among the last to get their power back. Not until 10:39 Thursday night, July 14, twenty-five hours after New York was first unplugged, was the entire city back up and running. Only one fire was still burning out of control in Brooklyn.

Many New Yorkers had followed the events of the night through the city's two all-news radio stations, WINS and WCBS. Some woke up the following morning to learn that their city had been ransacked. The *Times* was already on press when the blackout hit, but the paper's reporters and editors hastily cobbled together a new page one in their candlelit newsroom. POWER FAILURE BLACKS OUT NEW YORK; THOUSANDS TRAPPED IN THE SUBWAYS; LOOTERS AND VANDALS HIT SOME AREAS, read the six-column banner headline. The *Daily News* borrowed several generator-powered klieg lights from the crew of *Superman*, which was being filmed in the lobby of its building (the huge globe made it the picture-perfect newspaper lobby) and managed to publish a late edition. The wood, in tabspeak, was BLACKOUT!

But it was the local news broadcasts that really brought the story home, the searing images of tenements in flames, of twisted metal and broken glass, of shirtless young men strutting brazenly down crowded streets, pushing shopping carts filled with TV sets, or balancing new couches on their backs like seesaws. This was urban decay on fast forward. Watching the endless loop of destruction proved uniquely unsettling, not so much because of the ruination itself, devastating though it was, as because of what it seemed to suggest, or reveal, about the city. The conservative social critic Midge Decter likened the sensation to "having been given a sudden glimpse into the foundations of one's house and seen, with horror, that it was utterly infested and rotting away." She then carried the metaphor to its logical, if alarmist, conclusion: "No one will be at ease in the edifice again for a long time, if ever."

The final tallies were plenty unnerving in their own right: 1,037 fires, 14 of them multiple alarmers; 1,616 damaged and/or looted stores; 3,776 people arrested. This last figure may well have been the most shocking. In 1964 an off-duty white cop had shot a black teenager, touching off several days of rioting in Harlem and Brooklyn; 373 arrests had been made. Four years later, in the disturbances that followed the assassination of the Reverend Dr. Martin Luther King, Jr., 465 people had been hauled in. Taken together, then, the arrests from the city's two most recent disorders amounted to one-quarter of those arrested during the blackout of '77.

It was the largest mass arrest in the city's history, yet it had barely dented the momentum of the looting. As one commanding officer in the South Bronx put it, "The restoration of power and the sunrise were the main elements in containing the emergency." *The Chief*, the newspaper of the city's municipal unions, was quick to blame this reality on the layoffs two years earlier, which had reduced the size of the police force by five thousand to twenty-five thousand. The paper warned, ominously, that unless these men were rehired right away, it was doubtful that the Police Department would be able to cope with another citywide power failure.

The consensus quickly emerged that the cops had exercised commendable restraint. Department officials pointed proudly to their Firearms Discharge Review Board, which had been established several years earlier to discourage officers from firing too freely. "To put matters quite bluntly, we're shooting less . . . and hitting more," Deputy Police Commissioner Frank McLoughlin told *New York* magazine in an article headlined WHY THE COPS DIDN'T SHOOT. The NYPD reported that only two officers in the entire city had discharged their weapons the night of the blackout. According to the official record, in one case, a Staten Island cop's gun had gone off accidentally; in the other, an officer in Queens shot a looter's dog. Much had appearently been learned from the riots of the sixties, which had underscored the dangers of overreacting.

"But what about underreacting?" asked angry store owners who couldn't understand why the police hadn't been more aggressive. Commissioner Codd had left himself wide open to these attacks when he said on TV a couple of days after the blackout that "sufficient force," even "deadly force," would have been used if the rioters had tried to move beyond the confines of the ghettos. Conservatives quickly rallied to the cause. An editorial in the *Post* blasted what it called Commissioner Codd's "absurd order to go slowly . . . as the mobs ran wild." In the *News*, syndicated columnist Patrick Buchanan nostalgically recalled the far less measured response to the 1863 rioting, which had also erupted on July 13, by Irish immigrants who were protesting the Civil War draft. "With a clear conscience," Buchanan wrote, "President Lincoln dispatched the Army of the Potomac, which in turn dispatched a number of the rioters."

The commissioner of corrections, Benjamin Malcolm, had spent the night of the blackout visiting prisons, first Rikers, where eight inmates had escaped through a hole in the wall at the onset of the power outage, and then the Bronx House of Detention, where a riot had broken out. Prisoners were setting fire to their mattresses, breaking furniture, and clogging toilets to cause flooding. They had hurled a steel bed frame through a window and were lowering a string of knotted blankets down to the street when order was finally restored.

For Malcolm, a veteran of the prison riots of the sixties and the first black to hold his position, the biggest challenge was still ahead: what to do with all the arrested looters. Virtually every cell in the city's seventy-three precincts was full to overcrowding, as were the prisons. "City buses filled with black men in chains," wrote Timothy Crouse in *The Village Voice*, "were roaming from jail to jail looking for empty cells."

With nowhere else to house prisoners, paddy wagons and squad cars had started delivering them to criminal court buildings a couple of hours before dawn. Officers signed in the accused by flashlight and went about packing them into detention pens meant to hold prisoners for an hour or two before their arraignments.

Morning broke, and police wagons continued rolling up and unloading more prisoners. Before long, at 100 Centre Street, Manhattan's House of Detention, they were being stuffed into the windowless basement, where a gasoline-generated spotlight had made the already uncomfortably hot room unbearably so. Soon it too was full. Malcolm had no choice but to petition a judge to reopen the Tombs, a prison that had been ordered closed in 1974 for its inhumane conditions.

As the day wore on, the bottleneck continued to build. Arraignments were stalled by missing paperwork and missing officers, many of whom were still out in the streets making arrests, instead of hanging around the courthouse waiting for their cases to be called. Both evidence and witnesses able to make identifications from the dark, chaotic night were in short supply. So were the rap sheets and fingerprint records necessary for judges to set bail, as the power outage had knocked out communications with the central computer in Albany, where everything was stored.

As of 3 p.m. on July 14, the Bronx had worked through two cases, two more than Brooklyn could claim. At 4:30, the courts closed down on account of darkness. The office of the Manhattan DA had prepared 250 felony complaints over the course of the day, but without lights the judges couldn't read them. "The city was not ready," was the self-evident conclusion offered several months later by the state committee charged with assessing New York's "emergency preparedness."

Before long civil rights groups had been alerted to the squalid conditions in the overcrowded court detention pens. There was no bedding to cover the steel benches, a shortage of bathrooms, and no medical attention for the scores of drug addicts in withdrawal and accused looters sporting nightstick abrasions and lacerations from broken glass. Thirty-six men were in a holding pen twenty feet long and nine feet deep in downtown Manhattan. The president of the Corrections Officers Benevolent Association warned that if something wasn't done soon, "our prisons will explode and lives will be lost."

The Legal Aid Society urged the courts to grant the accused parole until their arrest records were located. When that failed, they drafted a statement calling attention to the "abhorrent conditions" in the cellblocks. The suspected looters, the statement went on, were victims of "extreme misery caused by extraordinary unemployment . . . and massive cutbacks in services." Hundreds of protesters marched in front of Con Ed's headquarters on Irving Place, waving placards that read, JAIL LUCE NOT THE LOOTERS and PUT CON EDISON UNDER MARTIAL LAW, NOT THE POOR AND HUNGRY. A new crisis was emerging. "On Wednesday night professional burglars and amateur scavengers disgraced us," wrote Murray Kempton, "and since then we have disgraced ourselves with our treatment of those arrested for looting."

Over the weekend, Corrections Commissioner Malcolm and a few of his fellow officials toured Brooklyn's criminal court building, which had been forced to house 510 detainees, roughly five times its capacity. Two dozen men had been packed into an eight-by-twelve cell for several days. The temperature outside was inching its way toward 100 degrees; the temperature inside was easily 120. There were puddles of urine and vomit on the floor. One of Malcolm's colleagues compared the pens with the galley of a slave ship. Malcolm, who had seen some grim prison conditions in his day, called these "the worst I've ever seen" and promptly barred the press from entering.

On Monday morning a suspected looter was found dead in a basement cell. That afternoon the temperature in the city hit a hundred for the first time in more than ten years. Con Ed appealed to New Yorkers to use electricity sparingly. (100 DEGREES AND THREAT OF A BROWNOUT, blared the front page of the *Post*.)

The next day the mercury touched 102, making it New York's hottest July 19 on record. It was the seventh straight day of the heat wave, with no end in sight. Thousands of gallons of water gushed out of hydrants across the five boroughs, triggering a citywide water alert. Beame announced that anyone caught watering his lawn or washing his car would be subject to a fine. On Thursday, the twenty-first, the ninth day of the heat wave, the temperature hit 104, making it the second-hottest day in the city's 108-year weather history.

By now, at least, the city's twenty facsimile machines and four computer printers were again spitting out fingerprints and arrest records from Albany. Emergency arraignment courts worked around the clock, dismissing cases, remanding suspects to prison, or setting bail. Most judges heeded Mayor Beame's call to prosecute looters to the fullest extent of the law, meting out stiff bails and refusing to plea-bargain with anyone whose record showed prior felony arrests. "Because this happened during an emergency," one Brooklyn judge told *Newsweek*, "it was more than just burglary."

All 3,776 prisoners had finally been arraigned. But the reckoning with the damage, both physical and psychic, had only just begun.

38.

IN 1969, Norman Mailer, who was pursuing a lark candidacy for the New York City mayoralty at the time, wrote an essay for *The New York Times Magazine* headlined CAN NEW YORK SURVIVE? In July 1977, the question no longer sounded rhetorical.

A few days after the blackout, Union Carbide, the manufacturer of Eveready batteries, took out a full-page ad in the *Daily News* headlined IT WASN'T A TOTAL POWER FAILURE. The ad pointed out that flashlights had helped lead people safely down dark stairwells and that portable radios had provided vital information to guide citizens through the crisis. "Whatever else may have happened Wednesday night, we can never forget that tens of thousands of New Yorkers rose to the occasion," it continued. "Eveready is proud of whatever part our products may have played in this service. We're even prouder of the New Yorkers who used them to help others."

What the ad failed to mention was that Union Carbide was in the process of moving its corporate headquarters out of New York City—not, as a company spokesman later pointed out, merely because of the crime and high cost of living but because of its "changing ethnic mix, which makes some people uncomfortable, and the graffiti on the subways, the dirt on the streets, and a lot of other things."

Between 1973 and 1976 the city had lost 340,000 jobs. How many more were sure to follow now? An executive recruiter from Chicago told a reporter that he had been handling an alarming number of résumés from people who were willing to go any place but New York, and that was *before* the blackout.

Ten days after the lights went out, stolen property recovered in raids or returned by citizens was still arriving at the property clerk's storehouse in Queens at the rate of five truckloads a day. The estimates from the blackout—the damage, the stolen merchandise, the lost business, the spoiled perishables—fluctuated daily, spiking as high as $1 billion before settling at $150 million. (A year later a definitive congressional study put the losses at a little more than twice that.) The debate was academic. Whatever the final sum, it was one that the barely solvent city would not be able to manage. Any hopes that Con Ed might feel obligated to help out were quickly dashed when Luce kicked the blame upstairs, calling the cause of the blackout "an act of God."

It seemed safe to assume that many of the looted stores would never reopen. Most of them were in dangerous neighborhoods where insurance was either unavailable or prohibitively expensive. A number of those that were insured had civil disobedience clauses in their policies, which precluded claims for losses incurred during riots. Moreover, most of the looted merchants had moved out of the neighborhoods years earlier and had no real stake in their survival. Given what they had just lived through, there wasn't much reason to believe that they'd be interested in rebuilding their businesses there.

The rest of the country was hardly sympathetic. In the late sixties the rioting in Detroit and Newark had served to draw attention to the plight of America's ghettos. The 1977 blackout looting in New York only seemed to confirm everyone's worst suspicions about the city. To go with the fictional portrayals of the dangerous, dystopian metropolis in recent movies such as *Taxi Driver*, there was now documentary footage.

The Washington Post set the tone, calling the looting "an indictment of the state of the city, its government, and its people." A spokesman for Miami's Chamber of Commerce pointed out that America had expected the worst, and New York had not let it down. Even *Christianity Today* weighed in, suggesting that God had sent his judgment on a city that had turned away from him. "The lack of electricity lit up the reality of people's minds and hearts," the magazine wrote. "That's what people are like when separated from light and *the* light." Writing in *The New Yorker*, Andy Logan summed up the popular sentiment thus: "Instead of comfort, what New York received in the first days after the disaster was often the punitive judgment that it had just got what it deserved, considering the kind of place it was."

President Carter also rebuffed New York, denying the city's request to be declared a major disaster area, a designation that would have given it access to badly needed federal funds. Since his election Carter had come to the aid of no fewer than fourteen regions, including some shrimping towns off the coast of his beloved Georgia that had endured a cold winter. But the blackout, the president insisted, was not a *natural* disaster and thus didn't qualify for the Federal Disaster Relief Program. The man who had vowed never to tell New York to drop dead was doing just that.

It wasn't the first time either. As a candidate Carter had criticized President Ford for having "no urban policy." To date, Carter's own urban policy had been one of studied indifference. Most noteworthy had been his failure to make good on, or even acknowledge, his campaign pledge to assume the city's welfare costs, which were currently exceeding its education budget. (Even Mayor Beame had written off the president. "Jimmy Carter still loves me," the mayor joked at the annual follies put on by the City Hall press corps. "The last time I met with him, he told me he had a whole list of items to help the city. But he left the list in his other sweater.")

Surely, in the wake of the blackout a presidential visit to one of New York City's devastated slums was in order. After all, during his presidential campaign, Carter had worked New York's black churches until his hymn-humming throat was sore. "We do not anticipate there being such a trip," responded the president's deputy press secretary at a late July White House press briefing. (First Brother Billy, meanwhile, was making plans to come to '21' to do a TV spot for Peanut Lolita, a new liqueur made from peanuts.)

Not even a pointed attack from Vernon Jordan, the executive director of the National Urban League, could stir Carter to action. "The sad fact," Jordan told some seven thousand league members at a conference on July 24, "is that the Administration is not living up to the first commandment of politics: Help those who help you." Instead of redoubling his efforts to help the urban needy, Carter summoned Jordan to the Oval Office to dress him down, assuring him that he had a "genuine interest in poor people . . . and that statements that argue to the contrary are damaging to the hopes and aspirations of those poor people."

When it came to New York anyway, the problem for Carter wasn't so much the black poor as it was the white middle class, one Italian middle-class enclave in particular: Howard Beach, Queens, an otherwise tranquil bayfront community that had managed to plunge the American president into an international crisis within months of his inauguration. At issue was a 1,350-mile-an-hour plane called the Concorde, whose manufacturers, Britain and France, wanted very much to land it at John F. Kennedy Airport, which happened to abut Howard Beach. It was bad enough, the people of Howard Beach complained, that they had to endure the constant roar of ordinary airplanes skimming their rooftops, but to add to the mix the boom of a supersonic jet breaking the sound barrier—and one that hadn't even been built in this country!—was too much to ask.

The angry protests against what one local politician called "the Edsel of the aircraft industry" paid off. The Port Authority of New York, which had jurisdiction over JFK, banned the jet indefinitely. The French, who considered a berth at the airport critical to the plane's commercial success and thus to the economic viability of the French town where it was being assembled, didn't take the news well. "The airport is on the sea, and the sea is crowded by fishes, not by people," sputtered a disbelieving President Valéry Giscard d'Estaing.

The president defended the Concorde—CARTER TO QUEENS: DROP DEAF, the headlines might have read—and tried to explain to his respective foreign leaders that the decision was out of his hands. To no avail. France threatened to sabotage future projects with the United States, and warned that it might well withdraw from NATO because of this " 'Oward Beach."

And President Carter offered a beleaguered, postblackout New York a paltry $11.3 million in grants and loans—"a sop . . . a cover-up for federal inaction," harrumphed Bronx congressman and long shot mayoral candidate Herman Badillo.

39.

BACK up off the canvas, if still a little woozy, in the weeks after the blackout New York found itself groping to understand the nature of the beating it had just endured.

The last citywide blackout in 1965, when crime had actually dipped, offered an obvious, and not exactly reassuring, basis for comparison. "In ghastly contrast to 1965, when a spirit of unity and common sacrifice brightened every section in the darkened city," the *New York Post* editorialized on July 16, "New York was transformed into a series of seething battlegrounds."

There were important distinctions between the two blackouts. In '65, the lights blinked off at five-thirty on a seasonably cool November afternoon, meaning that people hadn't been out in the streets escaping their steamy tenements as they were in the sultry darkness of July 13. What's more, most store owners hadn't yet shuttered for the night, so many simply decided to stay put and protect their property for the duration of the blackout. But the circumstantial details went only so far. The rampage that followed hard on the heels of the onset of darkness in '77 could not be reasoned away by the temperature and the time of day.

How to explain it then? Two possibilities quickly emerged. Either the looters were heirs to the urban rioters of the sixties, members of what one columnist termed "the most significant class uprising in this decade," or they were hoodlums.

That the darkness had illuminated the state of New York's ghettos, where black and Hispanic teenage unemployment was hovering at 70 and 80 percent respectively, was irrefutable. The argument soon followed that the looting was, at bottom, an indictment of the city's financial fumblings, which had left too many people without jobs or safety nets to break their fall.

Campaigning in the days after the blackout for City Council, Ruth Messinger, a Bella Abzug acolyte, hammered the point: "It is indefensible that the fiscal crisis has been worked out on the backs of people . . . Unemployment breeds hunger, resentment, and hopelessness. Low wages, heavy inflation, and loss of services convince people that government is not meeting their basic needs. Our society has been stretched too thin. It took the blackout to expose this to full and public painful view."

President Carter himself, while not actually setting foot in New

York, echoed the theme in an Oval Office interview with the National Black Radio Network, calling the looting a reminder that "deteriorating urban areas have been neglected too long."

Writing on the op-ed page of the *Times*, Herbert Gutman, a professor of history at CUNY, went even further, linking the blackout pillaging to the 1902 rioting by Lower East Side Jewish housewives protesting the artificially inflated prices of kosher meat. A flood of angry letters poured in, opposing both Gutman's piece and a pair of *Times* editorials. "These people," concluded one of the editorials, "are victims of economic and social forces that they sense but do not understand . . . they are locked in a once-promising city, watching jobs and opportunity evaporate across the suburban horizon."

The truth was, for most New Yorkers, regardless of ethnicity or political persuasion, it was hard to square the images of marauding mobs that had already been indelibly etched into the city's consciousness with some abstract notion of social protest. A "pained message" (as Gutman had put it) from the ghettos? No, this felt more like criminals taking advantage of the darkness, and the safety found in numbers, to rob stores and destroy buildings.

And so the blackout backlash was born. At its worst, it was bigotry, hatred, a blindness to the cause-and-effect rapport between poverty and crime. One *Times* reader, for instance, accused the city's poor, en masse, of being welfare cheats. "We either cut them off completely, or we will have to face a drastic evaluation of the situation," he wrote. "The Puerto Ricans can go back to P.R. They belong there anyway, and if the blacks do not shape up they can go back to the South."

At its best, the backlash took the shape of an enlightened awareness that it was possible—no, imperative—to feel the pressing need to do something about New York's hurting neighborhoods, to find ways to create full-time long-term jobs and promote urban renewal from the ground up, without excusing the looters from taking responsibility for their actions. To do otherwise was patronizing, paternalistic, racist even. Those who pointed to the misery of life in New York's ghettos to explain the looting weren't just missing its real cause; they were perpetuating it by fostering diminished expectations for the underclass.

"We must end the vicious double standard that now governs politics, the news media and the society," declared Bruce Llewellyn, the Harlem-born owner of Fedco Foods. "Whites are expected to learn, but black children are assumed to be uneducable, are allowed to graduate illiterate. Whites are expected to obey the law, but blacks are allowed to defy it—so long as they confine their depredations to other blacks." Fedco's blackout losses totaled one million dollars, a third of what Llewellyn had paid for the supermarket chain, leveraging everything he owned in the process, eight years earlier. Explaining what had moved him to speak out, Llewellyn averred that the looting had turned the minds of too many New Yorkers into "poisonous mush."

40.

FROM the start some of the most unequivocal denunciations of the looters had come from the black community, where one difference between the disturbances of the 1960s and the blackout looting seemed especially apparent. In the sixties rioters had spared merchants with the foresight to mount "Soul Brother" signs in their windows. During the looting of '77 not only were black- and minority-owned businesses not spared, but they bore the brunt of the destruction.

"When you see a black florist on Nostrand Avenue wiped out, and a supermarket on the same street suffer the same fate, both black-owned, how can I buy excuses that no jobs and poverty motivated this mob action?" asked Woodrow Lewis, a black assemblyman from Brooklyn, a couple of days after the blackout. "We can't coddle or pamper acts of vandalism." It was not lost on Lewis that as bad as unemployment in the ghettos had been on July 13, with hundreds of stores cleaned out, and hundreds more demolished, it was now going to be far worse.

In fact, the pillaging had been fueled as much by an antiblack sentiment as by an antiwhite one. LeMans, a stylish men's clothing store that catered to middle-class blacks, had been the first place hit on Amsterdam Avenue, miles from central Harlem. Its coowners had started the business in 1968, on the back of a twenty-five-thousand-dollar loan from the Small Business Administration. When they arrived at the store to find the plundering in progress on the night of the thirteenth, one of the owners screwed up the courage to ask a looter, whose arms were full of designer suits, why. The answer came: "Your things were too high, man."

"Buy black" had been the mantra during the struggle for civil rights in the fifties and sixties. Now local church leaders and politicians were urging the community *not* to buy black if the merchant in question was hawking stolen goods. The *Amsterdam News* wrote that the real power failure was within the city's black leadership and decried the community's willingness to tolerate lawlessness and violence. "It is not enough not to condone looting," the paper declared in a front-page editorial; "we must forthrightly and adamantly condemn it."

Manhattan borough president and mayoral candidate Percy Sutton shared this view. On the Sunday morning after the blackout, Sutton, a slender, cocoa-colored man with a thin mustache, took to the pulpit at the Abyssinian Baptist Church, the massive Gothic cathedral at 138th Street and Seventh Avenue where Adam Clayton Powell, Jr., had once held court. "You can't, on Tuesday, buy a television set that was stolen from the store around the corner," Sutton said, "and then, on Sunday, go to church and call yourself a Christian."

His calls for harsh treatment for "those who took advantage of the darkness to rip and plunder, to pillage, loot, and burn" echoed through the gleaming marble interior.

It was a stirring speech, worthy of the great Powell himself, but Sutton already knew he was finished. The blackout looting was not racially motivated, yet the vast majority of those arrested were black. The white backlash would be impossible for any black candidate to overcome.

It was an especially cruel fate for the fifty-six-year-old Sutton, a master builder of color-blind alliances, who had long ago been tapped most likely to become New York's first black mayor. (*New York* magazine titled a May 1974 Sutton profile "Guess Who's Coming to Gracie Mansion.")

The son of a man who'd been born into slavery, Sutton learned his craft at the feet of New York's original black power broker, the Harlem Fox, J. Raymond Jones. As a lawyer and civil rights activist during the 1950s and 1960s, Sutton fought for desegregation: He respectfully scolded Attorney General Robert Kennedy for moving too slowly to redress racial inequality and was even thrown in jail for sitting in the white section of a segregated diner in Maryland. But with his natty three-piece suits and slicked-back hair, Sutton would never be mistaken for a black militant. In 1968, when Martin Luther King, Jr., was assassinated and violence threatened to engulf Harlem, Mayor Lindsay asked Sutton to walk the streets, urging blacks to exercise restraint. Sutton was more than happy to oblige.

So it was perhaps no surprise that when it came time to launch his mayoral drive in February 1977, Sutton had focused his energy on white voters. "Our first task was to make him a candidate that was acceptable to whites at a time of great racial polarization in the city," recalls his campaign manager, Frank Baraff. "Percy knew that at that point in history you were not going to become mayor by being the black candidate."

Sutton's campaign headquarters were not in Harlem but in an

empty office building along a strip of abandoned factories and car repair shops in Queens, the least black of New York's boroughs save for Staten Island. His first celebrity campaigner was the former middleweight boxing champion Italian-American Rocky Graziano, who pledged to help Sutton "KO crime."

There had been seventy-five felonies committed every hour in New York in 1976, making it the worst crime year in the city's history. In his radio ads, Sutton blatantly played to white New York's growing sense of fear: "New York City is a great city, but it's a city turned sick with the fear of crime. And who doesn't know where the criminals are? You do and I do. They're on our street corners, openly selling dope. They're in our hallways and in our schoolrooms and in our subways and in our streets. They're mugging and crippling our people. They're operating nursing homes and Medicaid mills. They're cheating, stealing, and driving away our families and our jobs. Crime has laid its violent hands all over us."

Not everyone agreed with Sutton's strategy. William Banks, who ran the campaign's Brooklyn operation, could see that the terminal state of New York's ghettos and the steady stream of grim unemployment data were empowering a new generation of militant, self-styled community leaders whom Sutton risked alienating. The ideological heirs to Malcolm X, they were men like Brooklyn's Sonny Carson, who went on to lead the campaign to expel Korean grocers from the black neighborhoods of Bed-Stuy and Flatbush, inspiring a story line in Spike Lee's *Do the Right Thing*.

"If you're going to make a chocolate cake, you've got to have the cake first," Banks told Sutton early in the campaign in an attempt to persuade him to focus on his black constituency. "Then maybe you can have a white icing."

"That's not my style," Sutton answered. "I'm running for the mayor of New York City. I've got to relate to all the people."

Even before the blackout, Sutton was coming around to Banks's point of view. In May the candidate relocated his headquarters from

Queens to Lenox Avenue in Harlem—"lest my base feel neglected"—and then called together the ministers of hundreds of black churches to help mobilize their congregations on his behalf. In June he swapped Rocky Graziano for the militant black icon Muhammad Ali. Having just caused a stir on a local morning news program by lashing out at the Jewish and Italian managers who had "robbed" him over the years, the aging heavyweight champion campaigned all afternoon with Sutton.

In the wake of the blackout Sutton's frustration at his inability to bridge New York's racial gap turned to anger. His mayoral dreams deflated, his faith in the integrationist ideal dented, he accused the white press of ignoring his campaign: "I am treated as Ralph Ellison's Invisible Man." Sutton brought the Reverend Jesse Jackson, Jr., to Harlem to echo the charge. "The media have tried to destroy Percy with indifference," the Reverend Jackson thundered at a rally on 125th Street. After he "picked Abe Beame up on his shoulders and walked him across this community," Jackson continued, referring to Sutton's support for Beame in the 1973 mayoral election, "the Jewish community has turned its back on Percy Sutton."

At the end of 1977 a bitter Sutton resigned "forever" from public life, saying simply, "I no longer want anything from the city."

PART THREE

41.

TO Osborn Elliott, whose job as New York's deputy mayor for economic development was to attract business to the city, the real disaster wasn't the blackout looting. It was the *New York Post*'s coverage of it. After scanning the paper on the Friday after the blackout—the front-page headline bayed, 24 HOURS OF TERROR—Elliott hastily dispatched a letter to the paper's publisher and editor in chief, Rupert Murdoch. "So your *New York Post* has now covered New York City's first big crisis since you took over," wrote Elliott. "Are you proud of what your headlines produced?"

Not long after assuming control of the paper, Murdoch had stood in the *Post*'s newsroom and assured his staff that he had no dramatic changes in mind, just a little freshening up. "Don't judge me by what you've heard about me," he said. "Judge me by what I do."

The first sign of change had been harmless enough. On January 3, 1977, Murdoch added a thick red stripe to the *Post*'s otherwise black-and-white front page. That same day the paper's gentlemanly gossip columnist, "Midnight" Earl Wilson, finally got some company, Page Six. (In its first month Page Six, a gossip column assembled by a team of reporters, spotted Woody Allen canoodling with a "very young girlfriend" at Elaine's; reported that Dorothy Hamill was carrying on with Dean Martin's son, Dino, Jr.; and quoted Muhammad Ali saying that he'd like to star in an all-black remake of *Ben Hur*.)

Murdoch was an active presence in the newsroom, writing and rewriting headlines, peering over reporters' shoulders, even answering telephones. Men with Australian accents—gangaroos, as veteran Posties called them—were soon roaming the paper's halls too. They liked the feel of the city, and they loved that the pubs stayed open past ten-thirty, but they had a lot to learn about New York. One of the new editors, Peter Michelmore, asked veteran reporter George Arzt about the ethnicity of the staff.

"We're mostly Jewish," Arzt replied.

"I haven't met many Jews," said Michelmore. "We were always taught that they had horns on their head."

"Mine are retractable," answered Arzt.

The most reviled of Murdoch's new editors was Edwin Bolwell, a short, squat, beery-looking Aussie prone to shouting and turning red in the face. Among other ignominous acts, Bolwell decided that the reviews by the *Post*'s young film critic, Frank Rich, were "too windy" and ordered them halved. Murray Kempton, who called Murdoch "Mr. Merdle," after the unscrupulous banker in Dickens's *Little Dorrit*, might well have suffered the same fate had the *Post*'s new editors been more successful parsing his sentences.

Bolwell was under specific orders from above to punch up the paper's headlines and copy, but the rhythm of the tabloid beat eluded him. Fortunately for Murdoch, some of his other editors, most of whom had toiled for one of his papers in London or Sydney, had a better feel for the music. Topless women wouldn't fly in New York, but that didn't mean cheesecake was out. In March 1977 the *Post* ran twenty-one items on Farrah Fawcett-Majors, the feather-haired star of *Charlie's Angels.* Stories became shorter, pictures bigger, headlines louder. On the eve of the execution of serial killer Gary Gilmore, the first person put to death in America in a decade, a peaceful protest took place in front of his Utah penitentiary. THREAT TO STORM GILMORE PRISON, read the front page of the *Post.* Paul Sann quit in protest the following day.

Change was also afoot on the editorial page, where the aging anti-Communist Wechsler had become known as the Red Menace. By the middle of July the Murdoch makeover was almost complete. "Dolly Schiff's liberal backwater," writes Murdoch biographer William Shawcross, "had become a roiling, clamorous torrent of news, mostly conservative opinion and hucksterish entertainment."

Murdoch came into the paper's un-air-conditioned office at dawn the morning after the blackout and quickly sweated through his white dress shirt. The power outage prevented the *Post* from publishing that afternoon, but the paper's "Blackout Special," complete with a pullout section headlined A CITY RAVAGED, was on the streets the following morning.

Mayor Beame denounced the paper's arriviste publisher, calling Murdoch an "Australian carpetbagger" who "came here to line his pockets by peddling fiction in the guise of news." The *Post*, the mayor continued, "was making *Hustler* magazine look like the *Harvard* [*Law*] *Review*." Pete Hamill also turned on Murdoch, comparing the publisher to a guest who vomits at a dinner party: Everyone looks at him with alarm and pity, but no one knows quite what to do with him. "Something vaguely sickening is happening to that newspaper," Hamill wrote, "and it is spreading through the city's psychic life like a stain."

Murdoch himself could not have cared less. The *Post*'s July 15 blackout special exceeded the paper's usual Friday sales by seventy-five thousand. It was safe to say that the city was on the brink of its first newspaper war since the fifties.

> *Baseball has long merchandised its similarity of real life. But these Yankees seem stunned, unequipped to discuss what they are part of in the limited jargon of the locker room. Often, the Yankees cut too close to the bone. They resemble the suffering, everyday world far too much.*
>
> THOMAS BOSWELL, *THE WASHINGTON POST*

AT baseball's mid-July All-Star break, Chicago had two first-place teams and the Los Angeles Dodgers, who were being managed by a rookie skipper named Tommy Lasorda, had left the world champion Cincinnati Reds in the dust. But the biggest surprise of all was the close race in the Eastern Division of the American League, where the mighty Yankees were running third behind the streaky

Red Sox and an overachieving Baltimore Orioles team that started no fewer than five rookies.

Billy Martin's pitchers were refusing to stay healthy, and his boss, George Steinbrenner, was refusing to leave him alone. At a Baltimore Hilton on July 9, the Yankees' pilot had confided in Thurman Munson that his biggest concern was how he'd support his family, which included two ex-wives and children from both marriages, if he were fired. "As we spoke, tears welled up in his eyes," the catcher later remembered. "To avoid having anybody see him so upset, we took a walk around the block until he could clear the air a little."

Munson had no shortage of complaints himself. He was still bitter about his contract and the *Sport* magazine story, and he'd been taking an unholy beating behind the plate. The foul tips that were forever crashing into his mask had been causing throbbing headaches, his right pinkie was lined with stitches, and a loose pipe dangling from a batting cage had gouged a hole in his forehead. Adding insult to injuries, Carlton Fisk was on his way to outpolling him yet again in the All-Star balloting, and this year's game was going to be played in the Bronx. Not only would Munson be playing behind his nemesis, but he'd be doing so in his own goddamn ballpark.

The day after his walk with Martin, Munson took two reporters aside in the hotel lobby. After they agreed to refer to him only as a "prominent Yankee," Munson proceeded to carve up Steinbrenner for, among other things, forcing lineup changes on his embattled manager: "George doesn't care about anybody's feelings. To him, we're not professionals, we're all employees. He treats everybody like that. He's destroyed Billy. He's made him nothing."

It was just Martin's luck. Munson had meant to help his manager's cause; instead, he'd made him look powerless. When the story broke, the Yankees were en route to Milwaukee, and Steinbrenner was in a lather of his own. The moment the team arrived, he told Martin to call a press conference to insist that the front office wasn't meddling in his affairs. It was another humiliation for Martin: As much as he denied it, the newspapermen knew that Steinbrenner had dictated the statement.

By now Martin, never a fan of the free press—"if writers knew any goddamn thing, they would be managers," he once said—was getting more fed up than usual with the media. In Martin's day the papers didn't use quotes that made the team look bad. What's more, ball clubs were covered through their managers. Between his big-footed owner and loudmouthed players, even those who were only trying to help, Martin never had a clue to what was going to be in the papers, especially when it came to the scandal-mongering *Post.*

If he couldn't stop disgruntled Yankees from talking, Martin could at least threaten to keep the press out of earshot when they did. Before the first game in Milwaukee on July 12, he called a meeting with the beat reporters to warn them that he was going to bar them—"Not everyone, just certain writers"—from the clubhouse and the team plane and bus if they continued to use "off-the-cuff comments." The threat was based of course on an assumption that Martin knew to be false: Every one of the quotes that had stoked clubhouse controversy since the spring had been spoken with deliberate and malicious intent. Some of the beat reporters who covered the 1977 Yankees enjoyed the locker room intrigue; others just wanted to get back to writing about baseball. That wasn't an option.

On July 13, a few hours before darkness descended on New York, Steinbrenner turned up in Milwaukee. He was just in time to watch his team lose a heartbreaker. The Brewers had beaten up on Catfish Hunter, taking a 9–3 lead into the top of the eighth, when the Yankees scored five to pull within one. The tying run, in the person of Reggie Jackson, came up with two outs in the ninth and struck out on three pitches.

Munson and Lou Piniella went out for dinner after the game and talked, inevitably, about the state of the clubhouse. A few drinks later they decided to go have a word with Steinbrenner. It was after midnight by the time Steinbrenner came to the door in his pajamas and invited them in. Munson told him either to fire Martin or to get off his back: "Nobody can live with the kind of pressure you're putting on him." Piniella also defended his manager, urging Steinbrenner to strike the clauses in his contract that kept him on permanent parole.

At about two in the morning Martin came tottering upstairs. He had just closed the hotel bar, but he wasn't too loaded to recognize the voices in the owner's suite. Martin knocked.

"Do you have a couple of my players in there?" he asked.

"No," Steinbrenner answered, opening the door a crack.

Martin barged in and started looking around. Huddling together in the bathroom were Munson and Piniella, who somehow managed to reassure Martin that they weren't plotting against him.

This time, at least, the story didn't make the papers—not then anyway. (In a couple of weeks Steinbrenner told a reporter about it off the record. In his version, Munson and Piniella had urged him to take a stronger hand to the team's troubles.)

A few days later the forty-eighth All-Star game brought a badly needed respite, both for Billy Martin, who showed up late to the pregame press conference and never removed his sunglasses, and for New York. "For this night," wrote Maury Allen in the *Post*, "blackouts and brownouts will be forgotten, looting will not be a topic of conversation and the oppressive heat will be ignored."

The regular season resumed in 104-degree heat in the Bronx on Thursday, July 21, with a twin bill against Milwaukee. The Yankees came thundering out of the gate. Catfish Hunter blanked the Brewers in the afternoon affair, and Ed Figueroa took a 4–0 lead into the ninth inning of the night game. That's when the wheels came off. Three errors later the score was tied. The Brewers won it in the tenth. Still reeling come Friday, the Yankees lost again.

By the time Martin arrived at the ballpark Saturday morning, the heat wave had finally broken, but he was experiencing no relief. Reports of his imminent dismissal were again swirling, and this time

Steinbrenner made sure he was unavailable to deny them. Martin's friend Phil Rizzuto suggested that he request a meeting with the front office to ask about the rumors. Martin said he'd made that mistake before, in Texas. "I called Brad Corbett and said, 'What about these rumors?' He said, 'They aren't rumors.' " Neither were these. Earlier that morning Gabe Paul had interviewed Martin's third base coach, Dick Howser, for the job and had alerted Howard Cosell to stand by for a big story.

After a sleepless Saturday night at his apartment in Jersey, Martin waited for the fateful call. Sunday's *Daily News* carried a report that Howser had turned down the job but that "Yankee bosses are hot on the phone looking for a new man." Martin drove to the ballpark and sat in his office, drinking coffee and smoking a cigar beneath his mounted bonefish long past the time he usually changed into his uniform. With nothing left to lose, he told the newspapermen that he'd seen the handwriting on the clubhouse wall way back in Fort Lauderdale, when Steinbrenner stormed into the locker room after a game to berate him in front of his players, and Martin yelled at him to get the hell out of his locker room. "What all of this is doing," Martin said, "is making a martyr out of me."

The next day, Monday, July 25, it was Steinbrenner who summoned the newspapermen to a ninety-minute meeting around the polished wood table in his Yankee Stadium office. Martin was still his manager—by now Walter Alston, the erstwhile manager of the Dodgers, had also turned down the job—but Steinbrenner wasn't planning to issue a vote of confidence. "When is somebody going to have enough intelligence to say . . . maybe the guy's in the wrong profession?" he said. Later Steinbrenner produced a list of seven qualifications, which the newspapermen promptly named "the Seven Commandments," that he expected Martin to meet if he wanted to hang on to his job. Two stood out: "Is he emotionally equipped to lead the men under him?" and "Is he honorable?"

Steinbrenner hardly needed to be reminded of Martin's popularity in New York, but one of the writers did so anyway. "He's the little man and the people can identify with him," Steinbrenner acknowledged. "But . . . New York's a pretty sophisticated, astute place, and there comes a time when even the fans wake up."

The only thing that New York's fans were waking up to was a deep and abiding hatred of George Steinbrenner. After all, who was a man found guilty of making illegal donations to the Nixon campaign, a man whose company was being investigated by the Justice Department for fraudulent billing practices, to tell *Billy Martin* about honor? *New York* magazine, still an unfailing gauge of the city's temper, captured the consensus in an article headlined GEORGE STEINBRENNER, GO HOME! (Among other things, its author, Jeff Greenfield, observed: "Billy Martin was helping the Yankees win titles when Steinbrenner was dreaming of his first leisure suit.")

On Tuesday, July 26, the Seven Commandments were all over the papers. The first-place Orioles were in town for a three-game set, and it was no secret that if the Yankees didn't take at least two, it was Billy Martin who would be going home.

When the Yankees' skipper emerged from the dugout with his lineup card that night, 32,097 fans stood and whistled encouragement. Martin tipped his cap once, twice, three times.

The din died shortly thereafter, when the O's took a quick lead in the top half of the first on a single by Martin's old nemesis Elliott Maddox. Come the home half of the ninth, Baltimore was clinging to a 4–2 lead. With one on and one out, the Yankees' Cliff Johnson lumbered to the plate and hammered the second pitch he saw into the seats to square things at four. Reggie finished it off in the tenth, admiring his 420-foot line drive as it dropped from the sky into the fifteenth row of the bleachers.

The next night, July 27, the fans were roaring again, and the first pitch was more than an hour away. Steinbrenner, who was sitting in his office with a reporter from *Newsweek*, went to the window to see what all the fuss was about. It was Martin playing a little pregame pepper. "He hasn't had a bat in his hand on the field in six weeks, but after he got an ovation last night, he needs to milk the fans for more," Steinbrenner snarled. "The sad thing is that it means so much to him, and he has no idea how shallow it really is."

On July 28 the O's took game two of the series, roughing up Yankees' ace Catfish Hunter in a manner that had become all too familiar. The stage was set. "Yeah, this is a big game," Munson said in the clubhouse before the rubber match the following afternoon. "But do we win this one for Billy, George or the team? I haven't quite got straight yet which one comes first."

The Yankees proceeded to pummel the Birds, 14–2, on fifteen hits. Reggie watched the feast from the dugout. According to his manager, he had hyperextended his left elbow during a recent collision with Mickey Rivers. No one remembered the collision, and in any case wouldn't he have hurt his *right* elbow if he had run into the team's center fielder? "Everybody knows that when you get hit on the right elbow, it's the left elbow that gets hurt," Reggie answered when questioned about the discrepancy.

42.

STORES were still tallying up their blackout losses, looters were still being sentenced, and New Yorkers were still living with the daily anxiety that the underclass might rise up again when the tabloids gave the fragile city another reason to be afraid of the dark.

For the past twelve months a serial killer, New York's first since the 1930s, had been preying on young women (chiefly brunettes) in the outer boroughs (chiefly Queens). Since July 29, 1976, when he first attacked two young women on a residential street in a working-class Italian neighborhood in the North Bronx, the so-called Son of Sam had killed five and injured six.

The approaching anniversary of his first attack prompted a flood of stories across the country—even public television's *MacNeil/Lehrer Report* devoted an entire show to the manhunt—but nothing compared with the frenzied coverage in the city's warring tabloids. For the *News* and the *Post*, anything Sam-related was newsworthy. Reporters visited the families of all the victims ("A Year Can't Erase Their Grief"), endlessly rehearsed the facts of the case, covered the nonexistent progress of the investigation, and wrote up a steady stream of psychological profiles based on interviews with so-called "expert psychiatrists."

Until recently the city's sense of fear had been building slowly. The Bronx detectives charged with investigating the first attack initially suspected an ex-boyfriend who had recently moved out west. In a city that averaged fifteen hundred homicides a year, the vast majority of which were committed by acquaintances of the victims, there was no reason to assume this one was any different, at least until they questioned the suspect and test-fired a .44-caliber gun that had been purchased in his New Mexico neighborhood. The bullets didn't match.

On October 23 there was another attack, this time on a young couple sitting in a blue Volkswagen Beetle on a quiet block in Flushing, Queens. A month later it was two teenage girls in Floral Park, Queens, a virtually crime-free working-class Italian neighborhood. The girls were chatting late at night on the steps of a white frame house when a man in an army fatigue jacket approached asking for directions. Before they could answer, he pulled a gun from his waistband. Neighbors heard nothing but the crack of the pistol and the subsequent screams. The *Long Island Press*, the only paper that covered the attack, quoted a Queens detective on the shooting: "This is not something that usually occurs out here. It may never happen again."

Two months later, on a bitterly cold Saturday night in late January, it did. The victims were sitting in a Pontiac Firebird in Forest Hills, Queens, waiting for the engine to warm up. Captain Joseph Borrelli, the head of homicide for Queens, arrived at the crime scene and noticed a .44-caliber slug sitting on the dashboard. One of the sergeants recalled that there had been a couple of unsolved .44-caliber shootings in Queens in recent months, plus the one over the summer in the Bronx.

The following day Borrelli brought the detectives on these various cases together for a private meeting in his Queens office. The similarities were hard to ignore. Not only had all the victims been young women or couples in the outer boroughs, but the weapon used in every attack, a .44-caliber Charter Arms revolver, was an unusual one. (It had been designed for sky marshals several years earlier in the wake of a rash of hijackings; because of the gun's low muzzle velocity, bullets fired from it wouldn't puncture the fuselage of an aircraft.) Still, Borrelli told everyone present to keep mum until they were certain. Someone apparently didn't. A few days later, the *Long Island Press* published a brief story reporting that police were considering the possibility that these attacks were linked.

Conclusive proof came when the killer struck again in Forest Hills in early March. The victim, a Columbia student named Virginia Voskerichian, was walking home from the subway shortly after sunset. As she turned onto Dartmouth, the dimly lit street that marks the start of Forest Hills Gardens, an upscale enclave of Tudor-style homes, a man with a gun jumped in front of her. Voskerichian lifted her textbooks to her face. The killer put his gun against them and squeezed the trigger.

The bullet was extracted from Voskerichian's head the next morning and placed under a microscope at the Police Academy on Twentieth Street in Manhattan. Joseph Coffey, a Queens homicide detective, was on the Columbia campus interviewing Voskerichian's acquaintances when a ballistics expert at the academy beeped him to say he'd matched the grooves on the Voskerichian bullet with the lines on the fragments from the other slugs.

The next afternoon, March 10, reporters packed into the 112th Precinct station house in Forest Hills for a news conference. With Mayor Beame standing beside him, Police Commissioner Codd made the announcement: The bullets that killed Voskerichian, Freund, and Lauria and that wounded DiMasi, Lomino, and Denaro all had been issued from the same .44-caliber revolver. "Be careful," Codd warned, "especially the young women."

In the weeks that followed, the side streets of Forest Hills were deserted by dusk. "I'm scared to death," a female student at City College told the *Long Island Press.* A neighborhood vigilante group was formed to patrol the neighborhood. Five hundred residents crowded into a public school auditorium to air their fears and demand more police protection.

The rest of March passed without incident, as did the first two weeks of April. Then, on April 17, the .44-caliber killer returned to the North Bronx. The victims were parked in a Mercury Montego on a dark service road off the Hutchinson River Parkway. When the detectives pulled their bodies out of the car, an envelope addressed to Captain Borrelli fell to the ground. Inside was a four-page letter, handwritten in slanted block letters. The NYPD refused to make its contents public, but the *Daily News* learned enough for a front-page story the following day: KILLER TO COPS: "I'LL DO IT AGAIN." (The actual wording in the letter was "I'll be back!") The *News*'s police source told the paper that the letter writer lived in "a nightmare world of blood-sucking vampires and Frankenstein monsters" and that he had "indicated his belief that homicide officers don't know what they're doing."

Days later the Police Department created a central unit, Operation Omega, to coordinate the investigation. Thirty detectives were to be posted to the new division. A few of the city's best men refused to go. They were sure the police would never catch the killer and worried that the assignment would damage their careers. Many of those who did join Omega were in their early forties, lived in one of the outer boroughs, and had teenage daughters.

Deputy Inspector Timothy Dowd, a sixty-one-year-old Irish-American with neatly combed gray hair and steely blue eyes, was placed in charge. Though he had some major homicide cases under his belt, Dowd was considered bookish by police standards. He had studied Latin and literature at City College, and he was famous for kicking ungrammatical arrest reports back to his men, a habit that had earned him the nickname Captain Comma.

Dowd's new task force was based on the second floor of the 109th Precinct, a modern brick building not far from Shea Stadium in Flushing. It was a sleepy station house chosen precisely because of its remote location. The walls of the office were soon covered with pictures from the various crime scenes; detailed maps of the Bronx and Queens showing the times, dates, and places of the shootings; two composite sketches of the suspect; and glossy photos of a black revolver with a brown handle, a .44-caliber Charter Arms Bulldog.

Leads were scarce, and the task force had no choice but to try everything. Psycholinguists studied the handwriting of the letter to Captain Borrelli, while psychiatrists studied its contents. The ensuing psychological profiles—the killer is a paranoid schizophrenic, a loner who lives in a cheap furnished room, who feels rejected by women and may even consider himself possessed—didn't help investigators much, but when leaked to the press, they immediately enhanced the suspect's aura of mystery and stoked the city's sense of fear.

Detectives tracked down and test-fired each of the 56 Charter Arms Bulldogs registered in the New York area by shooting a bullet into a large tank of water, where nothing could obscure the markings left by the barrel of the gun. When that yielded nothing, they set about trying to locate every one of the 28,000 Bulldogs manufactured since 1972, an effort hindered by the fact that 677 of these guns had been reported stolen. Detectives pored over the medical records of local mental hospitals, exhaustively researched the various victims in hopes of finding any connection, and followed up on hundreds of tips called into a .44-caliber hotline.

Borrelli brought a psychic to the scenes of the various crimes. Dowd read tracts on demonic possession and even studied the Bible, looking for clues. Astrologists were brought out to Omega headquarters to match the strange symbols adorning the letter to Borrelli with the movement of the stars. In that letter the killer had claimed to be directed by a father figure named Sam. He was Sam's son, the Son of Sam. (Hence the *Daily News*'s nickname for him.) But what did that mean? Was he a Vietnam veteran, a son of Uncle Sam? Was Sam somehow a reference to Satan? Was it short for Samson, a reference to his affinity for women with long hair? Or to Sam Colt, the inventor of the revolver he used? Several survivors remembered seeing their attacker fire his weapon with both hands, the combat stance taught in New York's Police Academy. Could the killer be a laid-off cop? Police suspects were placed in a separate file that quickly grew to three hundred men.

Detectives were able to lift a palm print off the letter to Borrelli, a fact that they somehow managed to keep from the media, but they had nothing with which to match it. "Our focus," remembers Coffey, who had joined the task force, "was catching him in the act." To that end Omega mapped the popular nightspots in the Bronx and Queens and set up decoy teams in unmarked cars. Often a detective positioned himself beside a long-haired mannequin as his partner hid nearby, or two detectives, one wearing a wig, would pretend to neck. When the Police Department decided these tactics were too dangerous, the task force tried ordering bulletproof cars from the company that manufactured vehicles for the Secret Service.

Apparently frustrated with the lack of progress, in early June the .44-caliber killer decided to communicate with the city again. This time he borrowed a page from George Metesky, the so-called Mad

Bomber who had terrorized New York in the 1950s. Only instead of writing to a newspaper, as the Mad Bomber had done, the .44-caliber killer went straight to the city's most famous columnist since Walter Winchell, ensuring that the story would dominate the tabloids for months to come.

It was Jimmy Breslin's secretary at the *Daily News*, Ann Marie Caggiano, who first noticed something strange about the letter—namely, the return address:

Blood and Family
Darkness and Death
Absolute Depravity
.44

Breslin told his secretary to call the cops. Later that night he stopped by Omega headquarters to ask Deputy Inspector Dowd how to proceed. Dowd asked him to publicize the letter.

That was not a problem. The front page of the *News* hinted at its contents for days—NEW NOTE: CAN'T STOP KILLING; .44 KILLER: I AM NOT ASLEEP; COPS: .44 KILLER IS TAUNTING US—all the while promising that the paper's star columnist would answer the letter on Sunday, June 5. When he did, Breslin urged the killer to turn himself in, "to me, if he trusts me." He also quoted at length from the letter, which began: "Hello from the gutters of N.Y.C. which are filled with dog manure, vomit, stale wine, urine and blood. Hello from the sewers of N.Y.C. which swallow up these delicacies when they are washed away by the sweeper trucks. Hello from the cracks in the sidewalks of N.Y.C. and from the ants that dwell in these cracks and feed on the dried blood of the dead that has settled into these cracks."

In late June the Son of Sam struck again. The victims, Sal Lupo and Judy Placido, again a young couple, had just left Elephas, a popular discotheque in an old stone building in Bayside, Queens. Placido usually wore her long brown hair up, but she'd let it down that night in defiance of a police warning. She and Lupo were smoking cigarettes and talking in his Coupe de Ville when a figure appeared on the passenger side and fired four shots through the window.

Deputy Inspector Dowd passed Elephas every night on his drive home from Omega headquarters. Spotting the crowds of young men and women waiting outside, he had told his detectives to keep an eye on it. At the time of the attack two Omega officers were parked only a few blocks away. They saw a suspicious-looking man, stocky, carrying a brown paper bag, and were about to question him when word of the shooting came over the radio. They promptly left the man and rushed off to the crime scene.

In early July, Mayor Beame added more men to the Omega force. The city had only a thousand detectives, down from three thousand before the fiscal crisis, but the pressure to catch the killer was intensifying. Omega now had fifty detectives working the case, with twenty more on standby, and well over one hundred uniformed and undercover officers. Another seven hundred cops volunteered for duty in their off-hours, against the wishes of the police union, which didn't want anyone working for free until the city had rehired all their laid-off brethren. It was easily the largest manhunt in New York history.

Rupert Murdoch was stepping up his pursuit of the .44-caliber killer as well. Tired of getting his clock cleaned day in and day out by Breslin and the *Daily News*, he threw his ace reporter and fellow countryman Steve Dunleavy at the story. Lanky and pasty-faced with a gravity-defying pompadour and an eagle beak profile, the thirty-eight-year-old Dunleavy had come to New York via Fleet Street ten years earlier. He drank vodka-tonics with the rest of New York's British and Australian journos at Costello's on the East Side, but Dunleavy was different from the other expatriate hacks whose principal attraction to the city was its late-hour pubs. Aside from his right-wing politics, he was, as Mario Cuomo told *The New Yorker*'s John

Cassidy for a profile many years later, a real New Yorker: "He's feisty, he's resilient, he's self-made, he stands up for what he believes in, and he can even, on occasion, be charming."

As of July '77, Dunleavy had been at the *Post* for only six months, but he'd already established a reputation. "Steve drank a lot and fucked a lot," remembers his managing editor, Robert Spitzler. Legend has it that one snowy winter night, after doing quite a bit of the former, he and a Norwegian heiress were engaged in the latter when an approaching snowplow ran over Dunleavy's foot. He was so busy pumping away that he scarcely noticed. ("I hope it wasn't his writing foot," Pete Hamill quipped the next day.)

Dunleavy went after the Son of Sam story with a similarly single-minded lust. Along the way he produced a few legitimate scoops and yards of grisly, emotionally overwrought copy. What he lacked in police sources, he more than made up for in imagination. One day Dunleavy took a tape of the Jimi Hendrix song "Purple Haze" to an "audio expert" on Madison Avenue who separated and amplified the lyrics. Someone was apparently singing, "Help me, help me, help me, Son of Sam," in the background. LYRIC MAY YIELD SON OF SAM CLUE, explained the headline.

The frenzied coverage fanned the growing sense of fear; the growing sense of fear fanned the frenzied coverage. Salons reported a sharp increase in brunettes who wanted their long hair cut above their shoulders. "Parking"—necking in the car—was out of the question. "If a guy asks me to park with him now, I'd be very, very insulted," one young woman in Queens told a TV reporter in late July. "He should have the respect to know what's happening and not even ask."

By the middle of July the Omega task force was receiving a thousand tips a day. Every hour a thousand more callers couldn't get through because all twelve hotlines were busy. Women were naming husbands, ex-husbands, and boyfriends as suspects. Leads were categorized as low, medium, or high priority.

On July 28, the day before the anniversary of the first attack, the *News* advertised Breslin's Son of Sam column on its front page. Breslin dedicated the column to the killer on the occasion of "his first deathday" and resurrected the letter the killer had written him almost two months earlier, quoting one especially newsworthy passage: "Tell me Jim, what will you have for July 29 . . . You must not forget Donna Lauria and you cannot let the people forget her either. She was a very sweet girl but Sam's a thirsty lad and he won't let me stop killing until he gets his fill of blood." Breslin couldn't help wondering: "Is tomorrow night, July 29, so significant to him that he must go out and walk the night streets and find a victim?"

The *Post* answered the following day with a page one story headlined GUNMAN SPARKS SON OF SAM CHASE. Not until the penultimate paragraph did the reporter, Steve Dunleavy, alert readers to the fact that the police had already determined that the gunman was definitely not the Son of Sam.

That night, the Omega task force blanketed the Bronx and Queens in unmarked cars, vans, and taxis. Uniformed and off-duty volunteers were stationed at the on- and off-ramps of bridges to seal off escape routes. Back at Omega headquarters, Dowd studied the large map on the wall and, like a general in his war room, moved his troops around the city.

The anniversary passed without incident, but the following night the killer struck for the eighth and final time. The victims, a secretary named Stacy Moskowitz and her date, Robert Violante, who had recently applied for a job at Con Edison, both were twenty years old. As the night wound down, the couple left Jasmine's, a disco in Bay Ridge, and drove to a service road off the Belt Parkway in Bensonhurst. They got out of Violante's Buick Skylark and walked over a small footbridge leading down to the shore. A full moon illuminated the New York Harbor, and the necklace of lights adorning the Verrazano-Narrows Bridge sparkled in the distance. A few minutes later the couple returned to the car. The .44-caliber killer emerged from the bushes of an adjacent playground. Moskowitz was dead in a couple of days. Violante survived, but he lost one eye and most of the use of the other.

At the time Omega detectives were tailing their twelve best suspects, seven of whom were former cops. All of them were a safe distance from the site of the attack. What's more, the killer had ventured into a new borough, and the victim was a blonde. To the *Post* the leap of logic was easy. NO ONE IS SAFE FROM SON OF SAM, blared its August 1 front page. Dunleavy and Breslin both filed "exclusives" with the families of the victims. Breslin's name had been enough to secure his interview; Dunleavy had followed Mr. and Mrs. Moskowitz into the hospital at 4 a.m., donned a doctor's smock, and posed as a bereavement counselor. "When I held their hands and hugged Jerry and Neysa Moskowitz," he wrote, "I was stunned, shattered and angry." Over the next several days the *Post* outdid itself, reporting, among other farfetched things, that the Mafia had joined the hunt for the killer and serializing a suspense novel that "prefigured Son of Sam and–some believe–may actually have been read by Son of Sam."

For New York, the bad week got worse. On the morning of Wednesday, August 3, as Stacy Moskowitz was being eulogized in a crowded chapel on Flatbush Avenue in Brooklyn, bombs planted by the Puerto Rican terrorist group FALN exploded in two midtown Manhattan office buildings. An additional wave of bomb threats quickly followed, and a hundred thousand people were evacuated from more than a dozen buildings.

The following day, Mayor Beame ordered the rehiring of more than one hundred laid-off cops and doubled the number of officers assigned to the Omega task force. Having just reversed his lifelong opposition to capital punishment, the mayor now called on Governor Carey to reconsider his recent veto of a state death penalty bill. Beame said he was "damned angry" at the "the reign of fear" caused by the blackout looting, the .44-caliber killer's latest murder, the rash of arson, and the terror bombs of the FALN. The city's vigilante fury hardly needed the extra fuel. When a man with two revolvers was arrested near the harbor in Sheepshead Bay, Brooklyn, an angry mob surged out of a nearby bar, shouting, "Kill him!"

"For those who have lived through this mad week in New York there is a shared sense of outrage and impotence," the *Times* editorialized on Friday, August 5. "Is New York City, after all, a failed ultra-urban experiment in which people eventually crack, social order eventually collapses, and reason ultimately yields to despair?"

Arriving for roll call that day, New York City police officers watched a three-minute training film detailing the killer's method of attack. They were instructed to clear people out of the parking lots, service roads, and parks that were usually dotted with young couples; there was scarcely anyone to clear out.

The nightclubs were equally deserted. In recent weeks discotheques in Queens, Brooklyn, and the Bronx had been reporting an 80 to 90 percent drop in business and were, according to a story on the front page of *Billboard* magazine in early August, "teetering on the brink of financial disaster." A number of them, including Elephas and the Enchanted Garden in Queens, had tried adding security and valet parking, but to no avail. The Enchanted Garden, which had been averaging a thousand people a night only a couple of months earlier, was now logging barely over a hundred. (On the anniversary of the killer's first attack, fewer than a dozen people passed through its doors.) The extra cops who now loitered around outside in hopes of catching the killer only reminded would-be patrons of the danger of going out.

Like the tidal wave of looting and arson that accompanied the blackout, the .44-caliber killer hysteria had altered New Yorkers' relationship to their city. The vague sense of unease that washed over city dwellers whenever they found themselves walking along a quiet avenue late at night had been transformed into a real sense of fear.

Police sketches even made it possible to visualize its source. This had the peculiar effect of rendering the vast, violent city into a small town. Or perhaps two small towns: the boroughs, where the killer represented a true source of terror, and Manhattan, where he was already becoming a symbol of kitsch, as evidenced by the Son of Sam T-shirts—emblazoned with the police sketch and the words *Son of Sam: Get Him Before He Gets You*—now being sold on midtown street corners.

43.

I would simply say, "You put two more dingers in the center field bleachers, and all of your problems will go away." That was my constant refrain. "You just keep banging that ball into the seats, and all this will go away."

RALPH DESTINO, RECALLING HIS ADVICE TO REGGIE JACKSON DURING THE SUMMER OF 1977

REGGIE was following his friend Ralph Destino's advice. Hitting in the number five spot, sometimes lower, Reggie had been averaging an RBI a game for most of July and early August. That is, when his manager wasn't benching him against left-handers.

But Reggie's problems still weren't going away. On the contrary, they were multiplying. His fielding had not improved, a fact that his teammates were not letting him forget. One mid-July evening in Kansas City, after hustling into the right field corner to retrieve a Hal McRae line drive, Reggie bobbled the ball like a Little Leaguer as McRae raced around the bases for an inside-the-park home run. When Reggie returned to the dugout at the end of the inning, Sparky

Lyle told him to get his head out of his ass. "He was speaking for the whole team, and we were both fully aware of that," Reggie reflected later.

The fans were no better. In New York, Reggie had been signing autographs after the All-Star Game when a thirteen-year-old kid called him a motherfucker. Reggie chased the kid across the parking lot. Moments later the kid was on the asphalt. Criminal harassment charges were filed. When Phil Pepe called Reggie at home, looking for a comment—JACKSON: I DIDN'T STOMP THE KID, read the back page of the next day's *Daily News*—Reggie gave him a good one: "I don't want to be in New York anymore." There was also the constant jeering in the Bronx and in ballparks around the country, where Reggie was a convenient symbol of the greed that had overtaken the national pastime. (In Chicago, White Sox fans greeted him with an enormous banner that read: REGGIE: YOU GET PAID WHAT? FOR A .245 AVERAGE?)

Reggie endured this torture the only way he knew how—publicly. He stuck a "Be Yourself" button above his locker and talked about an escape clause in his contract that would enable him to leave after two years. "Get a good picture of that fucker," he told one writer, gesturing toward his uniform. "It's gonna be a collector's item." The escape clause didn't exist. Reggie had no more control over his Yankees' contract than he did over his deal with *Greatest Sports Legends*, the syndicated television program that fired him as a host in late July. ("He was arrogant, egotistical, and extremely hard to work with," said the show's executive producer.)

With all the fuss, it was easy to overlook Reggie's statistical line as it ticked past respectable and toward impressive. Come August 5, he was hitting .291 with eighteen home runs, ten stolen bases, and fifty-eight RBIs, eleven of which were game winners. That night he recorded his nineteenth dinger, a two-run drive to right-center, the three hundredth of his career.

The Yankees, for their part, were in the tank. After pulling within one game of the Red Sox and Orioles at the end of July, they had proceeded to lose four of their next six. Boston meanwhile was in the middle of an eleven-game run, the club's longest winning streak in more than twenty-five years.

Eight days into August, on the heels of a 9–2 drubbing by the Seattle Mariners, the Yankees flew back East a season-high five games out of first with fifty-three left to play. Two of Martin's starting pitchers, Ed Figueroa and Don Gullett, were coming home via Los Angeles, where they had appointments with an orthopedist to discuss their recurring shoulder problems.

Martin's pain was elsewhere. He had a sit-down scheduled with Steinbrenner and Gabe Paul. The word was that Frank Robinson, an old pal of Reggie's, was going to be replacing him. "Just say that Jackson smiled for the first time all year," responded Reggie when asked to comment on the rumor.

The meeting took place on August 9. Martin maintained in his 1980 memoir, coauthored by Peter Golenbock, that he had already decided to try Reggie in the number four slot. That was not true. A few nights before the meeting, Martin stumbled into the hotel room of the *Post*'s Maury Allen and told him that Reggie would never bat cleanup. Golenbock himself corrected the record in his 1994 posthumuous biography of Martin. "Steinbrenner," wrote Golenbock in *Wild, High, and Tight: The Life and Death of Billy Martin*, "gave Billy one more chance—bat Reggie fourth or else."

And so, on the afternoon of August 10, Reggie found himself penciled into the cleanup slot. He responded with a run-scoring single up the middle against his old Oakland teammate Vida Blue. After the game Martin got in another jab at Reggie—"I can bat Chris Chambliss at any spot in the lineup and he won't complain"—but the Yankees had a new number four hitter for the remainder of the season.

44.

THE first real break in the Son of Sam case came a couple of hours before sunrise on August 1, the morning after the attack on Stacy Moskowitz and Robert Violante, courtesy of Detective John Falotico, a thirty-one-year veteran of the NYPD who had never before worked a murder case. A small, clean-shaven man with bushy white hair, Falotico had only recently been transferred to the tenth homicide zone, which was responsible for all murders in West Brooklyn. For Falotico, who was always grousing about something, the reassignment was one more thing to complain about. But beneath the grumpy exterior was a steady, conscientious detective who was still on the force at fifty-eight, well past retirement age for most officers. He had split with his wife and the Catholic Church years earlier. Aside from his three teenage daughters, everything took a backseat to the job.

Within an hour of the shooting, Falotico was at the crime scene, interviewing a man who said he saw the attack in the rearview mirror of his car. Falotico brought the witness, Tommy Zaino, back to the scene the following afternoon to test the consistency of his recollections. Zaino provided the most detailed description of the killer to date.

According to protocol, as the lead detective on the Moskowitz case, Falotico should have been absorbed into the Omega task force the moment the link to the Son of Sam was established, but he wanted to stay put in Coney Island, where the tenth homicide zone was located. Deputy Inspector Dowd and Captain Borrelli reluctantly agreed, but they wanted Falotico to work with a more experienced homicide detective, Ed Zigo.

Falotico knew this area of Bensonhurst well from his years in the Manhattan district attorney's office, where he'd investigated the Columbo crime family, which kept a real estate office nearby. He spent his first two days on the case, a Sunday and Monday, scribbling down license plate numbers, ringing doorbells, and passing out his card to local residents. On Tuesday night a woman called the station house looking for him. He had given her his card a few blocks from the scene of the murder.

Falotico was tied up with Zaino and a police artist, trying to complete a new sketch of the killer, so another detective, Joseph Strano, a tall, strapping man with wavy brown hair and thick sideburns, took the call. The woman explained that her friend Cacilia Davis had been out walking her dog, a fluffy white terrier named Snowball, at the time of the latest attack. Davis, the woman told Strano, was almost positive that she'd seen the killer up close.

It took a few days of coaxing, but Davis eventually agreed to meet with Strano and his partner, Joe Smith. The man, she told the two detectives, had emerged from behind a tree. He was wearing a jacket and walked with his right arm straight down, as though he were hiding something up his sleeve. Strano asked if she had seen anyone else there. She said no. The detectives continued to press her. Davis eventually recalled seeing cops ticketing cars.

Hoping to find another eyewitness, Strano and Smith checked with the local precinct, but no corresponding tickets had been issued. They went back to Davis and asked her if she was sure. She was. Strano and Smith tracked down the young officer who'd been assigned to patrol the area that night. The officer insisted that he hadn't written any tickets. Either Davis was wrong, or in all the excitement this young cop had failed to hand in his summonses and was now trying to cover it up. The next day Strano and Smith had another detective call the officer to assure him that if he'd forgotten to submit them, it was an understandable mistake, one for which he wouldn't be punished. The young cop's tickets soon materialized.

Another detective in the tenth homicide zone, James Justus, followed up on the tickets. One for thirty-five dollars had been issued to David Berkowitz of 35 Pine Street in Yonkers, who had parked his cream-colored Ford Galaxy sedan too close to a fire hydrant. Justus tried calling him several times, but there was no answer.

On the evening of August 9 the NYPD saturated the city with new WANTED posters describing a man with a "good, athletic build," a "sensuous mouth," and "dark, almond-shaped eyes." That same night Justus put in a call to the Yonkers Police Department in the hope that it might be able to help him track down Berkowitz, who he hoped might be a witness. Justus identified himself to the switchboard operator and explained why he was calling. "When the name David Berkowitz was mentioned," Justus later wrote in his report, "she got very excited and asked if he lived at 35 Pine Street." The operator told Justus that her backyard faced Berkowitz's building, and that he had sent the sheriff threatening letters in the past. She insisted Justus speak with her father, Sam Carr.

"A short time later the father, Mr. Sam Carr, called the undersigned," Justus's report continued. "He stated that . . . he saw who he believed to be Berkowitz shoot his dog and further stated that there were four shots fired and one hit the dog. And another was found and is in the Yonkers property clerks at this time . . . The bullet is described as a large led [*sic*] slug with brass or copper jacket. Mr. Carr further stated that the subject lives alone and he had never observed him with a woman and stated that he has a small yellow Ford. He describes him as follows: M/W/24/5 feet 10 inches/165 pounds/long brown hair/thin face with high cheekbones . . . Mr. Carr stated that there are two police officers with the Yonkers P.D. that have further information on Berkowitz and they are P.O.s Chamberlin and Intervallo."

Justus called Officer Chamberlin. The report recounts their conversation: "He [Chamberlin] saw the composite in the *New York Post* and he stated that Berkowitz bears a striking resemblance to the sketch. He further stated that their department did a psychological profile on him and that he is disturbed."

The following afternoon William Gardella, the sergeant for the tenth homicide zone; Falotico; and another detective from the tenth by the name of Charlie Higgins made their way toward the Pine Hill Towers in Yonkers, a bleak city of boarded-up red-brick factory buildings that marked the beginning of Westchester County.

They were not the first to arrive at Berkowitz's building. Falotico's partner, Ed Zigo, and another detective had heard what was going on and quickly drove up to Yonkers on their own. Zigo didn't have a search warrant, but that hadn't stopped him from entering the Ford Galaxy, which was parked nearby. In the backseat was an army duffel containing a rifle, a toothbrush, and a pair of dirty Jockey shorts. In the glove compartment was a letter addressed to the Suffolk County Police Department promising an attack at a disco in the Hamptons. Zigo's hands shook as he read the note.

Falotico's group arrived on Pine Street, and Sergeant Gardella sent Zigo out for a search warrant. Falotico and Gardella stayed behind. More and more officers and detectives appeared as the afternoon turned to evening. Residents started monitoring the scene from their windows. At one point a passenger van pulled up near Berkowitz's car. Falotico asked him to park as close to the Galaxy as he could. In case Berkowitz managed to get to his car, Falotico wanted to make it harder for him to flee.

As officers continued to assemble outside, Berkowitz remained upstairs in apartment 7E, a $238-a-month studio with pornographic magazines strewn about the floor, a box spring sitting on a shag rug, and manic red scribblings covering the walls. ("My neighbors I have no respect for And I treat them like shit. Sincerely, Williams.") Dirty sheets hung over the windows, obscuring what would otherwise have been an uninterrupted view of the Hudson.

At ten-thirty that night Berkowitz finally emerged from the building in frayed jeans, tennis sneakers, and a wrinkled light blue sport shirt over a white undershirt. Falotico saw him walking casually down the hill toward his Galaxy. The detective moved briskly to the car, his gun drawn, as Berkowitz started the engine. Falotico put his pistol against the window and ordered him to cut the ignition and step out of the car. Resting against Berkowitz's thigh was a brown paper bag with something resembling an apple turnover inside. Falotico recognized the shape immediately; in the summer, when it was too hot to wear a jacket, he himself often carried his gun in just such a brown paper bag. It had to be the .44.

Their exchange was brief.

"You got me," said Berkowitz.

"Who are you?" Falotico asked, his heart pounding.

"You know me."

"I don't."

"I'm the Son of Sam."

"I looked at him, and he had that Mona Lisa smile," Falotico recalls. "I drew him out of the car, and he was still smiling at me. Nobody with a gun facing his nose would stand there and smile."

45.

THE convoy of police vehicles arrived at Centre Street at around one the following morning. The plaza was already choked with reporters, camera crews, and cops. Roone Arledge, the head of ABC News, was on the scene, personally directing his network's coverage with a walkie-talkie.

Falotico, Gardella, and Zigo, who was still fuming about having been tied up with paperwork when the suspect was collared, hustled Berkowitz through the sea of flashing bulbs. New York got its first glimpse of the man who'd been terrorizing it for more than a year. He was about five feet eight and pudgy, with thick black hair and bushy sideburns. His small belly drooped over his snug belt. His mouth was slightly open, and he smiled wanly.

It was perhaps inevitable that when the .44-caliber killer became a man, not a nameless, faceless demon, he wouldn't square with the city's image of him. But even discounting for inflation, this twenty-four-year-old postal clerk was a pathetic-looking character. Detective Coffey, the first to interview him, says it was like "talking to a head of cabbage. I walked into the conference room in a rage," Coffey recalls, "but I wound up feeling sorry for the guy."

Mayor Beame, who had been awakened in Gracie Mansion minutes after the arrest, was waiting upstairs for Berkowitz to enter the building. When he did, the mayor rushed down to congratulate the arresting officer. Mistaking Berkowitz for a detective, Beame moved toward the killer and tried to shake his manacled hands. "The photo op from hell," as the mayor's press secretary, Sid Frigand, later described it.

At 1:40 a.m., Beame entered the packed press room at police headquarters: "I am very pleased to announce that the people of the City of New York can rest easy tonight because police have captured a man they believe to be Son of Sam."

The arrest was page one news across the country and overseas as well. London's *Daily Express* gave it bigger play than Queen Elizabeth's visit to Northern Ireland. *Izvestiya*, the official organ of the Soviet government, noted in its coverage that mass murder was not uncommon in capitalist cities with such high rates of crime and mental illness. In America, a new joke made the rounds: "New York is a place where you can get away with murder—unless you're parked near a fire hydrant."

Murdoch's *Post* ran its banner headline—CAUGHT!—in red. Inside were sixteen stories and thirty-six photographs, as well as the first in a series of installments from another gory crime novel "that might have inspired" the killer. The paper sold more than a million copies, nearly twice its average daily circulation, prompting a proud follow-up story the next day: "Kids who usually bought comic books bought *The Post* and tourists snapped up souvenir copies to take back home." The *News* also opted for saturation coverage, including a Breslin column headlined A DOG TOLD HIM TO KILL; it sold 2.5 million copies, 600,000 more than usual. All the local TV stations ran lengthy special reports. There were endless interviews with the families of the victims, psychiatrists, and men and women on the street. Dunleavy paid a visit to John Diel, the bartender boyfriend of the killer's fourth victim, for his reaction. "I wanna feel the guy's blood," said Diel. "I wanna put my hands around his throat . . . and I want him to know he would be dying by my hands."

When Berkowitz was arraigned in Brooklyn's Central Courts Building, the mob outside chanted, "Death to Sam," and, "Kill! Kill!" Five young men, friends of one of the victims, were arrested as they tried to enter Kings County Hospital, where Berkowitz was being held. Stanley Siegel, the host of New York's most popular morning news show, compared the bloodthirsty atmosphere in New York with that in Dallas in November 1963, when Lee Harvey Oswald was apprehended.

In the days following the arrest, the appetite for Son of Sam stories was heartier than ever. Four journalists were arrested for breaking into Berkowitz's Yonkers apartment. Not surprisingly, two were from the New York tabs, but the third was from *Time* magazine, and the fourth from *The Washington Post.*

A portrait of Berkowitz quickly came into focus. He had been adopted and raised by a childless Jewish couple, Nathan and Pearl, in the Bronx. He graduated from high school and logged one year at Bronx Community College, as well as several months as an auxiliary police officer, before joining the army, where he learned to handle an M-16 rifle and experimented with hallucinogens. ("Paunchy postal worker David Richard Berkowitz took a series of mind-bending LSD trips while a soldier in Korea and returned to the Bronx . . . destined to terrorize the city," the *News* reported.)

After a stint with an infantry division in South Korea, Berkowitz finished out his tour in Fort Knox. While he was stationed in Kentucky, he attended a church with an army buddy and became a fervent Baptist overnight. Berkowitz stood out among his fellow Bible thumpers. "Anytime a Jewish person comes forward to take a stand in a Baptist church, it's a little special," his pastor told the *Louisville Courier-Journal.* Berkowitz moved back to New York after his discharge in 1974. By the time he quit his job as a private security guard to pursue a career in civil service, he had already struck twice. And that was before he'd met Sam Carr's black Labrador, who, according to Berkowitz, had conveyed the message from Carr—"the devil"—to kill.

Murdoch's *Post* sank to a new low in the wake of the arrest, publishing a series of letters that Berkowitz had written to an old girlfriend. The headline read, HOW I BECAME A MASS KILLER. (The byline, naturally, belonged to David Berkowitz.) But the paper also hit a new high with a grainy front-page photo of Berkowitz lying on a cot in a mental ward beneath the banner headline SAM SLEEPS.

It was, in a sense, the perfect postscript to the .44-caliber killer's reign of terror. The headline writer was alluding to Berkowitz's oft-quoted letter to Breslin, in which he'd warned: "Don't think that because you haven't heard from me for a while that I went to sleep." But with those two words, the *Post* had done much more. In an essay a few years later in *Harper's* magazine, Ron Rosenbaum captured the headline's tabloid genius: "How do we know that any of us ordinary citizens—looking just as ordinary on the surface as Sam there—might not be harboring a Sam sleeping within us. SAM SLEEPS might be the single most grim and poetic summation of the horror of the whole case."

The opinion shapers of the time were less generous, to both the *Post* and the New York media in general. In addition to citywide hysteria, the Son of Sam had touched off a heated debate about the coverage of the case. Now that Sam was sleeping, the hand wringing could begin.

The New Yorker had fired the opening salvo in its August 15 issue, which hit newsstands a few hours before Berkowitz was arrested. By transforming the .44-caliber killer into a celebrity, the magazine charged in an unsigned "Comment," the tabloids hadn't simply made a bad situation worse for New York; they had encouraged, perhaps even driven, Sam to strike again.

Breslin answered the charge himself and leveled one of his own, that of elitism. *The New Yorker* was, Breslin hastened to point out, a magazine whose blackout coverage featured a full page on fashion maven Diana Vreeland's candlelit dinner in Greenwich Village. "In the world of the *New Yorker* writer, one sits in the Algonquin lobby and sips daiquiris while discussing such as the Herb Society of America and the Third Annual Great Connecticut River Raft Race," Breslin wrote. "When you go into the Algonquin these nights, here is everybody sitting around and talking about this Son of Sam story and these grubby people on tabloids—tabloids!—who receive letters from killers. Letters they reveal to the public! God, isn't there one of us left to maintain some taste?"

The New Yorker's case was, at least in part, vindicated by the discovery among Berkowitz's meager possessions of a thick scrapbook of newspaper clippings about the .44-caliber killer. The killer had already professed to be a fan of Breslin's in his letter to the columnist. (Apparently, Berkowitz enjoyed the *Post* too. HE ASKS TO SEE THE POST, read a *Post* headline a couple of days after the arrest.) It was also true that in its heaps of stories on Berkowitz, neither of the tabloids allowed for the possibility, minute though it might have been, that he was actually innocent. Still, as Thomas Powers, in a rare voice of dissent, wrote in *Commonweal* magazine in September '77: "Criticizing the tabloids for their all-out pursuit of Sam is a bit like criticizing the lion for gorging upon the lamb. It neglects the nature of the beast."

In the end the mounting backlash had less to do with concerns about prejudicing potential jurors—after all, Berkowitz had already done that with his epistolary rantings—and more to do with a distaste for the sensationalism that tabloids trafficked in. Rupert Murdoch had made his mark. Not since the days of Hearst, Pulitzer, and the *Daily Mirror* had New York's newspapers pandered so shamelessly to the city's id. Yet in his own hamfisted, irresponsible way, Murdoch deserved at least a little credit for reminding New Yorkers that reading the newspaper, like living in the city, was an emotional experience.

46.

THE candidate's bald head glistened with small beads of sweat as he stood before the growing crowd of weary Staten Islanders at the Battery Park ferry terminal at the end of a long workday in August.

"All those who thought we should have called in the National Guard during the blackout, raise your hand!" the candidate bellowed through his battery-powered bullhorn, thrusting his own right hand in the air.

"All those who are in favor of capital punishment, raise your hand!" Again, the candidate's right hand shot straight up.

The doors on the opposite side of the terminal flung open, and the crowd spun around and began surging toward the arriving ferry. But the candidate was not done yet. "Society has the right to express its moral outrage," he barked at the departing masses.

The candidate, Edward Irving Koch, had surely been expressing his. While Beame was busy campaigning against Con Edison in the weeks following the blackout, Koch had been calling for Police Commissioner Codd's head and demanding to know why the mayor hadn't summoned the National Guard, not to help New Yorkers manage without power but to intimidate the looters. It was a genuinely bad idea: Even the law-and-order *Daily News* recognized that bringing in the Guard would have caused even more violence. Still, there was no denying its emotional appeal to the ravaged city. "There is naked fear here," wrote Evans and Novak on August 4, "that the looters may reassert their impunity some ordinary evening at sunset without waiting for a power blackout."

Reviving capital punishment, now *that* was a cause the *Daily News* could get behind—COME BACK, LITTLE HOT SQUAT, the paper editorialized—as could many New Yorkers, especially those in the fragile outer boroughs: in Brooklyn and the Bronx, where the worst blackout looting had occurred; in Queens, the Son of Sam's borough of choice; and in the historically conservative Staten Island. In all, 62 percent of the city favored reinstituting the death penalty and only 25 percent were opposed. So Koch took his show on the road, to the Staten Island ferry terminal, to the senior centers and nursing homes of the Bronx, to the beach clubs and boardwalks of Brooklyn and Queens.

What was a Greenwich Village liberal, a man who'd given up his 1964 summer vacation to do pro bono legal work for the ACLU down South, a man who had vehemently opposed the war in Vietnam and vociferously championed gay rights, a man whose annual approval rating from Americans for Democratic Action had never dipped below 90 percent, doing promoting the return of the death penalty? It wasn't even an issue over which the city had jurisdiction. "It shocked the shit out of the archliberals," Koch remembers. "They were absolutely beside themselves with rage."

Koch's soon-to-be-erstwhile allies dismissed it as pure political opportunism. "[T]here is a feral mood in the city," wrote Nat Hentoff. "And so Ed Koch became a panderer to savage fantasies . . . This once and former man of plain decency has become an advocate of mindless barbarism." The *Voice*'s Denis Hamill suggested a revision to Koch's campaign slogan: "After eight years of charisma, and four years of the clubhouse, why not try the chair?"

Koch insisted that he'd always supported capital punishment. It was a technically accurate, if a bit disingenuous, defense. He had endorsed a 1974 bill allowing death sentences for convicted skyjackers, but he'd never before mentioned his position on the issue, let alone campaigned on it. Even now, his campaign team was printing two different sets of literature. The leaflets for the outer boroughs emphasized his position on the death penalty; those intended for distribution in Manhattan made no mention of it. (*The Nation* called it Koch's "forked-tongue operation.") "It happens that the death penalty is not popular in Manhattan," says Koch, "so why should I put it on my Manhattan literature? There's nothing fraudulent about that."

But Koch was doing more than simply exploiting New York's bloodlust. Much as the city's beloved baseball team and its cherished tabloid, he was changing colors with New York's temper like a mood ring. Koch's metamorphosis had been under way for more than a decade. In August '77, even his campaign manager, David Garth, was a little surprised by how far he'd come. "I felt as though I had made the same mistake as the rest of the city," Garth recalls, "which was mark him down as a Greenwich Village liberal when in fact he was more conservative than that."

Koch speaks to his ideological journey in a 617-page oral history conducted with Columbia University in 1975 and 1976, a refreshingly straightforward antidote to his subsequent procession of triumphalist memoirs. Koch recounts, for instance, his change of heart on school busing. In the early sixties, when New York State was urging the city's Board of Education to integrate all of the city's schools, Koch had fought to bus white schoolchildren out of the Village and into black neighborhoods. He was shocked to hear Hilda Stokeley, a black political leader from Harlem, undercut the wisdom of integration at a meeting of New York's district leaders in 1963. "We're not interested in having our black kids sit next to your white kids on a bench in the school," Stokeley had said. "What we're interested in is equal schools, equal education. That's what we want."

"But Hilda," Koch stammered, "what you're saying is terrible. You're saying separate but equal, and the Supreme Court says there can't be such a thing as separate but equal."

By 1977, though, Koch had become an ardent opponent of busing. Surrounded by better streets and homes than their own families could afford, black children, he worried, were liable to become resentful and lash out at their white, middle-class schoolmates. The white families would, in turn, move their kids into private school, and New York City's public schools would suffer.

But for Koch, as for many other New Yorkers of his generation, the seminal moment was Mayor Lindsay's 1972 proposal to build a low-income housing project in middle-class Queens. As Cuomo had discovered, the Forest Hills project made for a knotty issue for most liberal New Yorkers. The scale of the plan—three twenty-four-story high-rise towers in a neighborhood dominated by houses and small apartment buildings—made it totally inappropriate, heavy-handed social engineering at its worst. Yet to anyone committed to racial and economic integration, the concept of scatter-site housing as a means of moving poor families out of the ghettos held an irresistible appeal. What's more, the poor needed housing desperately, however imperfect this proposal was. ("We cannot afford to do nothing as we wait to do everything," as Cuomo had put it.)

To Koch, the matter of Forest Hills could not have been more clear-cut: He'd objected to it in theory and in practice. Convinced that the Forest Hills community was being railroaded, Koch had turned up one morning in 1971 at a demonstration at the Forest Hills construction site, where he gave an impromptu address, cheering on the mud-splattered crowd of two thousand in their fight against City Hall.

Koch's old friends from the Village were aghast. Several took him aside to express personally their concern at his apparent betrayal of principle. Koch wasn't merely undeterred; he discovered that he rather enjoyed igniting the wrath of limousine liberals. "Having these people—the radicals, the politically correct—against me has been a source of strength because it gets my juices going," Koch says now.

In later years Koch told and retold the story of Stanley Geller, the head of his former political club, the Village Independent Democrats, calling to dress him down in the heat of the Forest Hills flap. Koch insisted that the project would destroy the neighborhood; Geller replied that the Jews of Forest Hills had to pay their dues. "Stanley," Koch answered, "you have this wonderful brownstone on 12th Street . . . And you have this marvelous home in the Hamptons . . . On the day your kids were born, you registered them in private schools. And you're telling me that the Jews of Forest Hills have to pay their dues? I'm telling you that they're willing to pay *their* dues. They are not willing to pay *yours*."

Thus transformed, Koch was well positioned to tap New York's mounting fury. As August wore on, that's precisely what he did. The marketing of the death penalty was only part of the effort. Koch promised to protect middle-class neighborhoods from "the nuts on the left" and inveighed against the "poverty pimps" and "poverticians" who embezzled money from federal antipoverty programs.

More striking still, Koch questioned if it was really necessary to rehire the city workers who'd been laid off during the fiscal crisis. This would once have been political suicide. There were too many votes at stake; the number of civil servants in the city had long since eclipsed that of blue-collar trade workers. What's more, attacking New York's public employees was tantamount to attacking the city itself. They were, after all, the men and women who propped up the city's network of parks, schools, libraries, hospitals, and subways. But by August 1977, as city services continued to shrink and the city's welfare population continued to grow, that network was sagging. New York's faith in its civic culture had cracked.

Koch pounced. Merely to denounce the "power brokers," as candidate John Lindsay had done a little over a decade earlier, would no longer suffice. "Up until then, everyone said that you don't go after the unions directly," Garth says of the Koch campaign. "We decided that was bullshit."

Nothing spoke as loudly as schools and crime. The *New York Post* was—uncharacteristically—not engaging in hyperbole when it wrote in August '77: "The problems plaguing virtually every aspect of public education in New York can be described in three ways: critical, severe, or merely serious." In the critical category was the student to teacher ratio, which routinely exceeded fifty. (Some thirteen thousand out of fifty-six thousand full-time teachers had been laid off during the fiscal crisis.) There was a time when New York's middle class, the children of immigrants who had used the city's public school system as their avenue to better lives, would have raised its collective voice in protest. That time had passed. "As middle-class whites withdrew from the city's public-education system, the schools became yet another minority service," wrote Jack Newfield and Paul Du Brul in their 1977 book, *The Abuse of Power: The Permanent Government and the Fall of New York.* Now here was Koch vowing to introduce rigorous performance standards for both principals and teachers, pledging to put an end to their "exorbitant salaries," questioning the number of hours they spent on the job.

Albert Shanker, the combative head of the teachers' union, fired back, pointing out that the average New York City teacher made just nineteen thousand dollars a year—not the twenty-six thousand dollars that Koch claimed—and that time logged in the classroom represented only part of their workday. The child of two ardent trade unionists, Shanker argued that Koch's efforts to stir up antagonism toward city employees threatened to make matters only worse for New Yorkers: "If you should succeed in pitting the public against its policemen, teachers, firefighters—and shattering the morale of our employees—will this improve services?" As it turned out, with his verbal assaults, Shanker only helped burnish Koch's image as the candidate with the courage to take on the special interests.

The cops made an even fatter target. It wasn't merely the large number who had failed to report for duty the night of the blackout; it was a growing sense that the police union, the Patrolmen's Benevolent Association, was more concerned with wringing a 6 percent raise from City Hall than with protecting neighborhoods. Much of New York had lost its sympathy for the police in the fall of '76, when a heavyweight title fight at Yankee Stadium was interrupted by roving gangs of gatecrashers, while off-duty officers drank beer and picketed outside. Koch promised to stand up to the PBA: to require that all cops live in the city, to take away the two free days they received for giving blood ("All I get is a Lorna Doone and a cup of coffee," the candidate quipped), to punish policemen who went out on strike.

Championing capital punishment, pummeling the unions, decrying government waste: This was not your typical liberal rhetoric. One prominent Republican pundit and former New York City mayoral candidate himself, William F. Buckley, Jr., took approving note, calling Koch "a liberal in the actuarial sense of the word, but a man who has always been ready to look ideology in the face long enough to recognize its glass eye."

Meanwhile, Koch's steady drumbeat of clever commercials, produced in Garth's state-of-the-art three-monitor studio—"Mayor Beame is asking for four more years to finish the job. Finish the job? Hasn't he done enough?"—coupled with the eighteen-hour days campaigning in a Winnebago blaring "N.Y.C.," the hit song from the Broadway musical *Annie*, were having their intended effect. Koch could feel himself gaining momentum. The polls confirmed his suspicions. Before the blackout he'd been at 6 percent, a distant fourth behind Abzug, Beame, and Cuomo. By the middle of August, with less than a month to go before the Democratic primary, Koch was still running fourth, but he'd moved up to 14 percent.

And he only needed to take second place. Several years earlier the city had enacted a law intended to give the winner of the quadrennial bloodletting that was New York's Democratic primary a mandate to govern the ungovernable city. If no Democrat captured

40 percent of the vote, the top two finishers would face each other in a runoff a little more than one week later.

Then Koch got his biggest break yet. On the morning of August 19 his phone rang. The caller identified himself as Rupert.

"Rupert?" asked Koch. A second later he recognized the Australian accent. "Ahhhh, *Rupert*."

The *Post*, Murdoch told Koch, was going to endorse him. In the event, the paper did much more than that, playing the editorial on its front page and generating enough pro-Koch copy in the ensuing weeks to prompt fifty *Post* reporters and editors to sign a petition complaining about their tabloid's biased coverage. (Murdoch invited them to quit; twelve did.)

What did Murdoch get in return? Some penny-ante patronage—Koch agreed to appoint a particular lawyer to a senior position in his administration—but more than that, Murdoch had deduced that Koch represented his best shot at becoming a kingmaker in his new town. Abzug was far too liberal, Beame too Establishment. As for Cuomo, he was sure to be the candidate of the *Daily News*.

After ignoring Koch for months, his opponents were now paying attention to him—or to his campaign manager anyway. "I was a person before the campaign, but David Garth has made a different person out of Ed Koch," Abzug complained. "What has Garth wrought?" asked Cuomo.

47.

UP in the Bronx, the drama on the field was finally overshadowing the melodrama off it.

Having taken his rightful place in the lineup, Reggie was flourishing. On August 11, his second day batting cleanup, he singled home a key run in a defensive battle with the A's. The next night, a sticky one in New York, he exploded for four extra-base hits and five RBIs in a twin bill with the Angels. He started with a double and a triple in the opener. Then, in the nightcap, he led off the bottom of the sixth with the score tied—the crowd chanting "Reggie, Reggie, Reggie," for the first time in months—and pulled a line drive into the upper deck. With two down the following inning, he lashed another homer, this time deep into the right-center field bleachers. The following afternoon, Reggie showed off his once-feared arm, cutting down Bobby Bonds, one of the fastest men in baseball, when he tried to score the go-ahead run in the top of the ninth.

The Yankees were winning, and more often than not with a maximum of theatrics. A few nights later, in the final game of the home stand, they scored four runs in the bottom of the eighth to take a 9–4 lead against the free-swinging Chicago White Sox. In the top of the ninth a weary Ron Guidry served up a two-run homer before ceding the mound to Lyle, who was battered for three hits and two more runs. With two on and two out, Lyle gave the ball to rookie Ken Clay, who walked the bases loaded, then surrendered a two-run single that put the White Sox on top 10–9. The Yanks would get one last shot. Munson led off the ninth with a walk, and Piniella moved him over to second. Chambliss came to the plate thinking, "Base hit," and sent a slider into the upper deck to give the Yankees the win.

Two days later, in Detroit, it was starting pitcher Ed Figueroa's 7–2 lead that started evaporating in the final frame. When Lyle trotted in from the bullpen to replace him, it was already 7–4, with two men aboard and only one out. Yankees' fans had every reason to be nervous. Not only had they watched Lyle get roughed up the other night, but they knew all about his tendency to fall apart after the All-Star break.

Lyle induced the first man to ground out, though the Tigers scored on the play, making it 7–5 Yanks, with the dangerous Ben

Oglivie coming to the plate. Lyle got ahead 0-2, but Oglivie fought back, taking two balls and fouling off three hanging sliders with menacing cuts. Lyle rubbed up the ball, rocked back, and uncorked one last slider. This one stayed down. Oglivie, recognizing the telltale spin a split second too late, thrashed at it for the final out.

The next night, August 18, the Tigers broke a scoreless tie in the fifth with a two-run bomb, but the Yanks rallied for three in the seventh inning, sweeping the two-game series in Detroit. The Yankees were ten of their last eleven, three and a half games behind the first-place Red Sox, who had won seventeen of their last nineteen.

The whole lineup was pounding the ball now, and Martin was making the most of his ailing pitching staff. With Don Gullett, the 10-3 staff ace, on the disabled list until the end of August and Catfish Hunter requiring five full days to recover from each start, Martin had taken to using the six-foot-five-inch Mike Torrez on three days' rest. Having won just five of his first fourteen outings, Torrez now found his stride.

But the biggest surprise was Ron Guidry, a wispy, bowlegged left-hander with molasses-colored eyes who had barely made the regular season roster after getting knocked around in six relief appearances in the Grapefruit League. The Yankees had drafted Guidry, the simple, soft-spoken son of a railroad conductor, midway through his third year at the University of Southwestern Louisiana in 1971, risking a ten-thousand-dollar signing bonus in the hope that he'd fill out. He never did; the '77 roster lists him, generously, at five feet eleven, 151 pounds. Not that it mattered. As unimposing as he looked on the mound, his spindly arms dangling from his slight frame, Guidry had an uncommon and inexplicable gift: For as long as he could remember, he'd been able to throw a ball a lot harder than everyone else.

Guidry's mid-nineties heater carried him through the minors, though he was quickly demoted to the bullpen, and in 1976 he was called up to the Bronx for a brief stint. Getting loose in the Yankee bullpen one afternoon, the veteran Lyle told Guidry what he already knew, that he needed another pitch. "He said you could get by with a fastball, but you won't get by with it all the time," Guidry recalls, "but if you've got something else to complement it . . . there's no way that guys are going to be able to look for a breaking ball off of you and expect to hit a fastball."

Lyle threw one of the filthiest sliders in baseball. Unlike a true slider, which cut across a more or less horizontal plane, Lyle's dipped as well. Guidry had never been able to throw a curve—he kept his pitching arm too straight—and his experiments with a slider in summer ball as a teenager had nearly destroyed his pitching career before it began. He asked Lyle to show him his grip. Lyle told him to forget about the grip and focus on the release. Then he showed Guidry how to rotate his wrist and yank the ball down and hard at the last moment, "like you're pulling down a window shade."

Guidry spent the '76–'77 off-season hunting in the duck blinds of rural Louisiana. He reported to camp in the spring of '77 for the first half of a two-year sixty-thousand-dollar contract, having not thrown a baseball since the fall. Guidry vainly set about trying to blow waist-high fastballs by every hitter he faced. Martin's patience quickly wore thin. "Tell me somebody you can get out," he told Guidry, "and I'll let you pitch to him."

Guidry was beginning to wonder if he could get anybody out. By the end of the exhibition season his ERA had swelled to 10.24. Both Steinbrenner and Martin, in rare agreement, wanted to send him back to Syracuse, but Gabe Paul convinced them otherwise.

Guidry did some mop-up work during the first few weeks of the season. On April 29, with the Yankees set to host the Mariners at the stadium, Martin found himself in a bind. His scheduled starter, Mike Torrez, whom the Yankees had just acquired for Dock Ellis, had not yet reported to New York. Martin's only rested starters, Catfish Hunter and Don Gullett, both were hurt. An hour before game time Torrez was scratched. Guidry would be starting for the first time since the Carolina League, circa 1973.

Ten minutes into the game, Guidry still couldn't find the plate. There was one out, and the lowly Mariners had loaded the bases on a hit and two walks. Guidry stepped off the rubber, kneaded his Levi Garrett chaw, discharged a mouthful of brown juice, and started snapping off sliders. Two strikeouts later he was out of trouble. He went on to pitch a 3–0 shutout.

When Torrez showed up, Guidry was sent back to the bullpen. With all the injuries to the Yankee staff, though, he continued to make spot starts and eventually worked himself into the rotation. The more Guidry threw the slider, the more it came to resemble Lyle's, only harder.

By the middle of August, Guidry was leading the team in strikeouts, and his ERA was just a shade above 3.00. He was still unknown, untested, so no one dared say it out loud, but the way the left-hander dispensed with hitters—hypnotizing them with heat and then bringing them to with that hard, tumbling slider thrown from the identical arm angle—was reminiscent of Sandy Koufax's fastball-curve one-two. Of course, all he was doing, as Guidry himself said, was throwing a baseball as hard as he could in the vicinity of Munson's mitt: "Usually my ball is so alive it's not gonna do what I want."

Guidry's postgame routine was no less straightforward than his approach to pitching. He'd drink a grape soda in front of his locker, give the writers a few quotes in his Cajun drawl about how he'd felt on the mound that night, then drive home to his apartment in Bogota, New Jersey, where he'd open a Coors and set a couple of steaks on the grill for him and his wife.

In Texas on August 21, a week before his twenty-eighth birthday, Guidry fanned eight, picking up his tenth victory of the season and pushing the Yankees past the Orioles and within a half game of the Red Sox. By now both Martin and Steinbrenner were claiming credit for sticking with him.

Two nights later, a rainy, miserable one at Comiskey, Torrez was on the mound and the Yankees and White Sox were knotted at three in the seventh when Mickey Rivers drove in the go-ahead run. In the eighth, Reggie delivered Munson with a single to give the Yanks some breathing room. Graig Nettles made it a blowout with a three-run home run through the wet, whipping Chicago wind.

The Yankees returned to New York early the next morning. They were fourteen of their last sixteen, and twenty-three and nine since the All-Star break. With a little help from the suddenly slumping Red Sox, they led the American League East by a half game.

48.

ON August 24, two weeks before the Democratic primary, the results from the most recent *New York Times*/Channel 2 News survey put Abzug and Beame in a dead heat, with both Cuomo and Koch within striking distance.

Beame had nothing to complain about considering that five weeks earlier, in the aftermath of the blackout, his prospects had seemed dimmer than ever. "[I]t is too much to expect you to recover once you wake up on a morning when your city is thoroughly ashamed of itself and you are its Mayor and its symbol," Murray Kempton wrote on July 19, reckoning that the blackout had reduced the field of legitimate mayoral contenders to two, Abzug and Cuomo.

Kempton had underestimated the privileges of incumbency. Between his daily press conferences and regular walking tours of looted, burned neighborhoods, the city's mayor was at the center of much of the media's postblackout coverage. Beame had also made some savvy political moves, writing off the uncertain prospect of a presidential endorsement, opting instead to assail Carter both for his unwillingness to declare New York a disaster area and for his failure to make good on his preelection pledge to federalize welfare. Out of fidelity to the code of the Democratic clubhouse, almost all the local union leaders and political bosses were lining up to endorse Beame. By the end of July he was climbing steadily in the polls. His reversal on the death penalty was followed by a series of anticrime commercials. One, a radio spot, quoted Abzug pontificating on the social and economic causes of the blackout looting. Another, this one on TV, showed the tiny mayor, crowned by a hard hat, before a sea of blue uniforms, against the tagline "Mayor Beame. He's fighting your fight against crime." By the middle of August, Beame was again a front-runner.

But Kempton had made an even bigger miscalculation with respect to Abzug, the leading candidate through the first half of July. Abzug had been out of town when the lights went out, but her campaign staff hustled her back to New York, where thousands of new leaflets—"Vote Bella: She's the Greatest Energy Source in America"—awaited her. Abzug promptly launched an attack on Con Ed, urging New Yorkers to "refuse to pay any more to this rapacious monopoly."

On Friday, July 15, Abzug became the first mayoral candidate to visit what was left of Bushwick. After touring the decimated neighborhood, she stopped by Bed-Stuy's Eighty-first Precinct, which had worked alongside Bushwick's Eighty-third during the long night of looting. Looking smart in a polka-dot sundress and white straw hat, Abzug defended her increasingly unpopular position of giving cops the right to strike.

"But what would you have done if the police had been on strike during the blackout?" one distressed community resident asked.

"Mobilize the community organizations and get them into the streets," Abzug replied.

"The community *was* mobilized," another resident volunteered. "They were all out looting."

Abzug held her tongue, but in the subsequent weeks, as she moved about the boroughs of a changed city, it became harder and harder for her to keep her infamous temper in check. As she campaigned one late July afternoon at the pool of a beach club in Canarsie, Brooklyn, an Italian enclave surrounded by poor black neighborhoods, Abzug's lap around the ring of card tables was halted by a man questioning her support for school busing. They argued, and the man called her a bigot. "Hitler spread the big lie too," she screamed back at him.

Abzug regained her composure and pressed on, but moments later, as Roberta Kapper recounted in the *Soho Weekly News*, Abzug was arguing with someone else who believed that the cops should have shot the looters. Abzug said that if she'd been mayor, she would have called in the National Guard. Now an older woman chimed in, telling Abzug that she didn't believe her, that Abzug didn't care about people like her. "Then go vote for that schmuck we have now," Abzug spit back. "I'm ahead in the polls."

Not for long. As July gave way to August, Abzug's popularity was ebbing. That one of the candidates gaining ground on her was Ed Koch made her all the more spiteful. Abzug and Koch were enemies of long standing. Their feud had begun in 1968, when Koch refused to march in an anti-Vietnam protest organized by a group Abzug chaired, not because he was in favor of the war but because he believed the group was a Communist front. Since then, neither one of them had missed an opportunity to say something nasty about the other. During Abzug's '76 Senate race Koch had volunteered to a reporter that New York State would be better off with someone else. Abzug stormed up to Koch on the floor of the House an hour later and called him "a divisive bastard." She had not spoken to him since.

Upon hearing in late July that Koch had accepted a three-thousand-dollar campaign donation from Al Goldstein, the publisher of *Screw* magazine, Abzug had her staff produce a new leaflet: "You can't claim to be against pornography—and then take money from the smut peddlers. Ed Koch thinks he can." ("The treasurer of the

Episcopal Church gave me $3,000, but that doesn't mean I'm Episcopalian," answered Koch, who'd been imploring Abzug "not to be the demagogue you usually are.")

The truth is that liberalism's retreat was throwing Abzug off stride. In the past she had always buttressed her stridency with a lawyerly attention to detail. During her movement days, she'd produced pamphlets that laid out exactly how many schoolteachers New York could employ for each B-52 bomber being sent to Vietnam. But as the '77 campaign entered its final weeks, she was resorting increasingly to generalities. Following Abzug one sweltering mid-August afternoon in Rego Park, Queens, *The Village Voice*'s Geoffrey Stokes heard her answer a question about what she'd do for the neighborhood with what Stokes, an Abzug supporter, described as "a disconnected attack on 'the special interests.' "

This was no longer the New York Abzug had once known. "She thought the city was out of control," her press secretary, Harold Holzer, recalls. "She thought it was beyond our control to remind people of what Lincoln would call the better angels of our nature, to remind them of possibilities, to remind them that harmony was more important than punitiveness. God knows it was impossible to say that people who pillaged in some pathetic effort to express anger should be pitied almost as much as punished. There was no way to get through the mood, between the murders and the heat and the blackout looting."

There were some bad breaks too. *Rolling Stone* was working on a story with Abzug, a first-person account of her favorite spots in the city, only instead of photographing her, editor Jann Wenner had commissioned Andy Warhol to paint her portrait. It was all set to run on the cover of a special issue devoted to New York, the magazine's new home. For Abzug, the timing could not have been better; the magazine would be on newsstands from the last week in August right up to the September 8 primary. But just as *Rolling Stone*'s editors were making their final tweaks, Elvis Presley died. The New York issue was promptly shelved. When it was resurrected a little more than a month later, the introductory editorial still wished Abzug "good luck," but the primary had already passed.

At least *US* magazine managed to run its feature on Abzug's diet, which began, "With a Little Help from Shirley MacLaine, Buxom Bella Abzug Is Losing Pounds While Gaining Votes." Actually, *US* had it backward. Abzug's campaign staff had discovered the virtues of food as a sedative and kept a cooler filled with nuts and yogurt in the back of the campaign car. By late August, as Abzug's once-comfortable lead continued to shrivel, she had added about ten pounds to her already full figure. Unable to fit into her dress when the *US* photographer arrived, Abzug was reduced to holding it up in front of herself.

49.

IN 1860 an Illinois lawyer and Republican presidential candidate named Abraham Lincoln gave his first speech in New York—his soon-to-be-famous "Right Makes Might" address—in the Great Hall at Cooper Union College. Some fifty years later, in the wake of the Triangle Shirtwaist Factory fire, thousands of immigrant workers gathered in the same room for the rally that launched one of the most important uprisings in the history of the labor movement. And on August 30, 1977, an event far less memorable yet still irresistibly symbolic took place within these hallowed halls. In the waning moments of a debate for the upcoming mayoral primary, an evening punctuated by frequent intervals of hooting and jeering, a chubby, balding man rose from his seat and hurled an apple pie at Mayor Beame.

The pie completed its journey just seconds after Beame, reaching the end of his ninety-second summation, had said: "Tough decisions were needed, and I made 'em." It was one of Beame's campaign slogans, a line he'd been using to good effect all summer, but the events of the past two weeks, surely the worst stretch of the seventy-one-year-old mayor's political career, hadn't merely undermined the claim; they had made a mockery of it.

Beame's troubles began in mid-August, when word leaked from Washington that the Securities and Exchange Commission was about to release its long-awaited report on New York City's fiscal crisis. The SEC had started its investigation, one of the largest in its history, in early 1976. Six months later Beame's lawyers were in court, trying to block the probe, arguing that the federal commission didn't have the right to examine how the city went about issuing securities. In late '76, Beame, who had just sat through a five-hour interrogation by the commission's lawyers, dropped the case. As the mayor explained later, he'd done so because the SEC assured him that the report was imminent. He figured its findings would be long forgotten when it came time for New Yorkers to choose their next mayor.

The report never came, and by the middle of July the conventional wisdom was that it would be delayed until after the primary. Joel Harnett, a long shot mayoral candidate, accused the Carter administration of deliberately holding up the report and filed his own suit in federal court demanding its prompt release. Several other candidates quickly echoed Harnett's charges. Wary of leaving the impression that it was meddling in local politics, the White House made it clear that it too wanted the SEC report out as soon as possible. On July 31 the *Daily News*'s Ken Auletta quoted a lawyer for the commission saying he would be "dramatically surprised if it was not out before the primary."

The commission kept quiet about the progress of the investigation, but a couple of weeks later Beame learned that it had dispatched a task force, including several high-ranking officials, to New York to expedite its completion. Beame grew nervous. Desperate to do something to get out in front of the report, to blunt its potential impact, he decided to release the transcript of his lengthy interrogation. On the morning of August 17, as the mayor's staff handed out copies of his 222-page testimony to reporters, Beame accused the SEC of playing politics by suddenly rushing to complete its investigation. The mayor said he was making the transcript public in order to encourage "a reasoned public evaluation prior to the primary election."

The actual effect was closer to that of a good movie trailer. By offering a glimpse of the SEC's line of questioning, Beame's testimony only whetted the public's appetite for the full report. Among other things, the commission had grilled the mayor about inflating anticipated revenues and understating expected spending as a means of balancing its budget. Beame insisted that he knew of no such practice. "The mayor," he said, "has got enough things to do besides sitting down and estimating revenues for the city."

More tantalizing still, the transcript revealed that Mayor Beame had met several times with David Rockefeller, the chairman of Chase Manhattan, and Walter Wriston, the head of Citibank, in early 1975, when Beame was still assuring investors that the city was on firm financial footing. The SEC asked the mayor if Rockefeller, Wriston, or any one of the other high-level bankers present at the meetings had warned him that New York was at risk of being cut off from the credit market, a critical source of badly needed capital. Beame said he couldn't remember.

The press was merciless. "To hear His Honor tell it, he was nothing but an innocent bystander, a detached observer," the *Daily News* sputtered in an August 19 editorial headlined SIMPLY INCREDIBLE. "This, remember, comes from a man who won election in 1973 by convincing voters that he knew municipal finances from A to Z, could put more cops on the street, improve services and balance the books . . . With that attitude at the top, it's a wonder New York didn't wind up being auctioned off at a sheriff's sale."

A few days later Beame managed to dig his hole even deeper when he publicly questioned the integrity of Robert Haft, the author of the forthcoming report. "It seems to smell to high heaven," the mayor charged on the radio station WINS, after explaining that Haft had recently resigned from a Manhattan law firm where several principals were involved in the Cuomo campaign. Beame also fired off a letter of protest to Harold M. Williams, the chairman of the Securities and Exchange Commission, who answered that it was the mayor, not his commission, who was guilty of playing politics.

The report was finally completed thirteen days before the mayoral primary. The members of the New York press corps wedged themselves into the classroom-style desks arrayed around the press room of the SEC's Washington headquarters and waited for their copies. No fewer than forty staff members had been involved in its preparation over the course of the past nineteen months, perusing 250,000 documents and twelve thousand pages of testimony along the way. This was to be the definitive analysis of how the biggest, richest city in the world had gone bust. "Is it too late to drop this class?" joked the *Times*'s Steven Weisman when copies of the ten-pound report were distributed around the room.

At least no one had any trouble finding the headline. The *Post* was the first of the New York papers to hit the street with the story on the afternoon of August 26. Its editors had whittled the 952-page report down to four words set in towering type across page one: BEAME CONNED THE CITY.

As Beame's testimony had suggested, much of the report turned on the question of disclosure. The SEC determined that the bankers had warned the mayor, not once but on four separate occasions between the end of '74 and the spring of '75, that the city's securities offerings were in jeopardy. Moreover, the commission accused the mayor of "deceptive practices masking the city's true and disastrous financial condition."

Beame promptly decried the report as a "shameless, vicious political document . . . a hatchet job" and told New York he'd have more to say on the subject after his staff had studied the SEC's claims in greater depth. The next day, a Saturday, at a hastily convened news conference at City Hall, Beame cried cover-up. Quivering with anger, he told reporters it was the banks that had misled him, assuring him that they were continuing to invest in New York–backed securities, while in fact—and now he jabbed his finger at his invisible slanderers—"rapidly unloading" those securities on unsuspecting small investors. "We kept the city from going under," Beame said. "We avoided bankruptcy."

It was an unconvincing performance. Everyone knew that averting bankruptcy had come at a terrible cost, self-rule. Had the state not intervened in 1975, transferring the management of the city's financial affairs from City Hall to the Emergency Financial Control Board, a group that comprised more nonelected businessmen (three) than city officials (two), New York would surely have fallen into receivership.

Seen in the right light, though, it wasn't an entirely unsympathetic performance. There was a curious nobility to the mayor's indignation. After all, he was being accused, at bottom, of harboring a stubborn, if blind, faith in his city. Municipal notes and bonds represented a murky area. Existing securities laws were not entirely clear about what cities, in contrast with corporations, were required to disclose to the public. And as Beame himself put it, was it really fair to expect a mayor to speak to his people in the language of an investment prospectus?

The mayor had a point about the banks too. The SEC had devoted a comparatively slender seventy-four-page volume to the city's underwriters, and with a few exceptions, notably the *Voice*'s Jack Newfield, the local papers hadn't devoted much ink to them either, but the commission's report left little doubt about their complicity in the city's financial collapse. In early 1975, the SEC concluded, nearly all of the city's banks, Chase, Morgan, and Citibank included, had been selling off their own New York–backed holdings, even as they continued to market them to the public as safe and secure investments.

A truly comprehensive narrative of New York's fiscal crisis would have reached back at least into the mid-1960s, when the city initiated the precarious practice of issuing notes that it intended to redeem a couple of years later with as yet uncollected tax revenues, a practice that seemed, at the time, like the surest way to keep the beneficent city humming. Instead, the SEC report focused almost exclusively on a narrow five-month window, from the fall of '74 through the spring of '75. "It [the fiscal crisis] wasn't anything that occurred during that period," Beame later reflected, accurately, if defensively. "It was the result of moves which had been made in years gone by . . . The city had a big heart, bigger than its pocketbook."

Yet rather than trace the demise of the social democratic city, the SEC report foretold the demise of its mayor. On August 31, Governor Carey added his voice to the growing Beame Must Go chorus, calling the mayor a "weakling" who lacked "the integrity" to run New York. "When we had the fiscal crisis that befell us in 1974 and 1975, I did my utmost to find leadership on the part of the incumbent," the governor told a couple of hundred Jewish businessmen and religious leaders at the Waldorf. "For whatever reason, it was not there."

It was hardly the first time the governor of New York State and the mayor of New York City, with their culturally and often geographically distinct bases, had fallen to feuding. In the late sixties, Nelson Rockefeller and John Lindsay, Republicans both, were forever sparring. But the mutual enmity that flowed between Beame and Carey was especially fratricidal considering that the two men were longtime colleagues in the tight-knit world of Brooklyn Democratic politics. Beame had even worked behind the scenes to help Carey land the Democratic gubernatorial nomination in 1973. Now, with the New York City mayoral primary a little more than a week away, the governor returned the favor by taking to the hustings on behalf of one of Mayor Beame's opponents, Mario Cuomo.

Whether Carey's support was something to be desired was another matter.

50.

ALL summer Mario Cuomo had been denying that he was Governor Carey's *Mario-nette*, an apparatchik dispatched from Albany to help the statehouse tighten its grip on City Hall. "Is the Governor really some kind of Dr. Frankenstein?" an exasperated Cuomo asked at a fund-raising breakfast in late June. "And I'm a monster with a stick in my neck that responds to his electrodes?"

The governor's staff had their own gripes about their boss's partisanship. By urging Cuomo to run, Carey had alienated most of the Democratic Party chieftains, whose fidelity to the clubhouse compelled them to back Beame. If Cuomo didn't win, Carey would pay dearly. What's more, the governor had been hitting up his wealthiest supporters for donations to the Cuomo campaign, making it more difficult for him to raise money for his own reelection fight in 1978.

Cuomo responded to this apparent generosity by rebuffing most of the governor's attempts to steer more experienced political muscle to his campaign. "Carey's neck was on the line," says James Vlasto, the governor's press secretary. "Everybody made that clear to Cuomo, but he wasn't grateful."

Cuomo didn't see why he should be grateful. "This was not a risk I asked the governor to take," he says. More to the point, Carey's endorsement made him uncomfortable. It was nothing personal, but Cuomo liked seeing himself as the outsider, the underdog. Even at this early stage in his political career, Cuomo had absorbed his own story: the smart, tough, proud kid from the outer boroughs who owed his success to intelligence and fearlessness, not to the benefits of entitlement. Cuomo ran best when running from behind, and the governor's backing had given him an unwanted head start.

Since acknowledging in May that he had encouraged Cuomo to enter the race, Carey had largely contained his role in the campaign to fund-raising. ("He's like Idi Amin," quipped Koch. "They bring him in on a chair and carry him around the room.") But near the end of August, Carey dived headfirst into the mayoral breach.

It had already been a long, trying summer for Cuomo. He was still new to political campaigning, and many of its requirements—fielding questions without resorting to disquisitions stitched together by subordinate clauses, among them—ran counter to his nature.

Nothing disturbed Cuomo as much as campaign commercials, which was Gerald Rafshoon's personal cross to bear. With David Garth committed to Koch, Cuomo had hired Rafshoon in his stead. This was something of a coup. As Jimmy Carter's media man in the '76 campaign, Rafshoon had helped transform a peanut farmer into a working-class folk hero. In so doing, Rafshoon had become a kind of star himself. He was consulting for President Carter and entertaining offers to produce a feature film when Cuomo called. "I wasn't really planning on doing any more campaigns," Rafshoon says, "but I fell in love with Mario. He was passionate, interesting, smart, articulate, well-meaning, not a typical politician."

Rafshoon's job seemed easy enough. For image-making purposes anyway, Cuomo was the urban, ethnic version of Carter. Rather than lean him against a split-rail fence in rural Georgia, Rafshoon would shoot him on the sidewalks of Queens, talking about the city's neighborhoods, or in the foreground of the Statue of Liberty, with images from old Ellis Island documentaries spliced in, reminiscing about his immigrant parents. Cuomo needed to sound tough too, even in the campaign's early days, so Rafshoon's first TV spots, which started airing in mid-June, ended with the tagline "Put your anger to work. Make New York what it can be again."

Cuomo was mortified. After glowering through a press preview of the ads, he grumbled to a *Times* reporter that in a perfect world campaign commercials would be illegal. The spots had an immediate impact on Cuomo's public recognition ratings, his main hurdle to surpassing Beame and Abzug, but the candidate was still less than thrilled. "Just saying 'Mario Cuomo, Mario Cuomo, Mario Cuomo' for five minutes each time might have had the same results," he complained.

Rafshoon soon had some complaints of his own, chiefly that his candidate "kind of looked down on politics." (A few years earlier, when he was first toying with the idea of running for mayor, Cuomo had penned a poem for his family called "Politics." It began: "Politics, an incredible game, A lusting for power, money and fame. The rules are bizarre, the logic convoluted–Intentions inconstant, invariably polluted.")

Working for Cuomo was nothing like working for Carter, who had trusted Rafshoon implicitly, so implicitly, in fact, that he almost always saw his ads for the first time on national television. Cuomo, by contrast, brought an entourage of some thirty people to the edit room for screenings. After listening to a group of Cuomo's friends and Carey's financial backers critique his ads in early July, Rafshoon quit the campaign. Cuomo succeeded in luring him back, but Rafshoon's frustrations continued right up until the end.

The loose structure of the campaign team was a media manager's worst nightmare: a weak inner staff featuring a procession of short-lived campaign managers, surrounded by endless rings of opinionated informal advisers (including Jimmy Breslin and Jack Newfield), whose presence was almost universally resented by the field operators. At the center of this chaos stood a candidate who refused to delegate authority, even to his scheduler, but who insisted on examining and reexamining every decision from every angle.

There was an intense competition for Cuomo's ear that reflected the paradox at the candidate's core: His conservative, outer borough instincts were perpetually at war with his loftier liberal ideals. "He thought the liberal ideals were more admirable—he aspired to them—but by instinct and impulse he was not a liberal," recalls Cuomo's pollster, Robert Sullivan.

This dichotomy was borne out in strategic debates over where to focus the campaign. On the surface, the boroughs represented Cuomo's natural constituency; he was, after all, an Italian kid from working-class Queens, a point he'd been underlining throughout the campaign. "If I stand for anything in politics," he liked to say, "it is that neighborhoods may live." His campaign commercials, updated to incorporate lurid scenes of blackout looting, earning still more scowls from the candidate, played to the temper of these neighborhoods: "I'm as angry as you are about a variety of issues." There was a demographic reason to fix on the boroughs as well. Some three hundred thousand Jewish voters had left the city since 1973; for the first election in decades, ethnic Catholics such as Cuomo were likely to outnumber the Jews.

But Newfield, Sullivan, and several others argued vainly that Cuomo's real opportunity lay in Manhattan. They saw him as a true progressive, a Kennedy-style liberal who could overcome Manhattan's contempt for the ethnic boroughs. (Jackie Onassis made the Kennedy link explicit by sending Cuomo a check and then telling a reporter that "he reminds me of my husband.") The *Times*, the newspaper of choice for Manhattan liberals, was confident enough in Cuomo, and sufficiently concerned about his faltering campaign, to endorse him well over a month before the primary.

For some reason, though, Cuomo insisted on sticking to the boroughs, which, as the summer wore on and the city's mounting sense of rage morphed into dreams of state-sanctioned vengeance, came to feel more and more like hostile territory. In late August, as New York's newspapers and airwaves resounded with talk of the SEC report, he was confronted again and again with what he had come to refer to as "the question." In Queens, in Brooklyn, in Staten Island, everyone wanted to know the same thing: "Why are you against capital punishment?" "He was a new face on the scene, and that was the signboard he wore around his neck," says Sullivan.

Cuomo typically prefaced his response to this question by pointing out that it was an issue over which the mayor had no jurisdiction. He would then proceed to explain that the electric chair would not make his seventy-seven-year-old parents any safer; that the only time anyone would actually burn, it would be some poor miserable person who couldn't afford an attorney to go up the ladder to the Supreme Court; that the electric chair wouldn't produce jobs or alleviate racial tension; that we as a society are better than capital punishment.

But were we? At a beach club one afternoon in the Bronx, Cuomo hadn't even launched into his reply when someone stood up and shouted, "Kill them!" In Brighton Beach, Brooklyn, another day, Cuomo delivered his anti-death penalty diatribe—and an elderly woman promptly spit on him. "The city was scared to death, angry and frightened," he remembers, "angry at the police and angry at me for not supporting the death penalty."

Cuomo's patron up in Albany didn't support the death penalty either. Governor Carey had vetoed a capital punishment bill the day before the blackout, eloquently explaining that he shared the city's growing sense of outrage at rampant crime and its perpetrators' seeming immunity, but that the solace offered by the electric chair was illusory.

On the first day of September, however, Carey allowed for the possibility that he might reconsider—if Cuomo were elected mayor. The governor was campaigning with his candidate's wife, bantering with a row of women under curlers in a crowded beauty parlor in

Pelham Parkway, a largely white middle-class section of the East Bronx, when the suggestion passed through his lips. Give Mario Cuomo a year in office, Carey said, and if he doesn't bring crime down, "I personally will listen to anybody on a review of the death penalty."

When the *Daily News* reported the governor's comment the following day, he promptly denied having uttered it. By then Cuomo's opponents were already hectoring Carey for trying to blackmail the electorate in a desperate attempt to prop up his sagging candidate. For twenty-four hours the campaign wasn't a referendum on the death penalty; it was a debate about what the governor had or hadn't said. "What's the difference if today he's saying, 'Look, I didn't mean it?' " answered an exasperated Cuomo when pressed for comment.

Cuomo managed to keep his temper in check for most of the summer, save for one hot night in August, when Mike Long, an ex-marine and vocal street-corner conservative, accosted him after a speech at a high school in Brooklyn. When Long called Cuomo a liar, the candidate lunged at him, pushing him through the swinging doors at the back of the auditorium. They continued to shove and grab at one another in the hallway outside, and were about to start trading punches when the police broke it up. Fortunately, both men were sufficiently embarrassed by the incident to make sure it stayed out of the papers.

If anything, Cuomo was too civil, at least where his opponents were concerned. Koch's endless taunts—"That campaign is *Cuomotose!*"—had gone largely unanswered, and Cuomo had even abstained from the Beame free-for-all in the wake of the SEC report, wondering what good it would do to "jump up and down on this man's head."

What good had it done Cuomo not to? By the beginning of September it was clear that Cuomo had failed to live up to the optimistic predictions that had anticipated his candidacy. Even the *Daily News*, the paper that first urged Cuomo to enter the race, had abandoned him, endorsing Koch instead.

Yet for all this, Cuomo was still in the running. In the absence of specifics, there were evocations, rhetorical flights back to his childhood in blue-collar Queens and forward to a city where the poor would once again have the opportunity to work their way into middle class (much as his father had done). Even if Cuomo wasn't saying what angry outer borough residents wanted to hear, they still recognized him as one of their own. And while the *Daily News* had endorsed Koch, the tabloid's two most widely read columnists, Breslin and Hamill, were doing everything they could to promote Cuomo as New York's best chance for redemption. "What surprises some people is that he is tough on the side of reason, and won't churn up still more irrationality in this disturbed city," Hamill wrote near the end of August. "He could have presented himself these last few months as the big tough Italian who was going to club and electrocute people into lawfulness. He didn't do that."

Cuomo could do nothing right, but he could also do nothing wrong. Not even Murdoch was able to purge his pages of pro-Cuomo propaganda. In their syndicated column in the *Post*, Jack Germond and Jules Witcover made a virtue of Cuomo's struggles, calling him "a conspicuously rational man in the essentially irrational business of a New York mayoral campaign."

As the campaign entered its final week, the polls showed Cuomo, Koch, Abzug, and Beame running in a virtual dead heat. A runoff was now a near certainty.

Eager to give his candidate a final boost, Carey persuaded Cuomo that they needed the backing of hero cop–cum–Congressman Mario Biaggi. Cuomo was wary. Biaggi, who had taken ten bullets on his way to winning a chestful of police medals, still smelled strongly of scandal. A few years earlier the transcripts of his testimony before a grand jury investigating allegations of payoffs to congressmen had been released; Biaggi had taken the Fifth Amendment seventeen times. But if the disclosure had torpedoed Biaggi's mayoral candidacy in '73, it had done little to dent his status as, in his words,

"New York's Number One Italian." Better still, Biaggi, a handsome, silver-haired man who had risen from a childhood of abject poverty in what was now East Harlem, was as law-and-order as they come, an outspoken advocate of resurrecting the electric chair.

Cuomo reluctantly conceded, and Carey deployed his special assistant Raymond Harding, an old friend of Biaggi's from the Bronx, to make their pitch to the congressman. It took a little coaxing but Biaggi, no doubt flattered by the attention in his politically weakened state, eventually agreed to go along.

The night before New York's Number One Italian was scheduled to anoint his candidate, Carey, Harding, and Cuomo were in a late-night strategy session at the Upper East Side town house of ex-Mayor Robert Wagner, discussing how best to exploit the endorsement. Cuomo announced that he'd changed his mind; he didn't want the congressman's support after all. Harding, a thick-necked army veteran and Holocaust survivor, started screaming at Cuomo. "Who are you to foist this on me?" an indignant Cuomo shouted back at him. Carey sided with Harding.

The next morning, Labor Day, Cuomo walked into Ratner's, a kosher dairy restaurant on the Lower East Side, to find Biaggi sitting hunched over a plate of scrambled eggs and onions. "Do I have time for breakfast?" Cuomo asked one of his handlers. He didn't. Cuomo grabbed half a toasted bagel to go and set off with his newest supporter to tape a fresh campaign commercial.

The next day, forty-eight hours before the primary, the two Marios walked the streets of Brooklyn together. Asked about Cuomo's position on the death penalty, Biaggi answered, "If he wins, I think I can persuade him."

51.

BACK in Manhattan, Koch was busy campaigning with his own sidekick, one enlisted to protect a very different soft spot. Bess Myerson, who was out of town for much of August, had been summoned back to New York for the final push. During the waning days of the campaign the two were inseparable.

The press gamely played along. When a *Post* lensman snapped them hand in hand at a beach club in Canarsie on September 6, the photo graced the front page. The *SoHo Weekly News*'s Sherryl Connelly caught up with the candidate and his leading lady at the San Gennaro Festival. "Both have refused to discuss marriage publicly, but as they draw nearer to the seat of power it has become important to many people to determine just how close is very close," she wrote. The story continued: "Very close." And continued: "As they meet on the streets of Little Italy at the end of a long day, in the midst of a milling crowd lighted by a neon glow, their faces come alive. Forming a tight unit of two that the push of people can't break into, they share the day's anecdotes."

Earlier in the summer, it was Myerson whom the voters had recognized. By the end of August people were asking Koch, suggestively: "Who's that with you, Ed?"

But Myerson provided Koch with much more than an answer to those inclined to wonder about his sexual preference. After all, she wasn't just the first Jewish Miss America; she was *New York*'s first Miss America, a dark-haired daughter of the Bronx who had trained as a concert pianist and earned a degree from Hunter College before winning her title in 1945, the year the concentration camps were liberated. New York could not have been more proud of her, even if the rest of the country had its doubts. (On her postpageant tour Myerson tried to visit a World War II veteran whose mother barred the door. "Because of the damned Jews," she said, "my boy was maimed.")

With the exception of Bella Abzug, Myerson was the city's most public woman, a former commissioner of consumer affairs who might well have been elected to the Senate in 1974 had her bid not been derailed by an eighteen-month bout with ovarian cancer. Like New York itself, Myerson was a survivor, not just of the cancer but of a demeaning if well-compensated career as a TV game show host, one marriage to an abusive alcoholic, and another to a rich, high-profile attorney whom she wedded and divorced twice. By 1977 Myerson's tiara had lost its luster, but she was still New York's queen. And the balding, pear-shaped man by her side was her unlikely king.

52.

This muck heaves and palpitates. It is multidirectional and has a mayor.

DONALD BARTHELME, *CITY LIFE*

THE months of three-digit temperatures, of air so humid it might as well have been water, were finally over. On Thursday, September 8, a mild, partly cloudy day, a record number of New York City Democrats turned out to nominate their candidate or at least narrow the field to two.

As night approached, the candidates made their way to their respective locations to await the returns. Abzug barreled confidently into the Roosevelt Hotel, her brown suede hat flopping, to the strains of the theme song from "Rocky." A few hours later, when her fourth-place finish was all but confirmed, the band struck up a more somber tune, "Eleanor Rigby." Abzug conceded at a little after midnight.

Abe Beame, stubborn as usual, waited much longer. Not since 1917 had a New York City mayor duly elected to a four-year term been rejected by his own party. For hours Beame sat, his face creased with fatigue, watching the returns on the twentieth floor of the Americana Hotel before finally coming down to admit defeat at a little before 2 a.m. Now, in the same hotel where New York had gained a superstar less than a year earlier, it was about to lose a mayor.

In a sense, it was losing more than that. "I gave this city every ounce of my strength and my fullest devotion during its most trying years of crisis," Beame told his dwindling band of supporters. "I've not let this city down." Moments later the usually stoic mayor began to cry. His wife, Mary, hugged him, allowing Beame to collect himself, and he pressed on. As he did, New York's diminutive leader seemed almost to grow. He was no longer an easy object of derision, a pint-size emblem of the city's failures, but rather a dignified civil servant, the embodiment of a vanishing New York, a New York in which the sons of socialists overcame poverty and then quietly devoted themselves to making the city a better place to live, where the Democratic Party machine (however corrupt) and the labor bosses (however power-hungry) always took care of their needy constituents.

Meanwhile, at Charley O's, a nondescript saloon in the theater district, the crowd was chanting "First Lady Bess." Ed Koch handed a bouquet of red roses to Myerson—"the most important person of the campaign"—and celebrated his narrow first-place victory.

Across the river at a catering hall in the eastern reaches of Queens, second-place finisher Mario Cuomo squinted into the harsh glare of the TV lights and looked ahead to the September 19 runoff. Cuomo had recovered his underdog status but Koch's margin of victory had been less than one percent. A senior member of his campaign staff, Richard Starkey, felt encouraged. "Mario has nice things to say about all of his opponents save Koch," Starkey wrote later that night in his diary. "He wants to put an end to the charge that he isn't substantive enough. He wants to debate 'Eddie' every day for the next eleven days. He talks with a zest for combat that is familiar. Although he is tired he doesn't let himself become aggressive or arrogant, just self-assured."

The following morning the feminist Gloria Steinem told viewers of the *Stanley Siegel Show* that the election results confirmed that the once liberal city had lurched to the right. That was one way of looking at it. Another was that in eliminating Beame and Abzug and choosing Koch and Cuomo, the city's voters had narrowed the field to the two candidates least encumbered by the past.

53.

ED Koch and Mario Cuomo had landed in first and second place in the September 8 primary, but they had managed to capture just 39 percent of the votes between them. The remaining 61 percent was now up for grabs, setting off a furious ten-day scramble for support that quickly devolved into an orgy of deal making, backstabbing, and score settling.

The runoff began predictably enough, with each candidate sounding familiar campaign themes. The day after the primary Cuomo spoke of the need to "harmonize" New York's "magnificient mosaic" and warned of Koch's potential to divide. Koch told the *Times* that the last thing the city needed was a "pacifier" like Cuomo.

On September 10 the Patrolmen's Benevolent Association held its annual convention upstate. The PBA's president, Samuel DeMilia, invited both Democratic candidates to speak. Koch, who'd been hammering away at the police union all summer, declined, reminding voters instead that he wasn't afraid to take on DeMilia—"the same Sam DeMilia who asked police officers not to volunteer to work on the Son of Sam case on their own time."

Cuomo barely made it there himself. His helicopter pilot got lost in the Catskills and wound up landing on the fairway of a golf course. A man on the second tee managed to direct them to the convention center, where the cops stood and whistled for Cuomo when he told them the city wouldn't be such a mess if the politicians had only done their jobs as well as the cops. With the support of the police union assured, or so he thought, Cuomo hustled back to the city for a late-night meeting in Riverdale with Herman Badillo.

In such a compressed race, winning over large blocs of voters was going to be critical, and Badillo had a large bloc to deliver. Since 1960, the year he created a new Democratic club in East Harlem to help presidential hopeful John F. Kennedy register blacks and Latinos, Badillo, a magna cum laude graduate of City College, had evolved into one of New York's most forceful and persistent minority advocates and, owing to the recent explosion of the city's Puerto Rican population, one of its most powerful. As that community's premier spokesman, Badillo now held sway over roughly 10 percent of the electorate.

Moreover, on the day after the primary Badillo formed an informal coalition with two other losers, Bella Abzug and Percy Sutton. They planned to meet with the two candidates individually and then collectively endorse the one most committed to helping the city's minorities. Taken together, Badillo, Abzug, and Sutton had won 42 percent of the primary vote, more than Koch and Cuomo combined. Given Abzug's disdain for Koch, this boded well for Cuomo.

The Sunday morning after his meeting with Badillo, Cuomo brought his family to the Church of the Master, a black Presbyterian parish in Harlem. He at first declined to speak, then agreed to take to the pulpit and improvised his best address of the campaign. After sketching the history of the Catholic Church's awakening to the moral obligation to participate in the political process, Cuomo transitioned into the city's problems. If he'd had time to prepare, he might have thought better of merging matters of church and state. As it happened, the theological preamble gave his words a fresh urgency, especially among a congregation whose faith had been so sorely tested by rampant crime and poverty. Arriving, inevitably, at the "question," Cuomo said that if the election was to be won or lost over the death penalty, "then we have to win,"—and now the congregation was whispering amen, amen—"because we cannot say to the whole country, to the whole world . . . that we are a people who have come to believe that the only solution to our problem is death."

In two days Cuomo had won over a convention hall full of New York City cops and a church full of black Presbyterians. The comparisons to Kennedy were beginning to look prophetic. That was when Cuomo's troubles began.

Badillo had apparently not been satisfied by their meeting. "I couldn't get a straight answer from him . . . He kept giving me the typical Cuomo philosophical discourse," Badillo remembers. In exchange for his endorsement, Badillo wanted to control the hiring for the top job in New York's public housing program, a critical appointment for the city's minorities. More broadly, he wanted to know what Cuomo would do for the Hispanic community. "I said, 'Look, I'm not going to dish out jobs,' " Cuomo recalls.

Badillo brought the same question to Koch, who promised to appoint Hispanics at every level of the city government and, as an added incentive, offered to name Badillo cochairman of his campaign. Badillo broke with his short-lived coalition and announced that he was now supporting, and working for, Ed Koch.

Losing Badillo was a blow to Cuomo, but it had at least given Sutton another reason to back him. Not only had Koch lined up against the black community in the Forest Hills housing dispute a few years earlier, but during the primary Sutton had accused Koch of using "racial code words" like "poverty pimps" in his attacks on the city's corruption-rife antipoverty programs. Now that he'd been betrayed by Koch's new campaign cochairman—"Oh, Herman!" a disappointed Sutton had gasped upon hearing the news—he was sure to swing behind Cuomo. And when he did, Sutton would be bringing much more than his own weight to bear. At a secret postprimary meeting in Congressman Charles Rangel's Harlem office, the city's most prominent black leaders had empowered him to speak on behalf of the entire community.

Cuomo was about to capture Sutton's endorsement when a power struggle in New York City black politics rudely intervened. Led by Vander Beatty, a flashy state senator from Bedford-Stuyvesant, Brooklyn (who was later sent to jail for embezzling state funds from a local rehabilitation program), several of the black political and community leaders who'd been present at the meeting in Rangel's office gathered on the steps of City Hall on the morning of September 13 to preempt Sutton and endorse Cuomo on their own. Twice betrayed, Sutton was now fuming: at the Brooklyn leaders for upstaging him and at Cuomo for not informing him that they were going to do so. Sutton decided to remain neutral in the runoff.

With the black and minority coalitions ruptured, Koch began maneuvering for more African-American endorsements. On the afternoon of September 13, he invited Representative Rangel and twenty other black leaders to a private meeting in David Garth's office. Koch, as conciliatory in private as he was confrontational in public, told them he didn't realize he'd been using racial code words and that he'd be happy to change his rhetoric. He talked about his involvement in the civil rights struggle, registering black voters in Mississippi and marching with the Reverend Martin Luther King, Jr., in Alabama. "I was very eloquent," Koch observed of the meeting in his 1984 memoir *Mayor*. More to the point, he promised to bring more minorities into his administration than the previous three mayors combined. (Koch ultimately made good on that pledge, though not until midway through his second term.)

Sensing the shifting tides, several other local black leaders quickly moved to try to prevent Koch from gaining momentum. One state senator, Major Owens, wrote an open letter to the city's black leaders in which he called Koch a "race-baiter" who would scapegoat minorities, dismantle community-based antipoverty programs, and polarize the city. "Our only option is the total commitment of the Black leadership and electorate of this city to the candidacy of Mario Cuomo," Owens said. By now, however, many of the city's most powerful black politicians, Rangel and David Dinkins among them, were already lining up behind Koch.

Cuomo was growing frustrated. When the *New York Post*'s Joyce Purnick called him while he was preparing for the first debate of the runoff on the night of September 14, he told her he was too busy to talk, then blew off some self-righteous steam, remarking that he didn't want to win badly enough to engage in influence peddling. "This illusion that you can have one morality on the way there and another morality when you get there is not only the ultimate in hypocrisy, it is unreal," he said. "It is. It's nonsense . . . I don't work that way. If I do what I think is wrong, I am not going to be able to lead."

Cuomo's indignation carried over into that night's Channel 13 debate. He promptly went on the offensive, assailing Manhattan for turning its back on the outer boroughs and chiding Koch for supporting the death penalty. "I went into that debate feisty and as near to angry as I ever get, and it showed," Cuomo remembers. "I was impolite. I was extremely tough on Koch. I did an awful job."

Koch, following his media manager's advice, studiously avoided engaging his opponent. "Garth said, 'Ignore him, don't listen to him, don't talk to him, talk to the camera. He's a distraction,' " Koch recalls. "The danger was that there's no question that Cuomo is a sensational debater. I'm not sure he always tells the truth, but whether he does or he doesn't, he makes a wonderful impression, so if you get sucked into debating with him you're going to lose."

Later that night Cuomo campaign aide Richard Starkey scribbled a dejected entry into his diary: "The debate is a major disappointment because Mario is reduced to a sniping role. He's testy instead of smooth and unruffled. He harps too much on the death penalty issue . . . I had hoped for a decisive drubbing of Koch. This is at best a standoff, at worst a defeat for my man Mario."

54.

THE same night the Yankees and Red Sox were locked in their own standoff in the second of three high-stakes games at the stadium.

Only ten days earlier the Yanks had opened their lead on the Sox to four and a half. With a little less than a month to go in the regular season, it was almost time to start the pennant countdown. Then the Yankees stumbled. Not badly—they dropped a twin bill to Cleveland and two of four to the cellar-dwelling Blue Jays—but badly enough to enable the streaking Sox, who had won ten of their last eleven, to pull within one and a half games before boarding their charter plane for New York.

The two teams had not met since June, when they split six games. The upcoming showdown was to draw 164,852 fans to the Bronx, baseball's biggest three-day crowd in almost twenty years. In Boston, hope bloomed. The *Globe* slapped its September 13 series curtain-raiser above the fold on page one: "It is like the conclusion of some 1000-page novel, some epic paperback potboiler that has been carried around for an entire summer . . . Was there ever any doubt where the plot lines were leading?"

Guidry opened for the Yanks, mowing down the first three Sox hitters on ten pitches. In the top half of the second, a walk and a wild pitch helped Boston parlay two hits into two runs. It was the last time they'd get a runner past first. For their part, the Yanks got on the board with one in the fourth, then pulled ahead 4–2 in the fifth. With

Guidry in rhythm, the Sox went nowhere. He finished the game himself, following Martin's instruction to stick with his fastball in the ninth so as not to risk hanging a slider.

Then came the standoff. For eight complete innings on a cool mid-September night, the two teams swapped zeros. Yet it was not exactly a pitcher's duel. The Yanks were certainly getting their rips. Red Sox third baseman Butch Hobson collared one hot smash after the next, and with two on and two out in the home half of the third, Munson crushed a line drive to left that seemed destined for extra bases. The thirty-eight-year-old Carl Yastrzemski took off on a dead sprint after the ball and launched into a full-extension dive to spear it inches above the grass.

Figueroa was going for the Yanks, and the Sox were hammering him. Through the first four, Boston had put men on base every inning. In the fifth, with the bases loaded and nobody out, it looked as if the dam were about to burst when Fred Lynn hit a hard hopper back to the mound to start a 1–2–3 double play. The top half of every inning saw at least one towering fly ball pulled down in the meadows of Yankee Stadium's endless outfield. In center, Mickey Rivers, who'd been hit square in the back by Reggie Cleveland's first pitch of the night, reeled in three 410-plus drives. ("Rivers won't be able to play tomorrow," Yastrzemski said after the game, "because he has to go in for an oil change.")

For his part, Reggie Jackson made two very good catches look spectacular. The first had come in the fourth. With Jim Rice on second, George Scott lashed a ball to deep right. Reggie, who was nursing a bruised knee, backpedaled and backpedaled and, just shy of the wall, leaped and stretched and gathered the ball in. Three innings later, with a runner on second again, Reggie hesitated just slightly, then charged in at Bernie Carbo's sinking liner, diving at the ball just in time to slip his glove under it.

Now to the ninth. Figueroa somehow managed to hold the Sox at bay one last time, and the Yanks sent the fat part of their lineup to the plate for the final frame. Munson singled up the middle, and 54,365 fans stood and roared. Reggie was next. Martin started him off with the bunt sign. (Not that Reggie, who hadn't laid one down since 1971, knew the bunt sign. Third base coach Dick Howser had to trot into the batter's box and mouth the four-letter word. "Where's the best place for you to lay one down?" Howser asked. "I have no idea," Reggie answered.)

Reggie squared around and took ball one. Martin, guessing fastball at 1-0, let him swing away at the second pitch. Reggie fouled it back. At 1-1, Reggie squared around again. Another ball. On it went—the bunt on, the bunt off—until the count was full. Pitcher Reggie Cleveland checked the runner and uncorked a hard sinker, low and outside: ball four or, with a little luck, a ground ball double play. Reggie went down after it, meeting the ball near his ankles and driving it 430 feet into the bleachers in right-center, giving the Yankees a 2–0 victory.

The Red Sox won the following night to prevent the sweep, but their pennant hopes were fading fast. With fifteen games to go, they trailed the Yanks by two and a half and were headed south to play the Orioles, who had lost just once in their last nine outings.

Writing a month later in *The New Yorker*, Roger Angell invested the Boston series with two-pronged significance. It was the moment the Yankees won their pennant and the moment he stopped feeling comfortable bringing his wife and son to the Bronx ballyard. During the third game a group of fans in the upper deck showered their fellow spectators with beer, hurled darts and bottles onto the field, and engaged in a near riot with the stadium police. "There was nothing fresh or surprising about this," Angell remarked; "it happened all the time this summer at Yankee Stadium."

55.

WITH the September 19 Democratic runoff drawing near, the city's unions started stepping into the electoral fray. Given all the abuse that Koch had heaped on the labor bosses during the primary campaign, this should have been good news for Cuomo. Victor Gotbaum, the gruff, pugnacious head of District Council 37, didn't disappoint. Calling Koch "a pimple on the behind of civilization," he enthusiastically bestowed the blessing of his union, the city's largest, on Cuomo.

But for the most part the labor movement's support for Koch's opponent was surprisingly muted. Unable to abide Cuomo's opposition to capital punishment, the Patrolmen's Benevolent Association wasn't endorsing either candidate. More surprising still, neither was Koch's favorite piñata, Albert Shanker's United Federation of Teachers.

There was an explanation for this, though not one Shanker was eager to elucidate. Political candidates had once worried about alienating municipal labor bosses, but the fiscal crisis had inverted the equation. In agreeing to help save the city from bankruptcy by steering billions of pension fund dollars into New York–backed securities, the civil servant unions had become the city's largest creditor. (Imagine a corporation's employees bailing out the company by buying up its stock for their IRA.) For the first time, Albert Shanker's responsibility to his members went beyond wringing concessions from City Hall. He had to protect their pensions, and that meant working with City Hall to help restore New York's fiscal health. A few years earlier Woody Allen had nominated Shanker as most likely to instigate World War III in his futuristic comedy *Sleeper*. Now, in announcing his union's decision to stay neutral, Shanker meekly suggested that his constituents would take into account Koch's "very negative statements" when they went to the polls.

There were still more storms ahead for Cuomo. With Beame and Abzug, the two candidates Carey objected to most strenuously, out of the picture, the governor was starting to sound less committed to his secretary of state. Though he continued to raise money for Cuomo, Carey was hedging his bets; he would need the support of New York City's mayor, whoever it happened to be, for his own re-election bid in '78. Having promised in the spring to stick with Cuomo through the general election in November, even if he lost the Democratic primary and had to run on an independent line, Carey was now suggesting that he would support the candidate who won the upcoming Democratic runoff, be it Koch or Cuomo.

Carey's nemesis, Abe Beame, was less diplomatic and more vindictive. During the campaign Koch had been the most vicious of the mayor's attackers, accusing him, among other things, of "running the city like a second-class candy store." But Beame could never back the man whom the governor had handpicked to unhorse him. The mayor endorsed Koch.

At least Abzug, increasingly ill tempered at the growing prospect of a Koch victory, was planning to endorse Cuomo. This could have been a big break for Cuomo. In the primary Abzug had taken Manhattan, his weakest borough, and her fiercely loyal supporters were eagerly awaiting the call to arms. The trouble was that Cuomo, who was now turning paranoid in addition to angry and self-righteous, kept ducking her. For some reason, he was convinced that Carey had promised Abzug something–he wasn't sure what–in exchange for her support, and he refused to be party to it. For several days, whenever Abzug charged into Cuomo's Manhattan headquarters, hoping to catch him for a quick preendorsement meeting, the candidate wasn't there.

Again and again Cuomo refused to participate in the sort of deal making that had long been part of the city's political culture. It was true that New York's five county leaders, once the kingmakers of the city's electoral process, weren't the men they used to be. There were fewer municipal jobs and contracts to parcel out, and the changing racial and ethnic mix of their respective boroughs—Brooklyn, Queens, and the Bronx, in particular—was eroding their once-unchallenged authority. Still, the county leaders controlled their share of votes. More important, they commanded a valuable army of field workers who could get people to the polls.

No county leader had been more adept at clinging to power than Brooklyn's cartoon version of a political boss, complete with mob ties and masticated cigar, Meade Esposito. Having delivered his borough to Beame for the September 9 primary, Esposito was now up for grabs.

Cuomo would have had no trouble wooing him. The two men shared a son-of-a-shopkeeper outer borough Italian history and, if Esposito is to be believed, a love of literature. (Though he had no diplomas hanging on his wall—Esposito never graduated from elementary school—the Brooklyn county leader boasted of reading Plato in his free time.) But the zealously high-minded Cuomo was not in the business of wooing. He reluctantly met Esposito for a cup of coffee and promised him nothing. "He wanted to know that he could put his guy in the transportation department," Cuomo recalls. "I said no."

Koch, on the other hand, gamely descended into the basement of Esposito's mother's house in Brooklyn for homemade meatballs, a culinary rite of passage for all those seeking political favors from him. An informal deal was quickly struck. If Esposito marshaled his Brooklyn forces behind Koch, he would, if elected, provide plum positions to certain of Esposito's cronies. Thus did Ed Koch, the crusading reformer who had made his name in New York City politics by slaying the Tammany Tiger, Carmine De Sapio, win Meade Esposito's support. It had to be done discreetly, though, lest Koch's reputation as a political maverick be tarnished. "We made it clear that the one thing we didn't want him [Esposito] to do was endorse me in any public way," Koch reflected in his 1985 book *Politics*.

The debates continued, and so did Cuomo's sniping. "You've got your Garth cards there you're reading from?" he asked Koch on the radio one afternoon. Meanwhile, Koch never forgot his media manager's advice to avoid tustling with his opponent, which seemed only to frustrate Cuomo further. As Murray Kempton observed, the two men had switched roles: Cuomo was the hectoring bully; Koch, the mild-mannered pacifier.

Cuomo's self-destructive tendency to harp on capital punishment also continued. "He was defining himself to himself on the death penalty," says Robert Sullivan, Cuomo's pollster. "The argument that he was going to lose because of this only defined for him where he must stand." It got to the point where even Koch, who picked up more votes every time his opponent railed against the electric chair, was urging Cuomo to stop raising the issue. Cuomo almost seemed to be trying to martyr himself, or was he straining to make sure that he'd have an honorable excuse for losing?

The campaign grew nastier as the runoff approached. In the wake of the city's polarizing summer, it was inevitable that the venom flowing between the two camps would be colored by their respective ethnicities. Early in the runoff Cuomo had inadvertently fanned the city's smoldering tribalism when he said that if Koch were elected by what was perceived to be the Jewish vote and New York continued to struggle, "they'll say, 'Yeah, there's that Jewish mayor.' " A Jewish organization promptly responded by effectively accusing Cuomo of anti-Semitism in an angry letter distributed around the city on the eve of the Jewish New Year. *The Village Voice* reported that Cuomo trucks in Jewish Brooklyn were being pelted with eggs, while Koch workers campaigning in Italian Brooklyn had been hit by stones (and in one case, a sausage pizza).

Scrambling to reverse Koch's momentum in the waning days of the campaign, Cuomo's team unleashed a new television commercial. The spot showed Koch's face morphing into that of another former congressman from Manhattan's silk stocking district, John

Lindsay. The accompanying voice-over elaborated on the similarities between the two men, suggesting that Koch's promises to take on the power brokers would prove just as empty and that he'd be equally tone-deaf to the problems of the middle class.

In the near future, this sort of commercial would become standard campaign fare; at the time, though, it set off a flurry of finger wagging. "We decided to go negative," says Rafshoon. "It didn't work."

Cuomo promptly pulled the spot, but Garth already had the inspiration he needed for a new spot of his own, starring a wounded Bess Myerson. "Whatever happened to character, Mr. Cuomo?" the former Miss America asked, her blue eyes gazing earnestly into the camera. "We thought your campaign would be better than that."

Outside the enemy camp the sense of disappointment with Cuomo was no less acute. The man who had once effortlessly charmed reporters with his self-effacing wit and pathological ambivalence about politics was now losing supporters in the press corps. On September 18 a disillusioned Ken Auletta wrote a column for the *Daily News* whose headline said it all: FALLING OUT OF LOVE WITH MARIO CUOMO.

The following day New York's Democrats voted. Turnout was lower than it had been for the September 9 primary and was particularly weak among the city's minorities. "[L]ike a store destroyed by the blackout," the *Amsterdam News* wrote the following week, "the political confidence of the Black communities . . . will have to be built from the ground up."

The polls closed at 9 p.m. Fifteen minutes later the winner by a wide margin, Ed Koch, was announced.

56.

EMBARKING on his run for governor in the spring of 1982, Mario Cuomo would blame all of the perceived problems with his candidacy on the dark days he had endured in September 1977. The negative images of him as a campaigner "all arise out of the runoff of '77, and ignore completely my history before that nine-day period and my history after it," he wrote in his diary in March 1982.

As for his diary entries for the primary campaign and runoff of '77, Cuomo has since titled them "Fishing in Shallow Waters," the implication being that he'd never really committed to his candidacy. "I ran out of respect for the governor's wishes, and that was a mistake," Cuomo says. "My frame of mind throughout was reluctance . . . You get married reluctantly and your marriage is doomed. You stay in a job reluctantly and you underperform."

Given Cuomo's fiercely competitive nature, it's a difficult explanation to accept, and it is contradicted both by those who were close to him during the '77 primary campaign—"I understand the theory that he didn't want to win, but I don't buy it," says Sullivan—and by what happened next: Cuomo ran in the general election as the candidate of the Liberal Party.

Founded in 1944 by a group of social democratic trade unionists who wanted to bolt the Communist-infiltrated American Labor Party but were wary of the Tammany-controlled Democrats, the Liberal Party had once played an important role in local and national politics, delivering key blocs for Truman in '48 and Kennedy in '60. By the fall of '77, though, the party's days of influence were behind it, and its members were in disarray after the internecine power struggle set off by the recent death of its founder, the former head of the hat makers' union, Alex Rose.

In exchange for the Liberal Party's endorsement in the early days of the mayoral race, Cuomo pledged to remain on the party's line for the general election, even if he lost the Democratic nomination. It was the one deal Cuomo made during the primary, and he intended to keep it. There was no way he could win; there were just 105,000 registered Liberals *statewide*. This was no secret to Governor Carey. Already gearing up to shift his allegiance to Koch, the governor urged Cuomo to stand down and leave the Democrats united behind a single candidate. Others quickly followed suit, suggesting that by staying in the race, Cuomo would only drive the wedge deeper between the city's Catholics and Jews. The *Post* called on Cuomo to abandon his "doomed, divisive effort." Victor Gotbaum and Mario Biaggi went so far as to withdraw their endorsements.

In other words, Cuomo was once again where he liked to be: running from behind with no hope of victory and no support from the political establishment. Now that Governor Carey had deserted him, the campaign funds quickly dried up. Rafshoon took a full-time job as a special consultant to President Carter. The Boston-based firm that ran Cuomo's press operation packed up and went home. The big-ticket columnists who had taken such an interest in the campaign's strategy drifted away. Cuomo was left with a small crew, made up mostly of ex-Abzug staffers who had nowhere else to go. He still didn't listen to anybody—for that matter, he wouldn't until his son Andrew was old enough to run the show—but as the rings of handlers began to disappear, so too did the candidate's self-righteous anger and sanctimony.

Cuomo ran a superb campaign, the notable exception being his handling of the innuendos of Koch's homosexuality. (Cuomo's failure to prevent outer-borough field operatives from investigating the rumors and from posting the infamous handbills reading VOTE FOR CUOMO NOT THE HOMO may have been forgivable; his suggestion in one debate that Koch supported the right of gay school teachers to "proselytize" was definitely not.)

Come the November general election, Cuomo managed to capture more than 38 percent of the vote, pummeling the Republican candidate, giving Koch a scare, and salvaging his nascent political career. Before long it was almost as though the summer of '77 had never happened. In the spring of '78, the *Times* was once again referring to Coumo as "everybody's favorite candidate for something," and in 1982, when Coumo resurfaced as a gubernatorial long shot, he got the better of Koch in a statewide rematch.

57.

THIS was Koch's moment, though. Pete Hamill filed his post-runoff column in late September from Bushwick. More than two months had passed since New York's long night of looting, and the damage had been absorbed into this bleak landscape. A steady drizzle added to the gloomy scene—the charred, gutted buildings; the abandoned cars that had long since been stripped bare. "This is the city that Ed Koch will have to cure," Hamill wrote, "a city abandoned, a city unrepresented, a city cynical, the ruined and broken city."

Hamill, who had never wavered in his loyalty to Cuomo, was betting against the city's new mayor, but in many ways Koch rose to the challenge. He eventually was haunted by the ghosts of the '77 campaign. In the late eighties, three of his commissioners, Esposito cronies all, were convicted for corruption, and Bess Myerson unraveled, publicly, in a bribery scandal the tabs gleefully dubbed "the Bess Mess." Over the years Koch's confidence came to read as arrogance, his candor as insensitivity, his strong stomach for confrontation as an insatiable appetite for it.

But first, Koch—along with the rest of New York's emerging titans: Reggie, Steinbrenner, and Murdoch—would lead the city into a new era. They were flawed, farsighted, self-made men who intuitively understood the city's desire for drama and conflict because they shared it. They were not idealists but egomaniacs. To their hungry eyes, New York wasn't a "ruined and broken city" but the place where you go to make it.

It was clear now that their New York, the new New York, was going to be different. The city that had once dared to fly in the face of capitalism could no longer aspire to be all things to all its people. New York's future belonged not to labor bosses, political power brokers, or social visionaries but to entrepreneurs; between 1977 and 1985, the private sector created more jobs in the city than in the fifties and sixties combined. Koch's hero, Mayor La Guardia, used to ride around every Sunday looking for new things to build. During Koch's tenure, virtually all of New York's new construction would be undertaken by private developers (or, in the city's poorer sections, private-public partnerships).

After taking office on the first day of 1978, Koch ran the city much as he had run his campaign, ruthlessly and pragmatically. At the same time, though, a new Ed Koch, one that Garth had intentionally suppressed for fear that it might alienate voters, quickly came into focus. This was Ed Koch the irrepressible, wisecracking cabbie, the city's mascot as much as its mayor.

His handling of a transit strike in early 1980 underscores the point. In stark contrast with Mayor Lindsay, who encouraged New Yorkers to stay home when the transit workers walked out, threw the head of the union and his cohorts in jail, and *still* wound up submitting to a 15 percent raise, Koch was determined to prevent the strike from crippling the city or deflating its spirit. He expected everyone to go to work and cheered workers on from the Manhattan side of the Brooklyn Bridge as they did. He denounced union demands as "outrageous" and defiantly went about his daily business, occasionally pausing to dismiss prounion hecklers as "wackos."

As for Bushwick, its recovery was slow, halting, to this day incomplete, yet inexorable. Mayor Koch helped jump-start plans to fill the garbage-strewn hole in the heart of the neighborhood, the infamous urban renewal zone, with low- and moderate-income housing. An influx of Asian-Americans moved in from Chinatown and Flushing, Queens. St. Barbara's Church fixed its organ, repaired its leaky ceiling, and was soon drawing Sunday mass crowds approaching a thousand. An interracial coalition of East Brooklyn churches secured a grant from the city for its Nehemiah homes, single-family brick row houses designed for families with annual incomes between twenty and forty thousand dollars. No less important were two small weekly newspapers, first the *North Brooklyn News* and later the *North Brooklyn Mercury*, which charted the community's rehabilitation, commending its heroes, exposing its villains, flushing out corruption, and, most of all, keeping alive the story of a neighborhood that might otherwise have been forgotten as the long, hot summer of 1977 began to fade into New York's collective memory.

58.

NEAR the end of September, Yankee Stadium attendance passed the two million mark for the first time since 1949. Yankees' haters were no less committed to their cause than Yankees' rooters; the team drew nearly as well on the road.

For rhetorical purposes, the Yankees may have won their divisional flag during that dramatic mid-September series against the Red Sox, but it had been a long slog from there. Not until the penultimate day of the regular season in early October did they officially clinch, and they weren't even on the field when they did. It was pouring in the Bronx, and the Yankees and Tigers were in the middle of a three-hour rain delay. During the extended pause the Orioles beat the Sox, officially eliminating Boston from contention.

The play-offs would be a rematch of '76: the Yankees versus the Royals. After finishing the season with the best record in baseball, Kansas City had both the oddsmakers and popular sentiment on their side. "All of baseball wants us to win," said Royals' manager Whitey Herzog. "Not that they love us . . . they just hate the Yankees and their check writing."

The Yankees' clubhouse had been relatively calm for the last six weeks, but malice lurked not far below the surface. Near the end of the season *Newsday*'s Joe Donnelly, who'd been covering the Mets since mid-July, returned to the Yankees' beat and was shocked to find Reggie and Munson kidding around with each other. "I went to Thurman and said, 'I'm not going to print this, but what are you doing hanging around with Reggie? Are you guys friends now?' " Donnelly recalls. "And Thurman said, 'How could I ever like that son of a bitch after what he pulled? But we need him to win. We need him to win.' "

The first squall of the postseason blew in on the eve of game one, when Billy Martin's fleeting moment of contentment at having again piloted his team into the play-offs curdled into a more familiar sentiment, underappreciation. Emerging from a preseries strategy session with George Steinbrenner and several Yankees' scouts, Martin declined to talk about his opponents for fear of saying something that might help them. But he was more than happy to talk about everything else, including what he called the turning point of the season, standing up to Reggie in the dugout at Fenway. And his boss. If the Yankees went on to win the World Series, Martin told the writers gathered in his office, and Steinbrenner *didn't* both sweeten and extend his three-year, three-hundred-thousand-dollar contract, he was going to have to think seriously about asking for permission to talk to other clubs. With the first pitch scarcely more than twenty-four hours away, there was no way Steinbrenner could fire him. So Martin as much as challenged him to: "If he buys $50 million worth of players, I'll beat him with another club and he knows it . . . I'll make him cry."

The ritual resumed, it was now Steinbrenner's turn. "He's crazy if he tries to take credit for our success," the Yankees' owner told reporters, presenting them with evidence—the team's day-by-day won-loss record—that the season's real turning point had been August 10, when Martin finally started hitting Reggie at cleanup. "He is just trying to work up public support," Steinbrenner said dismissively.

Public support was one thing Martin didn't have to work up. When he was introduced before game one on October 4, which was played on a clear, mild afternoon in New York, the fans stood and cheered themselves hoarse. "This is in recognition of Billy telling off his boss," Dick Young wrote in the *Daily News*, "by 55,000 people who dream of telling off the boss."

Martin trotted out to the first base line and lifted his cap toward the sky. A wincing smile spread across his narrow face. Several Yankees joined the ovation. Martin looked younger than his forty-eight years, but he did not look good. There were dark circles under his eyes, and his shriveled frame had practically disappeared inside his increasingly baggy uniform. But for the moment anyway, he was happy.

Martin bathed in the clamor, unaware that his starting pitcher, Don Gullett, was having trouble getting loose. The lanky left-hander, who had torn his rotator cuff while fielding a bunt during the season, didn't tell anyone that the tightness in his shoulder was back. By the middle of the second inning, having surrendered four runs on four hits and two walks, he confessed to the team's trainer that he wasn't right. The trainer passed the word along to Martin, and Gullett was finished for the night.

So were the Yankees. Reggie went hitless, and the Yanks dropped the game, 7–2. The ailing Catfish Hunter, who hadn't set foot on a mound in three weeks, was already out for the series. Now Gullett appeared to be too.

59.

THE following morning the South Bronx got a surprise visitor. His presence was announced by a long line of motorcycle escorts and police cars. Sirens blaring, the caravan chugged up the Grand Concourse as helicopters buzzed overhead. In the back of the motorcade, peering through the windows of a cream-colored limousine at the grand façades of this once-opulent boulevard was President Jimmy Carter.

He was a couple of months late, but the president, in town to address the United Nations, had finally decided to pay a surprise visit to one of New York's worst ghettos, a neighborhood that had been ignored by most of the borough's blackout looters. By July 1977 there was virtually nothing there to steal.

Anticipating Carter's arrival a week earlier, the *Daily News* had taken the liberty of mapping out a more ambitious itinerary for him, beginning at St. Barbara's Church in Bushwick: "There the few working, middle-class families left in the dying neighborhood can give Carter the kind of first-hand knowledge of what's killing the nation's cities." But Carter had chosen to limit his slum tour to the South Bronx.

As the presidential caravan wended its way through this urban prairie on this mild, early fall morning, small clusters of people began appearing in front of burned-out and abandoned tenements, shouting, "We want money," and, "Give us jobs." The motorcade stopped abruptly along Charlotte Street, and the president disembarked to walk through the wasteland, a two-block stretch of rubble unbroken by so much as a single building.

It was a powerful image, a natural for front pages nationwide, and scores of politicians would soon follow in Carter's footsteps, all seeking to underscore their commitment to saving the neighborhood.

A closer look would have revealed that the neighborhood was already saving itself. By the time of Carter's visit local community development groups with mottoes like "Don't move. Improve," had already begun to form. They beat back the city's wrecking crews, rebuilt battered buildings, and fought for the 1977 Community Reinvestment Act, a federal law requiring banks to provide loans in low-income neighborhoods. In time the city did its part too, earmarking some five hundred million dollars a year for affordable housing, much of which found its way to the South Bronx.

But these seeds of rebirth remained buried beneath the debris on October 5, 1977, the day the South Bronx became the most famous slum in America.

60.

THAT night was a cool and windy one at the stadium. Guidry was serving smoke, but the Yankees still weren't hitting, even against Andy Hassler, the weakest of the Royals' starters.

It was 2–1 Yankees in the top of the sixth when Hal McRae came barreling into Willie Randolph, knocking the ball loose and sending the Yankees' second baseman tumbling head over heels toward the edge of the outfield grass. The Royals had tied the game, but they had also awakened the slumbering Yankees, who exploded for three runs in the home half of the inning. With Guidry going, that was more than enough to put the game away. They were now even at one, but with the series moving to the artificial turf in Kansas City for the last three games, the Royals still had the edge.

Whitey Herzog had been saving his best pitcher, Dennis Leonard, for game three in Kansas City and the young right-hander didn't disappoint. The Yankees managed just four hits, and Reggie was blanked. He was now one for eleven in the postseason, and his one hit had been an infield single.

For his part, Martin spent most of the night shrieking at the umpires. He knew there was more at stake here than a pennant. In case he didn't, Royals' fans held aloft a banner to remind him: BYE, BYE, BILLY. By the end of the night his voice had been reduced to a rasp. The next day would be an elimination game. Desperate for an edge, the Yankees' skipper set about tormenting the Royals' game four starter, Larry Gura, whom Martin had cut from his Texas Rangers team back in 1975. "If I had my way," Martin told every reporter he could, "I'd put a bodyguard around his house tonight and get him a chauffeur so he doesn't get into an accident on the way to the ballpark."

Gura made it safely to the ballpark but soon wished he hadn't. The Yanks touched him up for four runs on six hits in two innings. Just about everybody participated, with the exception of Reggie, who posted yet another oh-fer. When the Royals rallied to pull within one run in the fourth, Martin skipped right to his closer, Sparky Lyle, who pitched five-plus scoreless innings to force a winner-take-all game five.

61.

AT Royals Stadium the following afternoon, not long before the Yankees were scheduled to take the field for their pregame cuts, Billy Martin summoned his backup catcher, Fran Healy.

Poking his head into the manager's office, Healy, who'd been to the plate sixty-seven times all season, wasn't expecting to be told to be ready to play. He wasn't. Martin had an even more surprising request: "I'm sitting Reggie tonight, and I want you to tell him."

"I'm not telling him, *you* tell him," an incredulous Healy replied. "You're the manager."

"I don't want to tell him."

"Why don't you have one of the coaches tell him?" Healy asked.

"They don't want to tell him."

Healy pulled up a stool in front of Reggie's locker and told him.

Martin headed out to the dugout, took a seat on the top step, and informed the newsmen that Paul Blair, his late-innings defensive specialist, would be starting in right field. This time there were no winking references to Reggie's hyperextended elbow. The three-million-dollar slugger wasn't hitting for "spit" (as the papers wrote it), and he was butchering balls in the outfield. "If I played him and he dropped a ball that cost us the game, I wouldn't forgive myself for the rest of my life," Martin said. "I don't like to do this bastard thing, but if I don't do what's best for the club, I shouldn't be manager."

It was an act either of noble courage or of sadistic insecurity. An unconvincing argument could be made that starting Blair was the best thing for the club. Reggie was in the grip of a one-for-fourteen postseason swoon, and he looked about as surefooted as a beery weekend softballer on the artificial turf. What's more, he did have trouble with that night's pitcher, the left-handed junk baller Paul Splittorff. In fifteen at bats against Splittorff during the regular season, Reggie had picked up just two hits, a double and a home run.

But Martin never put much stock in stat sheets; number crunching, to his mind, was for managers who didn't trust their baseball instincts. More likely, the only calculus that Martin made was this one: If the Yankees won without Reggie, he would be vindicated. If the Yankees lost, well, he was going to be fired anyway.

Batting practice started, and Reggie, burning, remained in the locker room. Eventually he emerged and gave a disingenuously stoic interview to Howard Cosell, admitting that he was disappointed but adding—you could almost read the humiliation on his face now—that it had taken "guts" for Martin to sit him.

As the newspapermen stalked Reggie, hoping for a more honest comment, another bomb was ticking away. The Yankees' leadoff hitter, Mickey Rivers, was holed up in the trainer's room refusing to get dressed. He'd been having problems with his wife all year. Earlier in the season she'd reportedly chased him from their apartment in New Jersey up to the stadium and then repeatedly smashed into his car until a parking lot attendant intervened. Now she had racked up a huge shopping bill in their Kansas City hotel, and the front office was refusing to advance Rivers the money to cover it.

Rivers was eventually coaxed out, and the game got under way. By the end of the first the Royals' George Brett had slid into third spikes high, and the two benches had cleared.

The Royals took an early lead against a worn-out Guidry, who had pitched nine innings just three days before, and Martin quickly replaced him with Mike Torrez. The score was 3–1 Royals after three innings, and then the two teams started matching zeros. Every now and then NBC would advance the subplot, pointing a camera at the best-paid man in baseball history sitting on the bench in a warm-up jacket. No one believed it would end like this.

It didn't. In the eighth the Yankees mounted a rally, and Reggie got his chance. With one out and runners on first and third, Martin called on him to pinch-hit for the team's designated hitter, Cliff Johnson. The Royals' closer, Paul Bird, was on the mound. Reggie took ball one and then fouled off a pair of fastballs. Now Bird tried to sneak a slow curve by him. Reggie lunged, chipping the ball into center field for a run-scoring base hit, pulling the Yankees within one.

They won it in the ninth. The unlikely hero was Reggie's replacement, Paul Blair. Most baseball scouts believed that Blair had never really recovered from a cheek-shattering beaning a few years earlier and that he was at his most tentative when facing right-handed power pitchers, such as Dennis Leonard, who was brought in to finish the game for the Royals. Martin stuck with Blair anyway. After spoiling a good fastball and a couple of diving sliders, he caught a pitch on the bat handle and looped it toward shallow center for a base hit. Roy White followed with an eight-pitch walk. Mickey Rivers singled to drive home the tying run, moving White to third in the process. Willie Randolph finished it with a sacrifice fly.

Most of the nation's sports editors chose one of two images to illustrate their game stories: a first-inning photograph of Royals' third baseman George Brett on all fours, with Yankees' third baseman Graig Nettles's foot embedded in his chest, or a postgame shot of the Royals' five-foot-four-inch shortstop, Fred Patek, sitting alone in the dugout, head in hands, his pants torn from a nasty spiking. Goliath had apparently defeated David. As one *Kansas City Times* columnist wrote, "Truth doesn't prevail. There is no justice."

In the locker room after the game, Billy Martin, for whom victory always tasted more like vindication, went looking for Steinbrenner with a full bottle of champagne. "That's for trying to fire me," Martin said, after sneaking up on his boss and soaking him from behind. Steinbrenner, a protective raincoat over his navy blazer, wheeled around. "What do you mean, *try*?" he said, half grinning. "If I want to fire you, I will."

Paul Blair hugged Munson and thanked him for working with him on protecting the outside part of the plate. "Yeah," Munson said, "the beachball can't stir the fuckin' drink, but he can teach you how to hit."

A few lockers away Reggie ended his short-lived experiment with stoicism. "Can I explain what it meant?" he blurted, reflecting on his bloop single to a few writers. "I can't explain it. I can't explain it because I don't understand the magnitude of Reggie Jackson." Not that he had forgiven Martin. On the team's charter plane a few hours later, Reggie sat alone in silence.

Martin was several rows up, listening to country music on a cassette recorder and wondering if any manager had ever gone into his second consecutive World Series still fighting for his job.

62.

THE Yankees' charter touched down at Newark Airport in the predawn darkness of October 10, 1977. Five thousand fans were waiting for it. The Port Authority had called in reinforcements from the Newark Police Department, but the extra twenty officers who had been dispatched to help contain the crowd made little difference. When the DC-8 taxied to a stop at 4:19 a.m., the mob broke through the barricades and charged it.

Martin was the first to disembark. He descended the ramp, which was swarming with drunk fans, to chants of "We love Billy!" Martin's stature, never in doubt, was now more exalted than ever. "If our planners and politicians had brass and brains like Billy the Kid, we would be living in Fat City instead of Tap City," wrote *Daily News* political columnist William Reel. "Martin for Mayor!" Yankees' fans couldn't keep their hands off him. Pushing through the surging crowd, Martin had his pocket ripped from his pants, a chain torn from around his neck, and a shoulder bag looted.

Reggie poked his head out of the plane and promptly ducked back in. He emerged a few minutes later and pressed on through the swirling masses, spilling a drink on himself as he made his way toward the team bus. By now the fans had spotted the "N.Y. Yankees" lettering above the windshield and had swarmed it as well. The roof of the bus buckled beneath the weight of unsteady bodies.

63.

WHEN the Dodgers still played in Flatbush, the Bums provided the color and the Bombers provided the class. These days the two teams had taken the shape of their respective cities: the friendly, easygoing Dodgers and the tired, neurotic Yankees. (The same dichotomy happened to be on display in movie theaters across America in the 1977 Academy Award–winning film *Annie Hall.*)

They had last met in the 1963 World Series, a Dodgers' sweep. Whitey Ford, who pitched the '63 opener against Sandy Koufax, was now called in at the last minute to throw out the first pitch. He replaced Joe DiMaggio, who had left the stadium in a huff the day before, vowing never to return, after being kept waiting a half hour for his tickets.

It was a brisk night in New York, the Empire State Building was illuminated in blue and white, and more than 62 percent of the city's viewing audience had tuned in to ABC, which was debuting new disco-style bubble graphics for the World Series. Few could have been disappointed. The Yanks took the field behind Don Gullett, who insisted that his shoulder was now fine. After a shaky start—two runs on three walks in the first frame—Gullett found his form and yielded just three singles over the rest of the game.

His counterpart, Don Sutton, a lean right-hander with a dazzling overhand curve, was just as stingy. The Dodgers took a 2–1 lead into the home half of the sixth, when Willie Randolph poled a 2-2 pitch into the seats in left to tie it. The Yanks inched ahead 3–2 in the eighth but left the bases loaded, and the Dodgers knotted it in the ninth.

Now it became a stalemate. The Yanks got their leadoff man on in the tenth and eleventh, but both times failed to move him into scoring position. In the twelfth, facing the Dodgers' fifth pitcher of the night, Willie Randolph led off with a double. Munson walked, bringing up Paul Blair, who had replaced Reggie on defense in the ninth. Blair squared to bunt twice, fouling off the first offering and missing the second one altogether. At the stroke of midnight, he punched an 0-2 pitch through the infield to put the game away.

64.

GAME two was humbling for the Yankees—Catfish Hunter, pitching on thirty-two days' rest but still shaky, was torched—and humiliating for the city.

About an hour before the first pitch, a fire started in Public School 3, an abandoned elementary school a few blocks west of the ballpark. By the time ABC began its broadcast at 8 p.m., orange flames were licking toward the sky. The network cut to its camera in a helicopter hovering above for an aerial view. "There it is, ladies and gentlemen," announced Howard Cosell, who later misidentified the building as an apartment complex, "the Bronx is burning."

By the late innings the fire had grown to five alarms, and Yankees' fans were getting restless. Play was stopped repeatedly while stadium police chased fans across the field. Rolls of toilet paper, whiskey bottles, and firecrackers rained down on the field. The residents of the upper deck dumped beer on the owners of the box seats below. A cop was assaulted when he asked several fans to lower a banner that was obstructing the view of those behind them. One fan pulled down his pants and hung from the scoreboard. Another tossed a smoke bomb from the stands that beclouded the outfield in an electric green haze.

New York's nationally televised degradation was still not complete. During the final out of the game, a fan pegged Dodgers' rightfielder Reggie Smith in the head with a hard rubber ball. Smith required immediate medical attention and left town the next day in a neck brace.

Catfish Hunter, who had been driven out in the third inning of the 6–1 Dodger victory, didn't blame Martin for giving him the ball. "I'd rather pitch than ride the pine anytime," he said after the game. Reggie, hitless on the night and three for twenty-two in the postseason, was less supportive when a reporter asked him about it: "How could the son of a bitch have pitched him?"

The Yankees left for Los Angeles early the next morning. Martin didn't learn about Reggie's comment until the afternoon. By then the Yankees were working out in the warm sun at Dodger Stadium. The hot foam rose quickly through Martin's knotted stomach. "Reggie has enough trouble playing right field," he told the clutch of reporters. "Why should I pay attention to him? His teammates don't." Martin was by no means finished. "He was told in Kansas City, the day of the last playoff game, he would be playing in every game of the World Series, but if he's going to say things to hurt the ballclub and if he doesn't hit John [Tommy John, the Dodgers' game three starter] I may have to think about making a change."

It was perfect off-day fodder for the papers. The *Post* carried the news back to New York under the back-page headline YANKS ARE READY TO EXPLODE—OFF THE FIELD.

Reggie did hit John—once anyway—and the Yankees took game three, 5–3. The following afternoon they took game four, leaving them one win shy of the World Series. Reggie's double to right and soaring home run into the left-center seats were overshadowed by the big story, Ron Guidry's four-hitter.

Facing elimination in game five, the Dodgers came out swinging. By the sixth they had run the score to 10–0. It was already too late to matter when Reggie singled hard to open the seventh and then, in the eighth, caught Don Sutton's first pitch and sent it sailing through the smoggy Los Angeles sky. A screen behind the foul pole arrested the ball's flight, so the distance assigned to his second home run in two days—450 feet—was just a guess.

The series was to conclude in New York. Even the Dodgers knew it had to be this way. "Otherwise," said Los Angeles's first baseman Steve Garvey, packing up his gear for the final road trip of the year, "it would have been like a play without a climax."

65.

IF the 1977 postseason was going to be a microcosm of the regular season—and that was how things were shaping up—there was just one piece missing: the controversial magazine story.

The new issue of *Time*, which contained a story headlined NICE GUYS ALWAYS FINISH . . . ?, greeted the Yankees on their return to New York on the cold, rainy morning of Monday, October 17. In a single page of text the magazine had Steinbrenner saying that several Yankees had pleaded with him to fire Martin; Martin saying that if Steinbrenner fired him, he'd never live it down with the fans ("a little Dago like me fixed his ass"); and Reggie saying he would refuse to play another year for Martin.

To most of America and all New York none of this came as any surprise. By now everyone just wanted to see how this bizarre drama would end.

The following morning, October 18, the skies had cleared but the cool air lingered in New York through the early part of the day.

Reggie had breakfast with his agent, Matt Merola, and then lounged around his apartment with Ray Negron. He called Ralph Destino to make plans for later. Destino was going to drive his son and Reggie's father and sister home from the ballpark. Then, as was their custom, they'd meet up at McMullen's.

By dusk the temperature in New York had climbed into the mid-fifties. The home team went out for batting practice. A couple of Dodgers were sitting on ball bags in front of the third base dugout. Several more stood on the dugout steps.

Yankees' third base coach Dick Howser pitched to the last few of his men, a group that included Reggie Jackson. As he stepped in to take his cuts at around 6:40 p.m., a crowd gathered behind the cage. Reggie smashed three balls into the third tier and a fourth off the back wall of the right field bleachers, some five hundred feet from the plate. No one recalls exactly how many Reggie hit out during batting practice that evening—or rather the estimates vary widely—but everyone remembers it as an unprecedented performance. "Every ball flew like it was shot out of a cannon," says Roger Director, an editor at *Sport* magazine who was on the field at the time. "It was an electrifying thing. People were completely buzzed and amazed."

Fran Healy was shagging flies in left-center during the show. Healy, who swears that Reggie hit every pregame pitch out of the park, couldn't help remembering the old baseball saw that a good BP was a bad omen: "I thought to myself, 'Boy, is he gonna have a horseshit game.' "

66.

There isn't anything to say or at least it's beyond me. Reggie Jackson. Three million dollars to get him here. He has often said he doesn't want to come back here. I don't believe it for one second. I never have.

CBS RADIO'S WINN ELLIOT, DURING THE EIGHTH INNING OF THE STATION'S BROADCAST OF GAME SIX OF THE 1977 WORLD SERIES

IN the days that followed, some said it had to end like this, but watching Reggie Jackson's game six performance now, it seems like an odd conclusion to this long season of tension and torment, not anticlimactic, but somehow unbaseball-like. There is none of the subtle jockeying, the foul tips and worked counts that usually accompany memorable at bats. Reggie simply strides to the plate three consecutive times against three different pitchers and, before the commentators can even properly set the scene, strokes the first pitch he sees into the seats. One gets the sense that if this had been the first half of a twin bill—and Martin hadn't sat him in the second—he would have hit three more, not because he was so much better than everyone else but because something had been lit inside him. For this one night the all-too-human Reggie Jackson glowed with superhuman greatness.

He first appeared on center stage in the second inning, a black turtleneck under his double knits, the top button of his uniform unfastened as usual, with the Yankees trailing 2–0. Reggie had gone zero for four with a pair of strikeouts against Burt Hooton in game two, but the balance of power had already shifted. Hooton didn't throw him anything near the strike zone.

At the start of the fourth, the Yanks now down 3–2, Reggie knelt on one knee in the on deck circle and watched Thurman Munson rap a single to left. Expecting something hard and inside, Reggie took his usual spot in the box and then moved off the plate about six inches, glancing back to make sure the Dodgers' catcher hadn't noticed. Reggie tapped his bat lightly on the plate and turned his gaze to the mound. Sure enough, Hooton came inside with a fastball, and Reggie smoked it—a low liner, no more than fifteen feet off the ground. Unsure of the ball's fate, Reggie broke hard out of the box before it landed in the first row of the right field bleachers. He circled the bases briskly, his upper body bent forward, slowing to a trot about ten feet from home. As he bounded down the dugout steps, Martin—"the beleaguered little pepperpot," as Cosell referred to him on ABC—gave him an adoring pat on the cheek.

The next inning three men were scheduled to hit before Reggie, but he pulled his thirty-five-inch bat from the rack anyway as Elias Sosa, the right-handed fastballer who had relieved Hooton, finished his warm-up pitches. Three batters later, with two out and one on, Reggie came to the plate. He mashed down his helmet and turned on Sosa's first pitch, a fastball down and in, sending it screaming over the wall in right.

It was another line drive, so Reggie again sprinted out of the box and started motoring around the bases. Between first and second, he picked at his form-fitting uniform, pulling it away from his swelling chest, as the baying—*"Reg-gie, Reg-gie, Reg-gie"*—washed over the park. The ABC cameras found him moments later at the first base end of the dugout, the second button of his uniform now undone. In case anyone at home had lost count, he held up a pair of fingers, mouthing the word *two.*

In the home half of the eighth, a standing ovation greeted Reggie as he walked toward the plate. The din continued as he smoothed the dirt in the batter's box with his spikes. Then, for a split second, after Reggie reached down for Charlie Hough's diving knuckleball, a good pitch, the crowd fell silent—"choking on its own disbelief," as *The Washington Post*'s Thomas Boswell would write. This time Reggie knew. He stood and watched as the ball sailed toward dead center, touching down about halfway up the stadium's blacked-out bleachers, some 475 feet from where it had collided with his bat. As Reggie glided around first, Dodgers' first baseman Steve Garvey applauded softly into his glove.

Reggie's last home run put the Yankees on top 8–3. The Yankees' first World Series in fifteen years was almost won, and the Bronx ballyard was ready to explode. The stadium had quadrupled its security for that night's game. More than one hundred cops in riot helmets now took their positions in foul territory, crouching on the field side of the wall along the first and third base lines. On the other side of the wall, officers were swinging their nightsticks above their heads to keep fans back. The public-address announcements began: "Ladies and gentlemen, no one is to go on the field at the end of the game."

On his way out to his position for the final three outs, Reggie—his pinstriped shirt now buttoned only halfway up—doffed his cap and blew kisses to the crowd. It was a long half inning. Torrez was weary, but he wanted to finish it, and Martin didn't see any harm in letting him. The outs came slowly, but they came. The bleacher creatures were now sitting along the top of the outfield fence, their legs dangling over the wall in fair territory. Firecrackers and cherry bombs were exploding on the field.

With two down in the top of the ninth, Reggie called a timeout and started running toward the dugout. ABC's Keith Jackson narrated: "Reggie Jackson is leaving the field, and I don't blame him. The home fans are chasing their most valuable player off the field."

But Reggie was pointing at his head: He just wanted a batting helmet! It took a couple of minutes to find one—the equipment had already been moved into the clubhouse to keep it away from marauding fans—but Reggie eventually trotted back out for the final out, a little popup that Torrez handled himself.

In an instant, thousands of fevered fans were pouring onto the field. They came from every section of the stands, charging across the tables in the press box on their way down. The extra police and their five mounted horses were no match for this mass of swarming, shaggy-haired humanity. Reggie took off his helmet and glasses and started weaving in and out of the crowd, the fullback looking for daylight. Without his specs, he had poor depth perception; he was genuinely frightened. Gaining speed now, he sent a parka-plump, blue-jeaned fan sprawling with a shoulder block and disappeared into the dugout.

67.

ONLY Babe Ruth had hit three home runs in a single World Series game (twice, in fact), but never in consecutive at bats, let alone on three pitches.

A feat like this, after a summer like this, lent itself to many different interpretations. To defenders of baseball's emerging era, it was proof that free agency had reenergized the game by raising the stakes for its performers and the expectations for its fans. To baseball nostalgists, it was a vindication of content over form, a victory of on-the-field drama over off-the-field melodrama. "We live in an unprivate time, and the roar of personality and celebrity has almost drowned out the cheering in the stands," wrote Roger Angell in *The New Yorker*. "The ironic and most remarkable aspect of Reggie Jackson's feat is that for a moment there, on that littered, brilliant field, he—he, of all people—almost made us forget this."

The tabloids wove Reggie's three mighty blows into their narrative of the city's struggle for survival. "Who dares to call New York a lost cause?" a pumped-up *Post* editorialized.

After antagonizing Reggie earlier in the season, the *Amsterdam News* now canonized him, comparing his game six feat to Joe Louis's knockout of Max Schmeling and Jackie Robinson's first major-league home run. "Black residents of New York City reacted with a special jubilation and sense of triumph to the sensational performance by Reggie Jackson," the paper reported on its October 22 front page. "Much of the feeling appeared to be based on the widespread feeling among Blacks interviewed by *The Amsterdam News* that the white-dominated media and whites in the crowds, as well as the Yankees' white manager Billy Martin, had been especially hard on Jackson because he was Black, arrogant, and spoke his mind."

As for Reggie, he didn't see why he should be limited to one interpretation. In the dozens of interviews he gave in the ensuing weeks, his game six performance became a triumph of the Lord ("God allowed me to do that"), a humanitarian gesture ("I'll tell you what I was thinking . . . *I did this for all of us. Take it. Enjoy it. And let's do it again*"), and, naturally, an emphatic telegram from the once-embattled superstar to his enemies, real and imagined: "Those home runs delivered a simple message: Let me up now– I'm no longer gonna be held down."

After the game most of the Yankees headed to a team party at the Sheraton in Hasbrouck Heights, New Jersey.

A few hours before the first pitch, Martin had been given a thirty-five-thousand-dollar bonus, a Lincoln Continental, and the assurance that he'd have his job in 1978. Now he'd won his first World Series as a manager. But he still couldn't enjoy himself. He was exhausted, and the party was too crowded. Martin flung his scotch to the floor and repaired to a quiet bar nearby.

Reggie was late getting to McMullen's. The game ended at 10:43 p.m. and he and Destino usually met an hour after the last out. But at 12:30 a.m. Destino, who had brought along two dates for them, was still waiting.

Reggie eventually showed, pulling his blue Volkswagen up onto the sidewalk on Third Avenue. At around 2 a.m., Governor Carey arrived with a small entourage. The two parties merged and proceeded to drink champagne and eat cheeseburgers into the morning. Sometime after 3 a.m. Carey summoned two state troopers to guard Reggie's car and assured Jim McMullen that the rules that govern after-hours drinking had been suspended for the night.

At a little before dawn, Reggie dashed home for a quick shower and change of clothes and headed down to Rockefeller Center for an interview with the *Today* show. It was cool and drizzly in New York, the start of the Son of Sam's competency hearings and the day the first Concorde was scheduled to touch down at Kennedy Airport.

After the ticker tape parade for the World Champion New York Yankees had made its way down Broadway to City Hall, Reggie went back uptown to Cartier. Soon he would start trying to persuade Destino to drive with him to spring training in his new Rolls-Royce, which was outfitted with a CB radio. (Destino's handle was the King of Diamonds; Reggie's, in honor of the forthcoming REGGIE! candy bar, was the Candyman.) For now, though, Reggie just wanted to stretch out on the couch in Destino's office and close his eyes.

NOTES ON SOURCES

PART ONE

1.

My portrait of New York's bicentennial celebrations is drawn primarily from reports in the dailies—*New York Times, Daily News*, and *New York Post*—as well as a July 8, 1976, *SoHo Weekly News* story on Operation Sail ("Op Sail as a Performance Piece").

For my portrait of the 1976 Democratic National Convention, I relied on coverage in the New York dailies, in addition to a July 19, 1976, *Village Voice* piece ("City Welcomes Delegates to Potemkin Village") detailing New York's massive cleanup effort in advance of the convention.

Historian Douglas Brinkley, who worked with Hunter S. Thompson in compiling his letters for publication, characterized Thompson's view of Jimmy Carter for me.

Rolling Stone's editor Jann Wenner and former publisher Joe Armstrong recalled for me the details of the magazine's 1976 Democratic National Convention party. Other useful sources on this subject include *Rolling Stone Magazine: The Uncensored History* (Robert Draper, Doubleday, 1990), and "Rolling Stone's Bash" (Sally Quinn, *Washington Post*, July 14, 1976).

2.

In addition to New York's three dailies and several boxes of relevant papers that the Museum of New York History compiled for a 2000 exhibit, I relied on a number of books that deal with the 1975 fiscal crisis, including *Working-Class New York: Life and Labor Since World War II* (Joshua B. Freeman, New Press, 2000); *The Streets Were Paved with Gold: The Decline of New York, an American Tragedy* (Ken Auletta, Random House, 1975); *Political Crisis/Fiscal Crisis: The Collapse and Revival of New York City* (Martin Shefter, Basic Books, 1985); *Secrets of the Tax Revolt* (James Ring Adams, Harcourt Brace Jovanovich, 1984); and *The Abuse of Power: The Permanent Government and the Fall of New York* (Jack Newfield and Paul Du Brul, Viking Press, 1977). In July 1985, *The New York Times* ran a five-part series on the fiscal crisis, "Back from the Brink: The Enduring Legacy of New York's Fiscal Crisis," which is indispensable to anyone who wants to understand the lasting effects of New York's financial meltdown.

My portrait of Abe Beame was informed by a 1979 interview on file at Columbia University's Oral History Archive, as well as dozens of newspaper stories written over the course of his life. Two lengthy profiles in particular stand out: "The Realism of Abe Beame" (Robert Daley, *New York Times Magazine*, November 18, 1973) and "Beame's Scenario: How to Beat Bella" (Maurice Carroll, *New York Times Magazine*, June 26, 1977). Beame also appears in several aforementioned books, most notably *The Abuse of Power* and *The Streets Were Paved with Gold.*

John Lindsay died shortly after I embarked on the research for this book, and I had the opportunity to attend his memorial service at St. John the Divine in late January 2001. Having read so many indictments of Lindsay's mayoralty, it was refreshing to hear the various eulogies—from Mayor Rudolph Giuliani's to Representative Charles Rangel's—all of which evoked a man who, for all his failings, had clung nobly to a hopeful, if increasingly outdated, vision of the city. Another valuable source on Lindsay is Vincent Cannato's *The Ungovernable City: John Lindsay and the Struggle to Save New York* (Basic Books, 2002).

3.

Warner LeRoy was the subject of a number of obituaries upon his death in 2001, the most memorable of which was Frank DiGiacomo's—"Good Night, Sweet Restaurateur"—in the March 5, 2001, issue of the *New York Observer.*

My portrait of One Fifth Avenue is drawn primarily from my interview with its proprietor, George Schwartz.

4.

There have been two full-length biographies of Martin since his death. Peter Golenbock's *Wild, High, and Tight: The Life and Death of Billy Martin* (St. Martin's Press, 1994) is the more exhaustive; David Falkner's *The Last Yankee: The Turbulent Life of Billy Martin* (Simon & Schuster, 1992) offers a more sophisticated analysis of Martin's character. When Martin was still managing, Maury Allen published *Damn Yankee: The Billy Martin Story* (Times Books, 1980), which is less comprehensive than the two posthumous biographies but has the benefit of having been written by a reporter who covered Martin day in and day out. Martin's own autobiography (*Number One*, Delacorte Press, 1980) provides a useful window into his frame of mind but should be read with a skeptical eye, given his tendency to distort. There are a number of noteworthy profiles of Martin from his playing days, including "The Damnedest Yankee of Them All" (Paul O'Neil, *Sports Illustrated*, April 23, 1956); "He's Never Out of Trouble" (Al Stump, *Saturday Evening Post*, August 18, 1956); "Billy the Tiger" (Les Woodcock, *Sports Illustrated*, March 31, 1958); "You Think You Know Billy Martin?" (Irv Goodman, *Sport*, August 1958); and "Have They Overrated Billy Martin?" (Dick Schaap, *Sport*, June 1959). My account of Martin's trade after the Copa incident is drawn largely from the New York papers. In the aftermath of the trade, on June 30, 1957, the *Times'* Arthur Daley published an especially memorable column on Martin entitled "Still a Yankee at Heart."

My account of Martin's firing by the Minnesota Twins, and the public outcry that followed, is drawn primarily from coverage in the *Minneapolis Star* and *The Sporting News.*

There are a few particularly good profiles of Martin as a manager prior to his return to New York: "A Little Love, and a Few Punches Make a Team" (Myron Cope, *Life*, September 19, 1969); "Billy Martin Will Never Finish Last" (James S. Kunen, *Sport*, August 1975); and "Billy the Kid as Peacemaker" (Ron Fimrite, *Sports Illustrated*, June 1971).

My account of Martin's hiring by the Yankees in 1975 is drawn largely from the

New York papers. Especially useful was Dave Anderson's August 3, 1975, column in *The New York Times*, "The Prodigal Son."

The story of Martin's rise to popularity in New York over the course of the '76 season was told best by the tabloids, as well as in an approving July 12, 1976, profile by *The Village Voice*'s Joe Flaherty, "We've Got a Contender."

In addition to the daily papers, the best source on Martin's meltdown during game four of the 1976 World Series is Norman Lewis Smith's "The Cincinnati Reds Didn't Scare Billy Martin: They Just Made Him Cry" (*Sport*, February 1977).

In terms of understanding Martin's psychology, I received valuable insight from all the Yankee beat reporters (mentioned by name in the acknowledgments), whose recollections of him ranged from affection to pity to disgust.

Neil J. Sullivan's *The Diamond in the Bronx: Yankee Stadium and the Politics of New York* (Oxford University Press, 2001) is a valuable source on the history of the renovation of Yankee Stadium. New York's papers and magazines from 1976 to 1977 are filled with stories questioning the city's decision to underwrite the renovation. Among the more memorable are: "Was the Stadium Worth It?" (Nicholas Pileggi, *New York*, April 19, 1976); "The Stadium the Swag Built" (Dan Diamond, *SoHo Weekly News*, June 2, 1977); "Yankees, $100 Million; Bronx Zip" (Rinker Buck, *New York*, October 24, 1977); and "Did New York City Really Need the Yankees?" (David Norflus, *New York Affairs*, Spring 1978).

5.

There are numerous biographies of Rupert Murdoch. I consulted four in assembling my portrait of him: *Murdoch* (William Shawcross, Simon & Schuster, 1992); *Arrogant Aussie: The Rupert Murdoch Story* (Michael Leapman, L. Stuart, 1985); *Citizen Murdoch: The Unexpurgated Story of Rupert Murdoch—The World's Most Controversial and Powerful Media Lord* (Thomas Kiernan, Dodd, Mead, 1986); and *Rupert Murdoch: A Paper Prince* (George Munster, Penguin, 1985). Several articles also proved particularly useful. On November 29, 1976, *The Village Voice* published a rare interview with Murdoch conducted by Alexander Cockburn ("Who Is Rupert Murdoch, Anyway?"). *More*, the now-defunct journalism review, published several articles on Murdoch when he first took over the *Post*: "Old-Fashioned Newspaper War in New York?" (Michael Kramer, January 1977); "Murdoch Buys His 84th" (Doug Ireland, January 1977); and "Killer Bee Reaches New York" (Jon Bradshaw and Richard Neville, February 1977). *Time*'s and *Newsweek*'s cover stories on Murdoch (both of which ran on January 17, 1977) provide useful summaries of his newspaper career to that point.

Jeffrey Potter's 1976 biography of Schiff—*Men, Money and Magic: The Story of Dorothy Schiff* (Coward, McCann & Geoghegan)—offers an intimate portrait of the publisher, as does Gail Sheehy in a lengthy 1973 *New York* cover story titled "The Life of the Most Powerful Woman in New York." Robert Spitzler, who worked for Schiff for many years, shared his memories of her with me as well.

My account of the history of the *Post* was informed by the Schiff biography; James Wechsler's memoir, *The Age of Suspicion* (Random House, 1953); Steven

Cuozzo's *It's Alive: How America's Oldest Newspaper Cheated Death and Why It Matters* (Random House, 1996); Pete Hamill's *A Drinking Life: A Memoir* (Little, Brown, 1993), and a number of magazine stories, notably Jerry Tallmer's "The Mama of Us All" (*Dissent*, Summer 1961). James Brady recalled for me the details of the night Murdoch celebrated his purchase of the paper.

6.

In the spring of 2001 I interviewed Reggie several times over the course of two days at the Yankees' spring training complex in Tampa. In addition, two books were particularly illuminating: Maury Allen's *Mr. October: The Reggie Jackson Story* (Times Books, 1981), and Reggie's 1984 memoir, *Reggie* (Villard Books), a relatively introspective look at his life and career, coauthored by Mike Lupica. David Remnick's May 1987 *Esquire* profile, "The September Song of Mr. October," also offered important insights.

Sport magazine reported on Reggie's late-night arrival in New York in a brief item in its February 1977 issue.

George Beck shared his memories of Reggie's boyhood with me; Jeff Pentland told me about his life at Arizona State; Rollie Fingers spoke with me about Reggie's minor-league career, particularly his stint in Birmingham.

Sal Bando shared with me his memories of Reggie's tenure in Oakland.

A number of books have been written about Charlie Finley's A's, most notably Bruce Markusen's *A Baseball Dynasty: Charlie Finley's Swingin' A's* (St. Johann Press, 2002); Ron Bergman's *Mustache Gang: The Swaggering Saga of the Oakland A's* (Dell, 1973); *Charlie O* (Herb Michelson, Bobbs-Merrill, 1975); and *Champagne and Baloney: The Rise and Fall of Finley's A's* (Tom Clark, Harper & Row, 1976).

Reggie also published a diary of the 1974 season: *Reggie: A Season with a Superstar* (Playboy Press, 1975).

Among the more memorable profiles of Reggie from his Oakland days are: "Home Run King Reggie Jackson" (*Ebony*, October 1969); "Maris and the Babe, Move Over!" (*Sports Illustrated*, July 7, 1971); "One Man Wild Bunch: Oakland's Reggie Jackson" (*Time*, June 3, 1974); " 'Everyone Is Helpless and in Awe' " (*Sports Illustrated*, June 17, 1974); "Reggie Jackson: Blood and Guts of the Fighting A's" (*Sport*, October 1974); and "Says Reggie: A's Ain't Dead!" (*Black Sports*, June 1975).

For my account of Reggie's year in Baltimore I relied primarily on the stories of Thomas Boswell, who covered the Orioles for *The Washington Post*. An August 1976 interview with *Black Sports* magazine was also valuable.

William Fugazy told me about his lunch with Reggie and Steinbrenner at "21."

My account of Reggie's signing is drawn primarily from the New York newspapers and interviews with the beat writers who covered it.

7.

For my portrait of Abzug prior to the 1977 mayoral race, I relied on interviews with Harold Holzer and two of Abzug's other confidants, Doug Ireland and Ronnie Eldridge. Abzug wrote about her first year in Congress in *Bella! Ms. Abzug Goes to*

Washington (Saturday Review Press, 1972). Among the more memorable magazine profiles of Abzug are "Is Washington Ready for Bella Abzug? Is Anybody?" (Jimmy Breslin, *New York*, October 6, 1970); "Dilemma in the New 20th Congressional District" (Tony Hiss, *New York Times Magazine*, June 18, 1972); "Bellacose Abzug" (*Time*, August 16, 1971); "Bella vs. Pat . . . et al." (*New Republic*, June 26, 1976); and "Bella's Appeal" (*New Republic*, July 31, 1976).

8.

My portrait of Clay Felker and *New York* magazine under his stewardship is drawn from interviews with a number of his *New York* colleagues, including Tom Wolfe, Richard Reeves, Ken Auletta, Byron Dobell, and Milton Glaser. Aaron Latham very generously shared with me his unpublished oral history of Felker. Tom Wolfe's two-part essay, "The Birth of the New Journalism," which was published in *New York* when it was still an insert in the *Herald-Tribune*, recounts the history of the journalistic revolution Felker helped pioneer.

For my account of Murdoch's hostile takeover of *New York*, I relied on coverage in New York's dailies; a lengthy front-page story in the January 9, 1977, *Washington Post* ("Takeover in Gotham: How a Press Baron Bought a Magazine"); interviews with Felker and several of his investors, including Alan Patricof, Robert Towbin, and Thomas Kempner; the aforementioned Murdoch biographies; and Gail Sheehy's July 14, 1977, *Rolling Stone* feature ("The Struggle for *New York*"). For Carter Burden's perspective on the matter, I relied on his close friend and business partner Bartle Bull.

9.

A number of the Yankee's beat reporters—named in the acknowledgments—shared with me their memories of Reggie's first spring training with the team. Harry Stein's July 1977 profile in *Esquire*—"Meet Reggie (Dr. Jekyll) Jackson (Mr. Hyde)"—provides a portrait of Reggie in the 1976–77 off-season.

Martin Appel, coauthor of Thurman Munson's autobiography (*Thurman Munson*, Coward, McCann & Geoghegan, 1978), spoke with me about Munson. Several profiles also bear mentioning: "What Makes Thurman Run?" (Dan Lauck, *Sport*, June 1978); "Bitter Munson Still Hoping to Be Traded" (Murray Chass, *New York Times*, July 5, 1978); and most notably "The House That Thurman Munson Built" (Michael Paterniti, *Esquire*, September 1999).

11.

Ed Koch sat for several interviews. Moreover, he generously granted me access to a sealed 617-page oral history he conducted in 1976 with Columbia University. That oral history captured Koch at the ideal moment for my purposes. It was my most important resource in understanding his attitudes and frame of mind at this moment in his life and political career.

Koch's various memoirs—especially *Mayor* (Simon & Schuster, 1984) and *Citizen Koch* (St. Martin's Press, 1992)—were all valuable, as were two other books about him: *I Koch* (Arthur Browne, Dan Collins, and Michael Goodwin, Dodd, Mead &

Company, 1985) and *City for Sale: Ed Koch and the Betrayal of New York* (Jack Newfield and Wayne Barrett, Harper & Row, 1988).

Ken Auletta's two-part profile of Koch published in *The New Yorker* in September 1979 was especially illuminating, as were John Corry's October 30, 1977, *New York Times Magazine* cover piece ("The Koch Story") and Michael Harrington's *Dissent* essay from the fall of 1987, "When Koch Was Still a Liberal."

On Carmine De Sapio, a February 15, 1962, profile by Meg Greenfield in *The Reporter*, "The Decline and Fall of Tammany Hall," was noteworthy, as was an unsigned October 31, 1959, story in *The Nation* ("The Two Faces of De Sapio").

For the 1963 race between Koch and De Sapio I relied primarily on the coverage of *The Village Voice*.

John LoCicero, who started working for Koch during his 1966 race for the New York City Council, helped fill out my picture of Koch as a young politician.

12.

In addition to the daily newspaper coverage, two books, both published in 1978, served as indispensable blueprints for the 1977 season: Ed Linn's *Inside the Yankees: The Championship Year* (Ballantine) and Steve Jacobson's *The Best Team Money Could Buy* (Atheneum).

13.

Mario Cuomo spoke with me several times about his background and the 1977 mayoral race. Robert S. McElvaine's biography, *Mario Cuomo* (Scribner's, 1987) was a valuable resource on Cuomo's early years. Sidney Blumenthal provides an insightful portrait of Cuomo in *Pledging Allegiance: The Last Campaign of the Cold War* (HarperCollins, 1990).

Several profiles of Cuomo also bear mentioning: "A Curious Politician" (Murray Kempton, *New York Review of Books*, September 19, 1974). "Cuomo Rising" (Nat Hentoff, *Village Voice*, April 18, 1977); "Is Saint Mario the Ethnic Savior?" (Richard Gambino and Michael Novak, *New York*, September 5, 1977); Ken Auletta's two-part series in *The New Yorker* ("Governor—1" and "Governor—2," April 9 and 16, 1984); "The Question of Mario Cuomo" (R. W. Apple Jr., *New York Times Magazine*, September 14, 1986); and "A Hard Case" (Murray Kempton, *New York Review of Books*, July 19, 1984).

Jimmy Breslin writes about the Corona controversy in his Preface to Cuomo's *Forest Hills Diary*. Another noteworthy account is "Corona: Cause for a Day" (Ross Gelbspan, *Village Voice*, July 8, 1971).

Valuable sources on the Forest Hills controversy include Cuomo's *Forest Hills Diary* (Random House, 1974); Cannato's *The Ungovernable City; New York 1960* (Robert A. M. Stern, Thomas Mellins, and David Fishman, Monacelli Press, 1995); "The Battle of Forest Hills—Who's Ahead?" (Walter Goodman, *New York Times Magazine*, February 20, 1972); and "Not You, Not You" (Andy Logan, *New Yorker*, November 11, 1972).

14.

Roger Director, a former editor at *Sport*, shared his memories of the magazine with me.

Robert Ward recalled for me the details of his spring training interviews with Reggie.

Sy Presten told me about his role in publicizing the *Sport* story.

15.

Fran Healy recalled Munson's reaction to the *Sport* story for me.

Ray Negron told me about his journey from juvenile delinquent to failed ballplayer to Reggie's aide-de-camp.

16.

My account of the Seaver-Young feud was informed by interviews with Tom Seaver, Jack Lang (who covered the team for the *Daily News*), and Maury Allen and by the blanket coverage in New York's dailies. Especially memorable stories on the Seaver trade include "There Goes the Franchise" (Pete Axthelm, *Newsweek*, June 27, 1977); "The Year the Mets Lost 'The Franchise' " (Paul Good, *Sport*, November 1977); "Seaver Beaned by Columnist" (Joseph Valerio, *More*, July–August 1977); and "The Unmaking of Seaver as a Met" (Kenneth Turan, *Washington Post*, June 26, 1977).

For my portrait of Young, I relied on the torrent of odes in the New York and sporting press following his death in 1987, as well as Ross Wetzsteon's fine profile in the August 1985 issue of *Sport*: "Dick Young's America."

17.

David Wojnarowicz's journals are included in his papers: MSS 92, Fales Library and Special Collections, New York University.

Timothy J. Gilfoyle's essay "From Soubrette Row to Show World," published in the collection *Policing Public Sex: Queer Politics and the Future of AIDS Activism* (South End Press, 1996), sketches the history of public sex in Times Square.

Mayor Beame's campaign against pornography was covered by all the New York papers, most comprehensively by the *Times*.

Randy Shilts writes about the arrival of AIDS on New York's shores during the 1976 bicentennial celebrations in *And the Band Played On: Politics, People, and the AIDS Epidemic* (St. Martin's Press, 1987).

For my portrait of gay life in New York in the mid to late seventies, I relied on interviews with a number of participants in the scene; back issues of *Michael's Thing* (available in the Manuscript Room of the New York Public Library); back issues of *Christopher Street* magazine (also available at the New York Public Library); and Arthur Bell's columns in *The Village Voice*.

The definitive history of New York's bathhouses, Allan Berube's "The History of Gay Bathhouses," was published in the collection *Policing Public Sex*.

The book *Becoming Visible* (Molly McGarry, Fred Wasserman, and Mimi Bowling, Penguin, 1998), which began as a catalog for an exhibit commemorating the twenty-fifth anniversary of Stonewall, is a valuable resource on post-Stonewall gay life in New York.

The best description of the sex piers can be found in Edmund White's 1978 novel *Nocturnes for the King of Naples* (St. Martin's Press).

18.

For my account of Abzug's 1977 mayoral campaign, I relied on interviews with Holzer and Eldridge, local newspaper coverage, and several boxes of press releases, policy statements, and leaflets at Columbia University.

Craig Whitaker, a young architect at New York's Housing and Development Administration at the time, shared with me his files and memos on Wateredge (which later became Westway). *New York 1960* contains a detailed account of the history of Westway. *The New York Times'* Sam Roberts reviewed the history of the project in a two-part series in June 1984. One of the most forceful arguments against Westway is contained in an interview with Jane Jacobs in the February 6, 1978, issue of *New York* ("How Westway Will Destroy New York"). One of the most persuasive arguments in favor of the project is Ada Louise Huxtable's column in the January 23, 1977, *New York Times* ("Will Westway Turn into the Opportunity of a Century?").

19.

I relied on Catfish Hunter's autobiography, *Catfish: My Life in Baseball* (McGraw-Hill, 1988), for the broad outlines of his career. Several magazine profiles are also particularly noteworthy: "The Quiet Ways of Catfish Hunter" (Pat Jordan, *Sport*, November 1971); "Opening of the Catfish Season" (Roy Blount, Jr., *Sports Illustrated*, March 1975); and "The Catfish Enigma" (J. Anthony Lucas, *New York Times Magazine*, September 7, 1975).

20.

My portrayal of the dugout debacle at Fenway is drawn from New York and Boston newspaper accounts, as well as the radio and television broadcasts of the game. Fran Healy told me about his role in the afternoon's events.

Moss Klein shared with me his memories of tracking Martin down at Daisy Buchanan's. The Reverend Jesse Jackson told me about his conversations with Reggie over the course of the summer. Steve Jacobson and Phil Pepe described for me Reggie's outbursts in his hotel room.

21.

Reggie spoke with me about the difference between his views on race and those of the previous generation of black ballplayers. A number of beat writers shared their perspectives on the racial dimension of the Reggie-Billy feud. Elliott Maddox spoke with me about Martin.

The Associated Press reported in May 1987 that Reggie had been admitted to the hospital that he claimed had denied him access because he was black. Pat Cheevers, whose father was Reggie's Little League coach, provided me with the score sheets that show that Reggie had actually played in the state tournament that he denied having played in.

23.

Ralph Destino recalled for me the details of his friendship with Reggie.

Jim McMullen told me about his now-closed restaurant and about Reggie's food and table preferences.

Reggie remembered his New York nightlife for me.

24.

My account of New York's disco culture is drawn from interviews with more than a dozen disco devotees and deejays. Tim Lawrence's *Love Saves the Day: A History of American Dance Culture, 1970–1979* (Duke University Press, 2003) was a valuable resource. Journalist Vince Aletti's stories in *The Village Voice* (and elsewhere) provide an excellent record of the rise of disco in New York. A few other articles bear mentioning: "Hollyw-o-o-d! The Return of the Disco" (Mark Jacobson, *New York*, July 1, 1974); "Inside the Disco Boom" (Richard Szathmary and Lucian K. Truscott IV, *Village Voice*, July 21, 1975); "The New Wave of Discotheques" (Sheila Weller, *Daily News Sunday Magazine*, August 31, 1975); and "The Dialectics of Disco: Gay Music Goes Straight" (Andrew Kopkind, *Village Voice*, February 12, 1979). Carmen d'Alessio shared with me her memories of Studio 54. Anthony Haden-Guest's *The Last Party: Studio 54, Disco and the Culture of the Night* (William Morrow and Co., 1997) lays out the history of Studio, from inception to implosion.

For my account of the New York rock scene, I relied on interviews with participants, back issues of *Punk* magazine and the *New York Rocker*, and two books: *Please Kill Me: The Uncensored Oral History of Punk* (Legs McNeil and Gillian McCain, Grove Press, 1996) and *From Montmartre to the Mudd Club* (Bernard Gendron, University of Chicago Press, 2002). Several articles from the mainstream press were also useful: "A Conservative Impulse in the New Rock Underground" (James Wolcott, *Village Voice*, August 18, 1975); "Report from New York's Rock Underground" (John Rockwell, *New York Times*, February 20, 1977); "(In Search of) the Next Big Thing" (Roy Trakin, *SoHo Weekly News*, May 26, 1977); "Punk Inc." (Dave Marsh, *Rolling Stone*, December 29, 1977).

25.

David Garth shared with me his recollections of the Koch campaign. A few of the more memorable profiles of Garth include "David Garth's Dangerous Game" (Jack Newfield, *New York*, 1970); "The Wizard of Odds: David Garth, John Anderson's Media Mentor" (Myra MacPherson, *Washington Post*, September 19, 1980); and "Hot on the Political Trail" (Elaine Ciulla Kamarck, *Newsday Magazine*, August 20, 1989).

26.

A number of SoHo gallery owners and artists, including Paula Cooper, Ivan Karp, and Alex Katz, spoke with me about the cultural transformation of the neighborhood. *New York 1960* includes a detailed history of SoHo. *The Village Voice* chronicled the early evolution of SoHo's artistic community and its ongoing war with city planners in the 1960s and early seventies in such articles as "SoHo in New York: A Fight for Survival" (Ron Rosenbaum, November 6, 1969). Gilbert Millstein profiled the first wave of loft dwellers in the January 7, 1962, edition of *The New York Times Magazine* ("Portrait of the Loft Generation"). Ada Louise Huxtable wrote several important columns in defense of the neighborhood's cast-iron buildings in *The New York Times*, including "Good Buildings Have Friends" (May 24, 1970). Among other memorable accounts of SoHo's resurgence are *New York*'s May 20, 1974, cover package "The Most Exciting Place to Live in the City" and Stephen Koch's April 1976 article in *Esquire*, "Where the Avant-Gardest Work the Hardest." Michael Winkleman puts the story of SoHo loft conversions in the larger context of New York City housing in "The New Frontier: Housing for the Artist-Industrialist" (*New York Affairs*, vol. 4, no. 4, 1978). Richard Kostelanetz's *SoHo: The Rise and Fall of an Artists' Colony* (Routledge, 2003) provides a nostalgic reminiscence of the neighborhood during its bohemian heyday.

Sharon Zukin makes the case against the conversion of commercial space into residential space in *Loft Living: Culture and Capital in Urban Change* (Johns Hopkins University Press, 1982). Carter Ratcliff makes the argument that the transformation of SoHo was not necessarily good for art in "SoHo: Disneyland of the Aesthete?" (*New York Affairs*, vol. 4., no. 4, 1978).

On loft jazz, I relied on a term paper by Ben Looker, an American studies graduate student at Yale, as well as the transcripts of several of the interviews he conducted with the musicians themselves. Peter Occhiogrosso, who wrote about avant-garde jazz for the *SoHo Weekly News*, Stanley Crouch, and Sam Rivers (the owner of the first jazz loft) all shared their memories of the scene with me. Other useful sources on loft jazz include "Loft Jazz Goes on a Three-Day Toot" (Robert Palmer, *New York Times*, June 4, 1976); "Jazz Lofts: A Walk Through the Wild Sounds" (Stanley Crouch, *New York Times Magazine*, April 17, 1977); and John Litweiler's *Ornette Coleman: The Harmolodic Life* (Quartet Books, 1992).

PART TWO

27.

For my account of New York's loss of power, I relied on the reports from the three subsequent investigations (city, state, and federal), the depositions and testimonies given by the various principals, as well as the telephone transcripts of the conversations among the system operators (which can be found in New York City's municipal archive). William Jurith's son Edward provided me with some of the details of his father's career with Con Edison. Carolyn Kay Brancato and Jonathan Rosner, senior staff members of the city's investigation, both shared their recollections with me, as did Dr. Thornton S. Lauber, an engineer who served as a consultant on the city's inquiry. The most comprehensive article on the mechanics of the blackout is "Investigators Agree N.Y. Blackout of 1977 Could Have Been Avoided" (Philip Boffey, *Science*, September 15, 1978).

29.

My portrait of Bushwick during the 1977 blackout is drawn primarily from interviews with more than twenty cops and former cops who worked in the Eighty-third Precinct at the time. Michael Daly and Denis Hamill also focused on Bushwick in "There Goes the Neighborhood" (*Village Voice*, July 25, 1977).

32.

For details on the looting citywide, I relied primarily on special reports filed by the commanding officer for each of the city's police precincts, *Blackout Looting!* (Robert Curvin and Bruce Porter, Gardner Press, 1979), and local newspaper coverage.

35.

My account of the modern history of Bushwick is drawn largely from interviews with residents and former residents. *Blackout Looting!* includes a section on the neighborhood's soaring crime and poverty rates. In August 1977, a team of *Daily News* reporters led by Martin Gottlieb wrote an excellent five-part series on Bushwick, "Our Dying Neighborhoods." Thomas Plate details the neighborhood's arson epidemic in "The Blaze in Bushwick: Will the Burning Ever Stop?" (*New York*, July 18, 1977). Jason Epstein lays out some of the demographic and economic forces that devastated the neighborhood in an essay in the April 9, 1992, issue of *The New York Review of Books*, "The Tragical History of New York."

37.

For my account of the city's troubles processing jailed looters I relied on newspaper coverage and a subsequent report by the New York State Crime Control Planning Board on the city's response to the blackout. On this same subject, Timothy Crouse's August 15, 1977, article in *The Village Voice*—"How 'Proximity to a Salami' Became a Crime: The Criminal Justice System Copes with Largest Mass Arrests in N.Y. History"—is also valuable.

40.

For my assessment of the black community's reaction to the looting, I relied primarily on the coverage of the *Amsterdam News*. Orde Coombs detailed the tension between middle-class and poor blacks in the context of the blackout in "The Trashing of Le Mans: The New Civil War Begins" (*New York*, August 8, 1977).

My account of Percy Sutton's 1977 campaign is drawn from interviews with two senior members of his campaign staff, William Banks and Frank Baraff, as well as campaign literature and local newspaper coverage.

Among the more memorable profiles of Sutton are "Guess Who's Coming to

Gracie Mansion" (Nicholas Pileggi, *New York*, May 27, 1974) and "Percy Sutton Has the Last Laugh" (Orde Coombs, *New York*, August 17, 1981).

PART THREE

41.

Several former *New York Post* reporters and editors shared with me their memories of the paper's transformation under Murdoch. They include Robert Spitzler, George Artz, Roberta Gratz, and Robert Lipsyte. The aforementioned Murdoch biographies also address this subject. The November 1977 issue of *More* featured an article on the paper's coverage of New York's infamous summer, as well as a Q & A with its new owner ("Can the *Post* Survive Rupert Murdoch?").

My account of Billy Martin appearing drunk in George Steinbrenner's hotel suite is drawn from interviews with several beat reporters, as well as *Inside the Yankees: The Championship Year*, and *Wild, High and Tight*.

42.

For my account of Son of Sam's reign of terror and its effect on New York, I relied on local newspaper reports and TV broadcasts, wire service stories and interviews with Jimmy Breslin as well as a number of the detectives involved with the Omega task force, including John Falotico, Joe Coffey, Bill Clark, and Joseph Borrelli.

In addition to the blanket coverage in the New York tabloids and the *Times*, other noteworthy articles on the pursuit of the Son of Sam include "Hunting the 'Son of Sam' " (*Newsweek*, July 11, 1977) and "The Hunt for Son of Sam Goes On" (*Time*, August 15, 1977).

Three profiles of Steve Dunleavy were especially useful: "Mr. Blood-and-Guts" (Tony Schwartz, *Newsweek*, October 17, 1977); "Steve Dunleavy and the Rise of Tabloid TV" (Frank DiGiacomo, *New York Observer*, December 6, 1999); and "The Hell-Raiser" (John Cassidy, *New Yorker*, September 11, 2000).

44.

My account of the apprehension of Son of Sam is drawn from interviews with the aforementioned detectives, local newspaper reports, wire service stories, and local TV news broadcasts. Among the more noteworthy stories on Sam's arrest are: "'Son of Sam'; Mail Sorter Arraigned in Brooklyn in 'Son of Sam' Murders" (William Claiborne, *Washington Post*, August 12, 1977); "The Sick World of Son of Sam" (*Newsweek*, August 22, 1977); and " 'Sam Told Me to Do It . . . Sam Is the Devil' " (*Time*, August 22, 1977).

Two of the more memorable stories on the press coverage of Sam are "A Tale of Midnight" (Thomas Powers, *Commonweal*, September 16, 1977); "Sam Sells: Press Orgy Follows Arrest of .44 Killer" (*More*, September 1977); and "The Night TV Cried Wolf" (Carl Tucker, *Saturday Review*, October 1, 1977).

46.

Koch's campaign for capital punishment was best documented by Denis Hamill (" 'Hi, I'm for Capital Punishment. Are You?' " *Village Voice*, September 5, 1977). Koch spoke with me about his decision to emphasize his position on the death penalty in the outer boroughs but not in Manhattan. He also recalled for me his conversation with Murdoch in which the publisher offered his endorsement.

47.

For my profile of Guidry, I relied on an interview with him in Tampa in the spring of 2001, as well as conversations with Yankees' beat reporters and local newspaper coverage of his surprising emergence during the '77 season. Two noteworthy magazine profiles, both by Roger Director and published in *Sport*, are "Ron Guidry" (October 1978) and "The Top Performer" (February 1979).

48.

The best analysis of Bella Abzug's flawed 1977 campaign is "What Makes Bella Run Cautious?" (Geoffrey Stokes, *Village Voice*, August 22, 1977). Pete Hamill offered a picture of the flagging candidate in his September 7, 1977, *Daily News* column: "Even Garment Center Can't Dress Up This Campaign."

49.

For my account of the SEC report on New York's fiscal crisis, I relied primarily on the coverage in New York's dailies. Several articles stand out: "The Fiscal Crisis: Forgive, but Don't Forget" (Sam Roberts, *Daily News*, August 22, 1977); "How Big Guys Burned the Little Guys" (Mark Lieberman and Bruce Drake, *Sunday Daily News*, August 28, 1977); "Bad News for Beame" (*Newsweek*, September 5, 1977); "Banks Rape City: Will Beame Fry Alone?" (Jack Newfield, *Village Voice*, September 5, 1977); and "The SEC vs. New York: Why Nothing's Happened" (Charles Koshetz, *New York*, November 20, 1978).

51.

Susan Dworkin's book *Miss America, 1945: Bess Myerson and the Year that Changed Our Lives* (Newmarket Press, 1987) provides a detailed account of Myerson's childhood and rise to prominence. For my portrait of Myerson, I also relied on several articles published in 1987, when she was wrapped up in a bribery scandal involving a judge and her boyfriend, a reputed mobster. A few of the more noteworthy ones include: "New York Abuzz over Bessie's Mess" (Elizabeth Mehren, *Los Angeles Times*, June 29, 1987); "The Bitter Limbo of Bess Myerson" (Paula Span, *Washington Post*, July 23, 1987); and "The Trouble with Bess: How Did a Former Miss America Get into This Mess?" (Shana Alexander, *St. Petersburg Times*, September 13, 1988).

52.

Murray Kempton offers a humanizing portrait of Beame in defeat in "The Bloom Goes Off for Abraham Beame" (*New York Post*, September 9, 1977).

53.

Pete Hamill recounted Cuomo's impromptu sermon at the Church of the Master in "Cuomo, in Church, Preaches the Politics of Love" (*Daily News*, September 12, 1977). Robert McElvaine also writes about the sermon in his aforementioned biography of Cuomo.

57.

Jim Sleeper captured the essence of Koch's mayoralty in the context of a changed New York in two pieces in *Dissent* magazine, both titled "Ed Koch and the Spirit of the Times" (Spring 1981 and Summer 1985).

61.

Fran Healy recalled for me the details of his conversation with Martin before game five in Kansas City.

The New York Times's Murray Chass reported on the mood on the Yankees' charter in "Yankee Flight Home Unusually Calm" (October 11, 1977).

66.

My account of game six of the World Series is drawn primarily from daily newspaper reports, conversations with beat reporters, and radio and TV broadcasts.

67.

Martin writes about his miserable time at the postgame party in his memoir *Number One.*

Destino shared with me his memories of being at McMullen's with Reggie after game six. He also told me about his and Reggie's respective CB handles.

ACKNOWLEDGMENTS

Many invisible hands helped shape this book, beginning with the 1977 Yankees beat writers. Moss Klein, Henry Hecht, Steve Jacobson, Maury Allen, and Phil Pepe were especially helpful. In addition, Bill Francis of the National Baseball Hall of Fame indulged countless research requests.

Peter Occhiogrosso, Ben Looker, and Joe Levy and John Leland helped guide me through New York's 1970s music scene. Tim Lawrence graciously shared with me his thick rolodex of DJs and discos devotees. Bill Dobbs steered me to numerous sources on the city's gay life in the seventies.

Robert Curvin and Bruce Porter trusted me with their copies of the special reports that each of New York's precincts was required to file after the blackout. I am deeply indebted to all of the officers of Bushwick's Eighty-third Precinct—William Sekzer in particular—who shared their memories of the blackout and tolerated endless phone calls as I tried to piece together my narrative of that chaotic night. Thanks to all the Bushwick residents who spoke with me about the neighborhood; and a special thanks to Dr. Carl St. Martin for taking me on my first tour of Bushwick. Martin Gottlieb's and Jim Sleeper's heartfelt portraits of the neighborhood—Gottlieb's in the *Daily News*; Sleeper's in two North Brooklyn community newspapers and in his incisive book, *The Closest of Strangers*—gave me something to which to aspire. Mario Cuomo and Ed Koch both generously granted me several interviews, and Mayor Koch allowed me access to an unpublished and unvarnished oral history at Columbia University.

James Hamilton and Janie Eisenberg, two of New York's finest photographers during this era, unearthed wonderful images for me. Judith Phillips and Erica Toth did valuable research.

I was lucky enough to be able to publish several articles drawn from the book-in-progress and would like to thank a handful of editors who were not afraid of a little history. Connie Rosenblum of the *New York Times* City section invited me to recall the summer of '77 on its twenty-fifth anniversary; David Shipley of the *Times*'s op-ed page asked me to consider the differences between the 1977 and 2003 blackouts. Saving the best for last, *The New York Times Magazine* published a lengthy excerpt from my account of Bushwick's long night of looting. It was deftly edited by Ilena Silverman and Gerry Marzorati, and fact-checked with inspired vigilance by Sarah Smith.

Doug Century, Blake Eskin, William Brangham, Lyn Mattoon, Tom Watson, Sam Sifton, Liz Garbus, Tina Brown, Will Dana, Michael Megalli, Seth Lipsky, and Susan Mahler provided critical support during this book's long gestation. Jack Newfield, who passed away before I could thank him in person, was an extraordinarily generous source. Roger Burlingame graciously slogged through a sprawling early draft and helped me find my story therein. Jonathan Rosen and Mike Sokolove offered keen insights into later drafts.

I am incredibly fortunate to have Sarah Chalfant of the Wylie Agency in my corner. Not only did she help shape the proposal and see to it that this book found the perfect home, but Sarah also took every one of my neurotic phone calls along the way and expressed more confidence in me than I had any right to expect.

My editor, Josh Kendall, and his boss, Frances Coady, were vocal champions of the book from the get-go, when they had every reason to be wary. In the four years since then, Josh has been a constant source of encouragement and wisdom. His perceptive comments have improved the book immeasurably. Copy editors Kevin Doughten and Pearl Hanig helped smooth out numerous rough edges. I am especially grateful to FSG's publisher, Jonathan Galassi, both for his enthusiasm and for coming up with the book's title.

My greatest debt of all is to my wife, Danielle Mattoon, without whom my life—never mind this book—would remain incomplete.